AMONG MEN

LIBRARY
Tel: 01244 375444   Ext: 3301

This book is to be returned on or before the
last date stamped below. Overdue charges
will be incurred by the late return of books.

CHESTER COLLEGE

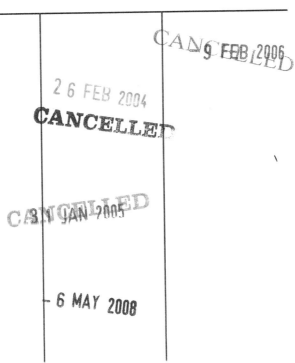

Among Men
Moulding Masculinities, Volume 1

Edited by

SØREN ERVØ and THOMAS JOHANSSON

ASHGATE

Published by
Ashgate Publishing Limited
Gower House
Croft Road
Aldershot
Hants GU11 3HR
England

Ashgate Publishing Company
Suite 420
101 Cherry Street
Burlington, VT 05401-4405
USA

Ashgate website: http://www.ashgate.com

British Library Cataloguing in Publication Data
Among men : moulding masculinities
   Vol. 1
   1. Masculinity - Scandinavia 2. Men - Scandinavia
   I. Ervø, Søren II. Johansson, Thomas III. Nordic Summer
   University
   305.3'1

Library of Congress Control Number: 99-073637

ISBN 1 84014 804 7

Printed and bound by Athenaeum Press, Ltd.,
Gateshead, Tyne & Wear.

Contents

Acknowledgements

We would like to thank the authors for trusting us with their material. The financial support we have received from "The Nordic Summer University," has allowed most of the contributors to meet at different conferences and enabled their papers to be proofread. Also thanks to Sidsel Ervø for technical assistance. And finally we praise the eminent work by our "proofreader" Rictor Norton, without whom this task would have been less manageable and the result less successful.

The article by Hans Bonde was earlier published in *The Scandinavian Journal of History*, vol. 21, 1996.
The article by Ella Johansson was earlier published in *Gender & History*, vol. 1, no. 2, Summer 1989.
The article by Helena Wahlström was earlier published in a slightly different form as a chapter within her Ph.D. thesis under her maiden name Helena Eriksson, *Husbands, Lovers, and Dreamlovers: Masculinity and Female Desire in Women's Novels of the 1970s*, Studia Anglistica Upsaliensis, Uppsala 1997.

List of Contributors

(for both volumes)

Hans Bonde, Ph.D., Assistant Professor, Department of Sports Science, University of Copenhagen, Denmark. <HBonde@ifi.ku.dk>

Mikael Carleheden, Ph.D., Associate Professor, Department of Sociology, University of Örebro, Sweden. <Mikael.Carlehede@sam.oru.se>

R. W. Connell, Professor of Education, Faculty of Education, University of Sydney, Australia. <r.connell@edfac.usyd.edu.au>

Stephan W. Cremer, Ph.D., Department of Health Service of the City of Utrecht, Netherlands. <S.Cremer@Utrecht.nl>

Claes Ekenstam, Ph.D., Associate Professor at the Department of the History of Ideas and Education, University of Göteborg, Sweden. <claes.ekenstam@idehist.gu.se>

Søren Ervø, M.A. in Film and History, Department of Film and Media Studies, University of Copenhagen, Denmark. <serv@vip.cybercity.dk>

Lena Eskilsson, Ph.D., Associate Professor, Department of the History of Science and Ideas, University of Umeå, Sweden. <Lena.eskilsson@idehist.gu.se>

Katrine Fangen, Ph.D., Assistant Professor, Department of Sociology, University of Oslo, Norway. <Katrine.fangen@sosiologi.uio.no>

Jeff Hearn, Professor of Sociology, Department of Sociology, Åbo Akademi University, Finland. <jhearn@ra.abo.fi>

Ilpo Helén, Ph.D., Assistant Professor, Department of Sociology, University of Helsinki, Finland. <IHELEN@valt.helsinki.fi>

Øystein Gullvåg Holter, Ph.D., Associate Professor, Department of Sociology, University of Oslo, Norway. <ogh@afi-wri.no>

Ella Johansson, Ph.D., Associate Professor, Nordeuropa-Institut, Humboldt-Universität zu Berlin, Germany. <Ella.Johansson@etn.lu.se>

Thomas Johansson, Ph.D., Professor, Department of Social Work, University of Gothenburg, Sweden. <Thomas.Johansson@socwork.gu.se>

Michael S. Kimmel, Professor in Sociology, State University of New York at Stony Brook, USA. <103321.1076@compuserve.com>

Christian Kullberg, Ph.D., Associate Professor, Department of Social Science, University of Örebro, Sweden.<Christian.Kullberg@sam.oru.se>

Martti Lahti, Chair, Department of Communication and Media Design, Laurea Polytechnic, Vantaa, Finland. <Martti-lahti@laurea.fi>

Philip Lalander, Ph.D., Associate Professor, SoRAD, University of Stockholm, Sweden. <Philip.Lalander@hik.se>

Jørgen Lorentzen, Ph.D., Assistant Professor, Department of Gender Studies, University of Oslo, Norway. <J.l.lorentzen@skk.uio.no>

Mairtin Mac an Ghaill, Ph.D., Professor, Department of Education, University of Sheffield, England. <M.m.a.ghaill@sheffield.ac.uk>

Paul McIlvenny, Ph.D., Associate Professor, Department of Languages and Intercultural Studies, Aalborg University, Denmark. <paul@sprog.auc.dk >

Ulf Mellström, Ph.D., Associate Professor, Department of Technique and Social Change, University of Linköping, Sweden. <UlfMe@tema.liu.se>

Michael Meuser, Ph.D., Assistant Professor, Department of Sociology, University of Bremen. <meuser.michael@t-online.de>

Wilhelm von Rosen, Dr. Phil. in History from the University of Copenhagen, Senior Researcher at the National Archives of Denmark. <wr@ra.sa.dk>

Victor Jeleniewski Seidler, Professor of Social Theory, Department of Sociology, Goldsmiths College, University of London, England. <soa01vjs@gold.ac.uk>

Juha Siltala, Ph.D., Professor, Department of History, University of Helsinki, Finland. <Juha.siltala@helsinki.fi>

Klaus Theweleit, Dr.Phil., freelance lecturer and author in Freiburg, Germany. <thewelei@ruf.uni-freiburg.de>

Arto Tiihonen, Ph.D., Department of Social Sciences of Sport, University of Jyväskylä, Finland. <artot@congcreator.com>

Helena Wahlström, Ph.D., Assistant Professor, Department of English, Gävle University College, Sweden. <hen@hig.se>

Geir A. Øygarden, Ph.D., Department of Sociology, University of Uppsala, Sweden. <Geir.Oygarden@soc.uu.se>

Foreword

MICHAEL KIMMEL

The study of men and masculinities has changed significantly in the past decade. Once, masculinity was as invisible as the air throughout the social and behavioral sciences, the unexamined norm, the "social" and the "behavioral" in the first place. So, studies of stratification could legitimately ask only of sons' and fathers' occupations and educational levels as measures of "social" mobility.

Feminism changed all that, of course, as women became visible as a gender, as a category of analysis. Then, we had a curious sort of mixture – one visible gender and one invisible norm against which women were measured. Finally, we discovered men. When social psychologists first "discovered" men they used sex role theory to describe the ways in which biological males and females were sorted, categorized, and socialized into their appropriate sex role. As had been the case when social psychologists had first explored women's experiences, differences between women and men were exaggerated by sex role theory, while differences among women and among men were downplayed.

If one were to look today at those first books on men in the 1970s, one sees this phenomenon most clearly. The terms "women" and "men" are used asunitary, universal categories. Men defined themselves by their relationship to a sex role, and those whose relationship to that role got their own chapter in the book. Thus a typical text on men would include chapters on the workplace, sexuality, friendship, sports, the military and the like. And then there would be separate chapters on gay men and on black men. One realized that the "men" who were included in the substantive chapters were actually heterosexual and white.

Since the late 1980s, the sociological inquiry into masculinity followed the transformative impact of multicultural feminism on our understanding of women. Specifically, we've begun to explore masculinities, the multiple constructions of masculinity as developed by specific cultural, racial, sexual, ethnic, or age groups. Masculinity is no longer a monolithic category, but a competing set of definitions constructed by different groups. Those constructions are constructed and articulated within a variety of institutional fields – the workplace, the family, the state. And so competing constructions of masculinity also must account for the differential crediting of different constructions, the play between the "hegemonic" definition of masculinity that sets the normative standards against which all other definitions are measured – and, often, found wanting.

This understanding further de-centers masculinity from its position as unexamined norm, because it exposes the way in which the formerly invisible is maintained by relations of power. Those "others" whose masculinity was problematized in their relation to hegemonic manhood were trapped by what we might call the "Goldilocks dilemma," named after the heroine in the old fairy tale. Goldilocks, you might recall, found everything "too" much – either too hot or too cold, too big or too small – but it was never "just right." So too for marginalized men: their expression of manhood was either insufficient or overly exaggerated as a compensation for insufficiency. It was seen as always out of line, always inappropriate.

To study the social and historical construction of masculinities means that we must (1) take into account the local articulations of specific forms of masculinity, within the context of the global domination of world-hegemonic forms of gender definition; (2) take into account the historically specific development of these local constructions as they work out locally, nationally, and globally; (3) the variations among specific national formations of gender ideology; (4) the variations over historical time of such specifications, and (5) the specific normative practices that transform the gender ideologies over an individual's life course.

The papers collected in this volume provide an extraordinarily rich and revealing illustration of this generation of studies of masculinities. The constant interplay between gender ideologies and actual gendered performances, the images and the acts; between the tension between global and local articulations of masculinities; the clear delineation of historically specific definitions; the specification of the institutional location of gendered actors; the ironic way male institutions reveal masculine fears and anxieties rather than express their power and dominance – these are the materials from which a new generation of scholars are building both the theoretical and methodological apparatus for, and providing the historical and culturally-specific material of a truly global inquiry into masculinities.

Many years ago, the great French medieval historian Marc Bloch provided a fitting admonition about the comparative method – that scholars would "learn not to attach too much importance to local pseudo-causes" but, at the same time, "learn to become sensitive to specific differences." The papers in this volume are exemplary in this regard: these are scholars who know how to keep their eyes clearly on the big picture, and their ears close to the ground.

Michael Kimmel is Professor of Sociology at Stony Brook, New York and has been the editor of the SAGE series on Research on Men and Masculinities. Kimmel is the author of *Manhood in America* (1996) and has edited *Changing Men: New Directions in Research on Men and Masculinity* (1987), *The Politics of Manhood* (1995) and has co-edited *Men's Lives* (1989) and *Against the Tide* (1992).

Chapter 1

Introduction

SØREN ERVØ AND THOMAS JOHANSSON

This two-volume anthology is the result of our efforts to collect innovative articles that in different ways represent a field, which we prefer to label pragmatically as "studies of men and masculinities."[1]

Many of the articles have earlier been presented at six conferences held between 1995 and 1997 by the Nordic Network for Masculinity Studies within the Nordic Summer University, arranged by the editors and financed by the Nordic Ministry Council. This early collection has been complemented by a few additional articles that have been presented at other seminars on "masculinities" in the Scandinavian countries during the same period. Finally we have included contributions from some of our visitors, among them some of the major researchers on masculinities, who have been promoting this hitherto predominantly Anglo-American subject.[2]

By enabling the first collective contribution from mainly Nordic scholars to "studies of men and masculinities" we hope to encourage further reading and research in other non-English cultures, which can contribute to an understanding of masculinities in a global context.

Instead of selecting articles with similar approaches, we have chosen to maintain a multi-disciplinary selection. This is not done in order to attempt a systematic overview, but rather to include the many different kinds of research that have been presented in the Nordic region under the label of "masculinity studies." Because the subject of gender transcends traditional structures and institutions in society, including the boundaries within academia, "studies of men and masculinities" necessitate a multi-disciplinary approach. The multi-disciplinary approach also helps to establish interesting links between otherwise very different subject areas. Though we welcome the "mainstreaming" of gender studies, and hope that our anthologies will contribute further to this development, we also believe that a multi-disciplinary approach is important in order to preserve the political and critical dimension of gender studies. "Studies of men and masculinties" is necessarily linked to the political struggle for a more equal society. If this were not the case, we might fall back to a kind of research on gender that merely reproduced traditional gender categories and cultivated an uncritical notion of the gender order.

The concept of masculinity is analyzed in a variety of ways – as forms of behavior, as specific ethics, codes and historical traits. Common to most of the authors is the belief that gender is socially constructed and negotiated, and that we need to maintain a close relationship between gender theory and case-studies in order to understand and demonstrate the dynamic and contradictory nature of gender. Our aim has been to show how different masculinities continuosly intersect and interact with specific individuals, groups and historical settings, in order to deconstruct static views of gender and gender relations.

Though "studies of men and masculinities" have grown steadily over the last few years, especially in the Anglo-American countries, the field is still very tentative and needs further development in many regards. This development may depend on more contributions from other parts of the world, enabling us to develop less ethnocentric perspectives. And though we acknowledge the need for more clarified theoretical agendas,[3] we also believe that diversity is still the best prerequisite for theoretical growth. The different approaches in our anthologies will hopefully enable the reader to envision "studies of men and masculinities" even beyond the present level of theoretical sophistication and diversity of subjects. We believe that it is too soon to evaluate the potential of "studies of men and masculinities" until they have been integrated into further subject areas and have been more developed internationally. Despite our belief that there is a need to develop the theoretical work – for instance to scrutinize and employ the dominant concepts of male crisis and hegemonic masculinity more critically[4] – we do not wish to distance ourselves from the multifaceted work already published, but are content to contribute further "pieces to the puzzle," believing that development in depth presupposes development in breadth.

The discussions surrounding the political implications of men engaging in feminism and gender studies have obscured the fact that "women's studies" have also always been "studies of men and masculinities." And if these concepts had been investigated with the same curiosity as women and femininity, "studies of men and masculinities" might have been integrated into gender studies much sooner. The monolithic accounts of masculinity as well as the lack of empirical studies of men and male cultures have necessitated a late corrective (and not merely a supplement): trying to find its place within the dispersed field of gender studies, and distinguish itself from the omnipresent public debates on "new men" and "fatherhood" fueled by women's magazines, popular psychology and the agendas of different "men's movements."[5] While "studies of men and masculinities" ought to challenge all accounts of men and masculinities (including these concepts) as well as omissions of these within gender studies, they also, supportive of feminism in general, entail criticism of traditional scholarship for its failure to include a gender concept and incorporate the insights produced by gender studies.

Basically, we feel that "studies of men and masculinities" are interesting and important, because they raise questions that are still unanswered. Though self-critical awareness and sincere respect for the many implications of men "tampering with feminism" are essential,[6] we should not let these concerns prevent us from developing the field beyond the constraints of political correctness. The important political loyalty toward feminism and theoretical dependency toward gender studies in general should not prevent us from committing ourselves professionally and critically when dealing with specific theories of gender.

The editors do not perceive "studies of men and masculinities" as a possible vehicle for contemporary men's rights or masculinist movements, nor has there been any evidence for such a connection yet. On the contrary, many of the authors included here have declared themselves as pro-feminists, and have on several occasions been active in pointing out backlash tendencies within different men's movements. Despite honoring the aspirations toward a politically engaged or even activistic scholarship, we do not believe that labelling research "critical," "pro-feminist," "gay-affirmative" and so on is sufficient to legitimize or establish the field within academia. Respectable political intentions do not produce new insights, nor do they prevent anybody from using this research with a different agenda.

Overall, we have tried to collect articles that employ the concept of masculinity in order to enhance or develop a gender perspective within areas where gender already seems to be so visible that conflicts, crises and changes within masculine identities would have profound effects on the perception and embodiment of masculinities and consequently on gender relations. In other words, we assumed that the best strategy would be to focus on dominant gender arenas, such as sexuality, the body, the family and subcultures dominated by men and male values. *Among Men – Moulding Masculinities, Volume 1* aims to contribute to the investigation of relational aspects of masculinity, in order to describe how different masculinities are moulded within specific structures and settings, especially how men interact with each other, and how they collectively react to and embody the changing concepts of masculinity within male-dominated subcultures. *Bending Bodies – Moulding Masculinities, Volume 2* aims to study changes within masculine identity and subjectivity and to discuss the constructions of masculinities that result from the relationship and understanding men develop toward their own and other men's bodies, sexualities and masculine dis/abilities.

By centering on the struggle and negotiation between different groups and discourses of masculinity and investigating the origin of dominant images and ideals of masculinity, the two volumes hope to widen our understanding of how historic forms of masculinities are interpreted, revived and combined in the process of moulding masculinities.

Among Men – Moulding Masculinities, Volume 1

Robert Connell discusses how we should understand the relationship of masculinity to the state, in a way consistent with a sophisticated contemporary understanding of gender. Connell believes that by seeing gender as a social structure, as one of the ways that collective social processes are shaped, it becomes possible to analyze the state as a gendered institution and inherently a site of gender politics. Reconsidering his earlier theses about the gender-state, Connell focuses on issues about masculinity, power, and globalization, in order to develop an alternative to gender-blind theory. Connell describes the gender dynamics that arise from different situations in the history of the two main patterns describing the relations between states, "international relations" and "imperialism." He looks at the differences between colonial, post-colonial, metropolitan and international states, and concludes with an example of how the American hypermasculine cult of weaponry is exported through the arms trade.

Øystein Holter also deals with the frameworks that we use for interpreting gender, including masculinities. He especially addresses the long-standing questions of the relationship between capital and patriarchy, by asking whether capital is genderless, or whether male dominance is reproduced through economic relations "by design." After outlining some common views of capital and gender, and some recent research on the capital/gender connection, Holter presents a critical gender theory that builds on this research. Finally, he discusses how a social-forms view of gender and capital may extend and nuance such a theory. Holter analyzes gender exchange as a two-tiered process. He believes that it is partly a symmetrical deal characterized by simple exchange, verging on gift and other relations, and partly a non-symmetrical deal that involves a particular form of reification of women and the feminine. He further argues that it is precisely the *combination* of the two levels that creates our concepts of gender. Holter also distinguishes between the gender system – as a social form that involves reference to the value form of gender – and patriarchy, which he defines as relations that lead to oppression of women, whatever their social form.

Mikael Carleheden investigates the very possibility of theorizing about any sort of gender identity in "late modern" society. His critique of postmodern gender theory, especially the work of Judith Butler, draws on Bourdieu and Benhahib to clarify the fact that gender is not something transparent, which we as subjects have direct control over. Historicity and sociality have a logic and a power of their own, which can be as powerful as biological forces, but in another way. Transferring the theory of Bauman to a gender-theoretical context, Carleheden concludes that postmodern identity, seen as an aesthetic self-construction, is not a real identity at all, since it cannot answer questions of self, questions that force us to deal with our own history.

Ella Johansson looks into the history of a Swedish male working environment – "the remote world of the lumbermen." The main source of her observations is a collection of over 200 memoirs – the life stories of loggers, born between 1840 and 1900, taken from a museum documentary project carried out in the 1940s. Johansson insists that the meanings and practices of masculinity have to be located within their particular historical context. Her way of identifying these particular patterns is to look at the loggers' life cycle, starting with boyhood and the socialization process. According to their memoirs it was the image of the lumberjack, and not the farmer, who represented the man the boys wanted to become. Johansson suggests that the loggers' winter lifestyle in the forests can be characterized as both egalitarian and individualistic. Most striking to her is the consistent avoidance of anything that could contribute to the formation of a hierarchy among men.

The historian Hans Bonde tries to combine men's studies with sports studies. According to Bonde, the linkage between men and sport was already established around the turn of the century. At that time, the family as an educational setting was increasingly left in the hands of women, and a proper mother cult developed. Because of the growing importance of

work outside the home, men were separated from the upbringing of their
own and other people's boys in domestic production. The fathers, however,
did not disappear from all upbringing, since some of them later undertook
to socialize boys and young men and teach them self-eduction in the world
of sport, developing the cult of the "coach." According to Bonde, sport
became a laboratory for masculinity, where men could create and cultivate
their body, motor skills, and a character expressing competitiveness in
modern society. Bonde emphasizes that the socialization and self-education
of men were based particularly on those virtues that mothers were not
expected to be able to impart to their little boys: individualism,
independence, fighting spirit, courage, and discipline. Bonde's source
material consists of Nordic books and magazines about sport from the
period 1880–1920.

Judging from heroic images of men in the Scandinavian wilderness,
Eskilsson proposes that these images of science and the North are also
images of masculinity; or rather, of one of the masculine ideals that
emerged in the decades around the turn of the last century. Eskilsson is
especially interested in middle-class masculinity, in which she believes
there exists a connection between masculinity and the North, and where the
status and conditions for mountain and arctic exploration comprise the
connecting link. Eskilsson's hypothesis is that the decades around the turn
of the century witnessed the development of a successful masculine type
featuring a connection between masculinity and the North, literally and
symbolically. This is primarily a middle-class phenomenon. Sheer physical
strength in itself – the hallmark of farmers and the working class – was not
a given element in middle-class masculinity; instead, the ideal was a
combination of physical strength, rationality, single-mindedness, stamina
and discipline. The masculine ideal held by leading groups in society
underwent a number of changes during the Victorian era. The emphasis on
male austerity and earnestness was complemented by respect for
"muscles," in both the physical and the mental sense. These Victorian
ideals of ascetic and athletic exercises complied well with the demands that
Alpinism and mountain sports made on their practitioners.

Based on an empirical study of young German men's collective
orientations, Michael Meuser raises the question how changes in women's
lives have affected the generation of men who grew up during the second
women's movement, and how they cope with the change in gender
relations. Meuser believes that the popular talk about a far-reaching crisis
of masculinity is overgeneralized, and he hesitates to define traditional
masculinity as obsolete. Instead he insists that cultural interpretive patterns

are marked by considerable longevity, and that they are still efficient, even when the social conditions that established them have changed. Even under the conditions of de-traditionalized gender relations, men are dependent on the culturally available symbolic inventory of masculine identity formation. As fundamental identities are tied to gender, a radical break with the cultural defining practices and discourses of one's own gender must be paid for by a deep habitual insecurity. Therefore any reconstruction of men's orientation has to pay attention to continuities as well as changes. Meuser distinguishes between two patterns of orientation among the young men: a threatened self-confidence caused by the feminist critique of traditional masculinity, and an egalitarian attitude based on pragmatic arrangements. Finally he discusses how masculinity can be "modernized" in the direction of egalitarian practice and what role men's consciousness-raising groups play in this process.

Ulf Mellström presents his anthropological study of Swedish engineers, and their professional identity and life career. He outlines two possible perspectives on how to study the construction of gender identity in daily technological practice. First, a perspective where microsociological situated activities are in focus. Secondly, a biographical perspective where the construction of gender identities can be studied from practices of socialization. A combination of these perspectives is, according to Mellström, the most processual and dynamic way of looking at the production and reproduction of gender identity. Mellström has found that the milieu of engineers provides insight into the reproduction of a masculine technical sociability in daily practice. This socialibity rests upon a reproduction of masculinity in the microsocial situations of everyday life as well as the masculine practices of socialization where a lifelong close relation to technology is of crucial importance and partly constitutes what it means to be a man in Swedish society. Mellström suggests that the "eternal youth" offered by the world of technology provides a peaceful existential corner, a social continuity, for men longing for a carefree existence in a world full of demands from both family and society.

Philip Lalander has analyzed the rituals of a group of young right-wing Swedish politicians through interviews and observation. His contribution is an attempt to problematize their construction of culture and identity, through an analysis of two positions, which are seen as valuable in this culture: the *Swedish hero* and the *perverted politician*. These ideological positions are shown to be closely linked to attempts to ritualize masculinity within this group. Though Lalander views this micro-culture as an alternative culture, he also describes how common cultural traditions (e.g.

of drinking) and concepts (e.g. of male honor) are reinforced as a temporary vaccination against feelings of uncertainty and ambivalence.

In order to understand what attracts Norwegian young men into the right-wing underground, Katrine Fangen has used participant observation to study skinheads. She describes how these men idealize masculinity and romanticize male heroes. In many ways the approval of fellow males is more important to them than that of female participants. This kind of homosociality might be seen as the core feature of such quasi-military communities, and the way the men express intimacy in this setting is physical and brutish. Fangen suggests that these men become addicted to a blend of adventure and excitement and the manifold possibilities for contesting a postural sense of masculinity. This is the reason the community becomes so important to activists, providing them with a sense of importance and commitment they would not experience with the same strength anywhere else. Through underground actions and street violence, right-wing activists are taken seriously as a threat by the outside world. According to Fangen, the resultant feeling of power contributes to their image of themselves as honorable warriors. They dismiss the view that honor is gained by education and work career. Instead, physical strength, discipline and a collective loyalty to their own group is what builds up their honor.

Victor Seidler discusses the way fathering has lost authority within the family structure since the 1950s, when fathering was more a position than a relationship. Seidler compares fatherhood within the modern and the postmodern family. In light of the radical changes within the meaning of fatherhood, he suggests that we need a moral psychology that illuminates some of the pain and tension involved, rather than simply celebrate the fluidity of postmodern identities in which people are supposedly free to create new hybrid identities out of what is culturally available. Following the tensions surrounding childbirth, Seidler believes that an involvement in supporting their partners through pregnancy and birth has been a powerful transformative experience for many men, which strengthens the relationship and allows men to bond. But according to Seidler this can be difficult to sustain as men return to work, since many men are able to split and separate emotionally as soon as the front door closes behind them. Since modernity has been implicitly shaped as a masculine project, it has been easy for men to talk in the impersonal voice of reason, before they have learnt to talk more personally for themselves. As men learn to talk in a different voice with their children, Seidler hopes they can begin to also open up a dialogue with a diversity of masculinities.

Christian Kullberg reviews the Scandinavian research on men and their families done in the past 10 to 15 years, by examining the "problems" concerning men's family orientation that these previous studies have reported. In this research it has been assumed that women have come "out" and strengthened their positions on the labor marker, while men have not taken a corresponding step "into" the family. According to this, the male position has been described as "a lack of concern with child rearing and domestic work." These results indicate that the current "problem" with men's family orientation can be divided into three parts: men's and women's household responsibilities, the division of labor, and the distribution of power between men and women. Kullberg attempts to show that these kinds of descriptions and explanations of the "problems" are oversimplified and in themself problematic. Kullberg's study concludes that men's "lack" of family orientation can hardly be explained by attributing decisions made in the family sphere solely to men's "rational choice" or "free will." Instead there is no clear-cut division between women's orientation to the labor market and men's orientation to family life. Men's and women's decisions within the family are instead intertwined and depend on each other, and the two phenomena are integrated and should be understood as two different aspects of the same process.

Thomas Johansson focuses on how different men deal with the problematic issues of being non-resident fathers and men of today. According to Johansson, many men today have difficulties in constructing a sense of masculinity and in developing an identity as fathers and men. When studying non-resident fathers and their relations to their children, one way is to focus on these questions. One of the key aspects of many fathers' failure to develop long-lasting relationships with their children is located in the problematic construction of contemporary masculinity and fatherhood. Even though it may seem to be problematic to use the concept of "hegemonic masculinity" when studying men who have lost their positions as heads of the family, Johansson suggests that the problematic issue of absent fathers must nevertheless be studied from this perspective. Instead of putting up a struggle for their relationship with their children, "absent fathers" avoid change and devote their time to their own careers and life-plans. In this way they reproduce a traditional male position and contribute to the strengthening of a certain type of limited rationality and hegemonic masculinity.

Jørgen Lorentzen contributes with an analysis of Strindberg's play *The Father*, focusing on the demasculinization and paranoia of the character the Captain. Lorentzen employs the definition of paranoia provided by Freud's "Schreber-analysis," which also enables him to distinguish between two types of demasculinization. One is bound up with being disenfranchised, the experience of having rights removed. The other is linked to the desire to become a woman, able to seduce God. Lorentzen describes the Captain as an example of a man who, in a desperate attempt to maintain his patriarchal power, has become remote from his body. He has wedded himself to rationality and renounced his body. A perception of his body has only been possible in the form of a demasculinization, an infantilization, through which he is able to experience fusion with the mother's body. Lorentzen analyzes how the Captain falls back on authority's traditional sovereignty and right, without listening to people or sense. Thus masculine rationality becomes the opposite of reason. The drama plays this out, as the text shows how the power that masculine rationality rests upon begets a counter-force that can grow mightier than itself.

While "images of women" have been given much attention by feminist literary criticism, female-authored representations of masculinity have largely been neglected. Helena Wahlström contributes to filling that critical gap, by looking at the ways in which various kinds of masculinities and masculine ideals are activated in a number of "women's novels" of the 1970s. Among the texts included are Erica Jong's *Fear of Flying*, Lisa Alther's *Kinflicks*, Gail Godwin's *Glass People*, Gael Greene's *Blue Skies, No Candy*, and Judith Rossner's *Looking for Mr Goodbar*. The novels, which deal primarily with a female protagonist's quest for personal, emotional, and sexual liberation, offer a map of contemporary stereotyped masculinities: the macho man, the successful businessman, the cowboy, the rebel, the hippie. After an initial discussion of the differences between representations of husbands and lovers in women's novels, Wahlström focuses on the significance of representing lovers as stereotypes in the texts. What is the meaning of female-authored "sexist" representations of masculinities? Wahlström's analysis emphasizes the function of representations of masculinity as sites for political and social critique, and stresses the ambiguous and multifaceted aspects of the novels' representations of gender and sexuality, as well as their destabilization of ideals of masculinity.

The last chapter is written by Thomas Johansson. The main object of the study is social work with lone mothers and their sons. The chapter in particular focuses on one issue, the part played by the father. In the cases Johansson refers to, the father is more or less absent. An issue often raised is what impact this has on the son. The need of a male "role-model" or a father surrogate is often discussed in the literature and also in everyday life. Social workers tend to work in the direction of creating a point of identification between son and an adult man. Against this background this chapter deals with how different discourses of fatherhood and the family intersect and intervene in discussions of and the treatment of "problematic" lone mother families.

Notes

1. As these two volumes also demonstrate, "studies of men and masculinities" is not a coherent or unified research paradigm, despite some dominant tendencies, such as the affinities toward Marxist sociology and psychoanalytical gender-theories. Maybe this explains why the discussion about an appropriate label continues. But the search for a common descriptive label is hardly worth the effort, considering the many different approaches already present, and the fact that no label gives a satisfactory presentation of all of the methods and theories employed. The efforts to agree on normative terms are similarly bound to fail. Whether we label it "men's studies," "pro-feminist research" or "male dominance studies," such labels will not be sufficient or even particularly helpful in solving the political challenges confronting each researcher differently, nor protect against unwarranted criticism. Only further research can hope to do that.

2. Although their work has created an important incentive to develop "studies of men and masculinites," an uncritical implementation of this work on a global level also risks obscuring its dependence on a certain geographical and historical context, as well as preventing the development of concepts and theories of a less generalizing nature, which in time could contribute to a more detailed and thoroughly researched global perspective on masculinities. For instance, the relative absence of racial and class differences in the Nordic countries, characterized by cultures of sameness, has led few Nordic scholars to evaluate theories based on differences attributed to gender, race and class. Though gender identities and gender relations are certainly structured and influenced in many ways by international relations and global institutions (mainly dominated by American culture, through advertisements for Coca-Cola and Marlboro or Levis clothing, through Hollywood blockbusters, through MTV and CNN, but also promoted by international organizations through implementation of Western policies concerned with birth control, AIDS, or gender equality), we urgently need more research into national and regional differences in order to understand how masculinities are intertwined and juxtaposed according to regional differences and national myths.

3. So far it has primarily been the concept of masculinities that has been

scrutinized for its lack of theoretical clarity and coherence. McMahon warns against the tendency that "all the attributes of men discussed in the literature [on men] are spoken of as aspects of masculinity" and that writers on masculinity seldom explicitly indicate what kind of concept they take masculinity to be, risking the reduction of the concept "masculinity" to an explanatory cliché (*Theory and Society*, 22 (5), 1993, pp. 675–96). Jeff Hearn (in *Understanding Masculinities*, 1996) lists a number of dangers resulting from certain usages of "masculinity" as an explanatory term and suggests that the term should be used more precisely, and particularly that we move back from the concept of "masculinities" to the concept of "men," that we further explore the multiplicity of "discourses on masculinities," and that we develop concepts that more ʳaccurately reflect women's and men's differential experiences of men. Hearn insists that "to begin the analysis of men with "masculinity/masculinities," or to search for the existence of masculinity/masculinities is likely to miss the point." According to Hearn "It cannot be assumed *a priori* that masculinity/masculinities exist. To do so is to reproduce a heterosexualizing of social arrangements" (p. 214). Suggesting that "gender, in the sense of an actually existing identity or social characteristic of men and women, does not exist," John MacInnes (in *The End of Masculinity*, Open University Press, 1998) proposes the abandonment of the concept of masculinity, understood as "the property, character trait or aspect of identity of individuals" (p. 2). He concludes that "trying to define masculinity or masculinities is a fruitless task," but immediately reinvents the concept by arguing that "masculinity exists only as various ideologies or fantasies, about what men should be like, which men and women develop to make sense of their lives." MacInnes's argument is directed against any confusion of identities with ideologies, thereby "reducing identity directly to ideology." Instead he proposes that we study "the specific historical conditions under which men and women ever come to believe that such a thing as masculinity exists in the first place, the different forms such beliefs take and the consequences that they have within such historical conditions" (p. 77). Kenneth Clatterbaugh has recently concluded that "It may well be the best kept secret of the literature on masculinities that we have an extremely ill-defined idea of what we are talking about" (in *Men and Masculinities*, 1 (1), July 1998) . Clatterbaugh's article is excellent, but unfortunately he does not seem to distinguish between conceptual clarity within a single text or research project, and the entire field of "masculinity studies." There is certainly a need for a clear concept of masculinity within every single research project, but there is not the same need for all researchers to agree upon a common concept of masculinity.

4.   The concept of hegemonic masculinity is often used as an explanatory concept, albeit seldom discussed or developed beyond the formulaic description given by Connell. This may explain why the concept hasn't been modified or challenged, even when employed outside the theoretical

framework presented by Connell. Mostly it simply refers, in a rather descriptive sense, to the mere existence of some kind of power structure between different groups of men, to emphasize the common notion of plural antagonistic masculinities (where masculinities can imply very different things). The concept of "male crisis" only makes real sense opposite a "normal" situation, that is hardly ever described in detail, for good reasons. According to both psychoanalytical and postmodern theories masculine identity is perceived as a permanent crisis, making the contribution made by the concept of crisis seem rather redundant.

5.   There are many examples among gender scholars that this insight has already been incorporated; one example is given by Lynne Joyrich, who writes: "The investigation of the construction and embodiment of the previously unmarked category of masculinity is part of this effort to emphasize the differences among and within (not simply between) definitions of masculine and feminine, men and women, male and female" (*Re-viewing Reception. Television, Gender and Postmodern Culture* (Bloomington and Indianapolis: Indiana University Press, 1996), p. 71). Susan Jeffords has also acknowledged the need for feminst discussions of masculinity because "there is an increasing understanding that many of the issues that affect women's lives cannot be adequately understood without a companion understanding of the intricate interrelationships between the constructions of women's and men's lives by and through the gender system" ("The Big Switch: Hollywood Masculinity in the Nineties," in Collins, Radner and Collins (eds), *Film Theory Goes to the Movies* (New York and London: Routledge, 1993), p.197).

6.   We include two examples of the criticism directed against the field of "masculinity studies," and encourage the reader to evaluate herself whether each of the authors included in these volumes has been sufficiently forthcoming in regard to the concerns raised here. Unfortunately there is a tendency among some critics to generalize from criticism of specific research to "studies of men and masculinities" in general. We would like to suggest that criticism of certain "studies of men and masculinities" could also be read as an argument for improving these, rather than rejecting the project altogether. Andrea Cornwall and Nancy Lindisfarne emphasize that "the scrutiny of men, as men, must also embrace prior studies of women and femaleness and locate discussions of masculinity in the history of gender studies" (in *Dislocating Masculinity*, 1994, p. 28). Christine Skelton expresses her concern that much of "the new men's studies canon is characterised by omissions or distortions of fundamental elements of feminism" (in "Feminism and Research into Masculinities and Schooling", in *Gender and Education*, 10 (2), 1998, p. 220) and that "these investigations do not sufficiently engage with what feminism is 'about' to provide insights which usefully satisfy and complement existing feminist studies of gender relations" (p. 221). Both arguments could be challenged, especially because of their attempt to simplify the rather difficult task of locating "studies of men

and masculinities" within existing feminist studies/history of gender studies, their belief that this embedding is a prerequisite for complementing gender studies, and the implicit accusation that omissions of any kind are politically motivated. It would be a simple task to find other examples within more traditional gender studies, which could be blamed for distorting or omitting earlier views. And these tendencies might also simply characterize new approaches and interpretations.

Chapter 2

Men, Gender and the State

R. W. CONNELL

Men, gender and the state

Almost every state in the world is controlled by men, and almost all states of which we have historical records have been controlled by men. Yet in a few cases women have gained high political power, and of course most men never exercise state power. In this paper I want to explore how we should understand the relationship of masculinity to the state, in a way consistent with a sophisticated contemporary understanding of gender. Wishing to move toward a dynamic, not just a static, analysis, and to make the argument relevant to practice, I will conclude with some remarks on the arms trade as a case in point.

The overwhelming predominance of men in positions of state power has always been a practical problem for feminism. Indeed, the modern movement for women's emancipation began with a struggle for the right to vote, that is for women's entry into the institutions of the liberal state. Contemporary feminism has a close practical engagement with the state, as Eisenstein (1991) wittily shows.

A theory of the state, however, has been slower in coming. This has been difficult to produce, because it requires a radical shift in the perception of gender. In everyday discussion, gender (or "sex") is always taken to be the attribute of an individual. In social science too, reference to "masculinity" or "femininity" is usually taken as reference to differences in personal traits, temperament or desire, produced by interpersonal interaction along the lines of "sex roles." With such a conception of gender, there can only be an incidental connection with the institutional system we call the state.

It has gradually come to be recognized that this view of gender is inadequate; gender is also an aspect of institutions and large-scale cultural processes (Connell, 1987). This can be seen clearly in the case of education. Schools have a gendered division of labor, and a curriculum marked by a history of gender division and patriarchal control of knowledge. Schools are settings for the drawing (and erasing) of gender lines in everyday interaction, for the creation of a hierarchy of masculinities, as well as for the contestation of gender subordination. To understand gender in public education it is necessary to "think institutionally," as Hansot and Tyack (1988) put it. And what is true for public education is true for other sectors of the state.

Seeing gender as a social structure, one of the ways collective social processes are shaped, makes it possible to analyze the state as a gendered institution and inherently a site of gender politics. During the 1980s such a view spread among thinkers influenced by socialist and radical feminism, resulting in a series of attempts to define a feminist theory of the state, the best-known being the work of MacKinnon (1989) in the United States. A few years ago I suggested (Connell, 1990) that the perspective could be summarized in six theses about the gender-state:

(1) The state is the central institutionalization of the power relations of gender (power relations being one of the major sub-structures of gender relations). Conversely the state is, at a fundamental level, constituted by gender relations. The state appears "masculine" because it is a condensation of men's gender power over women. Traditional state theory cannot see gender where only men are present. But where only men are present, we are dealing with a powerful gender effect (more powerful, indeed, than most effects discussed in social theory).

(2) The state is a gendered institution, marked by its internal gender regime. The social relations within the state are ordered in terms of gender through: (A) a gender division of labor among state personnel, (B) gendered power relations, for instance in the social definition of legitimate authority, (C) a structure of emotional relations, including the social construction of sexuality. It is typical of modern state structures that the centers of state power, such as the centers of military and economic decision-making, are heavily masculinized. Though women are not categorically excluded from the state, their interests tend to be represented in more peripheral state agencies, as Grant and Tancred (1992) point out.

(3) Through its position in gender relations, and its internal gender regime, the state has the capacity to "do" gender (as ethnomethodologists put it), and also has reasons to do gender. Put more conventionally, the state develops agencies and policies concerned with gender issues, and acts to regulate gender relations in the society as a whole. Recent research on

the welfare state, such as Quadagno and Fobes's (1995) study of the U.S. "Job Corps," shows in detail how state agencies reproduce the gender division of labor and promote gender ideologies. This is not a marginal aspect of state operations. It involves a whole range of policy areas, from housing through education to criminal justice and the military (Franzway *et al.*, 1989).

(4) State activity not only regulates existing gender relations. It also helps to constitute gender relations and the social categories they define. The best-analyzed example is the role of repressive laws and state-backed medicine in constituting the category of "the homosexual" in the late nineteenth century (Greenberg, 1988). "The prostitute" was a category constituted by similar processes; "the pedophile" is a category, once medical, now being constituted by law and electoral politics. In somewhat less dramatic form, the categories of "husband" and "wife" are also constituted by state actions ranging from the legal definition of marriage to the design of tax policy and income security systems (Shaver, 1989).

(5) Because of these activities and capacities, the state is the key stake in gender politics. It is the focus of most political mobilization on gender issues. Indeed, the rise of the liberal state, with its characteristic legitimation through citizenship, was the focus of a historic change in the form of gender politics. Gender politics, formerly almost entirely local, became mass politics for the first time through the woman suffrage movement.

(6) Since gender relations are historically dynamic, marked by crisis tendencies and structural change, the state as a gendered institution is liable to crisis and transformation. Current crisis tendencies center on problems of legitimation (often to do with violence), and on the tensions arising from the gender division of labor and the accumulation of wealth.

The above points are drawn from the first wave of feminist theorizing on the state. Broadly speaking, that research took as its model the Marxist analysis of the state as a condensation of class relations. It identified men as a kind of ruling class, with a common interest somehow embodied in the institutions of the state. This gave the analysis of the gender-state a certain solidity and toughness.

But that approach also had limitations, and has come under criticism. Watson (1990) questioned whether feminism needs a theory of the state at all; this is a category of patriarchal social theory, and feminism may be better suited by a more fluid understanding of power. There has been increasing recognition in sociology of the multiple forms of gender (Lorber, 1994), and feminist postmodernism has emphasized the shifting character of gender meanings and the lack of fixed gender identities. The attempts to construct a theory of the state have almost all been conducted in rich metropolitan countries; in developing countries, both gender issues and state structures may take very different shapes (Stromquist, 1995).

In this essay I will reconsider the gendered character of states in the light of these arguments, focusing on issues about masculinity, power, and globalization. I think the initial feminist critique of gender-blind social theory was entirely justified. The feminist theorizing of the 1980s provided a good first approximation to the problem, but not a complete analysis. We can now move on to develop a more sophisticated alternative to gender-blind theory.

Powers and genders

Mainstream theories of the state tend to erase other powers. For instance, the famous Weberian definition of the state as the holder of the monopoly of legitimate force in a given territory ignores the force used by husbands toward wives. This is a widespread social pattern, whose legitimacy is only now being widely contested (Dobash and Dobash, 1992).

Can we regard husbands as a *power*? To do so flies in the face of conventional political analysis. But in the context of gender relations, husbands may well be a group with definable interests and the capacity to enforce them. Where family structure is patriarchal, husbands' interests in their wives' sexual and domestic services are institutionalized on a society-wide basis. As shown by Hollway's (1994) study of employment practice in the Tanzanian civil service, state agencies may accommodate themselves to this power, to the extent of disrupting explicit equal-opportunity policy. Domestic violence commonly expresses husbands' claim to power over their wives. But as Segal (1990) observes, interpersonal violence is not usually the basis of power; rather, it is often a sign of its contestation or breakdown.

Gender-blind political theory has recognized limits to state power mainly in economic institutions – in corporations and markets, especially multinational corporations and international markets. There has been, without doubt, an erosion of state power over the economy in the last two decades, in the face of capital flight, global sourcing (in manufacturing), and currency deregulation. Discussions of these issues almost never register the fact that global capital is gendered.

International corporations are overwhelmingly controlled by men.

They are institutionally gendered in the same ways as the state, and depend on gender divisions of labor in their workforce, for instance in "offshore" manufacturing plants with female workers and male supervisors (Enloe, 1990). World capitalism involves a gendered accumulation process, whose dimensions have been shown with great clarity by Mies (1986). Most of the documentation of these facts has come from research on "women and development"; we are in dire need of research on "men and development," that is research on the masculinity of world economic elites.

Within the metropolitan countries, another power is emerging which might be called private states. There are said to be more private "security" employees in the United States than there are police. Corporations run surveillance programs to control their own employees, commonly using computer technology. Increasing numbers of the ruling class live in "gated communities," housing complexes with fences patrolled by security employees and designed to keep out the poor, the black and the card-less. These private states are gendered: controlled by men, mostly employing men, and in the case of the gated communities, en-gating women. (The motivating "threat" has its sexual dimension.) Because their legitimacy depends on property rather than citizenship, private states escape the political pressure of women which the public state encounters as demands for equal opportunity and affirmative action.

The gender-state, then, operates in a complex field of powers. This helps explain the phenomenon so forcibly brought to our attention in the 1990s, the disintegration of state structures – even apparently well developed ones such as the USSR.

Seeing the interplay of states with other gendered powers also gives some grip on what has surprised many people, the emergence of *ethnicity* as a basis of successor states. Given the importance of patriarchy in state legitimation, it is relatively easy to ground a new state on patriarchal local powers. Ethnicity is constituted in large measure through gender relations. The notion of extended "kinship" is central to the rhetoric of ethnicity – "our kith and kin," in the old language of British racism. As Vickers (1994) notes, ethnic politics lay heavy emphasis on women's reproductive powers. Gender relations thus provide a vehicle for new claims to authority (all the leaders of the warring successor states in the former Yugoslavia and the former USSR are men), and define boundaries of the group to which loyalty is demanded.

If we thus develop a more complicated picture of power, we must also recognize more complexity in the picture of gender. It has become common, in research on men and gender, to speak of "masculinities" rather than "masculinity" (Messerschmidt, 1993). In most situations there is a culturally dominant gender pattern for men; but this is a *dominant* pattern, not a universal one. Only a minority of men may actually live an exemplary masculinity, as defined, say, by Brahmin codes in India, or by Hollywood action-hero codes in the United States. Therefore we speak of "hegemonic masculinity," which means precisely that there are also subordinated masculinities (such as found among gay men), marginalized masculinities (for example in marginalized ethnic groups), and complicit masculinities, supporting the hegemonic code but not living rigorously by it (Connell, 1995).

In the overall structure of gender relations, men are on top; but many men are not on top in terms of sexuality and gender, let alone class and race. This introduces important complexities into gender relations within and around the state. The men of oppressed ethnic groups may develop aggressive versions of hegemonic masculinity, which are criminalized when state elites perceive a problem of order – note, for instance, the very high rates of violence and imprisonment among African-American men in the United States. They may also be tapped for the purposes of the state: the same group has a high level of recruitment to the U.S. Army.

The masculinization of the state identified in feminist theory is principally a relationship between state institutions and hegemonic masculinity. This relationship is a two-way street. While hegemonic masculinity is a resource in the struggle for state power, state power is a resource in the struggle for hegemony in gender (a fact clearly apparent to both Christian and Islamic fundamentalists in current struggles).

Where some earlier formulations saw the link between masculinity and state power as a constant throughout history, we must see this as a historical relationship, which has taken different forms in the past and is open to further change now. The pattern of hegemonic masculinity altered, in the North Atlantic world, during the transition from Ancien Regime states controlled by a landowning gentry to liberal imperialist states controlled by alliances of capitalists and technocrats. Metropolitan states in the twentieth century have seen struggles between forms of masculinity whose claim to hegemony rested on expertise, and forms whose claim to hegemony rested on qualities of toughness and fitness to command (liberals versus hard-liners, professionals versus managers, and so on). Specific forms of masculinity, often exceptionally violent, emerged in the process of imperial conquest: the conquistador, the brawling frontiersman or miner, the pastoral worker (cowboys, guachos), posing changing issues for the colonial states concerned (Phillips, 1987).

With increasing integration of world markets and mass communications, local gender orders are increasingly under pressure from a global culture centered in the North Atlantic countries. To some extent this makes for a standardization of gender categories. For instance, research on sexuality has shown, in countries as far apart as Brazil and Indonesia, diverse forms of same-gender sexual relationship among men being replaced by a "gay identity" patterned on the urban culture of the United States. Yet globalization is not flat-out homogenization. As Altman (1996) observes, the emerging homosexual identities of Asia are not all of one pattern; indeed the interplay between local and imported patterns creates a very complex array of sexualities and definitions of gender.

Clearly, not all gender phenomena follow a masculine versus feminine polarity. There is also a colorful variety of inter-gender and cross-gender identities and practices (Epstein and Straub, 1991). These can pose difficulties for the state. If the police arrest someone of mixed or intermediate gender, where is she/he to be imprisoned: in the men's jail or the women's jail? Lawsuits have already been fought over this issue. Wherever the state attempts gender segregation, in fact, difficulties arise about policing the boundaries.

States

Much of the writing in this area (including my own) uses the singular universal, "the state." Recognizing the plurality of powers and genders suggests that we should also call this habit of thought into question. What is true of one state is not necessarily true of another, nor of the same state at another point of time. We need to speak of "states," and think plurally.

As with genders, this does not mean that we have to think chaotically. The multiplicity of states in history is very definitely structured. In recent world history there are two over-arching structures of relations between states. The first is the competition and alliance of independent states, originating in the European system of sovereignty. This is the pattern analyzed by the academic discipline of "international relations." The second is the pattern of imperialism – the colonial empires, the successor system of neo-colonialism, and the world markets dominated by major states and giant corporations.

Both structures have a gender dimension. This is documented for the first structure by feminist critiques of international relations theory (Peterson, 1992); for the second, by feminist critiques of development theory and world-systems theory (Mies, 1986; Ward, 1993). Let us consider the gender dynamics that arise from different situations in the history of these structures.

Colonial states

Colonial conquest often involved a direct assault on the gender orders of indigenous societies. The Portuguese conquerors of Brazil forced indigenous "Indians" into slavery on plantations, or into village settlements rigidly controlled by the church, in which their pagan ways (and languages) would be lost (Burns, 1980). The Spanish conquerors of Mexico and neighboring central and north America did similar things, including a violent attack on "sodomy," nearly obliterating the intermediate gender category (the so-called "berdache") of indigenous society (Williams, 1986).

Economic exploitation under settler colonialism in Africa also involved the "pulverization" of indigenous society, as Good (1976) put it. A major disruption of gender relations was required to produce labor forces for plantations and mines. The resulting pattern of poverty, labor migration, male labor forces living in barracks, family separation, urban sex work and long-distance travel, has provided ideal conditions for the HIV/AIDS epidemic, now a major disaster in central, western and southern Africa (Barnett and Blaikie, 1992).

In constructing a social order after conquest, the colonizers produced racialized gender orders. Though initial conquest often meant widespread interracial sex (rape, concubinage, and sometimes marriage), by the high tide of colonialism in the late nineteenth century all the major empires were operating color bars connected to a gender division of labor. The colonial states were controlled by men, for whom wives were imported from the metropolis. The interpersonal relations of colonial society revolved around "white women" who directed labor forces of domestic servants but were forbidden political expression. (The resulting experience in Papua New Guinea is documented in a remarkable oral history by Bulbeck, 1988.)

Post-colonial states

The process of decolonization necessarily challenged the imperial gender order. Some anti-colonial movements mobilized women's support and contested traditional forms of patriarchy, the Chinese communist movement being the best known case (Stacey, 1983).

It is common, however, for the establishment of a post-colonial or post-revolutionary regime to involve the reinstallation of patriarchy. Mies's (1986) sardonic observations on the cults of Marxist Founding Fathers are all too apt. The intimidation of women by Islamic revival movements in Iran and some Arab countries is a current example, where feminist attitudes among women are seen as evidence of the Western corruption of religion and culture (Tohidi, 1991).

Yet the current is not all one way. Women have achieved a considerable level of influence within the Islamic republic of Iran. The post-colonial state in India has provided a political environment in which a feminist movement could develop, known internationally through the journal *Manushi* (Kishwar and Vanita, 1984). Of the five successor states to the British Indian Empire, three have had women Prime Ministers and a fourth nearly did.

Metropolitan states

Imperialism impacts society in the metropolis as well as in the colonies. The tremendous scale of the social surplus concentrated in the imperial centers, and now in the financial centers of the global economy, changes the conditions of gender politics. It supports, for instance, the rising expectation of life and the drastic drop in birth rate that has transformed the experience of married women. But global empire also raised the size of the patriarchal dividend, the volume of social assets controlled by men. This raised the stake of gender politics for men, and helped expand the public realm in which public masculinities were constructed (Hearn, 1992).

Women's political citizenship developed first on the frontier of European settler colonialism (in North America and Australasia), next in the metropolis. Citizenship, however, has been progressively emptied of political content and replaced by the status of consumer, as the commercialization of everyday life and culture intensifies. This has involved an extensive commodification of sexuality, constituting heterosexual men as collective consumers of women's sexual services (for example through advertising and pornography).

Thus women's increased presence in the public realm has been counterbalanced by a decline of the public realm itself, and a relocation of power into market mechanisms dominated by men. The old form of state patriarchy, with masculine authority embedded in bureaucratic hierarchies, was vulnerable to challenge through equal rights campaigns. New forms of management which commodify state services (privatization, corporatization, program budgeting), and neo-liberal administrative reform agendas (Yeatman, 1990), have reconstituted state power in forms less open to feminist challenge. It is no accident that these organizational reforms coincided with a "taxpayers' revolt" and tax concessions to business, budgetary attacks on social services (which tend to benefit women), and higher military expenditure in major powers (benefiting mostly men).

The international state

A striking feature of twentieth-century political history is the attempt to overcome the anarchy of the system of sovereign states through permanent international institutions. Some of these agencies link territorial states without themselves having a territorial base. The International Labour Organization is one of the oldest, followed by the League of Nations, the United Nations and its various agencies, the World Bank and International Monetary Fund, and the more selective club of the Organization for Economic Co-operation and Development. Other agencies follow the more traditional pattern of regional customs unions or trading blocs, gradually developing into federal states. The most important of these at present is the European Union.

These agencies too are gendered, and have gender effects. For the most part their gender regimes replicate those of the territorial states that gave rise to them. The international agencies have, however, a specific importance in gender politics as means for the globalization of gender relations. As Stromquist (1995) notes, gender policies at the international level may be more progressive than their local realizations.

In other respects international agencies have reinforced rather than challenged local patriarchy. The "male bias" in most development aid is familiar – so scandalous, eventually, that aid agencies such as the World Bank were persuaded to set up special programs for women. But the general economic policies pursued by international financial agencies since the debt crisis of the 1980s has disadvantaged women, since the austerity programs forced on debtor governments have squeezed the welfare sector, on which women are generally more dependent than men, and has favored market mechanisms, which are mostly controlled by men.

Realism demands that we should also acknowledge the size and importance of intergovernmental links in the realm of violence and espionage. Military aid is the largest single component of international aid.

The resources transferred go overwhelmingly into the hands of men. In many cases the armed forces supported by these links became the main political power; these cases include Indonesia, the largest Islamic country in the world; Brazil and Argentina, the largest countries in South America; Afghanistan, where rival military forces are currently fighting for control. Military dictatorships are, without exception, patriarchal dictatorships.

A case in point: the arms trade

The gender meaning of weapons is familiar, and has deep historical roots. Fernbach (1981) speaks of the "masculine specialization in violence" that can be traced from the first armies, in the first urban societies. Armed forces are overwhelmingly composed of men today. Recent research on civilians in the United States, which has probably the most heavily armed population in the world, shows gun ownership about four times as high among men as among women (Smith and Smith, 1994).

The masculinization of weapons is not a natural fact, but a cultural pattern. (So far as natural difference goes, guns are aptly called, in Damon Runyon stories, "equalizers.") It must be constantly regenerated and reproduced. A recent study by Gibson (1994) provides a striking illustration. Gibson traces the hypermasculine cult of weaponry in "paramilitary culture" in the United States, the cult of the "new war" developed in the period since the U.S. defeat in Vietnam. This was dramatically brought to public attention by the Oklahoma City bombing in 1995.

What is worked out culturally in gun cults and violent "action movies" is also an economic reality in the form of the arms trade. This ranges from government-to-government sales of high-technology weapons systems, to the private circulation of small arms in countries whose governments officially permit arms sales, or cannot prevent them. The largest part of the arms trade is the legal equipping of military and paramilitary forces. This is no small industry. United States arms exports in 1993 totalled $32 billion.

The metal does not come naked: it comes clothed in social forms. The army is a patriarchal institution. It is no accident that civil wars, from Bangladesh (at its separation from Pakistan) to the current conflict in Bosnia, include rape in the spectrum of military operations; this is a familiar form in which armies assert dominance over conquered peoples. Recent social research inside armed forces in the United States (Barrett,

1996) reveals an oppressive but efficient regime designed to produce a narrowly defined hegemonic masculinity. It is hardly surprising that institutions with such gender regimes have difficulty incorporating women under equal opportunity rules, and difficulty with the concept (though not the reality) of gay soldiers.

Because of the social forms in which armaments are embedded, the arms trade is a vector of the globalization of gender, much as the international state is. Indeed, the two overlap, since the arms trade is connected to the globally linked military and intelligence apparatuses of the major powers. The social forms of military masculinity are exported to post-colonial states by military aid and advice programs (the mechanism by which the United States became involved in the Vietnamese war in the 1960s, with U.S. advisers constantly urging greater aggressiveness on officers of the Saigon regime), and by the training of officers in the military schools of the metropolis. In a world perspective, the modest gains of women's representation in parliaments and bureaucracies at a national level may well be outweighed by the growth of the apparatuses of patriarchal violence at an international level.

Acknowledgements

This essay draws from a paper originally presented to the Symposium on Feminist Challenges to Social Theory, at the XIII World Congress of Sociology, Bielefeld, Germany, July 1994. I am grateful to all participants in this session, a notably successful occasion despite crowded conditions.

References

Altman, Dennis (1996) "Rupture or Continuity?: The Internationalization of Gay Identities," *Social Text*, 14 (3), pp. 77-94.
Barnett, Tony and Blaikie, Piers (1992) *AIDS in Africa*. Guilford Press.
Barrett, Frank J. (1996) "The Organizational Construction of Hegemonic Masculinity: The Case of the U.S. Navy," *Gender, Work and Organization*, 3 (3), pp. 129-42.
Bulbeck, Chilla (1988) *One World Women's Movement*. London: Pluto Press.
Burns, E. Bradford (1980) *A History of Brazil*, 2nd edn. New York: Columbia University Press.
Connell, R. W. (1987) *Gender and Power: Society, the Person and Sexual Politics*. Cambridge: Polity Press.

Connell, R. W. (1990) "The State, Gender and Sexual Politics: Theory and Appraisal," *Theory and Society*, 19, pp. 507-44.

Connell, R. W. (1995) *Masculinities*. Cambridge: Polity Press.

Dobash, R. Emerson and Dobash, Russell P. (1992) *Women, Violence and Social Change*. London: Routledge.

Eisenstein, Hester (1991) *Gender Shock: Practising Feminism on Two Continents*. Sydney: Allen & Unwin.

Enloe, Cynthia (1990) *Bananas, Beaches and Bases: Making Feminist Sense of International Politics*. Berkeley: University of California Press.

Epstein, Julia and Straub, Kristina (eds) (1991) *Body Guards: The Cultural Politics of Gender Ambiguity*. New York: Routledge.

Fernbach, David (1981) *The Spiral Path: A Gay Contribution to Human Survival*. London: Gay Men's Press.

Franzway, Suzanne, Court, Dianne and Connell, R. W. (1989) *Staking a Claim: Feminism, Bureaucracy and the State*. Sydney: Allen & Unwin.

Gibson, James William (1994) *Warrior Dreams: Paramilitary Culture in Post-Vietnam America*. New York: Hill and Wang.

Good, Kenneth (1976) "Settler Colonialism: Economic Development and Class Formation," *Journal of Modern African Studies*, 14 (4).

Grant, Judith and Tancred, Peta (1992) "A Feminist Perspective on State Bureaucracy," in Mills, Albert J. and Tancred, Peta (eds), *Gendering Organizational Analysis*. Newbury Park: Sage.

Greenberg, David F. (1988) *The Construction of Homosexuality*. Chicago: University of Chicago Press.

Hansot, Elizabeth and Tyack, David (1988) "Gender in Public Schools: Thinking Institutionally," *Signs*, 13 (4), pp. 741-60.

Hearn, Jeff (1992) *Men in the Public Eye: The Construction and Deconstruction of Public Men and Public Patriarchies*. London: Routledge.

Hollway, Wendy (1994) "Separation, Integration and Difference: Contradictions in a Gender Regime," in Radtke, H. Lorraine and Stam, Henderikus (eds), *Power/Gender: Social Relations in Theory and Practice*. London: Sage.

Kishwar, Madhu and Vanita, Ruth (1984) *In Search of Answers: Indian Women's Voices from Manushi*. London: Zed Books.

Lorber, Judith (1994) *Paradoxes of Gender*. New Haven: Yale University Press.

MacKinnon, Catharine A. (1989) *Toward a Feminist Theory of the State*. Cambridge, MA: Harvard University Press.

Messerschmidt, James W. (1993). *Masculinities and Crime: Critique and Reconceptualization of Theory*. Lanham: Rowman & Littlefield.

Mies, Maria (1986) *Patriarchy and Accumulation on a World Scale: Women in the International Division of Labour*. London: Zed Books.

Peterson, V. Spike (ed.) (1992) *Gendered States: Feminist (Re)Visions of International Relations Theory*. Boulder: Lynne Rienner.

Phillips, Jock (1987) *A Man's Country? the Image of the Pakeha Male - A History*. Auckland: Penguin.

Quadagno, Jill and Fobes, Catherine (1995) "The Welfare State and the Cultural Reproduction of Gender: Making Good Girls and Boys in the Job Corps," *Social Problems*, 42 (2), pp. 171-90.

Segal, Lynne (1990) *Slow Motion: Changing Masculinities, Changing Men*. London: Virago.

Shaver, Sheila (1989) "Gender, Class and the Welfare State: The Case of Income Security," *Feminist Review*, 32.

Smith, Tom W. and Smith, Robert J. (1994) "Changes in Firearm Ownership among Women, 1980-1994." Paper presented to meeting of the American Society of Criminology, Miami.

Stacey, Judith (1983) *Patriarchy and Socialist Revolution in China*. Berkeley: University of California Press.

Stromquist, Nelly P. (1995) "State Policies and Gender Equity: Comparative Perspectives." Paper presented to second annual Missouri Symposium on Research and Educational Policy, University of Missouri-Columbia.

Tohidi, Nayereh (1991) "Gender and Islamic Fundamentalism: Feminist Politics in Iran," in Mohanty, Chandra Talpade, Russo, Ann and Torres, Lourdes (eds), *Third World Women and the Politics of Feminism*. Bloomington: Indiana University Press.

Vickers, Jill (1994) "Notes toward a Political Theory of Sex and Power," in Radtke, H. Lorraine and Stam, Henderikus J. (eds), *Power/Gender: Social Relations in Theory and Practice*. London: Sage 1994.

Ward, Kathryn B. (1993) "Reconceptualizing World System Theory to Include Women," in England, Paula (ed.), *Theory on Gender/Feminism on Theory*. New York: Aldine de Gruyter.

Watson, Sophie (ed.) (1990) *Playing the State: Australian Feminist Interventions*. Sydney: Allen & Unwin.

Williams, Walter L. (1986). *The Spirit and the Flesh: Sexual Diversity in American Indian Culture*. Boston: Beacon Press.

Yeatman, Anna (1990) *Bureaucrats, Technocrats, Femocrats: Essays on the Contemporary Australian State*. Sydney: Allen & Unwin.

Chapter 3

A Theory of Gender, Patriarchy and Capitalism

ØYSTEIN GULLVÅG HOLTER

The present essay was originally written for my doctoral thesis (Holter, 1997). It does not deal with men as such, but rather with the frameworks that we use for interpreting gender, masculinities included. It especially addresses the long-standing questions of the relationship between capital and patriarchy, asking whether capital is genderless, or whether male dominance is reproduced through economic relations "by design."

I shall first briefly outline some common views of capital and gender, and recent research on the capital/gender connection. Next I present a critical gender theory that builds on this research. Finally, I discuss how a social forms view of gender and capital may extend and nuance such a theory.

Some common approaches

The conventional view of gender and capitalism in sociology has been of two phenomena that are fairly distant, or even separate. It is an "isolationist" view since it tends to isolate gender from other issues. For example, one can first discuss "the constitution of society" without reference to gender or feminist theory, as Anthony Giddens (1993) does in a recent work, and then eventually turn to gender as a separate phenomenon. This is still a fairly common approach in sociology, and one which I question. Capitalism, in this view, may have some impact on gender (or vice versa), yet this is not a central relation in order to understand modern society.

A second approach may be called "externalist," since the impact of capitalism on gender is seen as something external, coming from without; it is a relation crossing a great gap or distance. Gender, usually conceived as something which is there already, is among all those "peripheral" and partly "traditional" phenomena that are changed with the new age of capital. This is also fairly common in sociology. Both the "isolationist" and the "externalist" views exist in two main versions: a mainstream (and also fairly "malestream") version where capital is central and gender is peripheral, and a feminist and gender studies version where gender is central and capital is peripheral.

A third set of views that includes my own approach can be called "internalist." Capital and gender are not externally but internally related. This "inner" relation may not be a direct or simple one, but it is so important that it comes into the constitution of modern gender – and perhaps not only gender, but capital and society at large. Twenty years ago, this approach was discussed in terms of a "marriage" between feminist and Marxist theory (for example Hartmann, 1979), a failed marriage according to many, yet not entirely without offspring.

Before evaluating different theories in this field, it should be noted that much research over the past two decades has strengthened the broad assumption that the capital/gender connection is a central one, and weakened the "isolationist" and "externalist" views.

Research on the impact of capitalism

This research has been done in four main areas: historical sociology, institutional sociology, women's studies, and recently also studies of men. The findings in each area shall be briefly outlined here.

Historically, it has been shown that older conceptions of gender and sex were more radically transformed by capitalism than has commonly been believed. Premodern societies were characterised more by a patriarchal order with sex difference as one element, than by a gender system as such, and gender conceptions were often "unisexed" or not systematically polarized. For example, Thomas Laqueur (1990) has shown that even in the medicine of early modernity, women's sex was conceived along male lines as a kind of inverted maleness. Premodern images of men and women were occupied more with sin and salvation than with sex difference as such, and this difference was often toned down. Although the gender system that emerged in the eighteenth and nineteenth century built on older elements, these were put into a new framework, which was usually "archaized" and perceived as if it was based on natural characteristics. The word "sexuality," invented a hundred years ago, is an example. In the view of Michel Foucault (1977), a new sexual disciplinary system was in the making, and while Foucault focused on its classification and repression of homosexuals, I believe it was primarily a new ordering of men and women, a drastic transformation of the earlier patriarchal society.

What was new about it can be summarized in five main points. First, it is often forgotten that the introduction of capitalism was followed by a massive and historically unique victimization process that mainly hit women, in the form of witch hunts, a process that should be seen as a parallel to early capital's "primitive accumulation" discussed by Marx. This went together with a tightening of patriarchal control on other fronts, followed by an "indoctrination period" gradually legitimized by reference to women's special nature.

Second, a concept of democratic gender gradually emerged, together with industrialization and acceptance of working-class democratic demands. This system was characterized by individuals' free choice (on gendered premises), all very different from the old order of lords and dependants, and belonging to what I call the early "masculinatic" phase of modern patriarchy.[1]

Third, this democratized gender increasingly became a centre of institutionalization, for example as regards family formation, so that even the older traits of the gender system now played a new role.

Fourth, the gender system grew into a "meta-institutional" principle on a societal level, a system running through most institutions of society, both in implicit background forms in the production sphere, and in more explicit forms related to families and the sphere of reproduction.

I regard these last two processes as still in the making today, with gender as an increasingly powerful and absorbent paradigm of society, partially replacing the class paradigm.

In sum, historical studies have shown that our gendered ways are more modern than we usually believe, linked first to victimization and persecution, and later also to concepts of democracy, anonymity and personal freedom, and to new forms of institutionalization. Why is it that this change has not been more broadly recognized? This is not, I argue, only a matter of reification, of new social relations appearing as if they were based in materiality or biology itself. (It should be noted that the modern gender system, true to its commodity approach, has never been much interested in biology or inner content. What matters is external appearances, body form, as has been shown, for example, in studies of hermaphrodites. "Give me the right sex organs; who cares about biology" is in practice the ruling guideline of the modern gender market, creating a market for plastic surgery as well. So in a sense sociobiology fails to hit the mark, and socio-anatomy is created instead.) The lack of recognition is also due to the fact that theorists often fail to distinguish sex difference-related organization as part of some other order, such as patriarchy, and a sex difference system that becomes socially effective *on its own*, which is the case with the modern gender system, and which makes it so different from anything else that we should perhaps reserve the word "gender" for this system alone. No other known form of society effectuates patriarchal relations not through patriarchy itself, but through gender, through a system of presumably biology-based individual choices of men and women. This is the reason why premodern patriarchs mainly were not interested in women's so-called "nature" (except perhaps as ornamental philosophy), and why struggle over patriarchy – a very common theme – was not conceived as gender struggle, as today. Modern theorists tend to assume that since sex difference is there, gender is there also, and I think this mainly reflects our own local ideology, what I call the modern "gender fixation." This, in my view, is bound up with gender as economically submerged patriarchy and an intimate and efficient form of reification.

As soon as one looks at gender as something people *do*, things become more variable. Sexuality studies especially – and other praxis-related studies, rather than gender theorizing as such – have been important for extending our awareness of the historical character of gender, tracing the changes from broader conceptions of intimacy and erotics *within* a strong and open patriarchal order, to a sexual file system effectuated through self-discipline and individual choice, free from any external framework (Boswell, 1980; Gillis, 1995).

While critical theory has argued that capitalism is characterized by "labor mediation" of institutions, a labor value background of most processes (Postone, 1993), feminist research has been uncovering a "gender mediation" that seems to be as important as the traditional labor concept, and also closely related to it (Pateman, 1988; Jonasdóttir, 1991).

I only mention institutional sociology briefly here, since one main area was covered in my first presentation, concerning how a supposedly rational economic system re-creates male dominance. Family studies have been another important area (Moxnes, 1989). Often, however, this field has been investigated from the angle of gender's impact on capitalism, rather than vice versa, which leaves unanswered the question of where this gender came from in the first place. Analysts often turn to male hierarchies, yet these are not historical constants. Even if one believes they are old, we need an explanation of why some forms of male hierarchy persist in capitalism and are reorganized, while other parts are dissolved.

The impact of capitalism on gender was a topic in the emerging women's studies in the 1970s especially, with texts on the change from personal to structural dominance and the individuation of gender and family roles (Holter, 1970, 1976), femininity and alienation (Foreman, 1977), and similar works. At that time, the alliance between the new women's studies and ot er critical research was very important, and there was a tendency to portray gender oppression as a subdivision of capitalist oppression – a "masculinistic" tendency that contributed to the 1980s turning of feminist theory towards other approaches, such as psychoanalysis, phenomenology and postmodernism. Yet even if the capital/gender relationship was to some extent left behind by the main developments of feminist theory during the 1980s, important advances were made in this area also, and there has been a kind of renaissance in the 1990s, combined with an institutional focus and more nuanced mid-level theory.

Today, it is noteworthy that when one searches for gender, patriarchy and capital in social science data bases, one will find not only theoretical contributions, but also a growing number of empirical studies, in areas as diverse as the catering industry in the United Kingdom, carpet weaving in Iran and tea plantations in India (Bagguley, 1991; Balagopal, 1990; Ghvamshahidi, 1995). The catering study summarizes what has now become a fairly widespread view in this field: "The restructuring of gender segregation in the hotel and catering industry can only be understood through a grasp of patriarchal and capitalist processes in concert with a middle range conceptualization of how the two systems interact" (Bagguley, 1991).

In studies of men, the capital/gender relationship has often been a subdued background subject, yet recently it has also emerged as a more important topic on its own. One reason for the subduedness was that men's studies mainly took off from women's studies in the 1980s, focusing on men as gender in a fairly overt way – and not on men as presumed neutrals. This is what Helene Aarseth has called the "derived subject" tendency: men become important when what they do seem immediately important from women's angle, so we get studies of men and childcare, or men and violence, while what men do in presumed neutral roles has been given less attention. Recently, however, we have seen advances such as Robert Connell's masculinity hierarchy theory, which links masculine and capitalist ideals in the notion of "hegemonic masculinity" (Connell, 1995, 1993), Michael Kimmel's (1996) analysis of US masculinity as constructed around competition, market performance and anxiety, and Jeff Hearn's (1993) exploration of the masculine construction of the public sphere.

In sum, recent advances in all these fields shed new light on the capital/gender connection. Other areas should also be mentioned, such as social psychological research on gender as a means of personal valorization, the impact of commercialism on body and gender ideals and the sex-violence syndrome (for example Skårderud, 1997). Generally, however, the research is still mostly in a beginning phase, and the subject is often treated indirectly and unsystematically. Also, there is often a third party that knocks on the theorist's door: the concept of patriarchy, and the unresolved issue of the relationship of capital to patriarchy, which is still often only vaguely distinguished from the capital/gender relation.

A gender-critical theory

I shall turn to my own theoretical approach, which can be divided into two main phases: a gender-critical theory developed in the late 1970s and 1980s, and an extension and nuancing of this theory in terms of social forms analysis developed in the 1990s.

In a 1980 study of partner selection and the "gender market," I traced the changing meanings of gender through a key transition of the gender system: an area where gender is no longer a "potential" or embedded in other relations, but appears on its own, anonymously and abstracted in its own kind of public sphere, in the beginning of the process leading to couple and family formation. In the thesis (Holter, 1997), I discuss this as a praxis and institutional approach to gender – investigating gender not as a general concept but as a specific institutional process. I also discuss the gender exchange relation, which appears most clearly in the gender market, as a kind of lens for investigating the gender system as a whole. Certainly it is not the only kind of lens, and as we shall see it does not consist only of exchange elements. Yet as the main entry point to the family system and the point where the link between two main spheres of society is renewed, it remains an important and surprisingly often overlooked path of approach. This is true not only from a gender angle but also for investigating the renewal of class and ethnicity relations. I also find that a certain amount of rejection and denial is involved at this point, a theoretical aversion that can be found in practical partner selection, a common tendency to look away from exchange and concentrate on other aspects of what goes on, emphasizing the unique and the personal instead.

In the thesis, I do not just analyze how exchange comes into the gender relationship, but how a certain form of exchange *creates* gender, or contributes to the constitution of gender. In other words, given a certain relationship between two main social spheres and a certain way in which this relationship is renewed, gender is the outcome; a gender system becomes the social manifestation of background relations that do not directly appear by themselves. This kind of argument is characteristic of *value forms analysis*, which unlike conventional value analysis does not deal mainly with magnitudes of value or the value/price issue, but with the specific *socioeconomic form* in which background relations appear. Although the question *"why do they appear in this form"* is perhaps the most interesting aspect of Marx as a sociologist, it has mainly been neglected in sociology, in favor of either a humanistic, non-forms-aware interpretation of Marx, or an orthodox dialectical-materialist one. Both tend to put the concept, the abstraction, above historical change, which is precisely what Marx tried to avoid. They also tend to assume that economy is "basic," yet in the value forms tradition it is instead analyzed as a code, a medium, which is indicative of hidden background relations, although it also distorts things and tends to turn them upside down. So my questions are: Why does the relationship between society's production and reproduction processes appear as a gender relation, how does this constitute gender, and what does it tell us of the dynamics of the gender system? What I find, then, is a paradox: a relation that is egalitarian, exchange-based, and yet able to transmit asymmetry and dominance. How can that be?

I analyze gender exchange as a two-tiered process. It is partly a symmetrical deal characterized by simple exchange, verging on gift and other relations, and partly a non-symmetrical deal that involves a particular form of reification of women and the feminine. On the first, symmetrical level, one person is posited as being equal to the other, and differences between the two are incidental or personal. On the second, deeper level, there is not a meeting of persons in this sense, but of money and social control on the male side, and woman as sex or beauty object on the female side. Subsequent studies since 1980 have strengthened rather than weakened this argument. It is generally found that partner selection is indeed a gender-conservative area where the "money meets beauty" relation is still in force. I argue that it is precisely the *combination* of the two levels that creates our concepts of gender. This is the case because the symmetrical level relation basically only creates personal positions and identities, while the second level basically only creates men as subjects while women become their collective objects. The combination retains this second element and yet makes women themselves, as subjects, "in on the deal." An exchange of women (as objects) between men is thereby fulfilled through an exchange between men and women (as subjects).

Further, I argue that the two main positions in this double-level relation create two distinct world views, what I call the relative and equivalent position outlooks, characterizing masculinity and femininity respectively. For men, gender tends to be one element in a series, not something one feels forced to take into account (for example in sociology), but rather something that can be dissolved in a greater neutrality. The commodity in the relative (or production sphere) position in the asymmetrical relation does not depend on this relation for its realization even though it depends on it for its longer-term reproduction needs. It is not confined to this kind of exchange, so in a sense this position is "bigamist." The commodity in the equivalent (or reproduction sphere) position, on the other hand, depends on this relation for its realization, and therefore gender is not perceived as a minor matter or comparable to other exchange but rather as a *key link* to the world at large.

This analysis is a reworking of Marx's kernel reification theory, and although it does not solve all problems in this area, it does contribute to a more social explanation of de Beauvoir's classic idea of femininity as *immanence* and masculinity as *transcendence* than what de Beauvoir herself offers. In the thesis I also make it clear that this rather abstract model should be interpreted as a matter of tendencies: whatever is placed in the equivalent position, regardless of the physical sex of the person, will tend to be experienced in feminine terms, while the relative position will be experienced as masculine. I also believe this analysis works better than much current gender-as-performance theorizing. We cannot understand gender as action unless we understand why it presents itself to us as something which "simply is there," something we *are* before we *do* anything – and if gender is in fact part of a reification process, we are closer to understanding why this is so.

What are the hidden relations that, according to this view, are expressed through gender? Although my own approach has been work-oriented, I emphasize that we really do not know very much about what gender expresses, that we should be careful about hasty assumptions, and in the thesis I evaluate my 1980s contributions according to what seems to hold true, as fairly "robust" theory, yielding empirical knowledge in a variety of contexts. What remains, then, is a development of dual sphere theory in terms of the orientation of activities, towards people (reproduction) or towards things (production). This is developed in a more specific model of activity functions, a "function pyramid." This pyramid reaches from strategic production work at the top, downwards through production of means of production (heavy industry), further to production of means of reproduction (light industry), and further down to reproduction of producers, reproducers, and finally, at the bottom, reproduction of non-active, disabled people. Benefits usually pass upwards in the pyramid, burdens downwards.

It is a system of exploitation, but this is *not* visible; what appears, instead, is upside down, a view of producers creating all value and kindly paying for reproduction as well. This is why we have to look at *gender* in order to understand what goes on, for here, production's dominance over reproduction and the exploitation of the reproducers do appear, if we know how to look, how to interpret the gender value "code." Work life studies leave little doubt that the function pyramid model gives a useful and important map of power and exploitation in contemporary society, and one main answer as to why patriarchy is still around.

In the thesis I also go further into the division between production and reproduction and its historical background. I describe a "differentiation principle" of commodity economy, an inner barrier that becomes socially important given certain circumstances. Commodity economies, I argue, cannot fully reproduce themselves in their own way. They cannot possibly treat all activities equally, as commodity-creative activities, since if this were the case, with reproduction of people counting the same as production of things, the category of private ownership would disappear. The economy would be transformed into a complex redistributive system. The work that creates commodity owners cannot be counted as commodity-creative work, even when this work undoubtedly does create a key element, namely the labor force, which undoubtedly exists as commodities in our society. If it were, each producer's capacities would be owned by a chain of reproducers stretching backwards, and the free economic agent would suddenly be very much "embedded" in other kinds of obligations.

I think that this value differentiation approach is very important, as important as the traditional division between value and use value, and eventually one that may transform our ideas of critical political economy generally, although only some beginning steps are presented in the thesis.

Although it may be approached as a logical principle, value differentiation is primarily a historical process, becoming socially and institutionally effective only in certain historical circumstances. As long as commodity exchange is only one moment in society as a whole, an extension of a mainly household-based economy, the principle may be present logically speaking, and yet have little social impact. Things change, however, when commodity economy in the form of "realized," industrial capitalism sweeps the whole table, when older systems are finally broken down and dismantled. Now, it rises to the forefront; now we gradually get a major social division between two main spheres, one of which produces things, while the other seemingly stands as a counter-sphere to the first. This counter-sphere seems to be characterized by non-work or counter-work rather than work, a passive being, and so it is populated by a special race of "home-being" persons as the Norwegian expression goes ("hjemmeværende"). It becomes an ideal sphere of family and love. The household, formerly the centre of the economic sphere, now appears without any economic tasks at all except as a site of consumption, society's appendix. Only over the past decades have feminists painstakingly been able to *start* questioning some of this ideology, and it still dominates, although the increasing emphasis on human capital has made its dominance less absolute than before.

As can be seen, this critical gender approach mainly says that the dominance of production over reproduction, which is created by the differentiation principle, the fact that reproduction cannot take direct part in value distribution and cannot be given basic work rights like other kinds of work, is reflected in the gender system. It also says that this reflection is often backwards and distorted, in ways to be expected in non-monetary exchange forms, so that men's control of women appears as a characteristic of femininity (as does the exchange aspect of the whole relation, which is often attributed to the equivalent position), while women's work for men appears as a characteristic of masculinity, as men's larger "social size," responsibility, rationality, and so on. Further, it explains *why* this appears to be something biological given, so that we still in 1997 get serious research trying to weigh between the so-called natural and the social factors of the oppression of women – alias "gender." It even allows us to understand why such tendencies are *strengthened*, together with increased commercialization, even in the current context of greater gender equality.

On this basis I also distinguish between the gender system – as a social form that involves reference to the value form of gender – and patriarchy, which I define as relations that in consequence lead to oppression of women, whatever their social form. The function pyramid and the related economic concept of "horizontal" discrimination are important parts of contemporary patriarchy, or what I call the *masculinatic* form, while the older *paternatic* form of patriarchy relied on more open vertical dominance relations. I connect this shift to a shift in the mode of surplus value production, from absolute to relative surplus value.

In this analysis, gender and patriarchy are only partially overlapping fields; patriarchy can be addressed as a subject of study on its own, and the effects of gender fetishism, namely that oppression, also, is interpreted as if it somehow stemmed from gender as such, can be corrected. The gender system is a mixture of different elements, some of which are patriarchal, others not, and we can analyze people's gender-related aspirations not only as a matter of continued oppression but as attempts to move away from it, in more egalitarian directions. In this process, gender itself is so to speak dragged out of the exchange relation and into other kinds of relationships. This brings me to my final theme.

A social forms approach

In an early 1970s work, Jean-François Lyotard (1993) pointed to the tendency of critical theory to remain within the field of the object criticized. I think this is partially true also of my own 1980s approach, and of other capital/gender models – they tend to extend a masculine conceptualization, although this is done in a negative form; they do not really move beyond it and towards a more "radical other." My own approach was criticized for being "economistic" (Fürst, 1995, p. 138), and although some of this criticism seems mainly to have conveyed an unwillingness among feminists to consider gender as a value and capital process, some of it was true, and I have tried to change the course accordingly. Also, long-term cooperation with anthropologists played a main role here, as well as historical studies of patriarchy.

My point of departure, then, was historical studies as well as a new conceptualization of the equality agenda: not a movement away from questions of exploitation and oppression, but these *combined* with wider questions of *reciprocity*, not just who gets how much, but *how*, in what kinds of relations. Social forms analysis starts out from three dimensions: *power and exploitation* as the vertical dimension, *activity orientation* as the horizontal dimension, and *reciprocity form* as the depth dimension. Three main "elementary" forms of reciprocity are recognized: redistribution, gift relations, and exchange relations. Just as, in my view, capital consists of a hierarchy of different value forms, so this hierarchy coexists with other transfer forms, although these are often only latent, existing in the background in our society. One main example relates to the differentiation principle, the fact that *if* producers and reproducers should count alike, producers would no longer be independent owners: we know that this independence is important on the exchange level, yet it is also, in the background, surrounded by a "shadow economy" of other principles, other obligations, that we tend to think of in psychological terms (or in the masculine spirit: not to think of at all). To give a more concrete example: a so-called "care chain" for a child or a disabled person may involve people through gift relations, redistributive relations and exchange relations, quite different logics that do not always work harmoniously together.

I cannot go further into the social forms analysis framework here, but only highlight some of its possibilities in terms of gender. If what I have said of the gender equivalent position holds true, it becomes more understandable why women not only seek to address imbalance in this relation, but also to shift the whole relationship terrain away from exchange, towards giving and redistributing. *There* it is not they, but rather the men who are restricted. Generally feminists have argued that male theories of work and free time, the system and life world and so on, do not really fit women's lives; we may also say that the fit becomes worse, the closer "work" and "the household" are brought together. Work is usually clearly demarcated in exchange relations, and sometimes in redistributive systems, while in gift systems it tends to appear as a wider category: "life." We do not need to go to exotic societies in order to study these transformations, we can look for example at our own family sphere (Borchgrevink and Holter 1994). Further, the reciprocity dimension seems important (and overlooked) also in work life and organizational studies, for even if exchange and capital logic may dominate, it seldom rules the agenda alone, instead it interacts with background systems, seeking also to transform these. We may even argue that gifts have become a modern "ideology," created by capital (Carrier, 1990), yet this does not exhaust the issue.

On the basis of a broad analysis of historical, institutional and anthropological studies, I argue that the differentiation principle and the exchange form as a whole have been a much more stable basis for patriarchy than other reciprocity forms. It is in the historical development of commodity economy that we find the power of men in some spheres of society extended into the state patriarchal power, the power of patriarchs or free household heads over society as a whole, gradually creating male dominance as a general societal principle. Also, I find that this system existed in a long historical build-up process *before* there was much of a patriarchal *gender* system, which has often mistakenly been attributed to the distant past. It is something of a scandal, considering our current gender fixation, that it has been overlooked that for a couple of thousand years would-be patriarchs mainly legitimized themselves in terms of a fairly *egalitarian*, even female-prominent gender system, using female more than male religious images and so on in their efforts. This tendency can be found until the time of the great patriarchal monotheistic religions and in the early periods it dominates. Compared to this central build-up of patriarchal power in commodity societies, societies dominated by redistribution and gift-giving have been a much more varied lot, and an area where researchers have varying opinions. Mainly, the argument that these also were/are all patriarchal has been weakened by research over the last decades.

If this holds true as a broad historical generalization, we may examine whether it holds true today also, and investigate how different patterns of reciprocity affect gender-related outcomes in our own society. Here, questions of leadership and organizational design reappear. On the whole, social forms analysis is an attempt to extend the Norwegian tradition of "relational feminism" in a sociological direction.

Conclusion

The critical gender theory and social forms analysis presented here show that capitalism, based on the value differentiation principle, created a new, "economically submerged" patriarchal order, in the form of a gender system, a polarity of the gendered/feminine on the one hand and the neutered/masculine on the other. This system is historically and sociologically unique and can be understood without resorting to biologistic fetishism. We can avoid a gender fixation, which today often includes the use of a negative masculine mystique as explanation for continued inequality. The gender system includes older elements and a sex difference organization that by itself has no relation to dominance, yet is continually transformed into relations of stratification.

Further, I show that traditional critical analyses of capitalism have been one-sided by ignoring women's work and lives and neglecting other reciprocity forms that exist within capitalism itself. We cannot understand value and capital without looking at their reproduction, and this involves women, the differentiation of value, and the historical construction of a counter-sphere which is both a part of and an opposition to capitalism. Rather than static or deterministic structuralism, the structural parts of my theory emphasize the contradictory and partially independent and oppositional character of the gender system and of the latent and background forms of reciprocity in modern society. The theory combines a model of exploitation-based oppression, a value form interpretation of gender, and a qualitative view of reciprocity, generating propositions that are in principle empirically testable, like the exploitation of reproductive work and the specific contributions of gender. By disentangling the gender system from patriarchal structure, identifying more of their interconnections, it opens the way for more precise studies of both. Although the theory can be used in order to understand why gender-equal status is still a distant goal in many areas, especially in the vicinity of capital and commodities, the question of the future relationship between capital and patriarchy is left open, yet one which can now be addressed in more precise ways, focusing both on the wider reciprocity context of the economy, including the welfare state, and on the relational and human-capital-related changes within the economy itself. In sum, I hope it helps researchers venture into socially denied areas, break some of the theory barrier between private and societal life, ask new questions, conceptualize what they find, and go further on from there.

Note

1. As developed in my *Men's Life Patterns* (in Norwegian, Oslo, 1993), the three terms "paternate," "masculinate" and "androgynate" can be used for the three main modern forms of patriarchy.

References

Bagguley, Paul (1991) "The Patriarchal Restructuring of Gender Segregation: A Case Study of the Hotel and Catering Industry," *Sociology*, 25 (4), pp. 607-25.

Balagopal, Gopalan (1990) "Women in Tea Plantations - A Case from the Dooars Area of West Bengal," *Indian Journal of Social Science*, 3 (3), pp. 431-42.

Borchgrevink, Tordis and Holter, Øystein Gullvåg (eds) (1994) *Labour of Love - Beyond the Self-Evidence of Everyday Life*. Aldershot: Avebury.

Boswell, John (1980) *Christianity, Social Tolerance and Homosexuality*. Chicago: University of Chicago Press.

Carrier, James (1990) "Gifts in a World of Commodities: The Ideology of the Perfect Gift in American Society," *Social Analysis*, 29, pp. 19-37.

Connell, R. W. (1993) "The Big Picture - Masculinities in Recent World History," *Theory and Society*, 22, pp. 597-623.

Connell, R. W. (1995) *Masculinities*. Cambridge: Polity Press.

Foreman, Ann (1977) *Femininity as Alienation*. London: Pluto Press.

Foucault, Michel (1977) *The History of Sexuality Vol. 1*. Harmondsworth: Penguin.

Fürst, Elisabeth L'orange (1995) *Mat - et annet språk. Rasjonalitet, kropp og kvinnelighet*. Oslo: Pax.

Ghvamshahidi, Zohreh (1995) "The Linkage between Iranian Patriarchy and the Informal Economy in Production," *Women's Studies International Forum*, 18 (2), March-April, pp. 135-51.

Giddens, Anthony (1993) *The Constitution of Society - Outline of the Theory of Structuration*. Cambridge: Polity Press.

Gillis, John (1995) "En reise gjennom faderskapets historie:er vi på feil spor?" *Kvinneforskning*, 1, pp. 14-31. Originally titled "Bringing Up The Father: British Paternal Identities, 1750-present," paper presented at the "Men's families" conference, Copenhagen.

Hartmann, Heidi I. (1979) "The Unhappy Marriage of Marxism and Feminism: Towards a More Progressive Union," *Capital and Class*, 8, pp. 1-33.

Hearn, Jeff (1993) *Men In The Public Eye*. London: Routledge.

Holter, Harriet (1970) *Sex Roles and Social Structure*. Oslo: Universitetsforlaget.

Holter, Harriet *et al.* (1976) *Familien i klassesamfunnet*. Oslo: Pax.

Holter, Øystein Gullvåg (1980) *Kjønnsmarkedet (The Gender Market)*. Thesis (magistergradsoppgave) in sociology, The Institute of Sociology (Arbeidsnotat nr. 151), University of Oslo.

Holter, Øystein Gullvåg (1997) *Gender, Patriarchy and Capitalism - A Social Forms Analysis*, Dr. philos thesis (sociology), University of Oslo. Published by the Work Research Institute, Oslo.

Jonasdóttir, Anna G. (1991) "Love Power and Political Interest," *Ørebro Studies*, 7, Ørebro.

Kimmel, Michael S. (1996) *Manhood in America*. New York: The Free Press.

Laqueur, Thomas (1990) *Making Sex - Body and Gender from the Greeks to Freud*. Cambridge, Mass. and London: Harvard University Press.

Lyotard, Jean-Francois (1993) *Libidinal Economy* (orig. 1974). Bloomington: Indiana University Press.

Moxnes, Kari (1989) *Kjernesprengning i familien*. Oslo: Universitetsforlaget.

Pateman, Carole (1988) *The Sexual Contract*. Oxford: Polity Press.

Postone, Moishe (1993) *Time, Labour and Social Domination - A Reinterpretation of Marx's Critical Theory*. Cambridge: Cambridge University Press.

Skårderud, Finn (1997) "Vil gi år av livet for idealkroppen - skjønnhetsfokusering på ville veier," Interview in *Dagbladet*, 23 May, 1997.

Chapter 4

The Emancipation from Gender: A Critique of the Utopias of Postmodern Gender Theory

MIKAEL CARLEHEDEN

Some of the most apparent and important examples of the ongoing transformation of modern society concern gender and sexuality. R. W. Connell (1995, pp. 84ff) has summarized the most important changes in post-war gender order: 1) a historic collapse of the legitimacy of patriarchal power and the rise of a global movement for the emancipation of women, 2) a vast growth in married women's employment in the rich countries, and 3) women's increasing demand for sexual pleasure and control over their own bodies, as well as an increased acceptance of bi- and homosexuality. The continuing radical transformation of the situation and self-understanding of women has in turn been followed by a late-arriving and drowsy questioning of "the hegemonic masculinity" among men.[1]

Today, more and more of us in contemporary Western societies are thus in the process of losing, or becoming liberated from (depending on how one looks at it) what might be modernity's last unreflected certainties, the related ideas of natural gender identities and natural sexual orientations.[2] To capture the immediate result of this development we can borrow a term from the German weekly *Der Spiegel* (1996, No. 5), which describes the present situation under the heading of "die Verwirrung der Geschlechter" (gender confusion).

My primary intention in this article, however, is not to describe the actual changes of gender identity and gender relations.[3] The denaturalization of sex and sexuality here rather makes up the background which opens up to a general discussion of how we now should look at gender-related questions. In the field of gender theory one immediately comes across two conflicting meta-theories with normative implications – "essentialism" and "social constructivism." While the former to a great extent links gender to biological sex, the latter holds that gender first and foremost should be understood as a social and historical phenomenon. I am dissatisfied with both of these alternatives. The former obviously does not posses the theoretical tools to explain the ongoing *social* transformation of gender. Its normative implications are also highly questionable from the perspective of women's equal rights and worth. The latter is theoretically much stronger, but it is, to a very high degree, under the spell of postmodern philosophy. Social constructivism distinguishes itself by directly associating all mention of identity with essentialism and thus by an extremely radical critique of the concept of identity.[4] This theory thus tends to view the gender identity issue which people in a society without certainties grapple with as a form of "false consciousness." The situation which *Der Spiegel* terms "gender confusion" would be interpreted as freedom by a postmodern social constructivist. In this article I will criticize the equal sign between identity and essentialism which to a great extent dictates the postmodern gender theory's problematic. This criticism is the start of an attempt to develop a theory of gender between essentialism and postmodern constructivism.

The foundations of postmodern gender theory

It should be acknowledged to begin with, that the meaning of the term "postmodern," in spite of the fact that it has become a standard term in sociological textbooks, is still very unclear. Not only is the term used in many different ways, but also few of the people who are called postmodernists accept this mantle. Here we run into the recurrent problem in sorting theories into various schools of thought. Thinkers would rather highlight their own originality than be grouped together with others. As is well known, even Marx denied being a Marxist. The problem is even more acute when we are dealing with postmodernists, in that they are critical of identifying concepts in general. As we will see, it is, however, precisely this common point, the fundamental importance of non-identity, which justifies us in speaking of postmodernism.

Postmodern gender theory's fulcrum can today be said to lie in the USA.[5] In the following I shall concentrate on the thought of Judith Butler. I see her theory as one of the most developed postmodern gender theories.[6] With the help of her work we can see the outlines of a figure of thought that plays a central role in today's gender debate. Her primary thesis is that our bodies are "discursively" constructed. In a telling passage Butler (1990a, p. 337) writes:

If the inner truth of gender is a fabrication and if a true gender is a fantasy instituted and inscribed on the surface of our bodies, then it seems that genders can be neither true nor false but are only produced as the truth effects of a discourse of primary and stable identity.

The form of constructivism that Butler develops has its roots in French philosophical postmodernism, most importantly Foucault,[7] but also, for instance, Lacan, Lyotard and Derrida. From this philosophy, at least two fundamental assumptions are drawn, the first being the rejection of "philosophy of identity" and the second being the rejection of "philosophy of the subject." Philosophical postmodernism is primarily oriented against the modern conception of reason. I have argued elsewhere that this critique of reason has resulted only in a negation of Enlightenment philosophy and thereby remains negatively attached to precisely that which it criticizes (Carleheden, 1996). I believe that postmodern gender theory has acquired some of postmodern philosophy's paradoxes. To examine this, it is necessary to look deeper into postmodernism's critique of the philosophies of identity and the subject, before beginning a critique of postmodern gender theory.

The critique of the philosophy of identity

The term "philosophy of identity" can be traced back to Schelling, but it is most often the thought of Hegel and its claim to absolute knowledge which has come to represent this form of thinking. In it, differences are referred back to a universal principle or foundation and are thereby captured within a system or totality. The philosophy of identity is a holistic philosophy. Its purpose is to make the world comprehensible, but also controllable and manipulable.

The critique of this conception can be made clearer by utilizing Levinas's (1969) conceptual pair, "the same" and "the other," as well as Hegel's (1970) own concepts, "identity" and "non-identity." In a situation characterized by totality, "the other" as such is excluded, and at the same time subordinated to "the same." Here we can use Hegel's definition of what he called false identity: "The union is forcible. The one subjugates the other. The one rules, the other is subservient" (1970, p. 48; English trans. 1977, p. 115). Hegel believed, however, in the possibility of reconciliation, that is, "the identity of identity and non-identity" (1970, p.

87; English trans. 1977, p. 156). According to postmodernism, it is precisely this which was his great mistake. The same and the other are irreconcilable. The non-identical is the absolute other; that which cannot be apprehended in our knowledge; that which always eludes the subject's grasp, the foreign; that which comes from beyond; that which can never come under our control; that which we have not created. Every attempt to conceptualize and thereby incorporate the other in our world is to do violence to the other. Conceptions of identity always entail a disciplining, a normalization, a repression and exclusion of the other. Postmodernism has other goals: "The purpose of history, guided by genealogy, is not to discover the roots of our identity, but to commit itself to its dissipation" (Foucault, 1984, p. 95).

Transferring this critique of identity to gender theory has definite consequences. The basic assumptions behind this critique must be seen as fundamental preconditions in a paradigmatic theoretical sense and thereby set the limits for what is possibly conceivable within the framework of postmodern gender theory. It is almost beforehand deemed to be unimaginable to see any identity as anything but false and oppressive. To be identified as a man or woman implies being subjected to violence, as this can only be a false generalization, that is to say, something particular is made into something universal. To possess a gender identity means that things which for historical and social reasons are associated with the opposite sex are excluded, sublimated and repressed within oneself. At the same time, a specific relationship with the opposite sex is appropriated and reproduced. In a patriarchal gender order, man is constructed as "the same" and woman as "the other." The concept of identity not only has consequences for the relations between persons identified as men and persons identified as women, but also excludes differences between individuals with the same gender identity. Postmodern gender theory today continuously emphasizes that use of both the concept woman and the concept man carries with it associations of certain particular qualities, such as being white, heterosexual, Western, of middle-class background and the status of being "the same." As all other concepts, this also implies a false universalization of a particular historically and socially determined particularity and an exclusion of all other possible particularities.

Against this background, it is not surprising that Butler with great reluctance speaks of herself as lesbian. She writes: "The prospect of *being* anything ... has always produced in me a certain anxiety" (Butler, 1993a, p. 307; compare Butler, 1990b, chapter 1). We find a similar formulation in an interview with Kristeva (1980, p. 137) bearing the title "La femme, ce n'est jamais ca," in which she argues that "On a deeper level, however, a women cannot 'be'; it is something which does not even belong in the order of *being*." Kristeva then continues with a critique of conceptions of "sexual identities," which she calls naive romanticism.

That which appears to be the logical normative conclusion of such a critique of the philosophy of identity has recently been propagated in Sweden by Nina Björk. She takes her point of departure in Kristeva's division of feminism into three stages:

> One where women strive to achieve equality with men on the political and economic levels by arguing that women are like men, that there is no difference between the sexes; one where women emphasise their distinctiveness in positive terms, a type of "women are different from men, but they are different in a positive way"; and one where the concepts "man" and "woman" themselves dissolve, where these terms are seen as pure fictions which belong to metaphysics. ... It is this third stage which I see as feminism's present challenge. I wish for a future feminism which dissolves the narratives which create feminine and masculine; a feminism which does not upgrade the "feminine," but rather dissolves all sexual identities ... (Björk, 1996, pp. 13f; compare Kristeva, 1986).[8]

Perhaps we could call this the "utopia of the genderless society." Naturally, in such a society without genders, particular gender identities cannot be excluded or suppressed. In one sense freedom and equality has been reached. But the question remains as to whether it has occurred at the cost of an abstract universalism. Has a categorical mistake not been made which means that the *moral* devise "we are all human beings" without mediation is transferred to the level of personal identity, that is to say, the *ethical* level?[9] Shouldn't we ask ourselves "whose liberation?" and "liberation to what?" This identity critique is led by a normative conception that reminds me of a traditional, liberal conception that is usually referred to as "negative freedom," which builds upon an atomistic anthropology that does not see that human being *also* necessitates historical and social particularity. Here we have a good example of how postmodernism is caught in precisely that which it initially criticized; in this case liberalism. I will return to this.

Butler is, however, more sophisticated than Björk on this point. The political object of Butler's critique is what she calls the "reification of gender" or "the fixity of gender identity" (1990a, p. 339). She reacts against the rigidity of gender identity and sees "the promise of the possibility of complex and generative subject positions" (*ibid.*). It appears thus that she does not entirely reject the importance of gender identity, as long as it is "a site of permanent openness and resignifiability" (1995, p. 50).[10] But if this is the case, why then does she not accept the identity of lesbian, at least for a while? It is further hard to see how these normative propositions correlate with Butler's wider theoretical aim, "the deconstruction of identity" (1990b, p. 148). For even if every identity is temporally limited and open for revision, it is in any case an *identity*, implying suppression and exclusion of the other.

The critique of the philosophy of the subject

Postmodern philosophy is often associated with the idea of "the death of the subject."[11] To a great extent it has revolved around a deconstruction of the liberal conception of an autonomous subject; a free, knowledge-seeking and choosing subject, in principle unaffected by society and history – for example Kant's transcendental subject or Mill's (1982, p. 69) idea about the individual's sovereign control "over himself, over his own body and mind." This deconstruction has at the same time carried with it a critique of reason, as reason in the tradition of the philosophy of the subject is viewed as the property of the subject. In so far as the subject is situated in history, both the subject and reason lose the supposed sovereignty they previously possessed. Such an historicization of the subject and reason has become common fare in philosophy since Heidegger and the later Wittgenstein. That which sets postmodernism apart is its radicality on this point.

According to postmodernism, we are not masters of our own subjectivity. Foucault posits that our subjectivity, that is to say, that which we consider to be our will, our desire, our reason, is created by a causal, external disciplining of the body. Our subjectivity is a result of our contingent place in time and space. What is important to note is that history in postmodern theory is interpreted in terms of pure power and violence. The subject is seen as being discursively constructed and discourse is understood as something impregnated with violence and power. It is consequently not sufficient to suppose, in a Heideggerian manner, that our subjectivity or individuality is a result of us being "cast out" into history and society. Postmodern thought is more dramatic than this. It appears to imply that our subjectivity should be seen as a result of us being raped by time and space, so to say. Subjectivity, that which we experience as the innermost expression of our own personality, is created in this societal rape.

Based on such notions, it is not hard to see how the critiques of the philosophy of identity and the philosophy of the subject are linked in a gender theory context.

> [G]ender is not a performance that a prior subject elects to do, but gender is performative in the sense that it constitutes as an effect the very subject it appears to express. It is a compulsory performance ... (Butler, 1993a, pp. 314f).

Butler points out in *Bodies that Matter* that constructivism does not imply that we as autonomous subjects construct ourselves as gendered beings, but rather that through historical violence we are constructed as heterosexual men and women. "[E]xistence is already decided *by* gender" (Butler, 1993b, p. x and chapter 3). Our subjectivity is always already "gendered." That which we as individuals want is predetermined in a particular historical gender order. As we become human by being cast out into a world which is already gendered, we are fixed as men and women, which in turn predetermines our actions. Butler's term "compulsory heterosexuality" should be understood against this background. But as each determined identity also includes an exclusion of all other possibilities, the other, the non-identical, the foreign is also simultaneously constructed and suppressed. In the extension of this theory about the historically constructed subject, we find a utopia of freedom on the border between identity and non-identity. "Drag" ("cross-dressing"), like "queer" expresses this freedom (see Butler, 1993b, p. 110). The question that remains to be posed, however, is how such expressions are possible without some degree of autonomous subjectivity.[12]

A critique of postmodern gender theory

I will briefly criticize postmodern gender theory on three interrelated points. First (a), I make some remarks aimed at showing that identifying concepts are not only unavoidable, but also that the non-identical, as a normative foundation for critique, shows postmodernism's negative bond to metaphysical thought. Second (b), I will argue that the postmodernists' conception of personal identity does not hold in contemporary Western societies. Third (c), I direct my criticism toward the Foucauldian view of the social as a pure power and violence context. Once this view is brought into question, is it possible to argue that our fundamental historicity and sociality does not *a priori* eliminate autonomy. Taken together, these points of critique seek to show that gender identity, *a priori*, does not need to be seen as something enforced and freedom-depriving.

(a) *Postmodern philosophy as negative metaphysics.* The critique of the concept of identity, as noted above, is understood by the proponents of postmodern gender theory as a critique of essentialism. As a reaction against the essentialist reduction of gender identity to biology, postmodernists take exception to the concept of identity in a normative-political context. Identity concepts can, at the most, be useful only for strategic-political purposes. Such reasoning is negatively captive to the correspondence theory of truth, that is to say the belief that a concept should correspond to something in the physical reality outside of language. The negative connection to this theory consists of the tendency of postmodernists to throw the baby out with the bath-water, that is to say, the concept of truth with the correspondence theory of truth. If instead we apply some kind of consensus theory of truth, then decisive criteria for truth lie not outside of language, but precisely in language.[13] A certain interpretation of the meaning of gender can thus be descriptively true and normatively right, without this meaning being interpreted as predetermined by biological sex. If we furthermore seriously consider Popper's argument about truth necessitating fallibility, then the meaning of concepts like masculinity or femininity, just as all other concepts, cannot be fixed once and for all. But this does not prohibit us from using these terms and claiming that their use is true and right until someone convinces us that we use them falsely or that our use has unjust implications.

Another postmodern criticism of the use of concepts like man and woman is, as mentioned earlier, that these concepts obstruct our ability to see differences between different men and different women. This critique I believe can be easily rejected. To argue for the existence of trees is hardly to negate the existence of pines and palms. It is true that in the history of feminism, white, heterosexual, middle-class women have been the model of "woman" in general, in the same way that in patriarchal society, white, heterosexual, middle-class men have been the model of not only "man," but also "human" in general. One has not shown, however, that the concept of woman or man is false, but rather that a particular use of this concept is false. The conclusion we should draw from the postmodern critique is, rather, that we should use the concepts in the abstract manner when making universal claims and more contextually when we make substantial claims.

The theoretical basis for the postmodern gender theory's critique of concepts like woman and man lies undoubtedly in postmodern philosophy's scepticism of language as such. The idea appears to be that language in some manner always distorts, as it requires differences to be identified as the same. To speak of pine trees is to do violence to the individual pine's truth. Language is in itself – to speak with Jameson (1972) – "a prison house." The question is, however, how do postmodernists know that a particular concept distorts, when they at the same time deny the possibility of any direct access to "the thing-in-itself"? The general postmodern idea seems to be that if we cannot have a direct access to a pre-linguistic reality, then the whole conception of a true reality is false. All we have are fictions, texts, fantasies, illusions. But if this is all we have, on what basis can we make such a claim? Concepts like illusion seem to lose their meaning without concepts like reality. Again on this point the postmodern critique of empiricism shows its negative dependence. Postmodernists, like Derrida, dance on the border between metaphysics and non-metaphysics. They reject the possibility of reaching truth about the world, but they do it only in the light of the empiricist definition of truth as something directly related to something outside of language. Precisely for this reason concepts like "absence," "trace" and "*différance*" are so central. I would call this romanticism.

Instead, like Albrecht Wellmer (1991, p. 74), I would propose to see the repression, which postmodernists link to the logic of identity, as a "problem *within* language." It is not general concepts that do violence to the other, but rather "a specific *usage* of general concepts; and what is 'untrue' in such linguistic usage would have to be understood as untruth *in* the language (and not as untruth *by virtue of* the use of language)." Wellmer sees "the 'violent' aspect of identificatory thought in the sense of *specific* blockages, pathologies or perversions of linguistic communication or social praxis." Transferred to our gender theory problematic, this once again means that it is not the use of concepts of man and woman in general that is untrue, but rather specific uses of these concepts.

(b) *Modern identity.* Social theorists like Taylor, Habermas and Giddens, who all are critical of postmodernism, emphasize the importance of personal identity, but are at the same time quite aware of the changing premises that modern life pose for identity formation. Individualization and pluralization demand originality (Taylor, 1991). The declining direct legitimacy of tradition demands reflexivity (Giddens, 1991). Secularization means that identity can no longer rest upon transcendent assumptions that are beyond critique, but must rather be content with fallible foundations. A set and fixed identity is rather a pre-modern form of identity, or – in the case of gender – also an early modern form of identity. That we today feel a rupture in our hitherto certainties about gender and sexual practice means that gender-related patterns of action have been drawn into what Giddens calls "the reflective project of the self."[14] It thus becomes increasingly difficult to create a personal identity without reflecting upon one's own gender and sexuality.

According to these theories postmodern critique thus comes barging in through a door already opened by modernity's own dynamics. To have a modern personal identity demands not "fixity," but only the possibility, at least after the fact, to be able to tell a story about how and to justify why one's self-image has developed and changed.

(c) *Deriving freedom from oppression?* Foucault-inspired social theories present society almost as a prison. Norms are seen entirely as expressions of external compulsion which have been internalized. The fragmenting of the social which is usually associated with "the postmodern condition" is thus understood by some postmodern thinkers (such as Lyotard) to be a cause for a degree of hope. The only possibility of freedom appears to be freedom from the social, freedom from society. On this point postmodernism seems again to stand close to liberalism. But upon closer scrutiny such a hope of freedom is paradoxical, as the only theory about subjectivity available in the postmodern paradigm is the rape theory discussed above. There is no basis for conceiving of subjectivity as anything other than an enforced social construction and therefore it is almost impossible to develop a conception of freedom at all (see for instance Honneth, 1990, pp. 87ff). This of course has serious implications for a gender theory with political ambitions, which Benhabib (1992, chapter 7; and 1995), among others, has pointed out in her critique of Butler.

Butler paradoxically tries to see the subject both as a result of violence and as a force that can turn against this violence. To be discursively constituted is, according to Butler (1990b, pp. 142ff), not the same as being determined by that discourse. "The subject," she writes (*ibid.*, p. 144), "is not *determined* by the rules through which it is generated because signification is *not a founding act, but rather a regulated process* of repetition ....." This means that the subject as actor is, in a certain sense, involved in power. In this there should be the possibility of freedom, according to Butler. I cannot see how this solves anything. It only means that the subject contributes to his or her own oppression. In her response to Benhabib, Butler writes (1995b, p. 136): "[G]ender performativity involves the difficult labour of deriving agency from the very power regimes which constitute us, and which we oppose." But she never explains how subjectivity, understood as agency, ever can develop out of repression. The problem remains even if one says that repression to some extent is a matter of self-repression. In this case, all that is said is that power is transmitted via socialization and internalization. Butler seems to know that if she is to succeed in uniting her identity theory with her political theory, it must be possible to derive freedom from oppression. She formulates this paradox with what appears to be an almost desperate clarity. My conclusion is that Butler's political ambitions are held captive by the premises of Foucauldian theory.

These three points of critique of postmodern gender theory should of course not be understood as a general denial of the coercive character of subjectivity or gender. It is directed at the tendency to a *general* equation of gender and oppression. Under such premises, all normative and political claims become paradoxical or utopic. It becomes impossible for postmodern thought to account for the premises of its own critique of the social gender order. It lacks a stage of normative self-reflection that could lead to a clarification of the premises for agency and of the content of the political goals. Butler, as noted above, argues for a form of gender identity that is not reified, but she can neither describe the preconditions for, nor justify, this goal in a consistent manner. Each identity, no matter how temporary it may be, must be a prison according to the theory's own logic. But if each identity is a prison, then Björk's extremely liberal solution presented above at first glance appears to be the only way. But such a solution requires a subjectivity without history and without a body, that is to say precisely the autonomous subjectivity which Enlightenment philosophy is based upon, a divine subjectivity, which postmodernism in other contexts sharply criticizes as an oppressive illusion. Björk's solution is thus not just utopic in the negative connotation of the word; the normative ideal of an abstract or universal personality paradoxically enough ends with precisely the conception which initially was the object of feminist critique. Butler does not fall into this logical trap, but remains, as does postmodernism in general, negatively bound to Enlightenment thinking. With her theoretical idealization of transvestism, she dances in gender theory on the same loose thread that Derrida does in philosophy. It is possibly another variant of the abstract individual which attracts Butler's utopic energies. One senses between the lines of her writings the same omnipotent longing that Fernando Pessoa (1991, p. 21) expresses in his wonderful *Ode Triunfal*. The poem ends with the line "Ah, that I am not all people and everywhere." A person who strives after every identity remains without any identity, due to the fact that every identity is incompatible with some other identity.

The Danish literary critic Dag Heede's monograph on Foucault (1992) bears the title "The empty person." His point of departure is a quotation from the introduction to the second volume of *The History of Sexuality*, where Foucault (1985, p. 8) speaks of the possibility "to get free of oneself." There is much that supports the understanding of this line as not just a methodological point, but also as an expression of an implicit normativity in Foucault's thought. My claim is that this kind of normativity characterizes all forms postmodern thinking.

Beyond essentialism and social constructivism

The most important step to take in order to avoid the paradoxes of postmodernism, without falling back into the philosophy of the subject, is in my view to understand the social in a different manner than postmodernism does. In opposition to liberalism and essentialism, we should acknowledge the fundamental importance of the social for subjectivity and identity, but in opposition to postmodern social constructivism, we should understand the social as something not necessarily repressive. Postmodern thinkers seem only to overturn the way that the philosophers of Enlightenment saw the relationship between the subject and society. If the subject cannot be the master of history and society, then the implicit argument seems to be that history must be the master of the subject. In both cases, history is seen as something subject-less, in the meaning of being anonymous and violent, something which in itself contradicts human freedom. On this point postmodernist theory sounds just like Max Weber's analysis of modernity – the social is an "iron cage." Freedom according to this line of thought, if it can be conceived of at all, must lie beyond or prior to the social. It has its prerequisites in desire, the body, in the Dionysian, in the non-discursive; in other words, in the non-identical.

There are, however, a range of social theoreticians who see no inherent contradiction between sociality and freedom. They hold that the objectivity of the social at least partially has intersubjective premises. We can, for example, turn to the early Hegel's theory of recognition, to Mead's theory of "the social self," to Buber, to Bachtin, to Walzer's and Taylor's communitarianism, to Habermas's theory of communicative action or to Honneth's theory of the struggle for recognition. A theory that is based solely upon intersubjective social structures and thus emphasizes the participant's possibilities and importance is, however, equally as idealistic as iron-cage sociology is cynical. But if we can develop a theory of the social where intersubjectivity plays at least some role, then we have opened an avenue which is neither linked to the subject-object model of classic liberalism, nor to the object-subject model of postmodernism. According to this third way, society can never be entirely understood as subject-less sociality. Participation – that is a subject-subject relation – is seen rather as one of the fundamental conditions that make sociality possible. In the context of this article, this means that our subjectivity is formed by the social when we as subjects (with specific histories) *participate* in social life. In other words, we have the possibility to have an impact upon our own socialization through social participation. In this view oppression should not be thought of as socialization, but as hindrance to social participation.[15]

Such an intersubjective theory can be used in a normative way on the level of human rights to conceptualize the achievements of the political struggle for gender equality. The question of gender identity, however, is not primarily a question of the right (morality), but rather a question of the good (ethics). Gender identity is a part of the personal identity and personal identity cannot be understood as something primarily formal and universal (as the right), but should rather be conceived of as something substantial and particular (as the good).[16] Concerning the relationship between the right and the good I agree – in contrast to communitarians – with Rawls and Habermas on the priority of the right; as Rawls (1993, p. 174) puts it, "justice draws the limit, and the good shows the point." On one hand this means that the right does not allow identities that are unjust, and on the other hand it means that the logic of the right is too abstract to articulate the meaning of a particular identity. Neither Rawls nor Habermas has much to say about the good in itself. On this level the importance of intersubjectivity as participation has rather been developed by communitarians, most importantly by Taylor (1989, 1991).

The main communitarian argument is that in order to have a personal identity we have to be a part of and take part in a particular social life form; we have to belong to some kind of "community." This "belonging" should be understood in two connected ways. First, identity is seen as being related to the concept of authenticity. To find one's identity is to be able to relate to one's historical situatedness.[17] We can understand this situatedness neither essentialistically nor constructivistically. Social constructivism tends to regard the self as an object, that is as a result of causal force. Theories of authenticity, or to use a more popular term, self-realization, instead emphasize the possibility of relating to oneself in a dialogic-narrational manner. Relating to oneself should be seen as an intersubjective relationship. The subjective world should not be confused with the objective world. The self-relation should neither be seen as a subject-object relationship, nor as an object-subject relationship. Like postmodern constructivism, authenticity theory holds that subjectivity has social and historical preconditions, but the latter theory in contrast to the former has developed theoretical concepts to understand how, through a dialogic relationship to itself, the subject can "become itself." We could then even use Hegel's words and speak of the possibility of "reconciliation" with oneself, that is to say, "the identity of identity and non-identity."[18]

Second, personal identity presupposes recognition of others. Taylor (1991) argues that identity is a question of not only originality, but also significance: "Defining myself means finding what is significant in my difference from others" (Taylor, 1991, pp. 35f). This significance depends on the horizon of values that I share with others. Self-realization thus does not necessarily have anything to do with political passivity or conservatism. Self-realization is only possible in some situations through a "struggle for recognition." Good examples of this are the black struggle under the slogan "black is beautiful" and homosexual pride marches.

Communitarians regard identity as a fundamental need for individuals. Identities have both a descriptive and a prescriptive part. The attempt to realize an ideal conception of oneself plays an important role in guiding the actual actions of individuals. The process of reflexively creating the self, which in modernity is a lifelong process where each formation is contingent and continuously revisable, takes place at the intersection of the answers to the questions "who am I?" and "who do I want to be?" (Taylor, 1989). Martin Löw-Beer (1991) in a review of Taylor's *Sources of the Self* has called a life without answers to these questions "unbearable" and "existentially impossible." Concrete answers can of course only be arrived at by the individual concerned. But gender, like other dimensions of

personal identity such as ethnicity, class, race, nationality, age, and sexual
orientation, is not entirely subjective, but rather something we share with
specific others. This means that personal identity rests upon certain social
conceptions and values, the content of which is continuously recast in a
public discourse. I understand personal identity to be, to a great extent,
specific combinations of these dimensions' changeable cultural contents.
We can to some degree conceive of some of these dimensions losing
importance, others increasing in importance, new dimensions evolving,
others declining, but we cannot speak of personal identity if all particular
dimensions disappear entirely. A person without a specific identity ceases
to exist in a social and cultural meaning.

If we use communitarianism in the sense laid out above, it leads us to
develop a weak formalistic anthropology. While the adjectives "weak" and
"formalistic" stand in opposition to essentialism, the noun "anthropology"
stands in opposition to the utopias of postmodern social constructivism.
This anthropology says that human beings need – in contrast to animals –
personal identity to become human beings. To call this anthropology weak
and formalistic means that it does not prescribe a specific identity, only
some identity. In order to transfer this conclusion to a gender theoretical
context we must, however, be able to argue why gender should also be an
important dimension of personal identity under post-patriarchal social
conditions. I will end with giving two arguments. The first has to do with
bodily situatedness, the second with social or cultural situatedness.

The *first* argument takes it point of departure in the distinction
between man and woman on the one hand and the masculine and the
feminine on the other. We should understand this distinction in a similar
way to the distinction between sex and gender. Our conceptions of
masculinity and femininity are cultural narratives about how we should
conceive of the fact that men and women are born biologically different.
The biological difference says very little about its social significance.
There are no natural laws which should determine the relation between
woman and femininity or man and masculinity. The cultural context of
interpretation is for the human being a *conditio sine qua non*. Human
existence presupposes – in a fundamental sense – meaning. "Human beings
are self-interpreting animals" (Taylor, 1985, p. 45). To interpret does not
only mean to understand something given, but also to fill up the void which
to a high degree characterizes human nature. This, however, does not mean
that there is nothing outside of language, that everything is text – including
sex – as Butler claims. Sex is not – as Benhabib (1992, p. 236) has put it –
a *tabula rasa*. Sex is no less – and no more – a part of nature than, for

instance, age. That human beings are distinctive in their lack of behaviour-guiding instincts, does not exclude the existence of a human biological body. It means rather that this body does not *directly* determine our behaviour. Biological impulses have first to be filled with meaning through interpretation.

This anthropological side of the argument has also an epistemological side. Sex – like age – has a kind of objectivity, which social constructivism cannot grasp. Cultural narratives about sex are not completely independent of their object of interpretation. This is the difference between an interpretation and a construction. Interpretation, in contrast to social constructivism, involves – to use Habermas's expression – "a weak epistemological realism."[19]

The claim is thus that men and women need to understand their sexed body and make it a part of their personal identity. This task presupposes that we are able to relate to something non-linguistic with only linguistic means – culturally shared symbols, metaphors, concepts and so on – at our disposal. To explain the possibility of such a task, I will rely on Habermas (1996). In accordance with the later Wittgenstein, Heidegger and pragmatic philosophy, he takes his point of departure in the performative aspect of language. Such a view of language focuses on the fact that we do not only speak *about* the world, but, and more importantly, that speaking is a way of being *in* the world, that is, it is a fundamental dimension of the human way of living. In other words, we do our interpretations of the world in the world, or better, we live our interpretations. Hence, the linguistic and the non-linguistic dimensions of the world should not be understood dualistically, but as always already connected through life or praxis. This world that we, as language-using animals, are living in has, according to Habermas, not only social and subjective dimensions, but also objective ones. Like the other dimensions – but in its special way – the objective dimension puts limits on the possible ways of living and thus on possible interpretations. Some ways of living, some interpretations, are simply not successful. They don't work. Transferred to a gender-theoretical context this means that sex – as an aspect of our bodily situatedness – does not determine, but nevertheless puts *some* limits on identity formation. This is the reason why I claim that we have to include sex – through interpretation – in our personal identities to be able to live a good life.

The *second* argument is related to the first. If understanding our bodily situatedness is an unavoidable part of human life, then it is not surprising that some kind of cultural narratives about sex have been a part of every human society. However, as individual human beings we do not create these narratives ourselves. We are rather "cast out" into a specific historical and social context, which is built of more or less institutionalized cultural narratives. This pre-established social world provides us with the symbolic material we use when we try to understand ourselves. Hence, through such narratives, for example narratives about our sexed body, we become persons. Gender is thus a part of our social or cultural situatedness. It is a part of ourselves as much as sex, although in a different and a less permanent way. The important point to be made here is that we cannot relate in an instrumental way to something which is a part of ourselves, even if this part has a social origin. To try to abolish gender in a revolutionary way is to deny a dimension of our social selves instead of trying to change it in a dialogical manner.

Conclusion

My main point in this article is that we should not regard, as postmodern gender theory in a paradigmatic sense is forced to do, gender identity as something necessarily repressive. Gender identity can also be a way for men and women to relate to their different biological and cultural bodies. If we are critical toward the narratives of the social meaning of sex difference in a certain culture, the conclusion should not be that through political struggle we should try to dissolve all such narratives. Such an undifferentiated struggle would lead to inauthenticity, that is, we would lose our relationship to our biological and cultural bodies. Instead we ought only to oppose those gender identities that do not respect "the limit of the right" and then declare our solidarity with all attempts to find recognition for identities which stay within these limits. In late modernity such politics would mean the recognition of a plurality of more or less different conceptions of masculinity and femininity. It follows from what has been said above, that the human being, in principle, can relate to the fact of the sexed body in a wide variety of ways. However, the processes of gender formation cannot take place in the private sphere, they presuppose social participation.

The important distinction between the right and the good tells us thus that political struggle concerning gender should be of two different kinds; questions of the right demand politics of emancipation (politics of equality), while questions of the good demand politics of recognition (identity politics, politics of difference). A successful attempt to pursue the former without the latter leads, as has just been argued, to inauthenticity. A successful attempt to pursue the latter without the former could mean an acceptance of identities which presuppose inequality.

Notes

1. In Sweden during the 1990s we experienced a veritable explosion of interest in masculinity, especially in mass media.
2. Compare Henning Bech's (1997, pp. 174ff) discussion of homosexuals as avant-garde.
3. This has been done, for instance by Beck, 1986; Beck and Beck-Gernsheim, 1990; and Giddens, 1992. For "hard facts," see also Therborn, 1995, pp. 36ff, 104ff.
4. The subtitle of Judith Butler's much discussed book *Gender Trouble* is "Feminism and *the subversion of identity*" (my italics). See also Fraser and Nicholson, 1990, pp. 33f.
5. Many of the proponents of American postmodern gender theory, as well as some of its critics are collected in Nicholson (ed.), 1990. See also Benhabib *et al.*, 1995b.
6. Butler is one of those who explicitly questions this label, but she does so in a typical postmodern manner (see Butler, 1995a).
7. The primary model is Foucault's so-called "middle-period," first and foremost *Surveiller et Punir* and the first volume of *Histoire de la sexualité*. See McNay, 1992 on the connection between Foucault and feminist theory.
8. The same thoughts are common among masculinity researchers and persons who work politically to change the traditional male gender identity. Compare, ffor example, the telling title of a lecture (held 15 January 1997 at a conference on men and violence organized by the Swedish Labour Ministry led by Ulrica Messing, the Minister for Social Equality) delivered by Greger Hatt, a speech writer for the former Swedish Prime Minister Ingvar Carlsson, "There are no free men; a free man is a person."
9. Björk appears to leave herself defenceless to the communitarian critique of liberalism. On the distinction between morality and ethics, see Habermas, 1991.
10. Compare Fraser 1997: 24, who is quite clear on this point when she writes about the meaning of queer politics: "The transformative aim is not to solidify a gay identity but to deconstruct the homo-hetero dichotomy so as to destabilize all fixed sexual identities. The point is not to dissolve all sexual difference in a single, universal human identity; it is, rather, to sustain a sexual field of multiple, debinarized, fluid, ever-shifting differences."
11. Foucault (1974, p. 24) has said that he appropriated the concept of "the disappearance of the subject" from structuralism. Compare Flax (1990, pp. 32f), who speaks in a gender theoretical context of "The Death of Man."
12. It is the lack of clarity on this point which led some critics to understand the

thesis in *Gender Trouble* as a theory about the possibility of the self-construction of the subject, of gender identity as a masquerade. See Benhabib, 1995a, p. 109, note 4.

13. Compare Habermas's (1996) discourse theory of truth.
14. This project is to be understood as "the sustaining of coherent, yet continuously revised, biographical narratives" (Giddens, 1991, p. 5).
15. There are a few attempts to, more or less explicitly, use the concept of intersubjectivity in a gender theoretical context. See Benhabib, 1992; Benjamin, 1988 and 1998; McNay, 1992; and Weir, 1995 and 1996. I take my point of departure in none of these and my attempt is related to, but in one way or the other different from, all of them. Unfortunately, I cannot give an account of these differences here.
16. Rawls (1993) makes the distinction between the right and the good and Habermas (1991) makes a similar distinction between morality and ethics.
17. Compare Heidegger's concepts "In-der-Welt-Sein" and "geworfener Entwurf" (1986,: § 31).
18. We then of course cannot, like Hegel, understand reconciliation as being something absolute, that is, in this context, finding a true self in the meaning of reaching the end of a personal history. Modern identity formation is – as has been said above – something continuously ongoing in a changing culture. I have developed this further in Carleheden, 1996, chapter 8.
19. Compare Habermas (1996) who – in critiquing Rorty – defends the idea of an objective world without falling back on empiricism. Habermas does not argue that we can step outside of language, but that the grammar of language itself points toward the existence of a non-linguistic, objective world.

References

Bech, Henning (1997) *When Men Meet; Homosexuality and Modernity.* Cambridge: Polity Press.
Beck, Ulrich (1986) *Risikogesellschaft – Auf dem Weg in eine andre Moderne.* Frankfurt/M: Suhrkamp.
Beck, Ulrich and Beck-Gernsheim, Elisabeth (1990) *Das ganz normale Chaos der Liebe.* Frankfurt/M: Suhrkamp.
Benhabib, Seyla (1992) *Situating the Self.* Cambridge: Polity Press.
Benhabib, Seyla (1995a) "Subjectivity, Historiography, and Politics," in Benhabib, S. *et al., Feminist Contentions.* New York: Routledge.
Benhabib, Seyla *et al.* (1995b) *Feminist Contentions.* New York: Routledge.

Benjamin, Jessica (1988) *The Bonds of love – Psychoanalysis, feminism, and the problem of domination.* London: Virago Press.

Benjamin, Jessica (1998) *The Shadow of the Other – Intersubjectivity and gender in psychoanalysis.* New York and London: Routledge.

Björk, Nina (1996) *Under det rosa täcket.* Stockholm: Wahlström & Widstrand.

Butler, Judith (1990a) "Gender Trouble, Feminist Theory, and Psychoanalytic Discourse," in Nicholson, L. (ed.), *Feminism/postmodernism.* New York: Routledge.

Butler, Judith (1990b) *Gender Trouble – Feminism and the subversion of identity.* New York: Routledge.

Butler, Judith (1993a) "Imitation and Gender Insubordination," in Abelove, H. *et al.* (eds), *The Lesbian and Gay Studies Reader.* New York: Routledge.

Butler, Judith (1993b) *Bodies that matter – On the discursive limits of "sex."* New York: Routledge.

Butler, Judith (1995a) "Contingent Foundations," in Benhabib, S. *et al.*, *Feminist Contentions.* New York: Routledge.

Butler, Judith (1995b) "For a Careful Reading," in Benhabib, S. *et al.*, *Feminist Contentions.* New York: Routledge.

Carleheden, Mikael (1996) *Det andra moderna – Om Jürgen Habermas och den samhällsteoretiska diskursen om det moderna.* Göteborg: Daidalos.

Connell, Robert W. (1995) *Masculinities.* Berkeley: University of California Press.

Flax, Jane (1990) *Thinking fragments: psychoanalysis, feminism, and postmodernism in the contemporary West.* Berkeley: University of California Press.

Foucault, Michel (1974) *Von der Subversion des Wissens.* München.

Foucault, Michel (1984) "Nietzsche, Genealogy, History," in Rabinow, P. (ed.), *The Foucault Reader.* London: Penguin.

Foucault, Michel (1985) *The History of Sexuality*, Vol. 2 *The use of pleasure.* New York: Vintage Books.

Fraser, Nancy (1992) "The Uses and Abuses of French Discourse Theories for Feminist Politics," in Fraser, N. and Bartky, S. E. (eds), *Revaluing French Feminism.* Bloomington and Indianapolis: Indiana University Press.

Fraser, Nancy (1997) *Justice Interruptus - Critical reflections on the "postsocialist" condition.* New York and London: Routledge.

Fraser, Nancy and Nicholson, Linda (1990) "Social Criticism without Philosophy: An Encounter between Feminism and Postmodernism," in Nicholson, L. (ed.) *Feminism/postmodernism.* New York: Routledge.

Giddens, Anthony (1991) *Modernity and Self-Identity.* Cambridge: Polity Press.

Giddens, Anthony (1992) *The Transformation of Intimacy.* Cambridge: Polity Press.

Habermas, Jürgen (1991) "Vom pragmatischen, etischen und moralischen Gebrauch der praktischen Vernunft," in Habermas, J., *Erläuterungen zur Diskursethik.* Frankfurt/M: Suhrkamp.

Habermas, Jürgen (1996) "Rortys pragmatische Wende," *Deutsche Zeitschrift für Philosophie*, 44 (5).

Heede, Dag (1992) *Det tomme menneske – Introduktion till Michel Foucault.* København: Museum Tusculanums forlag.

Hegel, Georg W. F. (1970) "Differenz des Fichteschen und Schellingschen Systems der Philosophie," in *Werke 2 Jenaer Schriften.* Frankfurt/M: Suhrkamp.

Heidegger, Martin (1986) *Sein und Zeit.* Tübingen: Max Niemeyer Verlag.

Honneth, Axel (1990) "Foucault und Adorno. Zwei Formen einer Kritik der Moderne," in Honneth, A., *Die zerrissene Welt des Sozialen – Sozialphilosophische Aufsätze.* Frankfurt/M: Suhrkamp.

Honneth, Axel (1992) *Kampf um Anerkennung – Zur moralischen Grammatik sozialer Konflikte.* Frankfurt/M: Suhrkamp.

Honneth, Axel (1994) "Diagnose der Postmoderne," in Honneth, A., *Desintegration – Bruchstücke einer soziologischen Zeitdiagnose.* Frankfurt/M: Fischer.

Jameson, Fredric (1972) *The prisonhouse of language: a critical account of structuralism and Russian formalism.* Princeton University Press.

Kristeva, Julia (1980) "Woman can never be defined," in Marks, E. and de Courtivron, I. (eds), *New French Feminism.* Brighton: Harvester Press.

Kristeva, Julia (1986) "Women's time," in Moi, T. (ed.), *The Kristeva Reader.* New York: Columbia University Press.

Levinas, Emmanuel (1969) *Totality and Infinity.* Pittsburgh: Duquesne University Press.

Löw-Beer, Martin (1991) "Living a Life and the Problem of Existential Impossibility," *Inquiry*, 34, pp. 217-36.

McNay, Lois (1992) *Foucault and feminism: Power, Gender and the Self.* Cambridge: Polity Press.

Mill, John Stuart (1982) *On Liberty.* Penguin.

Pessoa, Fernando (1991) *Alvaro de Campos.* Frankfurt/M: Fischer.

Rawls, John (1993) *Political Liberalism.* New York: Columbia University Press.

Taylor, Charles (1984) "Foucault on Freedom and Truth," *Political Theory*, 12 (2), pp. 152-83.

Taylor, Charles (1985) *Human agency and language – Philosophical papers 1.* Cambridge: Cambridge University Press.

Taylor, Charles (1989) *Sources of the self.* Cambridge: Cambridge University Press.

Taylor, Charles (1991) *The Ethics of Authenticity.* Cambridge, Massachusetts: Harvard University Press.

Therborn, Göran (1995) *European Modernity and Beyond: The Trajectory of European Societies 1945-2000.* London: Sage.

Weir, Allison (1995) "Toward a model of Self-Identity: Habermas and Kristeva," in Meehan, J. (ed.), *Feminists read Habermas*. New York: Routledge.

Weir, Allison (1996) *Sacrificial logics: feminist theory and the critique of identity*. New York: Routledge.

Wellm , Albrecht (1991) *The Persistence of Modernity: Essays on Aesthetics, Ethics, and Postmodernism*. Cambridge, Massachusetts: MIT Press.

Chapter 5

Beautiful Men, Fine Women and Good Work People: Gender and Skill in Northern Sweden 1850–1950

ELLA JOHANSSON

As a little girl from Stockholm in the 1960s, visiting relatives in northern Sweden, I was worried and embarrassed by the behavior of my grandmother and her friends. Why did these old women consistently comment on how "beautiful" (skön) any young man was, whenever they happened to mention them in their discussions? Grandfather and his friends, on the other hand, would at rare occasions at the most describe a woman as "fine" (fin) – a word with overtones of moral, social and economic qualities, rather than personal appearance. Later on, working in the area as an ethnologist interviewing old lumberjacks, or reading their nineteenth-century life stories, I was again astonished by the gentleness of these men. There was an evident absence of a "machismo" type of masculinity, as well as the strong, hard, silent manliness which constitutes a widespread stereotype of the typical lumberjack. These men met me with striking confidence and lack of pretence, expressing their admiration for women's capacity, giggling when recalling girls' rude and witty talk or weeping openly at the memory of the unfaithful fiancée whose betrayal had caused their lifelong bachelorhood.

When such experience is combined with information on nineteenth-century social organization and folklore, it is evident that in northern Sweden – Norrland – a substantial part of gender-based behavior was distinctively different from most other European societies. That women in this area may have seemed "unusual" or "unfeminine" is, I believe, far less controversial than that the men apparently were unperturbed by such deviations from the widespread cultural norm. My overall impression is that these men abstained from creating ideologies of male supremacy or spheres of homosocial alternative culture. Although familiar to Swedish ethnologists, northern gender remains largely unanalyzed, and even less is known of this phenomenon outside Scandinavia. The following tentative reflections about masculinity, femininity and their significance for identity, the sense of self and the social construction of that sense of self, are based on my ethnographic material from Norrland, particularly the remote world of the lumbermen.[1]

A common presumption of the way masculinity and femininity are organized is the pattern of polarity and contrast: one concept provides the meaning for the other. It is likewise often assumed that an individual's level of gender identity is achieved through his or her relations with the other sex, a pattern said to be apparent in, for example, Mediterranean and Melanesian cultures, where men achieve their masculinity through their control over women. From the scattered materials available, it would seem that in northern Sweden an individual's relation to members of the other sex had little relevance to the issue of their masculine and feminine qualities.

Therefore, in considering gender in Norrland, perhaps the polarity model should be questioned, for it might exclude other more useful perspectives. My aim is not to dispute polarity as a valid method of analysis, but to explore what some other patterns might reveal. In this brief case study, the focus will be on masculinity in relation to members of the same sex, on work, on the handling of objects and animals, and on the process of maturing and the life cycle. In particular I will focus on the way lumberjacks related to a notion of professional skill. The main source of these observations is a collection of over 200 memoirs – the life stories of loggers, born between 1840 and 1900, taken from a museum documentary project carried out in the 1940s.[2]

The geographical area which is referred to here is the northern pine forest region which covers two-thirds of Sweden, most of it called Norrland. This area differs from the south in many natural, social and cultural aspects.[3] In particular, there was an absence of feudalism and the development of a yeoman-like, freeholding peasantry. Agriculture was possible only in the narrow valleys of the rivers which run eastwards to the Sea of Botnia. Between each of these inhabited valleys there are at least 100 kilometres of forested mountains. Up to this century, young women spent the summers away in these vast forests occupied with the care of cattle. In pre-industrial Norrland, women's livestock was perhaps the most significant part of the peasant economy. Shortages of resources were supplemented by exploitation of the communally owned vast forests for grazing, haymaking, slash and burn cultivation, or hunting. However, by the middle of the nineteenth century the woods were divided up as private property, and then usually sold or leased long-term to lumber companies.

With this development, men's logging became an important source of income. In an ecology of multiple and infinite – but meager – resources, private access to agricultural land had not been very important for the production of wealth. The hard work of men and women was the real source of successful survival, and work was a fetishized concept. It was considered to be inherent or internalized within certain individuals. To be a "workperson" or "workman" was a clear status that could be achieved by an assiduous individual, man or woman. This ability to work was always referred to whenever a person was spoken of, and it referred not so much to raw physical strength as to zeal and thrift. Nor was work understood in terms of producing things, but rather as keeping up and improving the conditions of the surroundings. The use of nature was not spoken of as a matter of extracting or making goods, but as a matter of allocating things to places where they were useful and which seemed proper to them.[4]

When the amount and quality of labor took precedence over access to land, farms tended to be of equal size, optimal for the local economy. Northern Swedish peasant culture was thus quite egalitarian and – before the rapid increase of population which accompanied the logging industry – most men stood a fair chance of becoming a yeoman or the head of a farm household. The importance of the ability to work and the relative unimportance of kinship and inheritance, made the choice of marriage partner a question which only concerned the young man and woman involved. Significantly, courting patterns showed a lack of parental control and a relatively high, although far from unrestricted, degree of sexual freedom.[5] This was also reflected in the absence of beliefs and taboos about the danger of illegitimacy. In southern Sweden unmarried mothers were believed to cause disease and bring harm to children and cattle, whereas in the north illegitimacy was both common and relatively easily accepted.[6]

Although this analysis will deal mainly with men's work and male skills in logging, it is first necessary to briefly describe the character of men's and women's work in the late peasant and early capitalist society of northern Sweden. Men and women not only did different types of work, but no less important, different parts of the work process were evaluated and stressed. One might characterize beliefs about women's work by stressing it as a form of bestowing care on humans, and perhaps even more so, on cows.

Cattle had great symbolic value for feminine identity and their care, particularly the milking, was taboo to men. Another significant feature of women's work was that it never started and never ended. Women rose earlier and went to bed later than men, and many lumberjacks remarked that they never saw their mothers in bed, in fact never resting at all. One aspect of the refusal to take breaks was that women did not stop working at meals to sit at ease at the table. Especially the mistress of the household performed a role of attendance and control, spending the meals moving to and fro between the stove and the table. Women tended not to describe their different tasks as being more or less heavy. Since neither heavy nor light work was distinguished, women could acquire equal admiration for everything they did, their constant occupation being an important part of their persona.

Light work, such as spinning or knitting – which was done even when walking – could thus be fitted into the day as invisible rest periods. In the loggers' life stories, the men are more than ready to give credit to women's part in the struggle for life. Fetching water and chopping firewood were especially pointed out as very hard work for the women, although the difficulties in organizing the fetching of water in the logging camps indicates – what hardly would be openly admitted – that this might have been seen as an effeminate task for a man.[7]

How was men's work regarded, how was it spoken about? For men, work was not the perpetual cycle of "bestowing care" as it was for women. Instead, work took the form of specific projects with a starting point and an ending. Days were described in terms of a schedule of work and rest periods. In contrast to the feminine work ethos, rests were deemed to be rightfully deserved. The loggers, for example, carefully describe their activities during the breaks in terms having a palpable scent of masculinity. Men's achievements were counted – countable – in contrast to the perpetual caretaking of the women. Loggers remember not only most of their earnings through the years, but also the number and dimensions of the logs they had cut. This extreme interest in counting and measuring was clearly related to the introduction of a market economy and piece-work contracts. Nevertheless, the division of work into projects seems to stem from an older feature of masculine identity.

The way gender is described among these loggers fits well with scholarly understanding of how gender identity is constructed and supported, and empirical similarities with the rest of Europe are evident. Still it seems worth trying to reach beyond simply identifying this pattern. For it has also been shown that such ideal divisions into male and female tasks have often been transgressed in practice, although this seems to have more often been the case among women rather than men, and especially among unmarried women of lower social strata.[8]

The Swedish lumber industry, to a great extent organized by British capital, was created in a relatively short period in the 1860s as a result of changed duty policies between Sweden and Britain. After its inception, logging occupied most men in Norrland during the winter season, and the workers lived more or less far away from home, isolated for months in the forests under poor housing conditions. These conditions and the organization of work were basically unchanged up to 1950. Logging remained an extremely tough occupation with a competitive work ethos and ruthless self-exploitation. Work was organized on the basis of piece-work contracts and yeomen sold the right to fell their forests to companies. The companies contracted horse-owning men, sometimes the same yeomen, to deliver the timber from a certain area. These contractors did the transport work and paid other men – who might be younger relatives as well as migrant workers – for doing the felling.[9]

The winter lifestyle in the forests can be characterized as both egalitarian and individualistic. Most striking is the consistent avoidance of anything that could contribute to the formation of a hierarchy among the men. Their meals and work processes were extremely atomized and individualized. The lifestyle lacked most of the elements that for an anthropologist would constitute cultural unity: food sharing, ritual initiations, rules of order and cleanliness. (This is not to say such matters were not culturally organized, but rather that they were done in such a way as to deny their existence.) Thus the loggers deviated not only from an inclination toward hierarchy found in many male collectives, but also from most other egalitarian cultures in their avoidance of sharing and cooperation.

The meanings and practices of masculinity have to be located within this particular historical context. One way of identifying these particular patterns is to look at the loggers' life cycle, starting with boyhood and the socialization process. In their memoirs it was without doubt the image of the lumberjack, and not the farmer, that represented the man the boys wanted to become. Boys often visited the felling areas and longed for the time when they would be allowed to follow their fathers to live for a full winter in the hauling areas. They retold loggers' folklore and could name important, distant places in the forest years before that day had come. The old men who recorded their memoirs can still recall the magical details of their image of the lumberjack, the object of their boyish longings: with the jack-knife in his belt, resin on his trousers, black slouch hat and icicles in his beard, he spat tobacco in the snow and outwitted the peasants with his sharp tongue. This mental picture was surrounded by "the smell of fried dumplings, tary firewood and sweaty horses, jingle of sleigh bells and clanking of chains." A boy's idea of masculinity had very physical and sensuous qualities; it was a sense of "being", a gestalt of the body more than a sense of "doing" or performing a skill.

The boys started work in the forest between the age of six and twelve, most commonly at eight. Even before then, however, many had been out alone in the forest, felling firewood "for mother's stove." The handling of wood-cutting tools and use of various techniques were thus not new when they arrived at the timbers. They already knew how to fell and cut up a tree, although under a child's conditions, that is, without time pressure or demands for advanced skill and thus without being overcome with feelings of inadequacy. This leisurely pace was promptly changed when the boys started working with their fathers.

Life at the timbers appeared to the boy as the place where he was about to become initiated into the male sphere. Other trades, like the guilds of the towns, as well as navy work, railroad construction and saw mill work (which, along with logging, characterized early industrialization in northern Sweden), all had their distinct rituals through which the men accepted newcomers. These rituals were based on patterns similar to many male groups, such as trials, bullying and demands on the newcomer to pay for drinks. In the haulings there were, in fact, not many practices which resembled initiation rituals. This was probably mainly due to the boys' close association with their fathers, but also to the widespread egalitarian attitudes. However, a muted form of ritual trial did appear when, for a short period at the end of the century, saws which were operated by two persons were in use. When a father made his son a partner using this type of saw, he put him through an inconspicuous ritual of manhood whose rules and type of challenge the boy clearly understood, although this was never expressed in words and possibly was not even recognized consciously.

> And it was habitual, that when we put the saw to the root of a tree, I was not allowed to straighten my back until the tree fell over, and by then I was usually so exhausted that I would fall over too.

Many men recall their first winter in the forest as an endless hell of bruised arms, secret tears, backache and chafing, and stiff frozen clothes. The previously held, romanticized physical image of the grown-up lumberjack was thus contradicted by the failure of the boy's own body. In the account of these experiences this contrast between childish prospects, and the disapproving confrontation with how hard and unromantic life in the timber turned out to be, is sharply stressed. There is no doubt that confronting this disappointment marked a genuine step or transition toward maturity and real masculinity, and was made with an understanding gained from a new angle, when childish illusions were left behind.

When the loggers recall that they started as forest workers at the age of eight, they mean that they started as members of the work force, if as yet inadequate to the role. Their place at the two-man saw they interpreted as a genuine position in which they were expected to do their best to increase the household income. A single exception among these voices, however, raises doubts about the validity of these memories. This man also started work at the haulings in his eighth year:

> I believe I ought to make clear from the start, that it was not as an active worker I made first contact with the lumberjack's life. Although it is often said by old people that they started hauling and felling timber at the age of eight or nine, this information deserves acceptance only with some reservations.

This writer was aware that his peers had misinterpreted the situation. They were certainly present at the haulings, but they have vastly exaggerated their own importance. I believe his insights are accurate and that his single observation gives an important clue to some of processes of socialization. The eight-year-old boy's presence at the haulings should not be seen primarily as child labor due to economic need of the rural proletariat in early industrialization (even if there were cases of exploitation due to economic necessity, and even cases of obvious sadism). On the contrary, early childish attempts at work were part of established peasant ideology about the boys' proper place in life at that age, that is, by the side of their fathers. As a rule no explicit pressure was put on the boys, yet they were made to feel that they were persons who could be counted on. To begin with, the boys played around, or watched what was going on. They were eager as observers and, when they were allowed to grab the tools, as followers of the grown-ups' behavior.

The learning of male skills was to a large degree a tacit process, based more on imitation than on the educational training modern man believes to be indispensable for the shaping of coming generations. Since the type of skill required for logging was physical, a part of the mastering of one's own body, the process of acquiring skill tended to be left to the boys to acquire for themselves. To such a socialization pattern of non-intervention, there was one exception. In a competitive felling "ritual," the fathers seem to execute intentional, although still tacit, training. This particular practice was concerned with the sons' ability for physical persistence. It was related to the creation of a sense of timing and estimating work in relation to a future which the fathers saw as a constitutive feature of a grown-up person. The concept of what constituted a grown-up man differed between the generations. The "pre-logging" boys' ideas have already been described in terms of a romantic physical image of a lumberjack. To the fathers, persistence, stamina and the taking of responsibility seem to have been the central values thought desirable to instil in the growing boy.

The Swedish language has two words for man: *karl* and *man*. Man refers more to sex and karl more to gender. Originally karl meant a free man, while both slaves and free men were man. In peasant society a karl meant a married man (men who never married were called old-boys), and a married man was – within the northwest European family pattern – at the same time a head of a household, in northern Sweden a yeoman. Before he became a karl he was a "youngster" (for whom the words change often, between different dialects and over time, but who sometimes can be called halv (half) karl). For ten to 15 years, the young man remained in this position, usually working as a farmhand. A boy was put through ritual trials and initiated into the group of youngsters around the age of 15, but it was through marriage that he became karl. The attributes and qualities of these two kinds of men were considered to be different, and these differences were particularly important in terms of masculinity in North European societies with their long period of pre-marital life as well as the many individuals who remained unmarried.[10] The lumbermen of northern Sweden appear to be part of this pattern.

In the logging, men who were married, fathers, heads of households and thus often yeomen or smallholders, tended to be the ones who signed the contracts with the companies and did the transport work as sleigh-drivers. Their role as entrepreneurs and risk-takers was important, although it was also significant that the fellers whom they hired also saw themselves as free entrepreneurs rather than dependent wage workers. In addition, the yeomen drivers were also responsible for the housing and the provisioning of the working team. These arrangements might have been expected to produce a paternalistic attitude on the part of the drivers, but this was not the case. Neither did they exhibit their higher social status to that of the fellers. So whatever sense of masculinity or self-esteem an ability as a driver might evoke, this was not put to use in interactions within the male group. The driver who speaks below was perhaps exceptionally expressive on these matters because he was speaking to his own son:

> To transport logs, you see Per, it is the worst and roughest and most devilish work of them all, Pelle Skog said one day. It is hard, though not a slave job! Certainly, most of it is toil and moil for both man and horse, but to a great extent it comes down to how you see things. He that hasn't got the head to calculate and see how things should be done; to see how a dragpath or a mainroad should be drawn so that one can quickly take the most trees from a plot; he that isn't brisk and fast in his movements – he will have to drudge the more with his body. And then there is Luck of course. It's a great adventure. But he that doesn't risk anything, he will never win.

A tree feller struggled to adapt his physical skill to the condition of the work, the tools and the trees. The driver's dangerous ride down the slopes with the fully loaded sledge, at the highest possible speed, also relied heavily on physical skills. Drivers often stood, straddling the sledge, so that they could use the strength of their legs to steer and feel what was going on through their whole body, to sense which movements were required at each moment, which might make the difference between an elegantly engineered ride or a road accident. Yet the overarching aspect of the driver's skill was his ability to see, understand and calculate his world, particularly the natural world. Like an untaught engineer, he negotiated serpentine roads and balanced enormous loads of logs. He also calculated prices on contracts and expenses, which involved considering market forces as well as converting the dimensions of the timber according to a complicated tariff of rates.

Between these two stages, the boy's image of a man, and the reality of his father's life as a driver, there was a substantial part of the life cycle in which the youngster or man worked as a feller. This was characterized by struggles to complete the techniques to perfect personal abilities. The achievement of skill was not acquired all at once, but rather was a lifelong process. There were, of course, occasions in every boy's life, not necessarily marked out, when he came closer to being a "real" lumberjack, but his work capacity continued to grow for most of his working life.[11] The earnings of a logger thus varied widely during the course of his life cycle, and the differences in income from one logger to another were also very great.

The implements used in logging were of a very simple kind. At the inception of logging and for some decades afterwards, the axe was used for virtually everything: felling, lopping the twigs and stripping the bark. Saws were originally only in use for cutting the tree into logs, but later were brought in for felling, and barking was eventually done with a special chisel. Technology remained on this simple level until the 1950s when the chainsaw was introduced. The youngest of the pre-mechanization generations comment on the tools of their predecessors with amazement that it was possible to work with them at all. Nevertheless, the change from axe to saw was due to the companies' wish to diminish the waste of timber and was only accomplished by banning the use of the axe, which was preferred by the workers. The barking of the logs took up about half the logger's time at work, even if not all logs were barked.[12] The introduction of the bark chisel did not actually increase work speed, although it saved energy for the worker, and older men carried on barking with the axe, as they were so deft at this task. For the most skilled men, a particular advantage of barking and felling with the axe was the ability to alternate between right- and left-handed work.

The mark of skill that was most visible to others was the ability to make the trees fall in the right direction, making them easy to remove. This involved a deep understanding of the nature of trees, similar to that of the driver's knowledge of terrain, weather conditions and the like. Failure in felling resulted in comments such as "a box full of matches turned upside down." Skill or deftness was more important to production than the intrinsic efficiency of the implements used. The ability to elicit the best out of these simple tools varied widely and their care was also regarded as a matter of individual skill. For example, the ability to file the saw and to adjust the angles of its teeth could determine the level of income, so closely did production depend on the handling of these basic implements, and physically weak men could compensate and overcome their disadvantage with well-kept tools.

The simplicity of tools made their use – the interaction between man and object – rich in potential capacity, capacity for both the shame of failure and dazzling success. However, it would appear that failure – as long as it was due to lack of the right knack and not to idleness – had few social consequences in terms of dishonor. Being skilled – deft and swift – on the other hand, did have strong social significance. This evaluation of skill and zeal was articulated in the loggers' folklore about their heroes: "the characters." The stories about these vagabond workers expresses how work capacity could overcome any other kind of social failure. These vagabonds' homelessness, alcoholism, irresponsibility with money, deplorable dress or other negative qualities were seen as irrelevant as long as they carried on their enormous tree-cutting performance, and showed good comradeship.[13]

When contrasting the vagabond to the husbandman in story-telling, the youngsters/fellers articulated their valued types of masculinity, in which responsibility and good husbanding are scorned. Such various meanings of masculinity at different stages in the life cycle were tied to particular age cohorts since the introduction of logging became the basis of a new masculinity for new generations. These particular boys and the youngsters into which they grew – and even a few men – longed to become tobacco-spitting, vagabonding lumberjacks. Yet their view was inconsistent with their well established fathers' attempts to make their sons responsible husbandmen. Similar examples exist in many other cultures and the different ideals of young people and older generations is often taken as common sense. But precisely such inconsistencies, if not contradictions, are what tend to be overlooked when gender organization is described of polarity, as two static, opposing identities.

Skill in logging before mechanization can thus be seen in terms of "having good hands with or having an eye for; as deftness and the ability of "handling" and seeing, rather than in terms of shared knowledge or mastering of technology. For this reason, the learning of the trade was not a simple transfer of knowledge from one generation to another, but each individual's personal adaptation to the objects on which he was working. Under these conditions, to speak of socialization into manhood through taking over a specifically and culturally defined masculine behavior is thus not entirely relevant.

In these subtle and particular relationships of certain qualities with masculinity, the issue of "skill" as usually understood becomes problematic. A feature of logging which more directly seemed to connote masculinity was competitiveness between the men. In spite of the autonomy of the individual in these egalitarian camp settings, the workers put tremendous pressure on each other through perpetual comparison and competition between themselves. Particularly the fastest workers, the Big-shots, encouraged this attitude. However, it was significant that all such competitions were never declared openly; taking part in an overtly competitive stance was thus never formally recognized. Yet competitive work activity could be a way of achieving respectability for the man who was not a householder, or whose household was very poor and incomplete within the peasant value system. The importance of work ability as well as the absence of at least part of what might be called mainstream European masculinity is demonstrated below:

> I worked with him during his last winters. He wept when he was drunk. In the
> end I cut more than he did, you know, since his arm went so bad. Boy, he was

weeping. He said he would stop cutting, since he had been defeated. There was something wrong with his arm. Yes, polio. His arm was completely twisted. He was a vicious cutter. He knew how to adjust the tools. And good at whetting too. Those things were a great help.[14]

This unspoken but constantly invoked rivalry indicates that competition flourished most of all among the drivers and the "husbandmen," those self-appointed responsible entrepreneurs. The roads in the forest were too narrow and too sloping for horse racing, which was a way of competing back in the villages, during work and on the road to church. In the forest, heavy loads and speedy driving was prestigious – unless strikingly foolhardy – but the final results of competitive driving were to be seen down on the ice of the lakes and the rivers where the logs were unloaded. There each driver had an area where he spread out his logs, making it possible, with a glance of the eye, to tell which man was leading the contest.

The perceived effort to comment on men and women as "work-persons" in everyday small-talk and gossip involved many discursive displays and elaborate ploys in trying to pin down an individual's pace, deftness, bent and likings, zeal, litheness, manners, suppleness – and their negative counterparts. In these evaluations, body, mind and work capacity formed a unity which constituted the central part of personal identity. Gender was relevant in the choice of words to describe such phenomena, but the qualities woven together, rather than vague connotations of masculinity and femininity, were what "constructed" a good man or woman. In spite of the contrast between the division into concrete projects in the case of men's work and the perpetual strenuousness of women's work, strenuousness was an essential part of the "work person" ethos which was attached to both sexes.

Work was mother's great passion. From work came all achievements as well as the life's ratification. A little moment of indolence she would count almost as a crime. Her eyes followed us everywhere in the field. This very day it still happens, when I take an accidental break, that I see the accusing face of my mother. Work is a part of my mentality, and I must admit that I am comfortable with the restlessness that constant zeal causes.[15]

In such memoirs, there is a strong tendency to idealize the mothers. This idealization differs from the Mediterranean patterns, as the boys did not see themselves in contrast to the purity of a worshipped mother, but in some sense looked upon her as a template, a model, to be imitated. The mother's part in the shaping of personality is even more evident than the role of the father according to the written memoirs from the logging area. This is not to say that the boys derived their masculinity from their mothers; nevertheless they did take qualities from mothers which were central to their self-esteem   as men. In most European thinking about gender, unmanly or unmasculine as applied to men immediately conjures up an association with effeminacy. This was not the case for the group we are considering.

Perhaps the differing nuances of their culture can be brought out by considering a different dichotomy, salient to their particular ideas of gender identity. This refers to attitudes about the possibility of sexual intercourse with animals, which carried deep taboos and evoked strong sanctions, both from the state and in local peasant cultures. At the same time there was an almost total absence of concern with or abhorrence of homoerotic relations between men, though this silence could be due to an absence of homosexual practices, as well as a non-recognition of their meaning. Historian Jonas. Liliequist[16] has suggested that the threat to Swedish masculinity from "bestiality" was its association with boyishness, immaturity and uncontrolled activity, as opposed to the threat of passive femininity that the presence of homoeroticism raises in many other European cultures. Such an interpretation of bestiality provides an important confirmation for the argument that masculinity in Norrland was more connected to maturity – and thus skill – than to the contrast with femininity.

Setting aside a dual model of gender construction does not mean that there was no such thing as gender polarity in Norrland. But in this study, doing so has served the purpose of helping to discover nuances and dynamics in both practice and subjective meaning which tend to become lost in a differently structured analysis. A polarized model, perhaps more than we care to admit, also raises the probability of transposing our own cultural assumptions of gender contrast to times and places where they are not appropriate. In Norrland – perhaps due to the fairly distinct and unproblematic sexual division of labor – gender does not seem to have been crucial to the dynamic center of people's identity construction. Gender was a muted discourse, and the ability to work took precedence in notions of respectability. In the continual interest in, and evaluations of, work ability within the community, there were constant challenges and disputes, but the covert competitions and the village gossip would rarely focus directly on gender. Yet gender evaluations were never far distant, for being a good "work person" also gave individuals the security of possessing a masculinity or femininity appropriate for his or her age and household position. And it is this unique historically specific combination of gender, skill and community recognition which not only gives the special flavor of late nineteenth-century northern Sweden but which also might be of some use in understanding other, very different configurations, including our own.[17]

Notes

1. The idea that different ideals of masculinity may depend on age and household position comes from discussions with Peter Loizos, my tutor during a stay at the London School of Economics during 1986-87. At the University of Lund I am grateful for comments made by Orvar Löfgren and Jonas Frykman.
2. The collection is called *Skogsarbetarundersökningen*, a part of *Etnologiska undersökningen* in the archives of Nordiska museet, Stockholm.
3. Sigurd Erixon (ed.), *Atlas över svensk folkkultur* (Uddevalla: Niloe, 1957); Gösta Berg, "Limes Norrlandicus," *Ethnologia Scandinavica*, 13, 1983, pp. 7-15.
4. Ella Johansson, "Träslott och timmerkoja," in Jonas Frykman and Orvar Löfgren (eds), *Modärna tider: Vision och vardag i folkhemmet* (Malmö: Liber, 1985), pp. 421-59; Ann-Kristin Ekman, "Det är för jaktens skull vi jagar, inte för köttets, älgjakt som kollektiv ritual och ekonomisk resurs,", in A. Hjort (ed.), *Svensk natur som resurs och symbol* (Stockholm: Liber, 1982).
5. Orvar Löfgren, "Family and household among Scandinavian peasants," *Ethnologia Scandinavica*, 4, 1974, pp. 17-52; K. Rob and V. Vikman, "Die Einleitung der Ehe. Sonderabdruck der Acta Academiae Aboensis," *Humaniora*, 11 (1), 1937.
6. Jonas Frykman, "Summary: Whores in peasant society," *Horan i bondesamhället* (Lund: Liber, 1977).
7. Ella Johansson, "Flat as a Pancake. Consumption, Commodification and Cosmology in 19th Century Swedish Logging," mimeographed paper presented at the 5th Interdisciplinary Conference on Consumption, Department of European Ethnology, Lund, August 1995.
8. Orvar Löfgren, "Kvinnfolksgöra. Om arbetsdelning; bondesamhället," *Kvinnovetenskaplig tidsskrift*, 3, 1982, pp. 6-14.
9. Being a logger or a farmer are partly different seasonal occupations, and at the same time they relate to different social categories in an extremely confusing way, since these changes are related to both the life cycle and rapid social mobility. See Ella Johansson, "Free sons of the forest: Storytelling and construction of identity among Swedish lumberjacks," in Raphael Samuel and Paul Thompson (eds), *The Myths We Live By* (London: Routledge, 1989).
10. John Hajnal, "European marriage patterns in perspective," in D. V. Glass and D. E. C. Eversley (eds), *Population in History: Essays in Historical Demography*

(London: Edward Arnold, 1965).

11. Jan Wallander, *Flykten från skogsbygden with Summary* (Stockholm: Almqvist and Wiksell, 1948), p. 260.

12. *Ibid.,* p. 104.

13. Johansson, "Free sons of the forest."

14. From fieldwork relating to the first half of the twentieth century, Johansson, "Träslott och timmerkoja."

15. Albert Viksten, *Mitt, liv, ett äventyr* (Göteborg: Författarförlaget, 1971).

16. Jonas Liliequist, "Peasants against nature – crossing the boundaries between man and animal in seventeenth and eighteenth century Sweden," paper presented at the conference "Man and the Animal World," Nijmegen, 1988.

17. This paper was first published in *Gender and History*, 1 (2), 1989.

Chapter 6

Masculine Sport and Masculinity in Denmark at the Turn of the Century

HANS BONDE

Introduction

> Language is incomplete without the language of the body. ... The science that prides itself on being based on observation cannot ignore facts just because they seem somewhat uncomfortable to the professors and can easily upset their neat results. Such phenomena will probably be referred to a different science, with the opportunity being taken to set up a special discipline, gestology, to study the language of arms and legs. This is the usual practice with uncomfortable facts, and this trick has succeeded in turning science into a whole factory town (Vilhelm Grønbeck 1956).[1]

In the course of the twentieth century, the sports coach has attained a central role in serving as a model and instilling norms for masculine behavior, particularly in boys who have been brought up in female-dominated institutional and family settings. If this is not regarded as education today it is because the emphasis on the character-forming potential of sport has been banished to the tenacious stuff of which mentalities are made. At the same time, words like "manliness" and the tough masculine virtues have not been *comme il faut* in the public debate as a result of the progress of feminism. In this unconscious way, sport is much more effective in the formation of consciousness.

This article should be seen as a combination of sports studies and men's studies. This linkage has a historical justification in the period around the turn of the century. At that time, the family as an educational setting was increasingly left in the hands of women, and a proper mother cult developed.[2] Because of the growing importance of work outside the home, men were separated from the upbringing of their own and other people's boys in domestic production. The fathers, however, did not disappear from all upbringing, since some of them later undertook to socialize boys and young men and teach them self-education in the world of sport. Sport became a laboratory for masculinity, where men could create and cultivate a body, motor skills, and a character expressing competitiveness in modern society. It is characteristic that the men's socialization and self-education was based particularly on those virtues that mothers were not expected to be able to impart to their little boys: individualism, independence, fighting spirit, courage, and discipline.[3] To quote from the first Danish sports "manifesto":

> Sport is thus to be perceived as an educational implement which we have hitherto lacked; it teaches our boys to accept the referee's decision, not because it is always correct, but because they themselves have chosen him as referee, it teaches them to obey their leader.[4]

Sport has been analyzed right from the start of men's studies. This is no doubt due to the fact that sport visualizes masculinity, which makes it conspicuous. Anglo-Saxon scholars in particular have worked in this field, but often from a one-sided theory of patriarchalism. A typical example is the book *Jocks, Sports and Male Identity*,[5] in which several chapter headings are explicit: "Sports and Sexism," "Violence, Sports and Masculinity," "Women, Sex-Role Stereotyping and Sports." There is no doubt that American sport can be rougher and more stereotypically masculine than sport in Scandinavia, but such ultra-feminist analyses[6] fail to explain why so many young American men do sports with such enthusiasm. Other Anglo-Saxon research, however, shows greater nuances, as evidenced in articles in *The International Journal of the History of Sport,* and not least in the anthology *Manliness and Morality.*[7] In Scandinavia there has not been any great interest in this research field, although it is used as a vogue word in titles without having any profound influence on the analysis of the problems.[8]

   This article seeks to show that physical culture is such a special research area that it requires untraditional methods. Sport is essentially about movement, and the actual bodily communication should therefore play an important role in sports studies in the humanities and social sciences. This also means that source material in the form of photography, film, video, painting, and instructions for movements are a crucial but neglected source group. My work is inspired by the history of mentalities. A typical feature of this tradition, according to Jacques Le Goff, is that mentalities work at the level of the everyday and the automatic. He also writes that the history of mentalities is linked to "gestures, behaviour, and attitudes."[9] Le Goff thereby places mentalities in both body and mind. It is not just the way a person or a group thinks, but also the way we stand or walk or move in general, that make up the content of the concept of mentality. When the focus is on the everyday, taken-for-granted dimension, an analysis of movement may contribute new insights which may be too unconscious or self-evident to the persons practicing the movements to be seen directly in the self-knowledge of the historical actors. I view the history of mentalities as a tool that sharpens the researcher's perception of the unconscious. It is therefore one-sided, in my view, to stress the unconscious sides of human practice. In human action we mix conscious, pre-conscious, nonverbalized, unconscious, and merely suspected ideas in a changeable web.

The sports movement that is the basis of this investigation is relatively new. The first Danish sports clubs arose in the mid-1860s, but it is not until the 1880s that we can speak of an incipient breakthrough for the sports movement. In 1896 the organizational high point of the period was the establishment of the *Danmarks Idræts Forbund* (Danish Sports Association). The word *idræt* goes hack to Old Norse, but by the turn of the century it was perceived as being roughly synonymous with *sport*, a definition which I follow.

Young men from the upper strata of society were the first to take up sport. For them sport was an activity that represented "leisure" in a society that for most citizens involved hard work from early in the morning until late in the evening. Some men from the bourgeoisie, however, viewed sport as a waste of time and socially degrading. Around the turn of the century, some young working-class men began to practice sports, despite scepticism among workers in the initial phase of sport. Women engaged in sport to only a limited extent, and there was a conflict about whether women should be allowed access to the men's clubs and types of sport. The compromise often arrived at was that women did other forms of sport, or at least that men and women did not perform the same sport together. The movement ideals were thus not the same for different genders and classes, and when we include different gender and class mentalities, we see the bourgeois-masculine cult of speed in relief. We are still on shaky ground, however, when it comes to achieving more exact insight into the patterns of class, gender, and age that sport showed.[10] What can be deduced from the sportsmen's patterns of movement? Which masculine ideals were cherished?

Most of the source material consists of books and magazines about sport from the period 1880-1920. These texts were almost exclusively written by men and are relatively homogeneous. In this article I shall call this *the sports literature,* although it also contains ample illustrations. Central works here were incidentally joint Nordic editions.[11] This British-inspired literature contained many different opinions and was in constant development. There were nevertheless some clearly dominant tendencies which justify us in using the definite article and calling it "the sports literature." To provide a tool with which to understand the link between the different sides of the masculine ideal of movement, I shall use the "figuration" concept,[12] which derives from "form, body, figure." The starting point is thus something spatial – in this context: "one or more figures in movement." Figuration analysis focuses on the forces in space that affect and are influenced by the figure of movement. For the following analysis, the figuration concept means taking a point of departure in human or equine bodies in movement or in one or more items of technology, such as a rowing boat. The movement structure of these figures can then be linked with associated elements, such as (1) perception of time, (2) perception of space, (3) standards of value, (4) records, (5) results, (6) technology and aids, (7) physique and bodily ideals, (8) character structure and self-understanding, (9) relations of age, gender, and class.

Let us take as an example a rower. If he leans forward, this can be seen in connection with temporal norms, that is, that he is trying to get to the finishing line as fast as possible. This effort also affects the shape of the technology: the boat is technically designed so that it can glide as fast as possible through the water. The straight course through the water gives an impression of perception of space (2) and should be seen in connection with the fact that the fastest way is along a straight line. The standard of value (3) is the number of measured seconds and not, for example, the aesthetic value of the rowing, and the aim is often to beat a record (4), not just to defeat the opposition. The result (5) brings a medal that incarnates the rower's mastery of the figuration: he was the fastest. To reach the finish as quickly as possible requires the rower to have the most modern technology with the most dynamic design (6). The form of movement can moreover be associated with bodily ideals and the physique that results from the activity, such as a taut, strong body (7). Furthermore, the mental demands and norms required by the activity can be emphasized, and the rower's perception of himself and the rest of the figuration can be considered, for instance, ideas about goal-directed behavior and ambition. Finally, the analysis of age, gender, and class factors (9) can be linked to the rest of the figuration; the question is whether rowing is practiced by everyone and in the same way, or more broadly speaking, whether the ideal of speed applies to all age groups, to both sexes, and to all social classes.

The analysis thus starts from a figure in motion, but this does not say anything at all about cause and effect. The figure is no more the cause of, say, the result or the perception of time than vice versa. We cannot localize a single point in the figuration which is the cause of the other elements. On the contrary, they are mutually dependent, and indeed they cannot be understood in isolation. This means that the elements mentioned in the figuration cannot be hierarchized, and there is no relative priority in the order. This said, it should be underlined that the perception of time is central to this analysis of rowing and to all other forms of racing. I shall therefore call this figuration a speed figuration.

Figuration analysis can reveal that the way we move is not unaffected by the course of history. Although most people regard their patterns of movement as a matter of course resulting from biology, figuration analysis can show that our movements are changed in connection with general social trends of development.[13]

The fast man

Speed became a central norm for masculine movement in sports culture in the years before 1900. In this section I shall describe in greater detail the speed revolution that arose with the coming of time sports such as horse racing, sailing, and cycling.

In bodily culture there was a development in the course of the nineteenth century away from aristocratic exercises in the form of fencing, dancing, and riding, toward a cult of speed sports among young men of bourgeois origin. One decisively new feature in particular was the spatial dynamics. Whereas the aristocratic exercises were based on fixed positional movements back and forth or up and down in space, the speed sports were based on a movement off into the distance, breaking away from the closed, strictly demarcated space.

The development of modern speed sports did not take place as a sudden transition from the exercises of the nobility to the sports of the bourgeoisie but against a background in which part of the nobility at the end of the eighteenth century began to abandon the traditional riding, fighting, and dancing to concentrate instead on open-air activities and pleasure sports such as hunting with hounds and angling.[14] Toward the end of the nineteenth century there were further decisive changes in bodily culture. To begin with, aristocratic amusements such as hunting and angling were eliminated from the concept of sport. Second, noble disciplines such as sailing and riding were increasingly reshaped into competitive sports. Third, completely new – and often technology-intensive – types of sport developed, such as cycling.

This development, however, did not take place at the drop of a hat. Even today features still survive from the aristocratic physical culture. Hunting and angling are still popular, and sailing and riding are often cultivated for pure enjoyment or (in the case of riding) as dressage. This nevertheless does not lessen the impression that sport toward the end of the nineteenth century acquired increasing importance for masculine sports culture. Unlike hunting and fishing, the aristocratic sailing and figure riding, riding to hounds, and riding for pleasure were better suited for transformation into competitive disciplines.

Time sports

Moving quickly toward a distant goal is not a universal ideal of masculine movement. Although the cult of speed can be found in many different bodily cultures, it was not until modern sport that the cult of time was erected into a system. The ancient Greek Olympic Games included some races,[15] but although it was technically possible, the Greeks did not think of measuring the time of the races. A race in Sparta thus could not be compared with a race in Athens, nor with an earlier or later race in the same place. Each race was unique, and there was no ambition to increase the speed year after year. The constant struggle to improve on current levels, expressed as records, is the most important characteristic of modern sports.

The American sports scholar Allen Guttmann, in his book *From Ritual to Record*, has argued convincingly that record sports are a unique form of physical culture which did not acquire pervasive significance until modern industrial society. Record sport is an incredibly abstract form of sport. A race in Boston can be compared with one in Copenhagen, even if there is a 20-year interval between them, and regardless of whether the athletes have ever been in the same room together, let alone on the same track. What ties it all together is the measurement of time, which makes it possible to compare races irrespective of where and when they take place. The central cult object of sport is the stopwatch.[16]

Modern science, epitomized by Einstein, pointed out that there is no fixed, objective concept of time. For Einstein, time was simply the same as what the hands on the clock show. And the clock he based on an infinite number of temporal rhythms: a chronometer, a religious calendar, the movements of the sun, and so on.[17] To underline the historical relativity of the concept of time, the German historian Wilhelm Hopf has launched the concept of "social time"[18] which reveals the ambivalence that the fixed concept of time which we view as natural and true is fiction, but because all citizens believe it and follow it, it is simultaneously a social reality which shapes not only our picture of reality but also the materiality of which we are part. This applies not least to technology, including sports technology.

Despite the relativity of time, time sport uses a one-dimensional perception of time. Time is assigned a place on an axis that can only point forwards and upwards. There are therefore no "bad records." A record is simply the quantitative high point in a discipline, and records can therefore never be cancelled. The very first Danish sports albums from 1899 onwards contained propaganda for record awareness. It became more and more important to achieve maximum speed. It did not always give the best result, however, in events such as cycling and racing, to rush off with no thought for the position of the competitors in the field; tactics could sometimes put a damper on speech.

Around the turn of the century there was actually disagreement about the justification for tactics. In cycling there were those who thought that it was morally reprehensible to adopt the tactic of cycling just behind the opponent and then defeating him in the final spurt.[19] This ethical angle was gradually abandoned, and two trends in tactics crystallized. On the one hand there was the "front runner" who took the lead at the beginning and strained every muscle to keep the lead for the whole distance. On the other hand there was the "kicker" who did not try to take the lead until the very end of the race, generally in the final spurt.[20] Such tactical differences did not mean, however, that athletes were indifferent to time technology. On the contrary, the occurrence of competitors in a race often led to an increase in speed. As a rule, all major races were timed, not least so as to determine whether a new record had been set. For individual cyclists, runners, and so on, it was important to think of the time, since saving time was synonymous with progress. A typical piece of advice was:

To assist you during training you should ideally have a reliable friend and an
equally reliable stopwatch to time the spurt, so that you can be sure whether
you are making progress or not.[21]

The modern cult of progress was taken to extremes in time sports. The very
word *progress* has a spatial dimension, deriving as it does from a Latin
word meaning "step forward," which was legitimated in sport where
stepping forward became a key word, whether on foot or on horseback.
Forward motion was largely only deflected when this was necessary for the
sake of the spectators, to give them a better view, but the tendency of the
movement was still expansive and directed forwards.

The first discipline in which the cult of speed caught on seriously was
riding. As early as the years 1832-36 there were annual horse races at
Noerrefaelled in Copenhagen.[22] In 1834, for example, these races attracted
a crowd of over 40,000 spectators. The early Danish horse races can be
seen as a stage in "representative publicness,"[23] with the prince displaying
his magnificent wealth in the form of thoroughbred horses reared at
incredibly expensive studs. At the same time the actual form of the race
heralded the interest of a new age in dynamics and growth.

Whereas the emphasis in school-riding and figure-riding had been on
perfection of form, on geometrically correct and choreographically
established movement in space, the breakthrough of horse racing brought a
total revolution in the horse's pattern of movement and perception of
space.[24] Speed and timed movement became the central yardsticks of
achievement. From having been master of close space, the rider now had a
new task – to break the bounds of this space.

Whereas the ballet horse of figure-riding had a great variety of
movements at different tempos and in different directions, such as
backwards and sideways, in horse racing there was virtually only one form
of movement, known as *career*, the horse's fastest gait. The word *career*
goes back to French *carriers* and ultimately to medieval Latin *carraria*,
meaning a chariot track. Today the word has two meanings: the horse's
fastest gait, and the course of professional progress.[25] I have analyzed
elsewhere the young man's endeavor to make a career as a central norm in
sports literature.[26] The concept of career thus had two meanings in sports
literature, and this psychophysical duality is a striking sign of a link
between the ideals of character and movement. In sport the general
masculine aspiration for progress – which is a characteristic feature of
modernity[27] – was ritualized through a pattern of movement in which
speed, drive, and a measurable result were the main things.

In sailing, rowing, and cycling, too, the fast pattern of movement acquired increasing importance toward the end of the nineteenth century. From having initially been confined to the bourgeoisie, the tricycle gradually became a more democratic means of transport and sport.[28] The well-known Danish author Holger Drachmann wrote several poems in praise of sport. In his "Cycle Song" he wrote enthusiastically about the dynamics of the tricycle:

Onward on fast-spinning wheels,
High above dust, through the rain and the wind at top speed.
Harden the body for hours,
Never take shelter from showers.
Riding for glory, compete for the prize on the "steed."
The steed is resolved, and the rider likewise.
It's time now to mount, and away the hike flies.[29]

This verse includes all three components in the masculine ideal of the sports literature: "Onward on fast-spinning wheels" (a dynamic pattern of movement), "Harden the body for hours" (a toughened body), and "The steed is resolved, and the rider likewise" (a resolute character). The numerous poems in the sports literature show the enthusiasm which young dynamic men could evoke.

The fascination with dynamics

The fascination with speed and drive was clearly seen in the use of club names. Among the 26 sports clubs registered in the Danish Sports Association in 1898 which did not reflect an occupation or a geographical origin, there were eight names expressing dynamism and forward movement: *Frem* and *Fremad* (both meaning "Forward"), *Go on*, *Kvik*, and so on.[30]

Sport and the cult of speed was so utterly urban a phenomenon that it is possible to see occasions in the sports literature when the rural populace were perceived as being almost unbearably slow. C. E. Staal, the chairman of the "Dansk Bicycle Club," for example, criticized the wooden clogs worn by country people because they "make walking heavy and troublesome, and generally deter the wearer from quick and agile movements."[31] To remedy this, he urged rural Danes to do sports with great zeal, which would give them a chance to develop the "speed and ease of movement" that they lacked.[32]

The fact that Staal's irritation over the more easy-going perception of time had a solid foundation is suggested by the observations of the museum keeper Peter Riismøller in the Danish army as late as 1925:

> The country lads still walked with the deep bend at the knee that characterizes peasants, and they were also exhausted by a few kilometres' march. As for running, they never learned that – but the Copenhagen men were the most mobile, with far more stamina when running and marching.[33]

In the sports literature, speed and strength were portrayed as ideal male qualities. I. P. Müller, the preacher of fitness and health who became world-famous after the turn of the century, was Danish champion in several speed sports, and through his newspaper articles he was an energetic advocate of the cult of speed.[34]

> No less a pleasure is associated with racing, especially if one can beat one's opponents. Those who have not tried it can scarcely grasp the love of life and joy of victory that flows through the soul when, after a protracted struggle, one still has the strength and the speed in the home stretch to spurt away from one's opponents.[35]

Müller was annoyed by the fact that many people still did not understand that the point was to run fast and not to run as far as possible.[36] This illustrates that not everyone around 1900 was mentally prepared for the cult of speed in sport. Müller noted that "sport nihilists like to bring up the argument that it does not matter a lot in this or that sport if one can cover a certain distance a few seconds faster or slower."[37] In gymnastics we can find examples of the extreme cult of speed being regarded as sheer nonsense, as in the following quotation from the doctor Valdemar Harslof. He had just attended the 1912 Olympic Games in Stockholm, after which he concluded that:

> The fact is that what was supposed to be a means in sport has been made into the end, so that the only ambition is to set a new record, to reduce or increase the time by a few seconds or minutes – even at the cost of one's life or health.[38]

The scepticism of the gymnastics supporters was based partly on the fear that the cult of the fast sportsman could lead to an "unmanly" self-centredness.[39]

The technological man

Modern man is fundamentally characterized by his relation to technology. Capitalist industrialization meant the creation of a society based on permanent and rapid technical development. As the main actor in the production sphere, modern men have acquired an advantage over women in that they master external nature by means of technology. The entrepreneur has become the practical hero of modern life; through hard work and inventiveness he has improved conditions for everyone, giving us all a more pleasant life.[40]

The development of modern technology did not just take place in the sphere of production, but also in the field of leisure, where technological man could be hailed and hail himself in particularly dramatic and physical situations. The development of modern speed sports therefore did not only take place on the level of movement; it also had deep roots in technical development. In the time-sports in particular, where the struggle against the hampering forces of water and air was vital, technology acquired a central position.

Being able to rush along the main road or through the ocean waves at violent speed became a privilege for the men who had the money, the time, and the courage to attempt it. Women, on the other hand, both in the sports literature and in the actual performance of sport, were confined to slower technology in the speed sports or simply expected to do less technologically demanding physical activities such as gymnastics or lawn tennis. The cult of expensive speed technology gave certain bourgeois men a chance to distance themselves socially from other men in their own class, and especially from men in lower classes who could not afford such luxury. With the aid of high-speed technology it became possible to move faster than all other people in society; to outdistance all those who could not keep up in the race.

In what follows I look more closely at what I call the revolution of the century in sports technology, a revolution that chiefly took place in riding, cycling, rowing, and sailing. The symbolic value of technology, as an expression of masculine drive, meant that the practitioner himself did not need to radiate physical dynamics, but by this economic and technical mastery of technology he could signal that his sights were set on the future. For example, a rich sports enthusiast could equip a jockey with a horse or sit behind the wheel at the earliest motor races (held on the island of Fanø off the coast of South Jutland but discontinued in the 1920s). Although a horse is not a piece of technology in the sense that a rowing boat is, I study changes in the form and movements of horses in connection with other changes in sports technology in the period. I do so because there was an element of design in horse breeding, and this design was closely connected with changes in sports technology proper.

The development of the horse race had a significance that went far beyond the actual change in speed. The movements of the horse's body in space were also changed, and this development was closely observed in the contemporary literature. There turned out to be a world of difference between the modern racehorse and the horse trained for traditional school-riding; despite the decline in aristocratic exercises the school-horse continued to play a major role in the art of riding:

> In the school-horse the centre of gravity is far back so that the horse can perform slow, high movements and tight turns; the ability to bring the centre of gravity further forward to develop considerable speed is not required. ... The flat racehorse, finally, needs only tremendous speed and places no emphasis on high movements and tight turns; essentially it requires only practice in keeping balance when the centre of gravity is moved as far forward as possible.[41]

The horse's pattern of movement had obviously undergone a profound change when the school-horse was seen in contrast to the modern racehorse. The development went from the slow, high movements and tight turns of the school-horse, filling a relatively limited space, to the elongated, fast, and expansive attempts to break through the restraining bonds of time and space. The bodily transformation that can be observed was not confined, however, to the time when the movements had to be performed. In purely anatomical terms, the racehorse had a completely different body from the school-horse. If one wanted a racehorse, one had to create it.[42]

British paintings of horse races from the nineteenth century often show a distinct development in bodily form and movement patterns from the school-horse to the flat racehorse. The depiction of the horse's shadows gives the viewer a sense of the spatial elongation of the horse's movements. The silhouette of the racehorse is sometimes portrayed virtually as a long narrow line, but this is an over-explicit representation of the forward-directed movement ideal of the time. The forelegs and hind legs point in diametrically opposite directions, stretching the horse to make it longer and flatter. Photographs of horse races, however, have shown that these paintings are physiologically incorrect; horses never spread their fore and hind quarters so far apart.[43]

In the traditional upper-class sport, sailing, there was a dramatic change in the design of the boats toward the end of the nineteenth century. As in the case of racehorses, the trend was toward long, narrow sailing boats. In England some rowing boats were made so narrow and deep that they were fittingly described as "planks set on end."[44] Perhaps the most extreme "plank-on-end cutter" seen in Danish waters in the 1880s was the *Muriel*, which was owned by Consul Broberg. Of this vessel it was said: "It is as narrow as a ruler, and sailing wits said that a well built man could not even turn in his berth." The problem was that the *Muriel* did not have any initial rigidity, which meant that it could be difficult to avoid drastic keeling. It keeled over flat on the water at the slightest breeze![45]

This example is extreme, of course, but it is a good illustration of the greatest and most widely discussed problem for Danish sports sailors at the end of the nineteenth century. One of the most important contributions to the debate came from Chr. Kroman, professor of philosophy, who in 1893 published a work entitled "The Logic of Sailing Races: Contribution to the Solution of the Measurement Problem." For Kroman the burning issue was whether one should use technological development for the aim of inventing the swiftest sailing machine imaginable, "and after having brought it into being to gallop off in it in pursuit of as many prizes as possible," or whether sailing races should be allowed to be "incorporated as an element in general pleasure boating and regarded as a means for the development of seaworthiness and general pluck and resourcefulness."[46]

Kroman himself preferred the second alternative, questioning whether the first "can in the long run please anyone but peculiar Englishmen and nervous Americans." Kroman's aim, and that of many other people, was to create a measurement system for sailing races which could ensure that virtually all existing types of boats (and hence also people with differing economic means) would have a chance to win first prize. According to him, "an unhealthy, one-sided emphasis is placed on certain characteristics, namely, those encouraging speed, while more or less neglecting the other qualities needed for a good boat, such as seaworthiness, a certain spaciousness, etc."

In short, Kroman wanted to prevent "the natural types" from slipping unnoticed into the "degenerate" types, with many ordinary pleasure yachts being designed on the model of the racing yachts. He did not succeed in this, however. Speed technology gained more and more ground in sailing, too, and in the mid-1890s there was a division into two classes, cruisers and racers, because it would be unfair to allow the two to compete against each other in the same race. This did not mean, of course, that sailing boats not intended for racing disappeared, but merely that the cult of speed around 1900 had a greater influence on yachting technology. The tendency of sports equipment to become longer and narrower was also seen in other types of sport, such as rowing, cycling, skating, and skiing.[47]

The change in sporting technology has a dimension of mentality history. The aerodynamic design of the racehorse and sports technology which could still make people's blood boil at the turn of the century has today become a self-evident part of our everyday life. The tricycle as we know it today seems natural to us. A tricycle is a tricycle! Today the traditional cycle model can be disparagingly referred to as a "boneshaker," or in Danish *vaeltepeter* (overturner). By using these terms we are praising progress: "How good it is that we no longer make bikes that overturn!" What is forgotten here is that all development also involves obsolescence. Many older models of cycles were often regarded as being more elegant and healthier than the newest models, because they allowed people to ride with straight backs so that the respiratory organs were not compressed.[48] At the same time, it was designed to allow good visibility. You could cycle off at a gentle rhythm and concentrate on looking at the things on either side of the road. All this was made difficult with the advent of the modern tricycle. Now it was more a question of cycling with a bent back, looking downwards and forwards. The tricycle had increasingly become a speed instrument.

All in all, sports technology can be seen as a set of tools to reinforce man's mastery of nature. Through the use of technology, the sportsman became capable of moving at much greater speed than the naked body could manage. The aura of forward-looking dynamism that surrounded sports equipment became a part of the image of the technological sportsman. By surrounding himself with the latest technology or by putting a jockey on a svelte racehorse, the bourgeois man was able to signal wealth, modernity, and enterprise.

A retrospect - the cultural history of the back

The new speed figuration revealed itself as more than just a new design for animals and implements. The sportsman too had to submit to development. In time sports such as cycling, horse racing, rowing, running, speed skating, and so on, it became necessary for reasons of aerodynamics to bend the back to get forward faster. The demand for a straight back had deep historical roots, so it was no easy matter to remove this norm from the movement situations of sport. Before I embark on a discussion of the bent back in sport, I shall try to paint a more general picture of the history of posture ideals.

Our bodies and our relation to the body are not unchangeable or God-given. The body changes according to the culture of which it is a part. Most people do not reflect on the fact that they have a back. The back is concealed from us. We cannot look at our own back. It is only when it begins to ache that we become aware of its existence. Then we experience it in a medical sense, as a bit of nature that is not working as it should. Very few people are aware that there are different ideals for the straightness of the back, or that the back is shaped differently according to the culture of which it is a part. A back is a back!

In his doctoral dissertation, the French historian Georges Vigarello has painted a picture of the civilizing of the body in France from the Middle Ages until the present day.[49] His point of departure is the posture of the body; crudely simplified, his finding is that the ideal of the straight back from the aristocratic culture of the fifteenth century until today was an important stage in the civilizing of individuals in society. The ideal of the straight back gradually achieved a broader response, first among the bourgeoisie, then in the other social classes. From the end of the fifteenth century, the courtly nobility in France began to take an interest in the back. Children of nobles were wrapped in swaddling clothes and women were straightened with the aid of corsets, to live up to the new ideal of the straight back. In the aristocratic fencing and riding of the seventeenth century, the straightness of the male body became a sign of the degree of civilization.[50]

The upright back can be seen as the attempt of the nobility to distance itself from other classes. By straightening the back, a nobleman could demonstrate his high state of civilization, his superior status, and his freedom from the physical labor that bent the peasant's back. The difference in height was further increased by the nobleman's use of wigs and high-heeled shoes. Class differences were thus justified on the basis of bodily postures. In the same way, the men of the bourgeoisie could make themselves into higher beings than bodily laborers, who had to break their backs to earn their daily bread. The erect bourgeois symbolized self-control and firmness of character. He was a man with backbone! The problem for the worker was just that the hard physical work often shortened his muscles. He simply could not pull himself together and straighten up.[51]

To my knowledge there has been no attempt to analyze the history of the backbone on the basis of Nordic evidence. If I assume that Vigarello's French history of the back also applies in broad outline to Danish history, I do so on the basis of circumstantial evidence.[52]

In the course of the nineteenth century the state began to show an interest in the erect back as a crucial educational instrument. From 1814 gymnastics were introduced in Danish boys' schools as an element in the national defence; this form of gymnastics involved an idealization of the severely erect military posture.[53] The peasantry, however, were not suited to these exercises.[54] Traditionally, the peasant was far below the mounted aristocrat, both literally and figuratively; he was expected to bow to the nobleman and he was often bent by hard physical labor. Around 1900, however, the rural population began to change the image of the subordinate, bowed-down peasant. In parochial halls and folk high schools they began to do the "fling gymnastics" that had been imported from Sweden.

The slogan of country gymnastics was "Straighten your back and tell the truth."[55] In the towns, however, the men had begun to do sports, and in their movements they proclaimed a completely different message: "Bend your back and get forward fast." Posture as an expression of both bodily stance and character is already implicit in the word *attitude*, which has both a physical and a mental dimension.

The forward-looking man

In the sports literature, a straight back was an ideal for the static sportsman posing for the camera, that is, while not actually competing. In sports culture, the erect male back became a sign of self-control and firm character. This posture was also maintained by the sports literature and in competition as the ideal, for example, in horse racing and speed skating. Oarsmen were generally recommended to keep a straight back, even though the aim was "to make a quick start."[56] Two rowing methods – the English style with an erect back and the American style with a bent back – were often confronted in races, which led to heated discussions about which was the better way to row.

On the basis of these discussions, I shall try here to describe the role of aesthetics in the cult of sport at the turn of the century. After the defeat of the Danish rowers at the first Scandinavian championship at Holtekilen near Oslo in 1883, a huge post-mortem was conducted not just in Danish but also in Swedish and Norwegian sports magazines.[57] One of the reasons for the defeat may have been that the Danish rowers competed in an outrigger boat which was said to be too thick and antiquated in comparison with the opponents' boats. The Danish oarsmen were also criticized for the way they rowed, and this led one of the Danish crew to make the following defence of the American-inspired rowing method:

> The Americans start from the assumption that the method that can bring a boat to the finishing line first must be the best to use in a rowing race. The consideration of beauty must take second place, and in any case it is only a matter of taste which of the different rowing methods can be considered most beautiful. In a horse race I am certain that a rider would look highly ridiculous if, instead of making the horse go as fast as possible, he let the beast do some voltes and other examples of the fine art of riding on the way, although probably everyone would admit that this is much more beautiful and pleasing to look at than all this furious galloping. The same applies to cycling, skating, and many other sports. Everywhere there is a distinction between speed skating and figure skating. ... For rowing, however, in my opinion, the American method must be used, since the aim is to finish first. The method that results in this is the best ... as well as being the most beautiful, since "handsome is, that handsome does [*sic*]."

Two pieces in *Tidsskrift for Sport* criticized the bent rowers for their posture, arguing that, although "it is not impossible that the American or French rowing method is better, giving better results as regards speed than the English method," the ideal should nevertheless be "the method of rowing which does not only ensure that the boat moves faster but also develops the rower's body in a healthy and all-round way." The chairman of the Copenhagen Rowing Club maintained from the aesthetic point of view that it was "impossible to perform attractive, classical rowing with such swift strokes." He supported the criticism of the Danish rowers and recommended the English-inspired rowing with a straight back.

This illustrates very well that early Danish sport was far from being totally dominated by the cult of speed. On the contrary, the traditional aesthetic and health aspects carried great weight for some people. These differences were also significant for the perception of the straight back. The ideal of speed gradually triumphed at the expense of the traditional ideals of beauty and health. In a great many time sports, the bent, forward-pointing back became the new sign of masculine energy, dynamism, and speed in movement. The erect back had to give way to this onrushing ideal.

The ball player

Ball games were not a new invention at the end of the nineteenth century, having been played in different forms by nobles and peasants alike for many centuries.[58] At the end of the nineteenth century, ball games became popular again and several new clubs were founded,[59] dominated by the urban bourgeoisie. Working-class men quickly followed by forming occupational clubs: there were clubs of sporting printers, painters, bakers, tailors, cigar workers, shoemakers, and railway workers.

The first ball club was founded as early as 1866 (Sorø Akademis Boldklub), but the real breakthrough came in the mid-1880s. From 1885 until October 1889, the number of clubs rose from about 15 to 83, which meant that some 4000 men were playing ball games (mostly cricket) in clubs as early as 1889.[60] This drastic quantitative development of ball games was followed by a qualitative change in relation to centuries of previous ball games. The main new feature was the revolutionizing of the young men's patterns of movement that took place as a result of the emphasis on speed in the growing hall sports; this is reflected in the names of the football and cricket clubs, some of which mean "fast" (*Rap, Kvik, Velo* from Latin *velox*), others "forward" (*Fremad, Frem*).[61] Although cricket and rounders were among the first ball games to be played, they were quickly superseded by more dynamic sports such as tennis and football.

The footballers' way of moving was at first glance a rather chaotic muddle of movements in every direction. On closer look, however, it becomes clear that both teams show a strong forward drive and both are literally and figuratively goal-directed. The only reason for the great variation in the patterns of movement is that both sides are trying with all their might to stop the opponents' motion toward the goal. The ideal direction of movement is therefore the straight, forward, fastest possible way to the opposing goal.

I have touched lightly on what can be called the alternating and spontaneous element in football. Unlike racing sports, which are based on a highly linear and predictable pattern of movement, the lightning-fast, intuitive ability to adapt to changing circumstances plays a major role in football. This spontaneity and ability to rethink undoubtedly had an effect on the men who played football instead of taking up, say, cycling. Conversely, different types of man have felt attracted to different sports. Throughout the twentieth century, football has been the working-class sport above all others. On the football pitch the workers could use the experience of teamwork that they had gained at the workplaces around the turn of the century, and they were able to develop the collective solidarity that had become the most important lever in their struggle for social and political liberation. In addition, the physical contact and the element of rough combat have undoubtedly appealed to many young manual laborers.[62]

In the course of this century, golf has become the bourgeois sport *par excellence*. The organizational start came in 1898, with the founding of Copenhagen Golf Club and the opening of Fano Golf Course. The refinement of the bourgeois man in contrast to the brute force of the proletariat is clearly seen in golf; although the long shots require great strength, there is a long time between each stroke, and the short strokes call for more accuracy than strength.[63]

Finally, it remains only to say that the lightning-fast, forward-pointing sport of handball in its Danish variant was created just after the turn of the century, but it was not until the 1920s that it showed any great upswing at club level.[64]

The strong man

Working-class sportsmen at the turn of the century were as much fascinated by strength as by speech. From the end of the 1880s some manual workers began to do power sports such as weight-lifting, wrestling, and boxing. In 1888 the first club for these sports was formed, *Københavns atletklub* (KAK, Copenhagen Athletics Club), on the initiative of men such as the social democratic agitator A. C. Meyer, who had understood that working-class men were much more interested in power sport than in cricket, which he had previously tried to inspire them to play.[65] KAK gave them a chance to do weight-lifting, and the club was dominated from the start by men from occupations requiring physical strength. In the words of another social democratic pioneer of sports, the journalist Norman Bryn, they were "Strong bricklayers, muscular blacksmiths and mechanics, energetic carpenters."[66]

Officielt Organ for Dansk Forening for Lystsejlads, Foreningen til den ædle Hesteavls Fremme, Selskabet til Travsportens
Fremme i Danmark, Kjøbenhavns Gymnastikforening, Kallebodstrands Sejlforening, Foreningen til Lystsejlads for Assens
Tolddistrikt, Sejlklubben i Kolding, Kjøbenhavns Roklub, Dansk Forening for Rosport, Øresunds Sejlforening, Dansk
Bicycle Klub, Fredericia Sejlklub, Dansk Cycle-Union og Kjøbenhavns Boldklub.

Nr. 42.   Redigeret af   Kjøbenhavn den 19. Oktober 1888.   Hovedexpedition: 5. Aargang.
             Kommandør T. Hansen   Emil Bergmanns Boghandel

Figure 1: *Danish Sports-Tidendes* vignette (1885-1895) is a fine presentation of early Danish sports and the range of the concept of athletics. As can be seen, sport was conducted as an outdoor activity, the main forms being sailing, rowing, hunting, fishing, horse-racing and velocipede cycling. Several relatively inexpensive activities such as cricket, football, longball, shooting and gymnastics, were mentioned only as ancillary, which underlines the newspaper's upper-class character. Women appeared only as erect riders, sitting side-saddle, in the specific style for women. *Source*: *Dansk Sports-Tidend*, no. 13 (1890).

Figure 2: I.P.Müller showing his perfect body in a demonstration of his 'skin gymnastics'. (From the Photographic collection at the Royal Library, Copenhagen.)

Figure 3: The straightened back, The Englishman Captain Darell.
(*Source*: Idrætsbogen [1909], p.42.)

Figure 4: The dynamic bent man, The American world champion William Beach.
(*Source*: Illustreret Idrætsbog [1890], p.197.)

Figure 5: The elegant man, Even Neuhaus with his 'monocycle' Beyerholm, 1941.

Figure 6: The strong man, celebrated by his worker colleagues in 1899. (*Source*: The Archive and Library of the Danish Workers Movement, Copenhagen, 33.1.[8].)

Figure 7: From 1902 to 1917 beauty contests for men were arranged in Copenhagen.

The extreme cult of strength that was practiced at KAK was clearly seen in the membership requirement: only men who could swing a 70-pound ball up in the air with outstretched arm could join.[67]

As a reaction to the fact that KAK had virtually "reached the stage where they judge a man according to his size,"[68] another pioneer of working-class sport, the fire-master P. L. Jacobsen, took the initiative in 1895 to form *Arbejdernes idrætsklub* (AIK, The Workers' Sports Club). Here the workers practiced a wider range of sports, such as gymnastics, wrestling, boxing, and athletics. The clientele was slightly different from that of KAK. Here, too, there was a predominance of skilled workers, but now they were mainly from trades requiring not so much physical strength as technique and adroitness: carpenters, painters, and tailors.[69] Despite this reaction to the extreme cult of strength, some power sports were nevertheless practiced in AIK – Greco-Roman wrestling and boxing – as they were in many other athletics clubs that arose around the turn of the century.[70]

Many of the earliest power sports clubs chose names indicating firmness and strength, such as names inspired by Viking mythology: *Dan, Hermod, Thor.*

Around 1900, show-wrestling was a highly popular form of public entertainment. Huge, powerful, often slightly obese men, such as the Danish world champion Magnus Beck-Olsen, fought fierce bouts to the great pleasure of large crowds of spectators. The outcome was often rigged in advance.[71] People gradually grew tired of and indifferent to show-wrestling, not least because of the slow pattern of movement. The last international show-wrestling contest ended in 1905, and the daily newspaper *Ekstra Bladet* expressed relief at seeing the last of the "fat men" falling on the mats. American boxing was promoted instead of wrestling, since the men looked completely different: "Strong, slim people whose muscles are like steel, whose skin is as bright as ivory."[72]

After the end of show-wrestling in 1905, boxing quickly took over as a great public favorite. One reason for this is that boxing, although based on strength, requires much greater speed than wrestling. Wrestling underwent great changes around the turn of the century. Traditional show-wrestling was abandoned in favor of modern sport wrestling, where the division into different weight classes was of decisive significance. This meant that it was no longer enough to be big and heavy to be able to flatten one's opponent. On the contrary, it became essential that all those kilos were muscles, except perhaps for heavyweights. The many lightweight wrestlers meant that the sport acquired a faster style. The infighting that slowed down a bout was relatively toned down in boxing,[73] but in wrestling it still remained the crucial aspect of the wrestler's pattern of movement.

As a whole, working-class power sports around 1900 should be seen as an expression of an independent class culture. Because of the sweat, bodily contact, brute strength, courage, and violence, power sports differed from other sports culture. Power sports can be seen as an undercurrent in bourgeois sports culture, an undercurrent pointing back to the peasant culture of strength and the struggle of earlier centuries. There seems to be continuity in the culture of manual workers as regards elements such as the direct physical fighting and the glorification of strength. The working-class sportsmen's growing fascination with the fast pattern of movement, for example in football, can be seen as a move toward the bourgeois cult of speed. Conversely, the very fact that bourgeois sportsmen began to perform large, sweat-producing, powerful movements and to cultivate the body in general although this had been taboo in Victorian culture, can be seen as reflecting that they were coming closer to the culture of the manual laborers.

The slow gender

When have described sportsmen at the turn of the century as belonging to "the fast gender" in their own self-perception, this implies that women are viewed in the sports literature as "the slow gender." As a contrast to the sportsmen, I now look more closely at the role of women in the movement revolution led by sport at the turn of the century, and at the norms of feminine movement found in the sports literature.

The sports literature made a strict distinction between what could be regarded as fitting patterns of movement for women and men respectively. Women as a rule were not supposed to attempt hefty, hard, or quick movements. Instead they were recommended to do (1) gentle sports for pleasure or (2) aesthetic sports, that is, those where style is crucial, or (3) female gymnastics.

If we look, for example, at the typical upper-class sport of riding, it was considered self-evident that women should not bother to gallop away post-haste. Riding in this period was exclusively an activity for "the ladies of our well-to-do classes,"[74] and the norms for these women's performances on horseback were chiefly concentrated on correct, decent, seemly, and pretty movement.

Not just riding but also fencing and cycling were pleasures for upper-class women in the period. Today we are not accustomed to making a conscious distinction between the way men and women ride a bicycle. Around 1900, however, the sports literature urged female cyclists not to move with excessive force or speed. Even as relatively progressive a man as the sport agitator Lieutenant William Hovgaard, who declared himself to be in favor of female emancipation in the world of sport, nevertheless maintained that the rule for women was that "violent spurts should be avoided."[75]

In rowing, women had already begun to make their presence felt before the turn of the century, although to a much lesser extent than men. The only specifically female rowing club around 1890, as far as I have been able to ascertain, was the Copenhagen Women's Rowing Club, with 18 active and 9 passive members. In contrast, the number of active male rowers was about 800.[76] We see once again the same pattern in the treatment of women in the sports literature. Women should not bother to row quickly or powerfully, as the following quotation shows:

> Above all, one should not over-exert oneself, for women are not expected to attain the greatest possible speed or develop the greatest strength, but to pursue the sport in a gentle, pleasant way.[77]

In Copenhagen the difference between the sexes resulted in races for women only. Here the decisive thing was not the speed; the emphasis was on "attractive, stylish rowing."[78] It seems absurd, however, that the sport was nevertheless arranged according to the configuration of a competitive sport, that is, with the contestants starting at the same time, with a fixed course, and with a forwardmoving pattern of movement; the only exception was that the value standard (the measurement of time) was missing. It is amusing that, when the starting signal went, the women nevertheless spurted off. In a report in *Politiken* from the ladies' race at a rowing event at Langelinie in 1905, for example, we read that "The competitive spirit was no less than in proper rowers. From start to finish they rowed with great energy."[79] For many years after this, women struggled to be allowed to compete in real speed races, but this demand was not granted until 1941. The board of the Danish Association for Rowing Sport then acceded and introduced a Danish championship for women, against the clock.[80]

In the sports literature there were also very different norms for the movement of the two sexes as regards ball games. An unfavorable view was taken of women participating in football or cricket. When these types of sport are discussed, women are not mentioned at all. It was presumably thought that the large, violent, perspiratory movements that developed the leg muscles were not suitable for women. Tackling and kicking, bending, shouting, falling, and getting dirty were regarded as aggressive and unfeminine behavior in the bourgeois public sphere. An extreme quotation from an article in *Idrætten*,[81] the official journal of the Danish Sports Association, in 1918 revealed how football ran counter to the traditional woman's role:

> There are male sports and there are female sports. Football is a male sport. Women should not run about a football field like idiots, shrieking themselves hoarse, kicking each other on the legs, and shaming their beautiful breasts, and getting men's legs and big wide feet, so that they need size 42 shoes, becoming round-shouldered, and suffering the other consequences.

Despite this warning, some women did risk their skins. In 1887 there was already a football club for well-off women, but this did little to provoke the public, since they played in a back yard in Copenhagen. Furthermore, the Copenhagen Women's Ball Club was founded in 1902; the women had already been playing for three years. At Hanne Adler's school in Copenhagen for the children of the liberal bourgeoisie, football was played after 1900 by girls and boys together.[82]

That football was regarded as a masculine activity is clearly illustrated in the utterances of a man who in 1902 attended a match between women's teams from Copenhagen and Odense. The women were advised to avoid "tough play and violent clashes," "a woman who is exhausted and breathless after playing is a sin against femininity." The distaste for women's breathlessness may suggest a dislike of the sexual associations in the total surrender to the game and the aggressive animality of the body. Football was supposed to be a male preserve:

> We have all been aware that ladies can play tennis, row, ride and even sail, but all men have surely been sceptical about women as footballers. We thought that this game, whose charm is its strength more than any other game, would remain untouched in the possession of men – but the attempt has been made to wrest this sport from men.[83]

Tennis for a long time was regarded as a sport suitable for both sexes, unlike football. The chief ball game for women was thus tennis, which had been taken up after the turn of the century by women from the upper class. The two sexes had different standards of strength, speed, and mobility. For the sports agitator William Hovgaard, the great advantage of tennis was that it could be played by both sexes. It was in no way dangerous and could therefore be played by "ladies, elderly gentlemen, and children alike," while it could also be played so hard, deftly, and fast that no man should dismiss it: "The greater skill in the game makes such great demands of strength, adroitness, and a sure eye that no man should be ashamed to play it."[84] Tennis nevertheless became one of the first games in which women were given the opportunity to take part in competitions. The Copenhagen Ball Club (KB), for instance, arranged individual matches for women as early as 1891.[85]

Interestingly, ball games such as bandy (a kind of open-air ice hockey) and hockey were taken up by women.[86] The fact that hockey rather than football attracted women was no doubt due to the lower degree of brutality and physical contact in the sport.

Handball, although relatively tough and fast, was not regarded as being unsuitable for girls in the sports literature, at least not by the Danish creator of the game, Holger Nielsen. Nielsen described handball as a game in which there were far more changes and alternations than in other ball games,[87] and his rules also permitted players to hold opponents, but physical strength was not supposed to be an essential element of the game. Here, too, however, the difference between the sexes was underlined: holding was prohibited in girls' handball. As for the heavy power sports, such as weight-lifting, wrestling, and boxing, it remained unthinkable that women should be allowed to take part.

In *Man and Woman*, a book published in 1895 by the doctor and gymnastics teacher Abr. Clod-Hansen, the status of women as "the slow sex" was given a physiological grounding:

> Manifold experiences from gymnastics, from handicrafts and laboratories have taught us that, however fast women in general learn to perform a "speech exercise" well – even better than average (and they often perform faster than men do) – as a whole they are still far behind men when it comes to pressing speed to the utmost.[88]

Not all women accepted the attempts of male sports writers to monopolize speed in time sports. In the course of the 1890s, two female cyclists, Johanne Jørgensen and Susanne Lindberg, managed to break a number of records – set by men, it should be noted – an achievement that attracted international attention.

Conclusion

> Of all the ridiculous things, the most ridiculous seems to me to be in a hurry in
> the world, to be a man who is quick to eat and quick to act. When therefore I
> see a fly at that decisive moment alighting on the nose of such a businessman,
> or if he is splashed by a carriage driving past him at even greater speed, or
> when the Knippelsbro bridge is raised, or a tile falls from a roof and kills him,
> then I laugh heartily. And who couldn't help laughing? What do these busy,
> hurried people actually achieve? Do they not end up as the woman did who, in
> a flurry because her house was on fire, rescued the fire tongs? What more do
> they rescue from the great fire of life? (Søren Kierkegaard, 1843).[89]

It was precisely at the time when the family as an educational sphere
became a woman's sphere that Danish men more or less consciously
created spaces where they could investigate and shape masculinity in
themselves and in their own and other people's sons. Sport became a
laboratory for masculinity, where men could create a body, motor skills,
and a character that expressed competitiveness in modern society. In a
unisexual space they were able to cultivate physical achievements, in
which the average man was superior to the average woman. In sport men
were physiologically on their home ground, so they could develop an
independent gender identity in relation to women.

Norms and values from the new masculine working-class culture were
ritualized in the sports movement that made its first breakthrough in the
1880s. The effort to beat the stopwatch by fractions of a second is a
characteristic feature of modernity, in which the swift spinning of the
wheels becomes the norm in everyday life. There was a revolution in the
sportsman's pattern of movement with the transition from the elegant
figure skating to the race against the clock that is speed skating. This
development, however, should only be seen as a gradual tendency through
time, not an overwhelming sudden change. Today we still have artistic
forms such as figure skating and dressage. We can nevertheless note a
trend by which the male ideal in part of the bourgeoisie changed from
having been "the elegant man" – which in turn was based on the standards
of aristocratic exercises – to being "the fast man." This is not to say that
the fast (sports)man cannot be elegant; it was rather the case that a whole
new aesthetic developed, in which elegance was associated with the
rhythm that could arise in the endeavor to move as efficiently as possible,
whether the aim was to get off to a quick start or to kick the ball into the
net.[90]

Some working-class men also felt increasingly attracted to sport, which should be seen, among other things, as a reflection of the fact that physical and practical aspects dominate in sport and working-class culture alike. Working-class men were not much drawn to the time sports, favoring instead power sports such as weight-lifting, wrestling, and boxing, in which the ideal was the strong man, and where the experiences of sweat, close bodily contact, and direct physical struggle, man against man, were central. Football also played an important role at an early stage, because this sport incarnated a crucial feature of working-class culture, namely, teamwork and solidarity, which had become important elements in the workers' social and political struggle. At the same time football and boxing were dynamic speed sports, which also shows that working-class sportsmen took part in the creation of the new culture of sporting achievement and speed.

Concepts such as grace, style, and perfection of form, which had been central ideas in the nobleman's exercises, were banished from male sports but partly carried on in new forms as a specifically female culture. The sports literature left (sports)men little opportunity to perform gentle, soft, rounded, compliant movements. These limitations on the repertoire of male movements should be seen in connection with the male ideal of character in the sports literature, which had no room for softness, submissiveness, or sensitivity.[91]

The movement revolution was part of a greater figuration. Many sports implements were now shaped to suit the men's new social time. Sailing boats, bicycles, and even horses were now elongated and flattened to allow them to thrust forward with the least possible hydrodynamic and aerodynamic resistance, a tendency which had a great influence on everyday technology. Even human beings did not escape this streamlining process. With a slim body, taut muscles, and a bent back, the sportsman now began a fierce struggle against the clock, in a quest for ever new records. The dynamic, forward-pointing male back gradually became more important in the masculine ideal of movement depicted in the sports literature than the traditional straight but also slower stance. Self-control and strength of character were no longer perceived in the sports literature as being associated solely with an erect back, but now also radiated the dynamism of the efficient and energetic sportsman who struggled with a bent back and neck. The ideal of the sportsman's career-oriented, forward-looking character structure was thus legitimized in the sports literature.

My analysis of the sports literature may seem one-dimensional in its emphasis on the socialization of young men into dynamic and goal-directed individuals. If I had also considered the young men's own motives and experiences, the concept of sport would have taken on other nuances: in sport, bodily spontaneity and sensuality were blended with the demands of working life for performance and self-control. Precisely this alloy was necessary so that sport in the course of the twentieth century was able to celebrate triumphs as one of the great masculine rituals of all time. When the sports literature hailed drive, energy, and discipline, it was precisely because sporting activity contained the potential for the opposite: sweat, filth, savagery, softening, stillness, and sensual lust. This dialectic, in my opinion, constitutes the core of the fascination with sport. The masculinity that was established around the turn of the century contained an ambivalence – being both cultivated and devil-may-care. The civilized side of man was his official image, but underneath there lurked all the unseemly instincts and dreams. Sport became a place where the young man could learn the official masculine virtues in the official culture, while in the informal culture of the changing room and on the journeys to sports events, he could indulge in all the tabooed male fantasies.

Notes

1. V. Grønbeck, *Sprogets music* (Copenhagen, 1956), p. 62.
2. Cf. A. Løkke, "Foraeldrebilleder- Skitser til moderskabets og faderskabets historic," *Social Kritik*, 25-26 (1993), pp. 6-22.
3. On sport as deliberate character formation see H. Bonde, *Mandighed og short* (Odense, 1991), pp. 21-64.
4. W. Hovgaard, *Sport* (Copenhagen, 1888), p. 42.
5. R. Sabo and R. Runfola, *Jocks, Sports, and Male Identity* (Englewood Cliffs, New Jersey, 1980).
6. See for example the articles in *Arena Review's* theme issue on "Sport, Men and Masculinity" (Boston, 1985).
7. Edited by J. A. Mangan and I. Walvin (Manchester, 1987).
8. Cf. H. Meinander, *Towards a Bourgeois Manhood* (Helsinki, 1994).
9. J. Le Goff, "Mentaliteternas historia - en tvetydig historie," in the anthology *Att skriva historia* (Stockholm, 1980), pp. 247, 257.
10. Ever since *Idrætshistorisk Årbog* was started in 1985, however, it has printed some empirically oriented articles, often based on historical dissertations. Jim Toft has written one such thorough thesis on the early history of football until 1911, "Fodboldbanen kridtes op" (Copenhagen University, 1990, unpublished). The book *Den engelske sports gennembrud i Norden*, edited by E. Trangback (Copenhagen, 1990), presents a number of recent empirical studies, of which we may mention Laila Ottesen's article about women's football and Torn Hansen's about the history of horse racing. See also E.

Trangbaek (ed.), *Dansk Idrætsliv*, vol. I and II (Copenhagen, 1995) and P. Jorgensen, "Dansk Idrætsforbund Og Sportens gennembrud" (unpublished Ph.D. dissertation, Odense University, 1995).

11. This applies above all to *Illustreret Idrætsbog*, which appeared in Denmark in two volumes in 1890 and 1893, with a preface by the Swedish professor of physiology and social Darwinist, Frithiof Holmgren.

12. The figuration concept has been used by several scholars, including Norbert Elias, Michel Foucault, and in the context of sport theory, Henning Eichberg. My figuration concept integrates my own methodological observations with Eichberg's concept. My addition is intended to counter the tendency of the figuration concept to ignore the self-perception of the individual, which contains a danger of historical behaviorism.

13. In the following I shall not use the figuration schema slavishly, but regard it as an underlying inspiration.

14. O. Korsgaard, *Kampen am kroppen* (Copenhagen, 1982), p. 108.

15. Westergård, "Den antikke Olympiade," *Idrætshistorisk Årbog* (1988), pp. 5-14.

16. A. Guttmann, *From Ritual to Record* (New York, 1977), pp. 15ff.

17. E. T. Hall, *The Dance of Life* (New York, 1984), p. 15.

18. W. Hopf, *Sociale Zeit und Körperkultur* (Münster, 1981).

19. Ingemann-Petersen, *Cyclesport* (Copenhagen, 1891), p. 40.

20. Cf. *Dansk Sports-Tidende*, 1888, p. 85, and *Illustreret Idrætsbog*, 1890, "Cyclesport," p. 469. On the tactical element in athletic races, see *Dansk Idrætsblad* (Copenhagen, 1898-1908), p. 675.

21. *Idrætsbogen*, II, "Cykling," 1909, p. 7f on racing; R. Rasmussen, *Laerebog i fri Idraet* (Copenhagen, 1913), p. 370.

22. J. Hansen, "Sportens vej til Danmark – Hestevaeddeløb," in *Den engelske sports gennembrud i Norden*, pp. 163-73.

23. On "representative publicness," see J. Habermas, *The Structural Transformation of the Public Sphere: An Inquiry into a Category of Bourgeois Society* (London, 1989), pp. 5-13.

24. *Illustreret Idrætsbog*, II (1893), p. 730.

25. See under the Danish word *'karriere'* in the Dictionary *Ordbog over Det danske sprog"*, K, pp. 116f., and *Nudansk ordbog, I* (Copenhagen, 1980), p. 484.

26. H. Bonde, "Where Boys Become Men and Men Become Boys: Sport as Socialization to Masculinity," in *Fatherhood in Scandinavia*, edited by L. Jalmert and D. Sommer (Stockholm, forthcoming).

27. On the theory of modernity see A. Giddens, *Consequences of Modernity* (Cambridge, 1994); A. Touraine, *Critique of Modernity* (Cambridge, 1995); Fornaes and G. Bolin, *Youth Culture in Late Modernity* (London, 1995).

28. H. Bonde, "Den hurtige mand: Mandeidealer i den tidlige danske sportsbevaegelse," *Historisk Tidsskrift*, 88 (1) (Copenhagen, 1988), p. 33.

29. *Cycle-Tidende*, 1 (3), 1890. Part of the first verse is translated here.

30. *Aarbog for legems-idræt*, 1898, pp. 76ff, published by the Danish Sports

Association (Copenhagen, 1898-1905).

31. E. Staal, *Friluftssport* (Copenhagen, 1892), p. 17. Cf. also *Tidsskrift for Sport*, 1887, pp. 191-199, where rural Danes are criticized for their insufficent interest in horse racing; they have not developed enough sports sense to understand that horse sports make horses capable of "moving their bodies regularly, beautifully, and swiftly."

32. Staal, *Friluftssport*.

33. P. Riismøller, *Sultegraensen* (Copenhagen, 1977), pp. 8f.

34. Müller's book about home gymnastics, *Mit system (My System)*, was translated into 26 languages between 1904, when it was published, and 1930, and it sold one-and-a-half million copies. Cf. H. Bonde "I. P. Müller, Danish Apostle of Health," *The International Journal of the History of Sport*, 8 (3) (1991), pp. 347-69.

35. I. P. Müller, *Vink om Sundhedsrøgt og Idræt* (Copenhagen, 1907; a collection of previously published articles from the newspaper *København* and elsewhere), p. 203. On the fascination with speed see also *Illustreret Idrætsbog*, I (i) (1890), "Hurtigløb på Skøjter," p. 255.

36. Müller (1907), ibid.

37. *Ibid.*

38. *Gymnastisk Selskabs Aarsskrift* (Copenhagen, 1912), p. 152.

39. Cf. I. Sarup, *De danske i Stockholm* (Copenhagen, 1912).

40. The famous Danish author Henrik Pontopppidan (1857-1913), in his novels about Lykke-Per (Copenhagen, 1898-1904), has written the classic Danish work about the bridge-building engineer as the bearer of an optimistic vision of the future, as well as his resignation as a technical servant of industry.

41. *Illustreret Idrætsbog*, II (1893), p. 139.

42. *Ibid.*, p. 737.

43. E. H. Gombrich, *Kunstens historie* (Copenhagen, 1972), p. 10.

44. *Illustreret Idrætsbog*, I (1890), p. 19.

45. *Jubilaeumsskriftet Københavns Amatør-Sejlklub, 1891-1941* (Copenhagen, 1941), pp. 11ff.

46. Chr. Kroman, *Kapsejladsens Logik: Bidrag til løsning af Måleproblemet* (Copenhagen, 1893), p. 18. I have counted as many as 14 books dealing with the "measurement problem" between 1893 and 1907.

47. On the technological development of skating see *Idrætsbogen*, "Vintersport," 1909, pp. 39 and 41; and *Illustreret Idrætsbog*, 1890, p. 691. On the development of skiing, see *Idrætshogen*, ibid.

48. On cycling see *Idrætsbogen*, II (1909), pp. 1-28.

49. G. Vigarello, *Le Corps redressé* (Paris, 1978). It should be noted that the straightening of the crooked back was often intended as health education, and that the ideal of the straight back is found in many cultures.

50. *Ibid.*

51. Cf. H. Bonde, "Farmers' Gymnastics in Denmark in the Late Nineteenth and Early Twentieth Centuries: A Semiotic Analysis of Exercise in Moral Action," *The International Journal of the History of Sport*, 10 (2) (1993), pp. 193-215.

52. See for example B. Andersen, *Adelig opfostring: adelsbørns opdragelse i Danmark 1536-1660* (Copenhagen, 1971).
53. Cf. Korsgaard, *Kampen om kroppen*, p. 34.
54. *Ibid.*, pp. 37f.
55. *Ibid.*, p. 90.
56. Cf. *Haandbog i Roning*, published by Handels- og Kontoristforeningen (Copenhagen, 1868), pp. 19, 23, and 26, and *Illustreret Idrætsbog*, I (1890), pp. 140, 223.
57. For the Danish debate see *Tidsskrift for Sport*, 1884, pp. 145-54, 256-63, 415-17, 469-81, 534, 537. See also *Illustreret Idrætsbog*, I (1890), p. 257.
58. There has been little research into the bodily culture of feudalism, but see Troels Lund, *Dagligt liv i Norden, i det 16'ende århundrede* (Copenhagen, 1929-31, originally published 1879-1901) book 6, pp. 83-96 and 115-27, and book 7, pp. 72-91. See also Jørn Møller's four-volume work on ancient sports in Denmark, *Gamle idrætslege i Danmark* (Kastrup, 1990 and 1991).
59. Berthelsen, *A. W. Frispark* (Århus, 1983).
60. *Illustreret Idrætsbog*, I (1890), pp. 667-74.
61. *Ibid.*, pp. 667f.
62. *Ibid.*
63. *Ibid.*, p. 456.
64. *Ibid.*, p. 480.
65. A. C. Meyer, *En Agitators Erindringer* (Copenhagen, 1929), pp. 106ff.
66. I. Varnild, "Sport som folkelig forlystelse," in *For Sportens skyld* (Copenhagen, 1972), p. 91.
67. *Ibid.*
68. *Ibid.* and E. Hansen, "Arbejderidrætten i Danmark 1929-43," *Den Jyske Historiker*, 19/20 (1980), pp. 139-204.
69. *Ibid.*, note 9.
70. Cf. Müller, *Vink om Sundhedsrøgt og Idræt*, p. 263.
71. Meyer, *En Agitators Erindringer*.
72. Varnild, "Sport som folkelig forlystelse," pp. 97f.
73. *Idrætsbogen*, I, "Boksning," p. 42.
74. Hovgaard, *Sport*, p. 54. Cf. also Orlow-Andersen, *Hvad enhver Rytterske bør vide* (Copenhagen, 1908), p. 53. Other women, of course, could not afford to ride.
75. Hovgaard, *Sport*.
76. Cf. *Illustreret Idraeetshog*, I (1890), pp. 268ff. Rowing clubs could have female sections, however.
77. *Ibid.*, p. 268.
78. *Idrætsbogen*, II, "Roping," 1909, p. 9.
79. *Politiken*, 25 September 1905.
80. Korsgaard, *Kampen om kroppen*, p. 289.
81. *Tidsskriftet Idrætten*, 19 August 1918.
82. *Hanna Adler og hendes skole* (Copenhagen, 1959), p. 107; the teacher was the famous sportsman and historian of ball games, Frederik Knudsen.

114 *Among Men*

83. *Bold-Bladet,* 1:6 (1902); cf. Ottesen in *Den engelske sports gennembrud i Norden,* p. 206.
84. Hovgaard, *Sport,* p. 144.
85. *Kjøbenhavns Boldklub i 25 Aar, 1876-1901* (Copenhagen, 1901), p. 120.
86. *Idrætsbogen,* "Boldspil," H (1909), pp. 80ff., 107~.
87. *Ibid.,* p. 146.
88. A. Clod-Hansen, *Mand og Kvinde* (Copenhagen, 1895).
89. S. Kierkegaard, *Enten-Eller,* vol. 1 (Copenhagen, 1843; reprinted Odense, 1976), p. 28.
90. For a more profound look at this "functionalist" perception of sport, see S. E. Rasmussen, "Omkring sportens Aestetik," *Tidsskrift for Legemsøvelser,* 1941, pp. 4-53.
91. Any movement which could symbolize femininity or homosexuality was taboo in the male forms of movement. The clear boundaries for what a man could permit himself to do with his body were shown by the internationally known Danish sports physiologist Johannes Lindhard in his major work, *Gymnastikteori i omrids* (1914), p. 56: "It therefore appears unattractive and disorienting to the observer when men are allowed to hold hands during walking exercises. If one wants to make a man look slightly ridiculous on stage, this can be achieved by making him move in dancing steps."

Chapter 7

Masculinity and the North[1]

Lena Eskilsson

In a magnificent portrait of Adolf Erik Nordenskiöld, the famous Swedish explorer gazes out over the ice floes, with his ship *The Vega* looming in the background. He is dressed warmly against the cold. In one hand he holds an ice-pick, in the other a pair of binoculars.[2] In this setting signifying "the North," the heroic scientist appears. Nearly as heroic is the studio portrait of Axel Hamberg outfitted in full mountain-climbing gear (he too is clutching an ice-pick), to be found in his well known guide to trekking in the Sarek mountain range.[3] These images of science and the north are also images of masculinity; or rather, of one of the masculine ideals that emerged in the decades around the turn of the last century. Other "masculinities" might include the "conscientious worker," striving for modernity and the future, or the hardy, diligent peasant who venerated both God and Country.[4] However, my interest concerns another, middle-class masculinity in which I believe there exists a connection between masculinity and the north, and where the status and conditions for mountain and arctic exploration comprise the connecting link.

The connection I make between masculinity and the north comprises several aspects, including science, tourism, alpinism and a society in the throes of change – industrial revolution, urbanization, democratization and femininization (in the sense that women slowly but surely won formal and actual access to the public sector).

Masculinity

My premise is that "masculinity," like "femininity," is shaped by social and cultural processes. At the same time, that which is considered masculine and feminine is historically variable. Furthermore, it is relational, in that gender or social sex is created by the interaction between women and men, both individually and structurally. Masculinity is defined in relation to femininity, and vice versa. This process has interested researchers in women's studies, who have shown that the relationship between men and women (or masculinity and femininity) is often characterized by differentiation and hierarchization. Men are what women arent. Masculinity has a higher status than femininity.[5]

However, masculinity is also constructed in relation to other men. These gender relationships imply a struggle for a hegemonic or dominant masculinity.[6] Not only masculinity and femininity are ordered hierarchically, but also various masculine types. Thus those men who best fulfill expectations as to how a "real man" should be in a certain context have qualities which belong to the hegemonic masculinity.

My hypothesis is that the decades around the turn of the century witnessed the development of a successful masculine type featuring a connection between masculinity and the north, literally and symbolically. This is primarily a middle-class phenomenon. The background is that the modern subject, shaped by an historic process from the Enlightenment onwards, was not only a man but also a representative of the bourgeoisie. Physical prowess and energy, which in one form or another have always been attributes of the masculine subject, were not to be exaggerated if one was to maintain ones middle-class affiliation![7] Sheer physical strength in itself – the hallmark of farmers and the working class – was not a given element in middle-class masculinity; instead, the ideal was a combination of physical strength, rationality, single-mindedness, stamina and discipline. The masculine ideal held by leading groups in society underwent a number of changes during the Victorian era. The emphasis on male austerity and earnestness was complemented by respect for "muscles," in both the physical and the mental sense.[8]

This transformation is also reflected in ideas about the sound body at the turn of the century. A sizable and popular genre of health and exercise theories underlined the importance of physical exercise for the public good, both physical and mental. The idea of a sound mind in a sound body was ancient, but was intensified by middle-class, puritan ethics of asceticism and achievement. These Victorian ideals of ascetic and athletic exercises complied well with the demands that alpinism and mountain sports made on their practitioners.[9]

The decades around the turn of the century were also a period of growth within the natural sciences and their application to industry during the industrial breakthrough in Sweden. The natural sciences became significant factors in social evolution, and stood for progress and growth. This is also the background to the image of the scientist as hero. The role of science has changed over the years and with it, the image of its practitioners. The scientist has been a philosopher, theologian, servant of princes, revolutionary, man of letters and specialist. During the nineteenth century the scientist was transformed into hero – or madman.[10] I am interested in the image of the scientist as hero, even if a hint of madness may indeed be discernable – in the sense that a number of scientific heroes were prepared to sacrifice their lives for the sake of science and glory through daring, even foolhardy, expeditions and ascents.

Mankinds relationship to nature was an important theme at that time, both intellectually and practically. The scientist personified mankind's struggle to chart and subjugate nature. This struggle was particularly evident in two regions – voyages of exploration in Africa and expeditions into the northern arctic.[11] Arctic research was conducted in the north, which was also true for a great deal of other research conducted at the time dealing with charting and investigating unknown territories in Sweden. Many of the white spots on the map were to be found in inhospitable, mountainous regions. How high were the mountain tops? What sort of climate prevailed there? How big were the glaciers, and was their size on the increase or decrease? What was the vegetation like there? How was the bedrock constituted?

The ability to find the answers to these questions demanded not only theoretical knowledge but also the ability to plan and realize comprehensive expeditions. This meant that academic scientific ability had to be combined with certain, more practical skills. The ideal scientist thus became a sort of entepreneur. He had to be able to negotiate with Laplanders and homesteaders for help with transportation and guiding, buy or construct the instruments and equipment required in uncertain climates, calculate his own and his assistants' consumption of food (and tobacco), foresee possible injuries and load up on everything from medicine to material for mending shoes and patching trousers. Furthermore, physical strength and stamina were required. In other words, here were demanded all the characteristics deemed suitable to the modern, middle-class (male) subject – a combination of rationality, enterprise, physical strength and spirit.

The Swedish Tourist Association

To a large degree, this combination of qualities seems also to have been the ideal of the members of the Swedish Tourist Association (Svenska turistföreningen, STF) founded in 1885 on the Norwegian model.[12] The tourist association came into being at the same time as Scandinavian arctic research and the job of charting the whole of Sweden were getting underway.[13] Several geologists and glacial and arctic researchers (among them Nordenskiöld himself) sat on its first board. Thus there existed a clear link between early tourism and scientists with the north as their "beat." In fact, the dividing line between science and early alpine tourism was rather vague. In the STF's yearbooks and handbooks, scientific discoveries alternated with travel tips dealing with equipment and routes. This combination of science and tourism was also hinted at in the club's first charter. Alongside "developing and facilitating tourism in Sweden" was an ambition to "make an increasing amount of the regions of our country accessible to tourists, through systematically organized studies and works, whose results will be disseminated in the annual publications of the association."[14]

The man who perhaps most clearly personified this dual ambition was Axel Hamberg, who had participated in numerous scientific expeditions before he began conducting his own explorations of the Swedish mountain landscape. His name was well known to anyone with any interest in mountains, whether scientist, tourist or mountaineer. Captain H. N. Pallin, a dedicated alpinist and member of the Laplander Mountainmen's Club, wrote appreciatively of Hamberg:

> The Sarek mountain range was subjected to scientific exploration over the course of many years by one of the most exceptional of the Swedish alpinists, Professor Emeritus Axel Hamberg, who published an excellent alpine guide on the region. In said book it is stated that Hamberg himself was the first man to reach the peaks of no less than 46 of the mountains mentioned therein, eight of which are located at a height of over 1,900 metres. This feat of mountaineering is so extraordinary for Swedish circumstances, that the mountain range where this was achieved casts a giant shadow over all others in that respect.[15]

The guidebook mentioned by Pallin was published by the tourist association, to whose publications Hamberg often contributed.

The tourist association founded in Uppsala did not appeal exclusively to men with some form of scientific and/or alpine interest in the mountains and the north, even if these men did indeed comprise the majority of the club's membership during the first years of its existence. For a long time the tourist association was a men's club which seemed to appeal to "ordinary" middle- and upper-class men: officers, wholesalers and lawyers. Interest was primarily focused on the mountains, which is revealed in both the club's rhetoric and in its statistics. Between 1886 and 1915, the yearbook (with a total distribution of nearly one million) contained roughly one thousand essays. If one categorizes these essays by province, then Lapland was in first place, closely followed by Jämtland. Most of the capital invested by the association went to the mountain landscapes of Lapland and Jämtland.[16] The association's concentration on the mountains must be seen against the backdrop of the era's positively charged images of the north. Norrland was the land of the future.[17] Here were to be found enormous natural resources of both an emotional and a material nature. In other words, there was much for an enterprising man to experience, exploit, chart and conquer in that land of the future.

Love of mountain landscapes has been a significant component of the self-image or world view of most of the ideologues of STF. This emotion was also shared by its membership for quite a long time. In many ways, love of the mountains and the wilderness suited the ethics and world view of middle-class culture. The ethical aspect of hiking in the mountains and other hardships runs like a scarlet thread through many of the travelogues and words of advice appearing in the yearbooks. In an essay on mountaineering in the yearbook for 1889, Louis Améen, member and later chairman of the board of STF, expresses this in a number of ways:

> However, the possibilities that the passion of mountain-climbing offer can only be fully appreciated by he who understands that it is the gradual striving toward a goal, ultimately crowned with success, that is the real joy in this world; that the realization of an intention can give a person infinitely more pleasure than merely taking in beautiful natural scenery or any other of the passive occupations one usually calls "pleasure."[18]

One might replace "mountain-climbing" with numerous other, grandiose hardships. The main thing is to defeat difficulties with the right combination of reason, strength and single-mindedness. On this stage, where activity is superior to passive pleasure, the actors are almost exclusively men. Mountain-climbing and sojourns in the highlands were symbolic activities in man's struggle against nature. This struggle was sometimes described in clearly sexual terms.

Wilderness and mountain peaks were "virginal" – especially if they had never previously been conquered or mounted. Nature was a "she" to be studied and overcome. In the aforementioned essay on mountaineering, Louis Améer expresses the significance of mountains as opponents to be vanquished. However, he emphasizes the ethical aspect of the struggle:

> Galdhöppigen, the highest mountain in Norway and northern Europe, was
> hardly known to mankind in the 1850s. ... Today, however, hardly a bright
> summer day passes without this mountain being ascended by large groups of
> tourists, among them quite a number of ladies. Galdhöpiggen is nowadays
> viewed with something akin to contempt by every mountain-climber of the
> first water. It fails to offer sufficient hardships to be overcome. It is too
> accommodating. Fighting such an opponent is simply demoralizing.[19]

In this world, women were the exception to the rule, which is emphasized
by Améer. Mountain peaks were opponents which were to be subdued by
men. Hardship and mountain-climbing expeditions were not judged
suitable for women of the middle-class at the turn of the century. In 1889,
the tourist association's yearbook contained an article with special tips for
female tourists, wherein it was underlined that the route chosen by a
woman should be chosen so as to not entail any unnecessary hardships:
"Let the men celebrate the triumphs of the mountain-climber – and bear
them no grudge."[20]

Inferior men

The north was no place for the fragile women of the middle class. Instead
they might wander along low-lying, easily negotiated paths in the foothills,
preferably in male company. Women were not considered to possess the
physical and mental strength required for expedition-like journeys. Nor did
all men have the capacity for conquering the mountaintops and wilderness
properly. Even homesteaders, Laplanders and others engaged as guides and
porters lacked some of the (masculine) qualities required. This was due to
the hierarchies that existed between different "masculinities." One can say
that Laplanders and homesteaders, ethnically and socially subordinate men,
were considered inferior because they lacked a number of the qualities that
were part of this single-minded, middle-class masculinity. They might
possess the physical strength and stamina, but they lacked rationalism,
knowledge and, at times, courage and morals. In a number of the
travelogues I have perused, Laplanders, homesteaders and porters are not
infrequently described as cowardly, temperamental, manipulative and
generally not very bright.[21]

In his relationships with guides and porters, one can see how even a veteran like Axel Hamberg betrays a certain attitude of superiority, at times irritation at how protesting Laplanders and unreliable homesteaders spoiled the best-laid plans and delayed the carrying out of an expedition. These helpers were an absolute necessity for lengthy mountain sojourns, and he treated them neither rudely nor aggressively. Instead, he treated them like natural phenomena. Stubborn Laplanders were dealt with in the same way as foul weather – one set up camp, started a fire, brewed some coffee, smoked and waited for the storm to pass!

Any of the helpers' achievements (reaching the top of a mountain, for example), seem not to have counted as being equal to those accomplished by the leader or leaders of the expedition. Future geologist and arctic researcher Johan Alfred Björling ascended Kebnekaise in the year 1889. He is generally credited with being the first Swede to have accomplished this feat, despite the fact that Rabot, whose ascent was the first to be documented, had employed a Swede living in Norway as his porter and guide. A year after his triumph, Björling described it in the STF yearbook. He had had a Finn named Hartvig Johansson Fjellborg in his service. Judging by the description therein, the latter was a rather incompetent guide, unable to locate fjords and indecisive as to the choice of routes. Futhermore, his suggestion concerning the place from which the peak should be ascended proved to be impracticable. Later, when the company approached the top, after much toil and hardship, the Finn refused to budge. He was afraid of falling to a snowy grave. Hartvig Johansson judged nature to be too much for him, and saw no reason to risk life and limb merely in order to reach the top of a mountain. Such was not the attitude of Björling and his crew, who bravely struggled onwards and crept their way a further hundred-odd metres upward toward their highly coveted goal. By that time they had climbed for almost 13 taxing hours without a break.[22]

However, rational and ethical qualities and the readiness to confront danger were not the only aspects of manliness in the north. Emotional needs could be fulfilled, too. The majority of the early mountain travelogues appearing in the yearbook of the tourist association (even the most scholarly), included more or less respectful, well-formulated reflections on the grandness of nature's beauty and the majesty of its high mountain peaks. One recurring theme is the need to recapture a feeling of wholeness and being at one with nature. "Fly like the eagle to the mountains: here find isolated, silent places where you may confront yourself in peace," wrote Frithiof Holmgren, the first chairman of the tourist association, in his poem "Åreskutan," in which he captured the age's male longing for the healing properties of the mountain landscape.[23] A yearning for repose in an age of nervousness, constant labor and urban cacaphony is also expressed by Améen: The mountains are good "repair clinics for the worn out mechanisms of mankind."[24]

The crisis of middle-class masculinity

All of these explorers, alpine tourists and mountaineers (of whom Nordenskiöld, Hamberg, Björling and Améen are ideal types) acted successfully in the north in the decades around the turn of the last century. This fin-de-siècle was also a time when increasing numbers of people were made uneasy by the large-scale transformation of society that was taking place and the ideological reinterpretation that these changes brought with them. This social anguish was channeled into an identity crisis, which has also been characterized as a crisis of masculinity. The manliness/virility that was associated with creativity, strength, progress and logic was being threatened by a femininity that was seen as passive, self-effacing, weak and irrational.[25] When middle-class women – together with organized labor – begin to show signs of life and demand more room, middle-class masculinity was also challenged. Traditional, patriarchal masculinity with its structural base in the church, the factory and the farmstead needed to be shored up with new qualities in order to confront the threats and demands of the new age. For the men of the middle-class, the scientific heroes – armed with ice-pick, binoculars and knowledge – could function as objects of identification. These specimens, trained in the north, exhibited a physical prowess and single-mindedness which would prevail – not only over the emasculating sexuality of femininity but also over weaker, more timorous men. Or stronger men with their minds set on the class struggle.

Of course, not everyone could become an arctic explorer. But almost anyone could at least become a tourist and thereby exhibit masculine virtues by hiking, climbing mountains and writing reports for the yearbook of the Swedish Tourist Association. At the very least, one could read about, and perhaps be inspired by, the feats of others. The tourist association expanded rapidly and its yearbook soon became the most widely disseminated book in Sweden after the Bible and the Farmer's Almanac. The association began with 74 members in 1885, all of whom belonged to the upper classes. By 1915 the membership had surpassed 60,000, the majority of whom still belonged to the upper or middle classes. All members automatically received a subscription to the yearbook. In this manner, membership in the tourist association could contribute to the construction and maintenance of middle-class masculinity, for both young and old. The successful man was also a tourist; whether he was one in the real world or in the world of fantasy perhaps did not really matter.

From mountain top to *Heimat*

Once the democratization of society had begun early in the twentieth century, the activities and goals of the tourist association also underwent change. One's own native district *(hembygd)* began to replace the mountain ranges of Sweden as the foremost tourist attraction. In 1915, the yearbook of the STF dealt mainly with the province of Uppland, commencing the first in a series of provincial travelogues to be published in the long history of the yearbook. Therewith, the tourist association descended from the rugged mountain tops and began wandering through the more accessible summer pastures back home. At the same time that the provincial series made its debut, the STF began broadening its activities in an attempt to reach increasing numbers of Swedes. Even women and the working class were now apprehended as potential tourists and members, and the association no longer bore the character of an exclusive men's club. Middle-class, masculine attributes such as courage, strength and rationality were not as necessary in one's home province as they were up in the mountains. Housewives on bicycles and youthful hiking groups eventually replaced the scientific explorer as the ideal tourist type.[26] This process can also be seen against the backdrop of a change in mankind's relationship to nature. The old, productive landscape of peasant society was superseded by the consumer landscape of industrialism and the middle class.[27]

It was at this point that the Laplander Mountainmen's Club was formed, the purpose of which was "to bring together men wishing to uphold an interest in skiing in the mountain ranges of Lapland, and other related activities which the club may find worthy of pursuing." The charter dictated full alpine and skiing competence for those who wished to seek membership in the club. Membership was furthermore restricted to 20 persons, above which limit a maximum of three honorary members could gain admittance. The club's president was Axel Hamberg.[28] Among the recommendations to the first charter was the demand that the prospective member provide evidence of having been on mountain expeditions where he had been exposed to mortal danger, "unavoidable injury due to hardships, being the first to have ascended a peak exceeding 1,200 metres, a journey above the tree line of at least 80 kilometers in length or three days in duration, or some other comparable achievement."[29] This proposal, however, was struck off. On the other hand, in the undertaking of their excursions the members were expected to combine careful and meticulous preparation with stamina and enthusiastic execution. One was also expected to be courteous and to lend support to one's fellows up in the mountains. The club member was supposed to do his utmost to promote the scientific exploration of Sweden's mountain landscapes and to avoid card-playing and strong drink while sojourning there.

One can see the organization of these, the last genuine men of their sort, as a sign that something was in the process of change. The connection between middle-class, male virtue and northernness was weakening. There was an apparent need to emphasize the relationship between masculinity, mountains, snow and hardship in an age when democratization and feminization was on the increase in what was to become the modern Swedish welfare state. But the scientific heroes of this new society were no longer arctic explorers, but rather physicians, teachers, technicians and sociological experts of various stripes – and sexes. For this, other qualities than those possessed by the mountainmen and explorers with their ice-picks in hand were necessary.

Translated by Stephen Fruitman

Notes

1. The present article is based on a lecture delivered at the network conference "The Northern Space: Images, Knowledge, Aesthetics," held in Hundested, Denmark, 6-8 October 1995.
2. The portrait, which hangs in the National Gallery in Stockholm, was painted by Georg von Rosen.
3. Axel Hamberg, *Sarekfjällen. Vägledning för färder i högfjällen mellan Lule Älvs källarmar* (Stockholm: Rediva, 1982).
4. For these versions of "masculinity," see Ronny Ambjörnsson, *Den skötsamme arbetaren* (Stockholm: Carlssons, 1988), and Bo Larsson (ed.), *Bonden i dikt och verklighet* (Stockholm: Nordiska museet, 1993), respectively.
5. Yvonne Hirdman, "Genussystemet – reflexioner kring kvinnors sociala underordning," *Kvinnovetenskaplig tidskrift*, 3 (1988).
6. Robert Connell, *Gender and Power* (London: Polity Press, 1987).

7. Ida Blom, "Fra det moderne till det postmoderne subject," *Nytt Norsk Tidskrift*, 2 (1995).
8. Michael Roper and John Tosh, "Historians and the Politics of Masculinity," *Manful Assertions*, ed. Roper and Tosh (London and New York: Routledge, 1991), pp. 2ff. See also Norman Vance, The Sinews of Spirit: The Ideal of Christian Manliness in Victorian Literature and Religious Thought (Cambridge: Cambridge University Press, 1985).
9. Karin Johannisson, "Det sköna i det vilda," in Tore Frängsmyr (ed.), Paradiset och vildmarken (Stockholm: Liber, 1984), p. 71.
10. Tore Frängsmyr, Vetenskapsmannen som hjälte (Stockholm: Norstedts, 1984), p. 7.
11. Ibid., pp. 162f.
12. In her Kraftanstrengelse og ensomhet (Hovedoppgave i etnologi 1994, Institutt for kunsthistorie og kulturvitenskap), Heidi Richardson analyzes the cultural constructions of Norwegian outdoor life, wherein several parallels with the development in Sweden can be observed.
13. Gunnar Eriksson, Kartläggarna (Umeå, 1978).
14. Charter, Svenska turistföreningens årsstrift (STF:s årsskrift), 1 (1886), p. 4.
15. H. N. Pallin, "Ur en fjälltopps histona," Ultima Thule. Årsskrift för de lappländska fjällkarlarnas klubb, 20 (Stockholm, 1929).
16. Svenska turistföreningen. Några siffror och bilder från dess verksamhet 1885-1915, STF:s broschyr No. 55.
17. Sverker Sörlin, Framtidslandet. Debatten om Norrland och naturresurserna under industriella genombrottet (Stockholm: Carlssons, 1988).
18. Louis Améen, "Om bergsklättring," STF:s årsskrift, 1889, p. 54.
19. Ibid.
20. "Några ord till våra qvinliga turister," STF:s årsskrift, 1889, p. 92.
21. See for example Knut Winge, "Sommarlif i högfjällen," STF:s årsskrift, 1898, pp. 187ff. and Axel Hamberg, "Resor i Kvikkjokks högfjäll sommaren 1896," STF:s årsskrift, 1897.
22. Johan Alfred Björling, "En bestigning af Kebnekaisse," STF:s årsskrift, 1890, pp. 77f.
23. Cited in Carl-Julius Anrick, STF 1885-1935 (Stockholm, 1935), p. 13.
24. Louis Améen, "Om bergsklättring," STF:s årsskrift, 1889, p. 52.
25. Ulla Wikander, "Sekelskiftet 1900. Konstruktionen av en nygammal kvinnlighet," Det evigt kvinnliga. En historia om förändring (Stockholm: Tidens förlag, 1994), pp. 12ff.
26. Lena Eskilsson, "Svenska turistföreningen från fjäll till friluftsliv: Från den vetenskaplige vildmarksmannen till den cyklande husmodern," Historisk tidskrift, 1996, p. 2.
27. Jonas Frykman and Orvar Löfgren, Den kultiverade människan (Lund: Liber Läromedel, 1979), pp. 45-73.
28. "De lappländska fjällkarlarnas klubb," Ultima Thule, 1929, p. 29. The club was founded at a meeting at Hasselbacken in Stockholm, August 1920. See

also Halvar Sehlin, "De lappländska fjällkarlarnas klubb," Till Fjälls, 1990-91.

29. "Förslag till stadgar för De lappländska fjällmännens klubb." A copy of the original manuscript is in the possession of the present author.

Chapter 8

Modernized Masculinities?
Continuities, Challenges and Changes in
Men's Lives[1]

MICHAEL MEUSER

Introduction

In an article dealing with male dominance, Pierre Bourdieu describes the principle and how this dominance functions as follows: "Male dominance is sufficiently secured that it needs no justification" (Bourdieu, 1990, p. 5). There are practices and discourses that make dominance a taken-for-granted fact and by this reproduce it. Just as in every system of power and subordination, of domination and inferiority, the gender order works (or worked) "smoothly" so long as the status of the ruling class is taken for granted: a matter of course not only for men, but also for women, and strongly founded on cultural interpretive patterns and inscribed into the routines of everyday life.

Today, however, (most) women no longer agree with the social rule of men. The activities of the women's movement concentrate not least on making visible the "symbolic violence" (Bourdieu) that hides behind the self-evident functioning of the traditional gender order. Does male dominance still need no justification, however, at the end of the twentieth century, when all Western (post-)industrial societies are confronted with what is called the "feminist challenge"? Do the practices and discourses still work in a way that they can maintain male dominance? Is male supremacy still unchallenged and can it therefore be hidden behind an objectivation of being a male as being human, just as Simmel (1985) had analyzed it as an expression of dominance at the beginning of the twentieth century?

All this is hard to imagine in a society in which the employment rate of women has been continuously increasing during recent decades, in which there are women's departments, programmes of affirmative action and other plans for women's support, discussions about job quotas, and many other visible signs indicating that gender relations are in a process of change. The question, however, is how fundamental the changes are. Estimations vary. Even Bourdieu (1997, p. 226) finds "that male dominance can no longer be sustained as a self-evident fact." He nevertheless warns us not to overlook the continuities that hide behind the visible changes. According to theorists of reflexive modernization, we live in a "multi-optional society" (Gross, 1994) in which the individual becomes a "homo optionis" and will be able (or coerced) to decide for (almost) everything, even "life, death, sex ..." (Beck and Beck-Gernsheim, 1994b, p. 16). Reflexive modernization is described as an extensive de-traditionalization and de-routinization as well as individualization. The taken-for-grantedness of routines and habitualizations are at risk in virtually all realms of everyday life (Beck, 1992, 1996; Beck, Giddens and Lash, 1995; Giddens, 1991).

It is clear that an increasing number of women no longer submit to the traditional gender order. But there is little empirical evidence to show how men experience this change in gender relations. Only one thing is certain: the change that has been initiated by the women's movement forces men to react because, in any relation between two parties, changes on one side always have consequences for the other side. It will have to be examined, what kind of reactions these are. The thesis that men lose all their securities which have been guaranteed by tradition and that there is a far-reaching crisis of masculinity is very popular and often talked about in the media, but it is overgeneralized as the only current situation of men. It is obvious that this thesis wears the index of the social milieu from which it arises. A reflexive calling into question of one's own gender status can only be found – if it is found at all – in the intellectual-academic milieu, where social status is defined by possessing cultural capital rather than economic capital. If Anthony Giddens (1992, p. 59) is correct that men now find themselves for the first time "to *be* men," because they posses a "problematic 'masculinity'," it seems to me that the attachement to the reflexive culture of one's own milieu restricts the view beyond its limits.[2] Even if men increasingly have to justify their dominant position, their gender status does not necessarily appear to them as a problem, at least so long as their justifications are successful.

This essay examines how men experience the change in gender relations, how they react to demands and expectations of women and what orientations they develop. The main focus is on a generation of men who grew up with the second women's movement, men between 20 and 30 years of age. They had experienced their primary and secondary socialization at a time when this movement formed and established itself. At least for these men, one should think, male dominance is no longer assumed by the mode of evider ce. Whether they therefore simply give up the demand for a hegen mic position and – if this is the case – whether their masculinity becom s a problem for them shall be examined, among other things, in the following.

Even if gender relations have begun to move and the young men live in a gender order that is different from the one 20 or 30 years ago, the conclusion is not inevitable that traditional patterns of masculinity have become obsolete. Cultural interpretive patterns are marked by considerable longevity. They are still efficient, even when the social conditions that established them have changed. They constitute a dimension of social reality of their own (Meuser and Sackmann, 1992). Even under the conditions of de-traditionalized gender relations, men are dependent on the culturally available symbolic inventory of masculine identitiy formation. As fundamental identities are tied to gender, a radical break with the cultural defining practices and discourses of one's own gender must be paid for by a deep habitual insecurity.[3] Therefore any reconstruction of men's orientation has to pay attention to continuities as well as changes.

To begin with, I will outline how a traditional male existence is typically characterized and how the evidence Bourdieu describes manifests itself in everyday life. Among men who grew up before the second women's movement developed, the unquestioned taken-for-grantedness of male existence is still a widespread experience. The reconstruction of the orientations of these older men serves as a contrast to highlight how the younger men differ from traditional patterns of masculinity, and also how they contribute to reproduce these patterns. As far as the young men are concerned, I will distinguish between two patterns of orientation: a threatened self-confidence caused by the critique of feminism on the one hand, and an egalitarian attitude based on pragmatic arrangements on the other hand. Finally I will discuss how and under what conditions masculinity can be "modernized" in the direction of egalitarian practice and what role men's consciousness-raising groups play in this process.

The following remarks are based on an empirical study about collective orientations of men. Group discussions were conducted with numerous and varying groups of men: from the bourgeois gentlemen's club and the workers' drinking round to the "new" men. The age of the men ranges between 20 and 60. The groups are so-called natural groups, that is groups that have existed before and independently of our scientific interest.[4]

The power of tradition: unquestioned evidence, male hegemony and habitual security

According to Simmel (1985, p. 201) it is one of the master's privileges that he does not always have to think about himself being the master. Within an unchallenged system of domination, only the inferior side is permanently reminded of its position. As Simmel says, it is much more extraordinary for a woman to forget that she is specifically a woman, than for a man to forget that he is specifically a man. The result of hypostatizing being a man into being a human is that the woman is noticed as a gendered being, while the man is regarded as an individual who is relieved of the gender antagonism, as the administrator of an objective reality.

This is, in brief, the cultural interpretive pattern that determined the gender discourse of bourgeois society and has been the symbolic foundation for men's claim to dominance. Doubtlessly it is a relict of the nineteenth century, but its shadow extends to the end of the twentieth century. At least among men of certain social milieus and generations, the equation of being a man with being human still secures male hegemony. During the group discussions we asked the men, what it means for them to be a man. Older men from the bourgeois milieu[5] often reacted with a lack of comprehension or even with anger. They told us that this was a "stupid question" and in some way they were right. Those who experience their way of acting as not being influenced by their gender must indeed think of this question as being foolish.

Whereas these men describe and experience their own way of acting as being non-gendered, they see women's way of acting as being determined by gender. They consider themselves to be male individuals who are so different from each other that they cannot be put together in a gender category. This is shown in statements such as "Well, basically I wouldn't say that I am proud of being a man. I am only proud and happy to be the one I am." The value of a man is a result of his work as a non-gendered human being. About the value of a woman it is said: "The value of women is very considerable, ... for the preservation of mankind they are much more important than the men." No matter what a woman does, her value is defined in terms of her ability of reproduction. Women are experienced as gendered beings and the men can talk about them in a generalized way, whereas generalized statements about males seem to be impossible because of the individualized status of men.

According to this perspective a generalized way of talking about men would only be possible if they are not looked at as men, but as human beings. Only in this higher sense is man a generic being. This is shown in the following dialogue:

> The question is basically identical, one can say, how do you feel as a man or how do you feel as a human being. The result is the same. I *can* only feel like a man, because I *am* a man.

> Right. You cannot feel like a woman.

> Yes, so the question could also be, how do you feel as a human being, basically.

Simmel might have had in mind a dialogue like this one, when he wrote about the equation of man and human: "The common way of being a human, of which the sexual speciality shall be an exeptional case, is so identical with the way of being a man, that no specific difference can be found: the general *per se* cannot be defined" (Simmel, 1985, p. 214). The men were not able to answer the question about the meaning of being a man, because there had no experience of difference that would enable them to observe themselves as gendered beings. There had no other perspective than the one of being a human. A question which asks about the feeling of being a human, is stupid – there is no alternative to being a human. In the same way, these men regard their own gender status as being unquestionable ("I *can* only feel like a man, because I *am* a man"). Therefore being a man cannot be discussed, not even in an abstract way. Their own gender is taken for granted in a fundamental sense; it is basically beyond questioning within the horizon of the lifeworld of these men. The question about the feeling of being a man is as useless as the one about the feeling of being human.

   Being a man is given within the mode of evidence. The question about its meaning can only be answered – if it is answered at all – in an iterative-circular way: "Well, yes, how shall I put it, a man is simply a man." There is nothing else to say about the *definition* of man. And if there where not those sociologists who ask such strange questions, one would not have to think about this any longer.[6] "We have been involved in this discussion, with its depth, something we don't do normally," explains one man regarding the difference between the ordinary meetings and the group discussion. If it is true that modern identities are characterized by a high degree of reflexivity (Berger, Berger and Kellner, 1973), then the *gender* identity of these men shows a rather premodern organization. These men are strongly tied to undoubted traditions that are circularly explained by a reference to tradition ("because it has always been that way"), and they experience their gender status as unquestionably given. They live, as far as this aspect of their life is concerned, in a "condition of unreflected 'being at home' in the social world" (*ibid.*).[7] The gender behavior of these men is marked by *habitual security*. One knows without thinking how to behave as a man in the familiy or in public, toward women or men. The traditional inventory of the male presentation of self is at their disposal without any ruptures caused by reflection. The position of the head of the family is not only claimed but also filled. Rituals of obligation and courtesy which are "imposed" on the male gender as well as "belonging" to it are practiced in a self-evident way. The habitual fate, which has in store not only privileges but also responsibilities, is accepted with self-confidence.

The continuity of the traditional gender order remains largely unbroken. The hegemonic position of the man is undoubtedly the foundation for how how the relative positions of man and woman in general and the family constellation in particular are experienced. Nevertheless male hegemony cannot be choosed freely. The man is "inflicted" by taking the responsibility for his family on his shoulders. This responsibility demands a rationally oriented way of acting that women are not only less obliged to take but also less talented for. And the man must take this responsibility "from the beginning," he is the one who "is responsible for it from the day he was born." To these men gender is a biologically determined fate and the gender difference is believed to be physiologically established.

This unbroken continuity of male hegemony could not last if the wives of these men did not contribute to it. Bourdieu (1990, p. 26) consideres "female subjection" to be "an irreplaceable kind of appreciation." The habitual security of the man, who is tightly linked to tradition, depends on the fact that his wife appreciates the position he claims within the conjugal relation. The men are not aware of this "dependence," but it reveals itself in numerous statements, for example that they don't have to argue with their wives about their respective roles at home. These men believe that their wives fulfill the duties that have been given to them within the conjugal division of labor with pleasure. They state, for example: "My wife likes her duties very much," it is not the case "that she would rather do something else, she gladly accepts these duties." Another adds: "She is happy, she is happy." According to these men the women support the traditional male position of their own free will.[8] Only on this condition can the men can experience their marriage as a "constant factor," in which the own position is safe. In this way they feel accepted and respected as the head of the family.

De-traditionalized gender relations

Young men between 20 and 30 years of age can no longer expect that the women of their generation acknowledge the male claims of hegemony, and they do not expect it either. They experience the relation between man and woman in a different way from their fathers, because they grew up at a time when the gender order was being transformed. Working mothers are rather normal, and women of their age achieve the same educational levels as themselves. Even if not all young women give absolute priority to employment (Geissler and Oechsle, 1994), as the men still do, the young men have to deal with women who have turned away from "being there for others" and who claim – at the very least – "a share of a "life of their own'." The "processes of individualization in the lives of women" (Beck-Gernsheim, 1983) take place to a high degree among the generation of those women, among whom the young men search for and find their partners.

It is highly unlikely that the young men (are able to) reproduce the orientations of their fathers' generation without problems. But it is unlikely to expect as well that the "old" patterns have lost their impact totally. Based on the data from the group discussions, two patterns of orientation can be distinguished as ideal types. One is an orientation along traditional male patterns that shows a variety of ruptures and is always endangered when women are present. The other one is a pragmatically motivated egalitarian attitude. The former is typically found among the students, the latter among young skilled workers.

Endangered securities: young men of the students' milieu

The students consider the question about the meaning of being a man to be almost as useless as the men who are tightly linked to tradition. However, the difference is that they do not feel threatened by it. The request to talk about their being a man does not make them angry at all. Being a man "does not mean so much" to them. One "finds a way to come to terms with it." "You don't think about it, you just take it the way it is and you are rather glad about it." Their way of accepting it has no negative touch, it is not articulated resignedly. On the contrary: the fate to be a man is an occasion for a positive self-experience: they feel at ease in their gender.

However, their gender status has not been given to them in the same unquestioned way as to their fathers' generation. The acceptance of the fate to be a man has lost the "naivete" that can be found among the men tied to tradition. Perhaps the young men consider their gender status to be unproblematic, but they realize that a number of their contemporaries no longer take this attitude. After emphasizing that everything is unproblematic, there follows the defensive addition: "I don't have to apologize for this, I don't have to hide for this." They know about the (not only feminist) critique of men and state that men have a "bad image" in public discussion. But they refuse to adopt this bad image for their own self-image. Of course it takes a certain effort to realize this, something that the older men don't have to do. Self-evidence is replaced by a continuous achievement. Their attempt to regard the issue as being unproblematic is a plea for leaving untouched that which should be undoubted and a given, rather than a case of an unbroken taken-for-grantedness.

As students, they have to deal much more often than any other men of their age with women who confront them with feminist criticisms of men. The group discussions show that this confrontation is part of the everyday life in universities; more often it happens to students of social sciences and the humanities, a little less often to students of natural sciences and technical faculties, but for both groups it plays an important role within their everyday world. This causes touchiness – as a man "one is hardly allowed to say something at all" at the university – and this leads to sometimes vehement forms of rejection: feminists are "filth" ("Dreck"). Whenever the defence is articulated less explicit irony is at hand: the establishing of rooms exclusively for women is rejected with comments like "purple coffee-break-rooms" ("Lilapausenraum").[9] According to the men, the localities of feminist self-organization can be compared with associations of male bonding and their hypermasculine forms of self-presentation: "This would really be the same as if a chauvinistic club opened somewhere – but this will never happen at the university."

The everyday confrontation with feminist criticism is a clearly visible sign that the young men's experience of gender relations differs from that of the older men. But also on the basic level of interpretive patterns of gender difference, clear differences between the generations are found. The young men no longer explain gender-typical behavior with the help of biology, but refer to gender roles and the effects of socialization. But socialization replaces biology in the sense that fate is no longer biology but education. As well as the "natural dispositions," the dispositions created by socialization cannot be influenced. To know that gender-specific acting is a product of social conditions by no means leads to a critique of social relations and their restraints. The students rather practice "enlightened" double standards (Behnke and Meuser, 1997). Double standards are recognized as such and at the same time become the basis of their own judgements. Referring to promiscuity, for example, these men know that it is a matter of culturally produced standards which make it objectionable if a woman changes her sexual partners frequently, whereas for a man it is considered to be a positive sign of virility. Although they know that this is a question of social labeling and, in the case of the woman, of stigmatization – the woman is perceived as an "old slut," the man as a "real man" – they not only fall for these labels against their own intentions, but they also employ them with "moral engagement": "Recently a woman told me, that she had had about forty men, and I thought, uups, what a slut." Another one comments: "You better beat it, go away, far away."

An attitude that is "enlightened" in this fashion is not only limited to the perception of women. Even male stereotypes are recognized and yet practiced at the same time, for example "carousing like real men." They see that their way of acting corresponds to such stereotypes, but they do not feel obliged to change this. They may refer to "old stereotypes" of masculinity in a reflexive way. However, acting in accordance with the stereotype still seems to be attractive enough for them to go on practicing it *deliberately*. Not only the double standards, but also the traditionalism of these men is "enlightened".

In contrast to the unquestioned reference to tradition that characterizes the fathers' generation, the knowledge of double standards and stereotypes involves also ambivalences and precarious situations of life. These manifest themselves in certain divisions of the world of these men. For them it is a fundamental difference whether they are together with women or with men. Toward women, their way of acting is imprinted with caution and ready for defence. They behave differently, above all they talk differently from the way they would talk among other men. This means less the observance of gender-related rules of etiquette, which are so very important and self-evident for the older men, than a compelled observation of rhetorical standards erected by the women, as the men see it. Toward women they fell obliged to pretend. An unproblematic – and this means to them an authentic – male existence seems only possible within a homosocial association of males. This is the place where they can practice masculine stereotypes and rituals without criticism, here they can behave in a way that they themselves describe as "not ladylike." And above all, here they cope with the irritations they continuosly experience when interacting with women. A member of a male flat-sharing community comments on a conversation during which they made fun of feminist theses as follows: "This saying was dirty and hostile to women, but in our community even this is permitted, we can talk about this." Everything that is interdicted elsewhere is allowed here. Here they are secure in their masculinity, while outside of these protecting walls they feel unsure to what extent their very masculinity is accepted by others, especially by women. The habitual security that is experienced within the homosocial community is always endangered when women are present.

This precarious situation is documented in their conflicting descriptions of their behavior toward women. It varies between total withdrawal of their own person, shown for example in an inability to address a woman in a discotheque, and a hypermasculine stylized hegemony: time and again they would need to say something "brutal" to a woman, for example "Shut your trap!" Whether they really communicate with women in this way seems questionable. They do not want to have subservient women as partners.[10] But even if this is "only" a stylistic means of male self-presentation within a male community, it clearly shows the importance which is attached to the pattern of hegemonic masculinity (Connell, 1987, 1995) as far as the gender symbolism is concerned.

The fact that an orientation on this pattern is expected within the male community is proved by a discussion about "who wears the pants" in a partnership. In one group one member is reproached with the fact that it is his girlfriend who dominates in his relationship. The discussion, however, shows that this relationship has a mutual-egalitarian structure. Nevertheless the accused man feels the obligation to prove to the other group members that, though it does not seem to be the case, he is the one who could finally determine which decisions are made. "Theoretically speaking I could have my way." And even if the girlfriend had it her way, she would by no means be in the dominant position: "Yes, but this does not mean by any means that she has the whip in her hands."

Even on conditions of de-tradionalized gender relations, hegemonic masculinity continues to play an important part as a *foil of orientation*. Though it might be less suitable for describing everyday life within a partnership than it is for the generation of the parents' of the young men, its importance lies in being an interpretive pattern for locating oneself in the gender order. Above all, if this location takes place within the homosocial community. Here hegemonic masculinity is at least still efficient as expectation and demand. But the gap between demand and practice demonstrates the fact that one's own position in the gender order is no longer given to the young men in the mode of evidence. On the other hand, the persistence of the pattern of male hegemony demonstrates that these men have not broken with the traditional patterns of masculinity.

Pragmatically motivated equality: young skilled workers

The difference between the sexes plays an important part for the older men as well as for the students, as a condition for hegemonic practice and – referring to the students – for distinguishing those places of action where authentic acting is possible, from those where strategic acting is required. In contrast to this it is immediately noticeable that the young skilled workers vehemently emphasize the irrelevance of the difference. For them, man and woman are interchangeable labels that have no necessary relation to what they designate and which by no means describe different characters or allow predictions about the way of acting of those characterized in such a way. This view should not be understood as a transfiguration of inequalities caused by society, but as a postulate as well as a rejection of stereotypes concerning gender characters. Stereotyping is confronted with the demand that one judge human beings exclusively on the basis of their individual acts and on what they have achieved: "It depends on the human being."

The physiology of the genders is denied as being relevant to everything that is socially important. This is not surprising. But unlike the students, the young skilled workers do not consider the gender roles and socialization to be inevitable fate. Referring to gender role, an atypical way of acting seems possible to them; they accept it for their partners and practice it for themselves. One of them tells us, for example, that his girlfriend does the work if something in the flat has to be converted because as a joiner she is much more skilled to do this than he himself. In this case he wouldn't say: "Come on, this is my part or something like this, I am the man in the house." He knows what behavior would conform to the male gender role, but he distances himself from it. In practical terms, it would be stupid to orientate oneself according to gender role because individual competences would be left unused. This attitude does not seem to cause identity problems: "It wouldn't hurt my Highness," if he admits that his girlfriend has more handicraft skills than he himself.

The individualistic logic does not keep these men from noticing social discriminations against women. These are vehemently criticized as grievances, for example unequal payment for equal work. The principle of this criticism is the view that gender difference is irrelevant. This has a double effect: it motivates indignation, and it prevents the criticism of being fixed into a gender-political framework. The men can understand without any difficulty why women revolt against unequal payment: "This is totally normal," because they themselves would react in the same way, if they were discriminated against. But such women's protest would "not have anything to do with emancipation." The understanding of the protest is motivated by the individualistic ethics of achievement. On the other hand, a gender-political framwork would accentuate the difference of the genders by putting humans into social categories instead of comparing the efficiency of individuals.

The individualistic logic leads to a rejection of feminist arguments. The politicizing of gender relations made the men feel subsumed under a social category and therefore devalued as human beings, that is in their individual way of acting. For feminists men would be "all pigs." In their opinion such global criticism is not an expression of emancipation. A "really" emancipated woman would pursue her individual interests without framing her way of acting gender-politically: "You just do it, you don't talk, you just do it for yourself and not for the society."

The priority is placed on doing: talking obstructs practical action rather than encourages it. These men also describe everyday life in their partnerships in the context of this pragmatic fundamental attitude. The division of labor at home is done as a matter of course. It is a necessity that results from the fact that the man and the woman are both working. One man reports: "Then I am, let me say, more or less condemned to it, because I don't like to do the dishes and to vacuum. Never mind, we share the homework. My clothes, I have to iron them myself, too, these are quite common things." The – more or less given – equal division of domestic labor[11] is *not* motivated by an intention to contribute to the transformation of the gender order. The men sureley do not pursue such gender-political intentions, and, as far as one can tell from their descriptions, it is the same with their partners. Obviously the partners' demands are not "As *a man* you have to wash, clean, iron etc.," but "In my job I work as hard as you do, therefore at home you have to work as much as me." The individualistic logic seems to be shared by the women.

The young skilled workers had grown up just like the students in an era of de-traditionalization of gender relations, but in contrast to them they are not confronted with feminst criticisms in their everyday lives. Significant others of the female sex, above all their partners and wives, do not argue within this framework. If this were the case, a willingness to divide the domestic labor equally would probably turn into rejection of the demand for cooperation. Then they would feel "devalued as man," degraded simply because they belonged to the male sex. But this will not happen as long as their partners pursue the same individualistic and pragmatical logic as they themselves.

The sometimes radical egalitarianism implies a consequent de-gendering of the behavior of man *and* woman. As shown above, the men who are tightly linked to tradition also "de-gender," but only their own way of acting, and not that of the women. For these men it is only possible to describe the male way of acting in individualized categories, whereas women's way of acting is stereotyped. This one-sided "de-gendering" is a very effective instrument for the reproduction of male hegemony. The irrelevance of the gender difference assumed by the young skilled workers does not exhibit this one-sidedness. As a consequence no work exists for them which a woman could not do because of her sex. The egalitarian attitude also excludes the double standards of the students. In contrast to them, it is said: "If a woman for example had fifty men before me and I but one woman, then it is her business; she has to know for herself what she needs and what she does not need."

The young skilled workers represent a form of modernized masculinity that is not based on making a problem out of the male gender status. The lack of reflexive problematization implies that these men do not experience a habitual insecurity. The traditional symbolic resources of male self-location within gender relations do not mean much to them. Although they are no longer kept within the continuity of male hegemony, they do not execute a radical break for themselves. This seems to be made possible by the fact that the modernization takes place within pragmatical arrangements. This gives the change an inward looking framework.[12]

Here, the modernization of masculinity is an unintented consequence of a way of acting that pursues intentions other than gender-political ones. One can, of course, suppose that this modernization could not take place if it were not put into the framework of transformation of the gender order. Without the de-traditionalization of gender relations that has been pushed ahead by the womens' movement, and without creating a new image of women that focuses no longer on family or the work of reproduction, the partners of the skilled workers would hardly possess the self-confidence that allows them the demanding attitude described above.

Consciousness-raising and the modernization of masculinity

According to popular expectations, which are also supported by sociological theories of social change and modernization, one expects to find an egalitarian attitude and a willingness toward social change among men from the academic-intellectuall middle class rather than among skilled workers. Walter Hollstein, a german protagonist of the men's movement as well as of men's studies, describes the "prototype of the changed man" as follows: He "is between 27 and 40 years of age, graduated in humanities or in social sciences, is not only interested in but is also engaged in current events, works as teacher, psychologist, social worker or journalist, and is politically progressive" (Hollstein, 1988, p. 159).

This type of man is also represented in our sample. One finds him, equipped with the mentioned demographical characteristics, in men's consciousness-raising groups. The members of these groups meet for a critical examination of the male gender role. The discussions of these men, however, draw a picture that clearly modifies the expectations created by Hollstein. These men are prototypical in that they continuosly call traditional patterns of masculinity into question. Nevertheless, the institutionalized continuous reflection creates more problems and ambivalences, than it helps to find a direction and a way of changing practice. "We don't get any further than talking about it," says one group self-critically. These men have quite progressive opinions and an egalitarian attitude toward gender relations. However, the consciousness-raising groups serve to help them cope with identity problems rather than as the foundation for (gender-)political actions.[13] These men are perfect examples for Giddens's thesis, quoted above, that men find themselves today for the first time "to *be* men," because they possess a "problematic 'masculinity'." These men perceive their gender status in the context of crisis. Their being a man is imprinted with a fundamental ambivalence: on the one hand suffering from the traditional patterns and norms of masculinity and, on the other hand, longing for habitual security that is promised by a life adequate to the traditional male role. This yearning seems, on a latent level, to give to hypermasculinity and male hegemony – which are critcized in explicit statements – an attractive aspect, as the following examples will show.

In a discussion with a men's consciousness-raising group one member emphasized that he did not feel well among men and that he had better relations with women than with men. It seems that the world of women is more accessible to him than the homosocial male world: "In an extreme case I discover that, in principle, I could be a woman too." He does not experience this "border crossing" positively as an extension of room for manoeuvre, instead it causes strong anxieties. He tells many biographical stories, none of which is a success story. But there is one exception. Talking about sexuality, he first reports his anxiety "to be accepted as a man at all," and then he remarks: "If it really happens to me to sleep with a woman for example then the pressure disappears somehow, then I feel myself somehow as a man, and often just superior." Although for this man the traditional symbolic order of masculinity generates enormous conflicts and sufferings, the only way for him to keep up a male identity is to rely on what is at the heart of the traditional order: the superiority of men.

With respect to the extent and the intensity of his conflicts and sufferings, this man is extraordinary and not a typical member of men's consciousness-raising groups. But the ambivalence that is documented in his case is typical for these groups. On the one hand traditional stereotypes and patterns of masculinity are rejected by intention, while on the other hand, on a latent level, these men are attracted to the "old" patterns. Another member of the same consciousness-raising group reports on his time in the army. As a member of the generation of 1968 (the student's movement), he is critical of the military, but in retrospect there remains some fascination:

> For two years I wished most to get into there, with the rituals of initiation and of drinking. ... There was such a terrific wish to be accepted by *these* men, because these rangers never accepted me, ... as I would have had such a smell, and I always had this smell, like a smell that I am not a real man. And for an incredibly long time – but actually it still lasts, when I tell now, I never thought about it – it bothers me still now, time and again.

The male homosocial world of the army with its rituals of initiation is still fascinating after 20 years. Concerning his own masculinity, his integration within this world is made a validating condition. Even in retrospect, any failings at that time are percieved as a cause of his present feelings of uncertainty. There is a strong yearning to be accepted by the traditional male world, which, on the other hand, is criticized programmatically. In the same discussion the same man at first says that he does not identify with the world of machos and Rambos ("this doesn't effect me at all"). Then, a few seconds later, he says that he want to learn a macho-like behavior. What is criticized in the first place fascinates because the machos and the comrades in the army embody a habitual security, which the members of the consciousness-raising groups are missing, but yearning for. It is true that they do not want to live according to the traditional patterns of masculinity, and this is the reason why they look for alternatives and for new options. However, they wish to be secure in their own masculinity as much as those men who are tightly tied to tradition. Uncertainties and identity problems generate a yearning for the taken-for-grantedness that is given by the traditonal male habitus. It is the habitual security that makes the criticized patterns of masculinity attractive.

The men in the consciousness-raising groups are facing a serious dilemma, which is caused by the dialectics of determination and emergence. In order to define themselves as men they cannot avoid referring to the established cultural order and its symbolic resources. On the other hand, they suffer from the expectations and norms that are constituted by this order, and they want to change this order. At the outset of this essay it was shown how tradition is still powerful and that an unbroken continuity of the established gender order can be observed among older men. However, as the ambivalences found in men's consciousness-raising groups reveal, continuities are also discovered within a world of changing masculinities. What do the continuities consist of? What is the "nucleus" of these continuities?

The macho, Rambo, the military are to be seen as documents of a fundamental pattern: hegemonic masculinity. This is, as it were, the nucleus of male self-perception and self-identification, which is in effect even among those men who explicitly criticize the gender order. The figures that the members of the consciousness-raising groups refer to as symbols of a self-evident and secure masculinity are hypermasculine prototypes of male hegemony. The ordinary "doing" gender of men does consist so much of hypermasculine forms of acting. But in either case the pattern of hegemonic masculinity is to be seen as the generating principle of the male gender habitus.[14] By this it is not meant that all the behavior of men is hegemonic and that there are no differences in men's ways of acting and behaving; hegemonic masculinity is a generating principle, and not the practice itself. But because of its latency it often goes against explicit intentions and manifest attitudes. According to Bourdieu (1979, p. 544), habitus means a "sense of social orientation," a "sense of one's place" in society. Usually this sense is not accessible to the actor's "discursive consciousness" (Giddens, 1984). This constitutes the power of the habitus and its longevity.

Bourdieu (1990) describes male dominance as "symbolic rule" and states that this dominance unfolds its effect "in the obscurity of the practical schemes of the habitus where the relation of dominance is inscribed and often not accessible to reflection and to the control of volition" (p. 11). "The inertia of the habitus cannot be suspended by a simple effort of will founded on liberating awareness" (p. 13). Bourdieu's notion of habitus draws attention to continuities that are more or less hidden behind visible changes. Further, it lets one be skeptical that a deconstructionist strategy that assumes a multi-optionality of gender identities and propagates queer politics (masquerade, travesty) as a means for breaking up the established gender order will have the potential for change that its advocates assume. It has to called into question whether a subversive play with gender signs reaches habitualizations that are deeply inscribed into bodily routines. Certainly, there is no denying that, due to the de-traditionalization of gender relations, a variety of images of masculinity emerges. However, this development does not constitute a "homo optionis" in the sense that it would simply be a question of free choice which pattern of masculinity guides a man's doing gender. Patterns of masculinity, in other words, are not put on display in a postmodern supermarket of lifestyles to be selected by decision. Behind the variety of images of masculinity the male habitus as a fundamental and generating principle ensures that the social category "man" and masculinity as a distinct and distinctive social mode of existence and practice are not (yet) vanishing.

It seems important to me to emphasize the continuities because there is a strong tendency toward a voluntaristic understanding of the concept of doing gender within the recent (popular and cultural) discourse on gender and on masculinity (Meuser and Behnke, 1998). Often it is not sufficiently taken into account that what is socially constructed is at least as constraining as biological determinations, if there are any. But to draw attention to continuities is not to conceptualize masculinity in an essentialistic manner as a trans-historical phenomenon. What masculinity consists of is tied to changing historical, cultural, economical and political conditions. But one must also take into consideration that patterns of masculinity develop over a long history of male dominance. One cannot expect that deeply inscribed patterns will loose their effect within the relatively short time of 30 years, in which the second women's movement has challenged male dominance.

Conclusion

The question as to why a critically reflexive examination of one's own masculinity apparently obstructs rather than paves the way to a changing practice can not be discussed here in detail. The limits of self-reflection – for men – are probably related to the fact that, regarding to gender, identities are tied to something that cannot, according to male common sense, be dealt with by communication. As the men who are tightly linked to tradition see it, it is something that cannot be talked about. The destruction of habitualizations results first in confusion and the reflexive deconstruction only ruins that which apparently cannot be the basis for new constructions.[15] In opposition to this, the pragmatically motivated egalitarianism of the young skilled workers seems to enable a practical significant modernization of masculinity, because it needs no reflexive deconstruction of fundamental identities.

Contrasting bourgeois-intellectual men's groups with skilled workers should not generate the impression that an egalitarian practice on the basis of pragmatic arrangements is possible only in the workers' milieu. It is true that we found this practice only there, but this may be due to the sample of our investigation. It was an explorative study without claims to statistical representativeness, and it only reconstructs different patterns of orientation. American research about the family situation of dual-career couples (that is couples where both man and woman pursue a professional career) show that there is a tendency toward an egalitarian distribution of domestic labor even in the bourgeois milieu. In addition to this, these studies show, however, that this distribution is based on a pragmatic motivation. It is less the result of intented attempts than the unintented consequence of getting two careers under one marital umbrella. Gender-political motives do not seem to play a part. Hertz (1986, p. 33) describes the development of the egalitarian practice in a way that clearly shows parallels to the descriptions of the young skilled workers: "Far from being the avant-garde of a social movement, with an articulate vision of what they want to create, these couples are notable for their lack of ideological prescriptions about the equality of marital roles. Instead, combining two equally demanding (and rewarding) careers, *they simply practice such equality*" (my italics).

Of course, referring to the career couples, one has to take into account that, without the (gender-)politically pushed transformation of gender relations, women would hardly be able to pursue their professional careers in the same way that men have always done. Nevertheless, a modernization of masculinity, which can survive as *egalitarian practice*, because it does not have to be paid for by habitual insecurity, may probably most easily appear as an unintended consequence within a pragmatically arranged relationship, in which the man is *not asked as man* to abandon traditional male privileges. The reflexivity of being a man, and above all its institutionalization in the shape of consciousness-raising groups, does not seem to have the practical potential for change that numerous protagonists of a men's movement hope for.

Notes

1. This paper is an extended version of the article "Gefährdete Sicherheiten und pragmatische Arrangements. Lebenszusammenhänge und Orientierungsmuster junger Männer" (Meuser, 1998b) that integrates parts of the article "Kulturelle Deutungsmuster von Männlicheit. Veränderungen und Kontinuitäten" (Meuser, 1998c).
2. Almost notoriously the particularities of rural life with their powerful connections to tradition are left unconsidered (Behringer, 1993; Hüwelmeier, 1996, 1997; Wahl, 1991). But also in the bourgeois milieu of the towns, which is characterized by the possession of economic capital, working-class references to tradition and pre-reflexive habitualizations of masculinity are found that

stand in the way of a problematization.

3. This at least is true for those men who, with such a break, risk not only identities but also privileges. Such breaks and the resulting problems are found in the scene of the "men's movement" (see Behnke and Meuser, 1996).

4. The group discussions (n = 30) are part of a research project named "Collective orientations of men and changes in gender relations." It was funded by the "Deutsche Forschungsgemeinschaft" and conducted at the University of Bremen from 1993 to 1997 (Behnke, 1997; Loos, 1998; Meuser, 1998a, b, c).

5. This refers mainly to men who are older than 40 years of age and who work as managers, managing directors or freelances. According to Connell (1993) these men's way of acting (as the technocratic and professional elite) represents prototypically the pattern of hegemonic masculinity. For this reason I concentrate only on the bourgeois milieu. But this does not mean that undoubted evidence, habitual security and male hegemony are limited to this milieu. For unities and differences between bourgeois and workers' milieu see Behnke, Loos and Meuser, 1998.

6. The questions of the sociologists are considered to be not only strange, but sometimes even to be threatening. A man asks rhetorically "if this is not a grievance, well, to permanently ask oneself such questions." He draws the conclusion that sociologists are jointly responsible for the grievance: "And much damage is done, I mean, with this, that many things are so exaggerated, perhaps by the thing you're doing. You are doing it, too, somehow you are working in this field, too."

7. Such a traditional, pre-reflexive orientation does not determine the professional action of these men.

8. Whether women look upon it in the same way is another question, which cannot be answered on the basis of the mens' descriptions.

9. In Germany there is a chocolate called "Lilapause" ("purple break"). The students refer to this.

10. In this context they distinguish between "Emanzen," used as a code for feminists, and "emancipated women." They can imagine themselves living together with the latter "on a reasonable basis."

11. Of course it cannot be decided on the basis of the group discussions whether the relationships are really organized as egalitarian as the men describe it. It must be noted, however, that the young skilled workers do not refer to the pattern of male hegemony but to one of equality when describing their partnerships. In comparison to the other men this marks a considerable difference.

12. The pragmatic arrangements refer to a continuity other than that of the gender order, and this is the involvement in the workers' milieu. Even if hegemonic masculinity is a central symbolic resource of the self-location for older skilled workers as well as for the bourgeois men, the older skilled workers share the pragmatic reference to the gender order with the young ones (Behnke, Loos and Meuser, 1998). This indicates that gender habitus and class habitus intersect. The importance of this intersection and above all its way of functioning have hardly been defined as a topic of research, let alone been analyzed

(Bourdieu, 1997; Meuser and Behnke, 1998).
13. Whenever it comes to political action, most of the time it is some kind of symbolic politics (Behnke, Loos and Meuser, 1995).
14. The notion of male gender habitus is explained in Meuser, 1998a and Behnke and Meuser, 1998.
15. A look at current developments in the field of men's groups, as well as at recent tendencies in the discourse of masculinity, shows that the groups and patterns of orientation that become increasingly attractive are those which promise, with intentions of restoration, to gain back habitual security while emphasizing essential differences between men and women (Behnke and Meuser, 1996; Meuser, 1998).

References

Beck, Ulrich (1992) *Risk Society: Towards a New Modernity*. London: Sage.
Beck, Ulrich (1996) *The Reinvention of Politics: Rethinking Modernity in the Global Social Order*. Cambridge: Polity Press.
Beck, Ulrich and Beck-Gernsheim, Elisabeth (eds) (1994a) *Riskante Freiheiten. Individualisierung in modernen Gesellschaften*. Frankfurt a.M.: Suhrkamp.
Beck, Ulrich and Beck-Gernsheim, Elisabeth (1994b) "Individualisierung in modernen Gesellschaften – Perspektiven und Kontroversen einer subjektorientierten Soziologie," in Beck, Ulrich and Beck-Gernsheim, Elisabeth (eds) (1994a) *Riskante Freiheiten. Individualisierung in modernen Gesellschaften*. Frankfurt a.M.: Suhrkamp.
Beck, Ulrich, Giddens, Anthony and Lash, Scott (1995) *Reflexive Modernization: Politics, Tradition and Esthetics in the Modern Social Order*. Cambridge: Polity Press.
Beck-Gernsheim, Elisabeth (1983) "Vom 'Dasein für andere' zum Anspruch auf ein Stück 'eigenes Leben' – Individualisierungsprozesse im weiblichen Lebenszusammenhang," *Soziale Welt*, 34, pp. 307-41.
Behnke, Cornelia (1997) *"Frauen sind wie andere Planeten." Das Geschlechterverhältnis aus männlicher Sicht*. Frankfurt a.M.: Campus.
Behnke, Cornelia, Loos, Peter and Meuser, Michael (1995) "'Wir kommen über das Reden nicht hinaus.' Selbstreflexion und Handlungspraxis in Männergruppen," *Widersprüche*, 56/57, pp. 119-27.
Behnke, Cornelia, Loos, Peter and Meuser, Michael (1998) "Habitualisierte Männlichkeit. Existentielle Hintergründe kollektiver Orientierungen von Männern," in Bohnsack, R. and Marotzki, W. (eds), *Biographieforschung und Kulturanalyse*. Opladen: Leske & Budrich (in press).
Behnke, Cornelia and Meuser, Michael (1996) "Ausdiskutieren oder Ausschwitzen. Männergruppen zwischen institutionalisierter Dauerreflexion und neuer Wildheit," in Knoblauch, H. (ed.), *Kommunikative Lebenswelten. Zur Ethnographie einer geschwätzigen Gesellschaft*. Konstanz: Universitätsverlag.

Behnke, Cornelia and Meuser, Michael (1997) "Zwischen aufgeklärter Doppelmoral und partnerschaftlicher Orientierung. Frauenbild junger Männer," *Zeitschrift für Sexualforschung*, 10, pp. 1-18.

Behnke, Cornelia and Meuser, Michael (1998) "Gender and Habitus: Fundamental Securities and Crisis Tendencies Among Men," in Kotthoff, H. and Baron, B. (eds), *Gender in Interaction*. New York: Mouton de Gruyter (forthcoming).

Behringer, Luise (1993) "Leben auf dem Land, Leben in der Stadt. Stabilität durch soziale Einbindung," in Jurczyk, K. and Rerrich, M. S. (eds), *Die Arbeit des Alltags. Beiträge zu einer Soziologie der alltäglichen Lebensführung*. Freiburg i.Br.: Lambertus.

Berger, Peter L., Berger, Brigitte and Kellner, Hansfried (1973) *The Homeless Mind: Modernization and Consciousness*. Harmondsworth: Penguin Books.

Bourdieu, Pierre (1979) *La distinction. Critique sociale du jugement*. Paris: Les Édition de Minuit.

Bourdieu, Pierre (1990) "La domination masculine," *Actes de la Recherche en Sciences Sociales*, 84, pp. 2-31.

Bourdieu, Pierre (1997) "Eine sanfte Gewalt. Pierre Bourdieu im Gespräch mit Irene Dölling und Margareta Steinrücke," in Dölling, I. and Krais, B. (eds), *Ein alltägliches Spiel. Geschlechterkonstruktion in der sozialen Praxis*. Frankfurt a.M.: Suhrkamp.

Connell, R. W. (1987) *Gender and Power. Society, the Person and Sexual Politics*. Cambridge: Polity Press.

Connell, R. W. (1993) "The Big Picture: Masculinities in Recent World History," *Theory and Society*, 22, pp. 597-623.

Connell, R. W. (1995) *Masculinities*. Cambridge: Polity Press.

Geissler, Birgit and Oechsle, Mechtild (1994) "Lebensplanung als Konstruktion: Biographische Dilemmata und Lebenslauf-Entwürfe junger Frauen," in Beck, Ulrich and Beck-Gernsheim, Elisabeth (eds) (1994a) *Riskante Freiheiten. Individualisierung in modernen Gesellschaften*. Frankfurt a.M.: Suhrkamp.

Giddens, Anthony (1984) *The Constitution of Society: Outline of the Theory of Structuration*. Cambridge: Polity Press.

Giddens, Anthony (1991) *The Consequences of Modernity*. Cambridge: Polity Press.

Giddens, Anthony (1992) *The Transformation of Intimacy: Sexuality, Love and Eroticism in Modern Societies*. Cambridge: Polity Press.

Gross, Peter (1994) *Die Multioptionsgesellschaft*. Frankfurt a.M.: Suhrkamp.

Hertz, Rosanna (1986) *More Equal Than Others: Women and Men in Dual-Career Marriages*. Berkeley: University of California Press.

Hollstein, Walter (1988) *Nicht Herrscher, aber kräftig. Die Zukunft der Männer*. Hamburg: Hoffmann und Campe.

Hüwelmeier, Gertrud (1996) "Kreischende" Frauen – Singende Männer. Geschlechterbeziehungen in einem deutschen Dorf," in Kokot, W. and Dracklé, D. (eds), *Ethnologie Europas*. Berlin: Reimer.

Hüwelmeier, Gertrud (1997) "Kirmesgesellschaften und Männergesangsvereine. 'Rites de passage' in der dörflichen Kultur Deutschlands," *Zeitschrift für Sozialisationsfoschung und Erziehungssoziologie*, 17, pp. 30-41.

Loos, Peter (1998) *Zwischen pragmatischer und moralischer Orientierung. Der männliche Blick auf das Geschlechterverhältnis im Milieuvergleich.* Opladen: Leske & Budrich (in press).

Meuser, Michael (1998a) *Geschlecht und Männlichkeit. Soziologische Theorie und kulturelle Deutungsmuster.* Opladen: Leske & Budrich.

Meuser, Michael (1998b) "Gefährdete Sicherheiten und pragmatische Arrangements. Lebenszusammenhänge und Orientierungsmuster junger Männer," in Oechsle, M. and Geissler, B. (eds), *Die ungleiche Gleichheit. Junge Frauen und der Wandel im Geschlechterverhältnis.* Opladen: Leske & Budrich (in press).

Meuser, Michael (1998c) "Kulturelle Deutungsmuster von Männlicheit. Veränderungen und Kontinuitäten," in Mall, R. A. and Schneider, N. (eds), *Einheit und Vielfalt - das Verstehen der Kulturen.* Amsterdam/Atlanta: Rodopi (in press).

Meuser, Michael and Behnke, Cornelia (1998) "Tausendundeine Männlichkeit? Männlichkeitsmuster und sozialstrukturelle Einbindungen," *Widersprüche*, 67 (in press).

Meuser, Michael and Sackmann, Reinhold (1992) "Zur Einführung: Deutungsmusteransatz und empirische Wissenssoziologie," in Meuser, Michael and Sackmann, Reinhold (eds), *Analyse sozialer Deutungsmuster. Beiträge zur empirischen Wissenssoziologie.* Pfaffenweiler: Centaurus.

Simmel, Georg (1985) *Schriften zur Philosophie und Soziologie der Geschlechter.* Frankfurt a.M.: Suhrkamp.

Wahl, Peter (1991) "Wo der Mann noch ein Mann ist," in Böhnisch, L., Funk, H., Huber, J. and Stein, G. (eds), *Ländliche Lebenswelten. Fallstudien zur Landjugend.* München: Verlag Deutsches Jugendinstitut.

Chapter 9

Technology and Masculinity: Men and their Machines

Ulf Mellström

THIS is a book of Men at Work; men of courage, skill, daring and imagination. Cities do not build themselves, machines cannot make machines, unless in the back of them all are the brains and toil of men. We call this the Machine Age. But the more machines we use the more we need real men to make and direct them. I have toiled in many industries and associated with thousand of workers. I have brought some of them here to meet you. Some of them are heroes; all of them persons it is a privilege to know. I will take you into the heart of modern industry where machines and skyscrapers are being made, where the character of the men is being put into the motors, the airplanes, the dynamos upon which the life and happiness of millions of us depend. Then the more you see of modern machines, the more may you, too, respect the men who make them and manipulate them.[1]

In the preface to Lewis W. Hine's remarkably beautiful photography book, he poetically speaks about men's characters as being formed within engines, airplanes and generators. Could that explain why so many men love their machines dearly, and why many men tenderly care about their cars, motorcycles, computers, boats and other technical artifacts? Do men have a special relationship to technology that women lack? Do men have an ability to create close and intimate relationships with machines that women lack? If women, according to certain feminist theories (Chodorow, 1978; Gilligan, 1982), are supposed to have a superior ability to create close and intimate personal relationships, do men get an outlet for their emotional needs in relation to machines?

These are some of the questions that arise from studying the relation between technology and masculinity and which I will be dealing with in this article. The article takes its point of departure in an anthropological study of Swedish engineers, their work and life career,[2] and includes a general discussion of the relation between technology and masculinity as well as a more concrete discussion based upon empirical investigation. As an introduction, I discuss contemporary research on men and masculinities and the essential questions this emerging field are formed around. These questions are put in relation to my main interest, masculinity and the construction of gender in the world of technology. Two possible perspectives on studying gender in daily practice are outlined: first, a situational micro-sociological perspective where the practice of everyday life is focused, and second, a biographical perspective where the construction of gender can be studied from practices of socialization. A combination of these two perspectives is, I believe, a dynamic and processual way to see how our gender identities are produced as well as reproduced.

Technology and research on men

Despite the fact that contemporary research on men and masculinities is to be considered as a broad field of research with a large empirical scope,[3] little work has been done on the relation between technology and masculinity. To a certain extent that is surprising, since many men, not least in the Western world, spend a great deal of their everyday life with machines and different forms of technology. It is also surprising from an anthropological standpoint, since technology and science are the domains that have been and still are a common ground for global – political as well as economic – Western dominance. Furthermore, it is almost exclusively masculine social arenas in which men have struggled for prestige, power and influence. In other words, these are the social fields where masculine career-oriented forms of life have been given free play. In a comparison of different forms of masculinity, these career-oriented forms of life are usually defined as belonging to a hegemonic form of masculinity, and more precisely defined as a white, heterosexual, married, urban, professional middle class.[4] It is usually a dominating form of masculinity whose form of life and values have hegemonic pretensions over other forms of masculinity and femininity.

Science as a professional gendered field has been focused on mostly by feminist scholars. In a study of American and Japanese high-energy physicists, anthropologist Sharon Traweek (1988a, 1988b) demonstrates how they create an exclusively manly professional community which more or less presupposes the absence of women. The sometimes paradoxical masculine forms of science are crystallised in Brian Easlea's book *Fathering the Unthinkable* (1983), which describes the development of the first Atomic Bomb in the United States. Easlea effectively shows how Oppenheimer and his colleagues gave birth to their "baby" with great care and attention. A common ground for these studies is that they reveal how masculine ideology is made up of certain sorts of knowledge, beliefs, desires and practices in the world of science and technology.

In the few studies that deal with the relation between technology and masculinity, Judy Wajcman's work is perhaps the most celebrated, besides Cynthia Cockburn's important writings concerning male dominance and occupational hierarchies.[5] Wajcman (1991) outlines two dominant forms of masculinity in technology, one based on physical toughness and mechanical skills, the other based on the professional, calculative rationality of the technical specialist. The first form is often associated with working-class culture and its often outward and expressive masculine performance. A classic example of such a culture can be found in Paul Willis's book *Learning to Labour* (1977). Without having any outspoken focus on masculinity as such, Willis nevertheless convincingly shows how a strong masculine ethos pervades the lifestyle of "the lads." A ground component in such an ethos is the ability to master mechanics and machines. If the first form of masculinity in technology can be characterized by "working-class men," the other form can be characterized by "ruling-class men." Men with technical expertise often occupy crucial power positions in business organizations as well as social institutions. Their form of masculinity form has a more theoretical character, but in a similar manner it rests upon a mastering of machines and technology.

Both forms of masculinity are connected to mastering and controlling technology and nature, even though class often distinguishes them. Another common ground for both forms of masculinity is that they are expressive and constitutive forms of masculinity, and both forms conceptualize how men construct identity in relation to machines and technology. Engineering is a particularly interesting case for studies of masculinity, because as Wajcman (1991, p. 145) argues "it cuts across the boundaries between physical and intellectual work and yet maintains strong elements of mind/body dualism."

The fact that engineering and the world of technology is a world highly concentrated around men is of course no surprise. Numerically as well as normatively men dominate.[6] In 1921 the first woman in Sweden was accepted into a higher engineering program, but it was not until the 1970s that women started to make way into the classical masculine domain of technical universities. Women who were recruited to the engineering profession were for a long time seen as part of the "talent reserve," in a similar way that working-class men were recruited to the profession in the 1950s. The motifs for such a policy can be read against a tremendous lack of skilled technicians and engineers in Swedish industry during these periods, and these needs could not be met by the traditional middle-class engineering work force.[7]

Thus, the world of technology has until quite recently been a manly bastion where a pure masculine sociability has prospered. Therefore, it is also a most interesting social arena for studies of masculinity constructions. Using my empirical material, I will in the following try to examine how masculinity is produced as well as reproduced in both daily practice and during different life-courses.

Everyday life among cars and computers

The world of technology is heavily dominated by men, but the question is: what makes it masculine as such? On what ground, besides the purely numerical, is it relevant to talk about a production and reproduction of masculinity and masculine ideals? In other words, how is masculinity constituted in the world of technology and what is it that makes it masculine *per se*?

By focusing different forms of everyday interaction at two engineering milieus, Microchips and Automobile, I will give examples of how the construction of gender identity is formed in some of the micro-social situations that make up a day at work. I will also give examples of how such situations mirror a social continuity in the lives of different engineers. To situate my examples I will give a short description of the two different workplaces.[8]

Automobile, Inc.

Automobile, Inc. (hereafter Automobile) is one of the leading transnational enterprises of Swedish industry. The company was founded in the late 1920s and is today a multi-industrial corporation with many different lines of business. My fieldwork took place in the chassis department in the design and development division at the car corporation of Automobile's headquarters. The headquarters are located on a huge industrial site on the outskirts of a large city.

The work process at Automobile involves extensive coordination between corporate planning, product planning, finance, marketing, body styling, design engineering, and manufacturing engineering. This complexity generates numerous sequences of specialized tasks, meaning that design engineers within this industry in general and at the chassis department are highly specialized.

Microchips, Inc.

In many regards Microchips, Inc. (hereafter Microchips) is the very opposite of the large-scale Automobile environment. Microchips is a "spin-off company" from an Institute of Technology. It is a small high-tech enterprise within the semiconductor industry, founded in 1986 to provide specified integrated circuits to the Nordic market. Microchips has design, manufacturing and qualification facilities at its headquarters in the Plainland Science Park located in a middle-sized Swedish town; the company has altogether 23 employees. In contrast to Automobile, the engineering practice at Microchips constitutes itself around small-scale projects with a settler spirit based on a strong future orientation.

Metaphors, cooperation and competition

Everyday interaction in both organizations is mostly exerted through talk. The verbal interactions that take place in the form of meetings, and through shop talk, small talk, stories, and jokes are situated activities that are in the center of the "production of meaning" in the organizations. These activities are differently situated in time and space according to who is involved in the interaction and can be seen as different events that in themselves structure time and space within the organizations. It is through these kinds of routine activities that shared frames of meaning are produced and reproduced in everyday practice.

In the talk-based interaction of daily social practice of both workplaces, metaphoric process is a constitutive part of the communication of symbolic meaning in the organization. From an analytical standpoint, it is assumed that metaphors carry properties that are central and significant to everyday life.[9] Metaphors are here referred to as "conventional metaphors," that is metaphors that are embedded in everyday language and structure. In the words of Lakoff and Johnson (1980, p. 454), "Our ordinary conceptual system, in terms of which we both think and act, is fundamentally metaphorical in nature." The essence of metaphor in everyday life seems to lie in its capacity for understanding and experiencing one kind of thing or experience in terms of another (*ibid.*, p. 455).

The talk-based interaction and metaphoric processes of everyday life are strongly marked by gender.[10] Typically, the discourse at Automobile is continuously structured around what one usually associates with masculine social activities such as sport and hunting. The incessant flow of talk-based interaction shows how the engineers often use metaphors related to the world of sports when describing the components and design of their cars. These sets of metaphors capture both the collectiveness and the competitiveness of work in analogy with what usually characterizes different games and sports. The engineers are very concerned about how "the game runs" or how "the inter-play goes." Talking about other car manufacturers is a matter of "if we win over them" in this or that test, or if "we are leading in market shares." A favourite topic for such comparisons is the products of the other Swedish car manufacturer. A sibling-like relation between them pops up every time a new business or production measure is taken by that particular competitor. Needless to say, the comparisons often turn out in favour of their own brand.

The competitive element is time. A continuous talk about development time, lead time, and manufacturing time flourishes. It is something you can always cut down on, you can win time. The time element is closely connected to costs, and cost estimates pervade the daily life of design work. Just as with time, costs are possible to hunt and shoot. Cost-cutting is time-cutting. You cut, shoot, win, hunt, kill, take the lead, etc. The discourse here is structured through metaphors of an everlasting battle and time is the most valuable commodity in that battle.

Coexisting with the metaphors coming within the pattern of "more/less" and "dead/alive" is another set of metaphors describing the design and inner characteristics of the car. In contrast to win, hunt, shoot and kill, these metaphors represent "softer" qualities, such as the following ones:

I think we did a good job, the body and the chassis play wonderfully together.

We have given them a beautiful pass. (From design engineering to manufacturing engineering.)

The game is well off now, the interior lines are consistent, but you should have seen the misfit before, my God!!!

The artful interplay between different departments, components, people and design solutions is here at the core of the metaphorical expressions. Again, they are connected to a language associated with the world of sports, but this time with its hostile features are played down in favour of its cooperative qualities. The analogy with a football or hockey team is a recurrent one when people try to communicate the spirit of the ongoing project. The striving for a collective goal in which everyone on the team does his best is the given mental image and it is a most pervasive one that everyone can hold on to. For example, the head of the department, Bengt, explains: "This project is just like playing football, everyone has got to strive for the same goal to make sure that the ball hits the back of the net."

This kind of sports' metaphorical talk is derived from predominantly manly styles of interaction. It highlights the dimension of gender in engineering. It reflects a socializing continuity in the world of males (cf. Hacker, 1978, 1981) and how the technical language becomes gendered. At a department such as the chassis one this metaphorical function is furthermore strengthened by its direct relation to mechanics. An early and close relation to the world of mechanics is a very common feature in the personal biographies of the male engineers. It adds even more to the socializing continuity since it contributes to the homogeneity of a shared frame of reference. These mutually reinforcing factors offer a platform for interpretation of the ongoing flow of events of everyday life at the office. A male frame of reference is seen as the self-evident and natural one.

This socializing male-centered technical practice is shown in the way that the male engineers "talk cars." They amply use metaphors that embed their artifact in a language emphasizing a face-to-face relationship to it: the car talks to you, the car is stubborn, the car is friendly, and so on. When the engineers talk brakes, a truly vital part of the chassis system, they talk in terms of how slow or fast the different car models communicate with the driver. For example, they compare front-wheel drive to rear-wheel drive or oversteering to understeering. At a lunch conversation one of them, Olle, gives me his picture on how very different models may perform on slippery winter roads:

> The old 380 was marvellous in that sense [rear-wheel drive], it started to talk to you right away, as soon as it began to lose hold of the road. Then you had the time to react, but now and especially with X-brand new model [front-wheel drive], you sit and drive nicely and suddenly it just goes boom! It goes between extremes, from a pleasant and peaceful drive to sudden strikes.

The use of metaphors full of human analogies shows an intimate and internalized knowledge about the technology.

At Microchips the men have a similar way of talking about their machines. The most important machines and equipment are anthropomorphized in that they carry names such as "Lasse" (Laser scanner) and "Kalle" (the mask maker), thereby becoming more than machines, rather more like a friend towards whom one develops feelings. The "caretakers" speak about their machines in these terms, even though everyone knows that the machines are just mechanics; these obviously contain a humorous self-reflective dimension. Nevertheless, the machines do become more than neutral objects – they are actors "married" to their "caretakers," whose competence and personality they share and "live" with. At Microchips, identity and position are very much connected to the machines in relation to their caretakers.

That identity and status are related to the machines one has responsibility for is indisputable and a well known phenomenon, not least in different shop-floor occupational hierarchies, but the anthropomorphization also speaks of something else. It speaks of a relation to mechanics and machines that are something more than an object and means relationship. It speaks of an emotional relationship to the machines, a relationship that arouses both frustration and joy. In her now classic book *The Second Self* (1984), Sherry Turkle speaks about the young hackers' love of their machines as a "love for the machine itself." An essential component in that relation is what Turkle describes as the mastering and controlling of the machines. In the personal relations that are created with the machines, many of the ordinary wishes and frustrations which constitute other emotional relationships are certainly involved. The advantage with the machine is possibly, as one the engineers told me when I asked him why he once started computers, "They are silent and they don't speak and they mostly do as they are told to do."

At Microchips a significant dimension of work is precisely the strive for mastery of the machines and of new computer software. Computers are self-evidently at the center of the work practice. Engineers at Microchips have a playful and almost sensuous relation with their computers, using them with great virtuosity for all different kinds of work tasks. Almost without exception, they master new programs and the latest software within their specialized fields of microelectronics. This gives them pride and professional identity. On the door to a design engineer's room there is a note with the motto "Real Programmers don't Write Specs." It jokingly announces all the things "Real Programmers" do. Among other things it says: "Real programmers don't write in BASIC. Actually, no programmers write in BASIC, after the age of 12." This little note reflects a prevailing attitude among engineers at Microchips: mastery of the machines and new software is the criterion by which technical achievement is measured and status given.

Microchips is an engineering environment where technical talent is highly regarded and consequently generates a climate where technical creativity and playfulness prosper. In other words, it is a milieu where it is possible to cultivate one's love and fascination for the machines, and at Microchips it is exclusively men who cultivate this love. The women at Microchips have a much more sober relationship to electronics and the computers. But where lies the difference? and do women feel the same kind of emotional attachment in relation to technology as men do? By focusing on different forms of metaphorical use at the two engineering workplaces, it is possible to state that everyday engineering practice and technical language use are pervaded by metaphors derived from different forms of manly social interaction, but is it thereby any ground for speaking about any inherent relation between technology and masculinity? To be able to continue with that question I shall henceforth focus on both the workplaces and the life-histories of different engineers.

Technology as a manly direction in life

Mastering computers and computer systems is part of the personal biographies of most Microchips engineers, and has been for a long time. They have had a practical relation with microelectronics technology and with other technologies ever since their childhood, and to work with electronics and computers as a grown-up person is for many seen as a self-evident continuation of a life-long interest and in some cases a life-long passion. One of the engineers describes himself as well as his colleagues in the following way: "I guess we're all these kind of guys who take things apart and try to put them together in a different way."

For some of the boys at Microchips the work process seems to give as much satisfaction as the finished product. They are genuinely interested in technology in general and electronics in particular. The engineers at Automobile in a similar way often have an emotional relation to the car and it is a relation that has followed from their early adolescence. In general, it seems as if the car as a technological artifact tends to develop an emotionally committed practice. For many of the male design engineers, the design and construction of cars has become a life-long relationship. Quite a few talk about the comfort that comes from total absorption in a mechanical problem, when time stops and one becomes fully entranced by the machine.[11] In an interview a representative for the graduate engineers' union[12] at Automobile claimed that one of the factors making people stay at their jobs is that many of them have a profound and life-long interest in cars.

The emotional involvement that evidently many Automobile employees have with their jobs seems partly due to the open and highly visible technology that they deal with. Much of the design work still carries a character of craft and the work combines just as much practical sensibility as theoretical understandings. The workers have a direct and sensuous relation to the artifact. Those who do not share this relation to the technology are seen as marginal, as illustrated by one of the engineers' comment about a person who had left the department a few months earlier: "He was not a real chassis-man, he had something else, a lack of mechanical interest."

The real chassis-men are those who form the social core at the department. They are also the good story-tellers and can retell the history of the department, knowing the difference between skilled and less skilled chassis-men. A self-evident manly frame of reference is reproduced here.

Early experiences of machines constitute a common theme among these men sharing a practical relation to technology, as for instance in the case of Bertil, one of the engineers at Automobile, driving the tractor at the farm of his childhood:

> But then, this thing about vehicles and machines meant a lot since we had a tractor at home. Driving a tractor is fun – I still feel this way. Back then, you were expected to help out at home, and the thing I found most fun was driving the vehicles. And that interest is still with me. To drive a truck with or without a trailer, to drive a bus, and things like that, are in fact, almost like a dream – yes, they are!

These engineers testify to a technical interest that grew out of a childhood milieu where machines had been an integrated part of the local setting. Memories of a concrete practical skill and close relation to machines are recurrent. They describe their fathers as men who mastered a variety of skills such as carpeting, plumbing, small-scale farming and hunting. They said that taking part in those multi-skilled activities promoted their technical interest and practical relation to the surrounding world.

A permissive "do-it-yourself" attitude was pronounced and the engineers said that their parents promoted an early interest in machines and technical objects in general. A deft touch was considered as a positive social and cultural value. Machines and technical objects were within convenient reach. The boys' practicality was encouraged and given free reign. Another common denominator was that their families had their own houses, connected to the farm or the family business, offering much space to play as well as opportunities to keep outside the immediate supervision of their parents.

To the boys, this ability with machines milieu was an integrated part of their upbringing and a constitutive component of what it means to become a man. Technology is here an expressive part of various forms of masculinity. This is not least seen in the way that technical skills become a part of what it means to be a competent man, a man who can handle a variety of practical problems. Just as handling large quantities of alcohol, a practical multi-skilled ability belongs to a definition of masculinity in this context.

This also goes hand-in-hand with another recurrent theme in the childhood memories of these engineers. Microchips engineer Conny says:

> Yes, the thing is that one learns to become rather independent too. It is very much that your parents are not at home to take care of you, to look after you, so to speak, sitting next to you and watching what you do. Instead, one is outside playing, and then one comes up with the idea to build a cabin – one then get nails, a saw, and a hammer from the barn and builds oneself a cabin. At first, it might not look that great, but one had done it oneself. And one has watched one's dad hammer away and one has worked next to him ever since one was little ...

The virtue of being independent is strongly emphasized. It is learned early on in life. And to be independent means to be independent in relation to practical things. Conny continues:

CONNY: I think I'm rather practical. You know to repair, fix and paint – yes practical.
U.M.:   Mending and fixing up.
CONNY: At least I'm not all thumbs. I don't think I'm especially good at anything, but one manages. I believe that this is what one learns – to manage, so to speak.

The notion that "one finds a way" is seen as crucial. It is said to be the opposite of being practically helpless. Throughout their adolescence these engineers have continued along a similar path. They describe uncountable hours of repairing and fixing old cars, other motor vehicles and big machines. Olle, who was also brought up in the countryside, recounts the memories of his first car:

OLLE: Since one lived in the countryside, one was dependent on a car while in high school, while, at the same time, it was like a dream to be able to move around – the independence. I hardly had any money, so I was handed down a car. I spent an enormous amount of time on it. I got it about one year before I turned 18 – at that time it was a wreck.

U.M.:	What type of car was it?
OLLE:	A Mini Cooper. It had all imaginable problems, and one spent an enormous amount of time on it. That car took away a part of one's youth.

Another dimension of independence is here touched upon. An early technical interest, practical possibilities and living in the countryside coincide in Olle's case. To be technically skilled provides the ways and means to become independent by being mobile in the countryside. To have a car meant that he could visit friends in the vicinity, go to dances, and so on, that is, that he could acquire space outside the realms of his parents. To socialize and have a common interest in cars are things that Olle also mentions as being very important in his youth. In the center of these social activities stand vehicles of different sorts; as he explains: "It is a way of living." Others interviewed have had experiences similar to Olle's.

Most of the engineers[13] in the group portray themselves against a background that can be characterized as "technology as something self-evident." A technical interest during the early years of life self-evidently led to a subsequent career within the world of technology. Technological work is mapped out as the only feasible alternative, irrespective of social origin and gender. It has often been taken for granted and rarely been given much thought before, say several of the interviewees. Those who have the strongest understanding of "technology as something self-evident" are the engineers whose family background is working-class, farmers, or self-employed entrepreneurs. Their present occupations are described as a self-evident continuation of their early familiarity and fascination for technology, as illustrated by Microchips engineer Anton:

U.M.:	Were you involved with technology when you were younger?
ANTON:	Yes, I have always been fixated on technology, one was always working with bikes and mopeds and such things. That one always had to do. Sometimes more things broke than one repaired. I destroyed my brother's car once, one of the later ones, I had to later replace the engine. I have dabbled with electronics as long as I can remember. Yes, I still do.

In the life-story of Anton technology represents social continuity. It is something that maintains a path back to adolescence and often pleasant memories in relation to fathers. For those who, like Anton, have such a relation to technology, significant others that are referred to are exclusively male: a father, older brother, best friend, or, in one case, an enthusiastic teacher. No women are pointed out as significant others, and for the female engineers, the father seems to be of special importance for their way into the world of technology. In other words, to enter into the world of technology means entering a world of males and, irrespective of sex, the significant others referred to are exclusively men with the father standing out as the most important significant other.

What this shows, among other things, is that the gender codification of technology starts early and runs deep. As a parallel comparison to the strong gender codification of the world of technology, Nörvönen's (1994) biographical study of women's way into nursing shows that the significant others referred to are the mother, a sister, or an aunt, that is only female significant others. In their world an exclusive female world of care and nurturing exists early on and is being reproduced throughout life. The parallel is obvious and is also shown in the childhood memories of the engineers.

The childhood world described by both male and female engineers is also a world characterized by a strong spatial separation of work and leisure. In this world the gender roles of their fathers and mothers are described as being strongly differentiated. Memories of the father are often associated with him being absent because of work. The different spheres of the father and the mother also seem to have had different cultural directions and meanings. The world of work had come to symbolize turbulence and rapid change. In many ways family life is portrayed as being just the opposite; here stability and tradition are the emphasized values.

In all 17 life histories, childhood worlds are differentiated by gender. The domestic arena was solely directed by the women. Men rarely helped with housekeeping. The ideal of the housewife stands out as the dominate picture in all interviews. The "breadwinner" man of action complements the woman's domestic role. In this gender separated world, technology belongs to the men's sphere. This is especially true for men with a "practical-rural" background, and where a multi-skilled technical ability is part of what it means to be a competent man. A man who can take care of himself is a man who can manage a variety of practical skills, a man who never finds himself being practically helpless. In the different horizons of growing up in relation to technology that is described by these persons, the significant others are exclusively men. This is pronounced in spite of rural/urban orientations and gender. What these 17 engineers recall in the early memories of their way into technology is a world that is solely occupied by men.

However, in one respect there are clear differences as to how gender expectations work in relation to play, technical interests and the masculine world of technology. One telling example is the story of Anna. She is the only middle-aged woman in the group of engineers. In recounting her childhood, she says that her technical interests were continuously suppressed. She retells several episodes related to gender, technology and the resistance she met. She describes a continuous battle for her to get hold of desirable mechanical toys. One such episode is the following:

> My cousin who was two years older had got a model of a train set. I was five and he was seven. One Sunday just about the time when he had got his train set, he visited our house. He unpacked the train set and was about to run the set and my father was very interested and so was I. My cousin and my father started to run the set and then they say – "You are not allowed to join." "Why can't I?" "Well this is only for boys and not for girls so you can't be here." I was both sad and angry and it wounded me very much. I went out to the kitchen and complained to my mother. She would not understand how that could hurt me so much and said – "Well you have to help out here instead." – I think this was the time when I first decided to work with technology.

The story of Anna's adolescence is filled with similar experiences. Her father worked as a smith and her mother as a housewife. Anna is the only child in the family and she says that early on her father inspired her to play with tools, though he never encouraged her. But she persisted in her interests. Her father is described as a man who had a strong desire for learning. In Anna's description of her father, he also stands out as a most dexterous man. For example, he built the family's summer cottage. Whenever Anna was allowed to help her father with his different practical projects, she did. When Anna was seven years old, she managed to trade a few of her dolls for a Meccano set. Her parents refused to buy a Meccano set even though it was her number one wish on her list of presents. Anna mentioned that she always had to create her own space to play with technical things. There never was any self-evident space in her close environment where she was able to develop her technical interest. Accordingly, during her childhood she always had to face a certain resistance and she always had to strive for space. In her words: "Yes, there were reflections, many reflections when they said that it wouldn't work. Then one regretted that one was born a girl."

Anna's life within the world of technology has been marked with matching experiences. She recurrently portrays herself as one who continuously trespassed underlying gender-specific cultural boundaries by being a girl or later in life a woman engineer. The only significant other she mentions in relation to technology is her father, who is referred to throughout her life history. It is evident that her father has meant a lot to her, especially in relation to her technical interests. Her mother is hardly mentioned at all in the interview.

When I ask Anna about her occupational career, she replies: "You mean the absence of a career." Her understanding of her career is one of a non-career. She often compares herself to her male colleagues of the same generation. In most cases they have obtained far more responsible and prestigious positions. A theme in her life history is the resistance she has met and the hardships she has gone through. In recounting her life history, she recurrently returns to the adversities of her occupational career. For example, after Anna graduated as a mechanical engineer in 1968, she applied for altogether 50 different positions during a year. She applied for jobs from the very north of Sweden to the very south, but she was never accepted. To judge by Anna's experiences, there was solid resistance against women in industry at that time. She recounts that she drove around to many different manufacturing companies and personally presented herself, but even though many seem to have been positive toward her, none wanted to give her employment.

> I looked all the way from Skåne to the far north of Norrland. And everywhere the answer was no. Every time one got a no – of course, the first time one thought that it was rather natural that they didn't want me for just that job, but by the twenty-fifth job one began to wonder.

In retrospect, she cannot see any other reason besides her gender for not getting work at that time. Her male colleagues at Automobile who graduated the same year on average applied for two jobs and got at least one of them.

When we compare the experiences of Anna and the three younger female engineers of this study, it is clear that being a female engineer graduating in the 1980s has been a less laborious experience.[14] The experience of being a woman in a world dominated by men seems to have taken much less of their emotional energy, at least so far.

Microchips engineer Ingrid is the most articulate about her experiences of being a female in a male world. No doubt the reason for this is that she has two children. Becoming a mother has revealed certain features of her working life that she never thought about before. Before she had children, she worked many irregular hours. She took part in the gossip in the peer group at work and never thought much about it at the time. Now she feels that she misses the important informal discussions that take place after four o'clock. In Ingrid's words:

It is certain that nobody questions if one goes home at four o'clock, but in general there aren't many guys who must do it, therefore one is sometimes afraid of missing a part of the discussions which almost always takes place after four o'clock.

Consequently, social life at the company comprises those who do not have a family, that is the life and daily rhythm of the bachelors. They usually work late and arrive late in the morning. They work nights and weekends. A social rhythm circulating around times at the day care center as well as other family duties tends not to match up with the dominating rhythm of the bachelors at the workplace.

Generally, the company's male-centered social practice circulates around mastery, irregular working hours, social activities connected to technology, sports, alcohol and common educational experiences. The social life and informality of such an engineering practice is also due to social networks that stretch beyond the workplace and form an important part of the private lives of many engineers. Common experiences of life have generated a work style that more or less has become a full lifestyle. It is a microculture that predominantly has its preferences in a young male middle class. It is reproduced through culturally encapsulated institutional life environments such as the school, the common residential district close to the company, and the workplace. Sports and going to the pub are the most common forms of socializing. The engineers have had this style of interaction in common since their time at school. It does not exclude the women at the company, but during my stay at the company women rarely joined the men in activities during non-work time. In a few cases, a certain lack of experience in how to relate to women outside work was also discernible; these men socialized exclusively with other men and seemed to have more experience with computers than with women. Computers offered a predictable "partner" and a safe and secure environment. They even promised prospects for "eternal youth",[15] a state of pure juvenility, free from social intervention, in which one basically deals with the same problems one did as a technically interested child. One engineer, running air-battle simulations on two parallel computer screens in a project for the aircraft industry told me: "My work is just like playing computer games, the only difference is that this is reality."

Most engineers at Microchips share a deep fascination for technology that goes back to early childhood, which furthermore contributes to the production of common social and cultural frames of reference at the workplace. Thus, it is in these kinds of milieus that we clearly see how a masculine technical sociability is reproduced in daily practice. It is a sociability that rests upon a reproduction of masculinity in the microsocial situations of everyday life as well as masculine practices of socialization where a life-long close relation to technology is of crucial importance and partly constitutes what it means to be a man in Swedish society. In the world of "eternal youth" that the world of technology possibly offers, there is a secure social continuity to be at rest with. Perhaps the "eternal youth" offered by the world of technology promises a peaceful existential corner for men longing for a carefree existence in a world full of demands and obligations from both family and society.

Conclusion

Even though, by following the arguments raised in this paper, one may conclude that technical competence and practical ability comprise a fundamental component in the cultural construction of masculinity in Swedish society, is there any possibility or ground for answering the initial questions of this paper, namely, if there is an inherent relation between technology and masculinity?

   In the conclusion of my own work and with explicit references to the work of, for instance, Cockburn (1983, 1985), I would say that there is no reason for speaking of any such relation. Technology often plays a different role for men, and for most men in this study, the identification with technology is self-evident and taken for granted. It is part of what it means to be a man. It has been an essential part of their upbringing as boys. It closely connects to definitions of what is masculine and what is not. Owning a multi-skilled technical ability belongs to such a definition of what it means to be masculine. In contrast, to be practically helpless is not masculine, but is rather portrayed as feminine. As Wajcman (1991, p. 159) writes: "technical competence is central to the dominant cultural ideal of masculinity, and its absence a key feature of stereotyped femininity."

   If technology and technical skill are constitutive features of what it means to be masculine, the relation between femininity and technology is typically portrayed as one of non-existence. But, as for instance Cockburn (1985) shows, women use technology to the same extent as men do, and women are just as skilled in using machines as men are. Nevertheless, womanly technical skills are rarely defined as technical skills because technology is conceived to be basically a masculine cultural expression. For women technology is rarely part of their identity, whereas for many men it is. But there is nothing inherently masculine about technology and masculinity, like femininity, are culturally and historically constructed forms that are open to change. One of the important tasks of gender research on men and masculinities should then be:

> emphasising the subjectivity of masculinity as a way of unmasking and depowering men's pretensions to objectivity, one of the important elements in anchoring patriarchal privilege ... and thereby discredit their pretensions to universality (Hearn, 1989, pp. 39-43).

In regard to gender research, the form of professional middle-class masculinity that is being reproduced within engineering is something that can be refereed to as a hegemonic form of masculinity and a career-oriented form of life. In Western culture, this is the kind of masculinity that sets the standards for other men and women and against which other men and women are measured. Kimmel (1994, pp. 122ff) discusses this as the marketplace manhood. It is a notion of manhood rooted in the sphere of production, the public arena, a masculinity based on successful participation in the marketplace competition. He suggests that this is a model for masculinity for which identity rests on homosocial competition. Indeed he argues that masculinity is a homosocial enactment because what such a hegemonic form of masculinity strives for is to receive manhood and manhood is received in competition with other men. Such a manhood is also equated with power and domination of women and other non-hegemonic forms of masculinity.

Furthermore, this form of hegemonic masculinity and career-oriented form of life, where notions such as individualism, compartmentalization and periodization are crucial components, are to be seen as a reproductive cultural form at the productive heart of Western culture, that is science and technology. As such, it is just as much a cultural construct as any "exotic" form of life far away from the anthropologist's own cultural hemisphere. During the past two decades, several anthropologists have emphasized the need to anthropologize the West. As Rabinow (1986, p. 241) argues, we need to "exoticize" those domains which are taken most for granted as universal, to "make them seem as historically and culturally peculiar as possible; show how their claims to truth are linked to social practices and have hence become effective forces in the social world."

Technology is one of those domains because engineering and technological innovation are at the core of "universal" modernity. Yet, any such practice is far from universal, but instead is socially and culturally constructed according to varying contexts. Still, what often makes technology and technological practice peculiar is exactly its belief in a decontextualized universalism, and its hegemonic pretensions as tools and expressions of perceived cultural sovereignty.

Nevertheless, social practices and individual perspectives in this profession are constituted and formed at a micro level of social interaction, in a professional activity at the ideological heart of Western culture. What I finally argue for here is that such a microcultural approach also speaks to larger cultural processes in our society because social practices are always embedded within cultural systems of meaning, produced and reproduced in particular activities at particular places in particular relationships.

Notes

1. Preface to Lewis W. Hine's book *Men at Work*, 1932.
2. Mellström, 1995.
3. See for example Brod, 1987; Kimmel and Messner, 1989; Hearn and Morgan (eds), 1990; Brod and Kaufman, 1994; Connell, 1995.
4. Duroche, 1990; Kimmel, 1994; Connell, 1987, 1995, 1996.
5. See for example Cockburn, 1983, 1985; Wajcman, 1991; as well as Hacker, 1978, 1981, 1989.
6. However, here we see clear changes over the last 30 years. Of all the engineers with a Masters degree in 1960/61, 2.3 per cent were women. In 1988/89 the same figures were 25.1 per cent (Source: The Engineering Union, 1990).
7. Berner, 1984.
8. These names are pseudonyms.
9. For a discussion of metaphors and culture, see Merten and Schwartz, 1982; Fernandez, 1974; Levi-Strauss, 1966; and Douglas, 1966.
10. See for example Tannen, 1993; Henley and Kramarae, 1991.
11. None of the women talk about such a relation even though they have a profound mechanical interest.
12. CF, Civilingenjörs Förbundet.
13. Thirteen out of 17.
14. They were born during the 1960s and graduated in the 1980s, while Anna was born in the 1940s.
15. Tracy Kidder writes about engineers and boyishness in his book *The Soul of a New Machine*: "Part of the fascination, it is just little boys that never grow up, playing with erector sets. Engineers just don't lose that, and if you do lose that you can't be an engineer anymore."

References

Berner, B. (1984) "Women, Technology and the Division of Labour. What is the Role of Education?", *Tidskrift för Nordisk förening för Pedagogisk forskning*, 2, pp. 5-17.

Brod, H. (ed.) (1987) *The Making of Masculinities, the New Men's Studies.* Boston: Allen and Unwin.

Brod, H. and Kaufman, M. (eds) (1994) *Theorizing Masculinities.* London: Sage Publications.

Chodorow, N. (1978) *The Reproduction of Mothering: Psychoanalysis and the Sociology of Gender.* Berkeley: University of California Press.

Cockburn, C. (1983) *Male Dominance and Technological Change.* London: Pluto Press.

Cockburn, C. (1985) *Machinery of Dominance: Women, Men and Technical Know-How.* London: Pluto Press.

Connell, R. W. (1987) *Gender and Power: Society, the Person, and Sexual Politics.* Cambridge: Polity Press.

Connell, R. W. (1995) *Masculinities.* Berkeley: University of California Press.

Connell, R. W. (1996) "New Directions in Gender Theory," *Ethnos: Journal of Anthropology*, National Museum of Ethnography, Stockholm, Vol. 61, pp. 3-4, Scandinavian University Press, 1996.

Douglas, M. (1966) *Purity and Danger, An Analysis of the Concepts of Pollution and Taboo.* London: Routledge & Kegan Paul.

Duroche, L. (1990) "Male perception as social construct," in Hearn, J. and Morgan, D. (eds), *Men, Masculinities and Social Theory.* London: Unwin Hyman.

Easlea, B. (1983) *Fathering the Unthinkable.* London: Pluto Press.

Fernandez, J. (1974) "The Mission of Metaphor in Expressive Culture," *Current Anthropology*, 15 (2), pp. 119-33.

Gilligan, C. (1982) *In a Different Voice: Psychological Theory and Women's Development.* Cambridge, Mass.: Harvard University Press.

Hacker, S. (1981) "The Culture of Engineering: Woman, Workplace and Machine," *Women's Studies International Quarterly*, 4 (3), pp. 343-51.

Hacker, S. (1989) *Pleasure, Power and Technology.* Boston: Unwin Hyman.

Hacker, S. L. (1978) "Man and Humanism: Language, Gender and Power," *Humanity and Society*, 2, pp. 62-78.

Hearn, J. and Morgan, D. (eds) (1990) *Men, Masculinities and Social Theory.* London: Unwin Hyman.

Henley, N. M. and Kramarae, C. (1991) "Gender, Power, and Miscommunication," in Coupland, N., Giles, H. and Wiemann, J. M., *Miscommunication and Problematic Talk.* London: Sage Publications.

Hine, L. W. (1977) *Men at Work. Photographic Studies of Modern Men and Machines.* New York: Dover Publications (1932).

Kidder, T. (1982) *The Soul of a New Machine.* London: Penguin Books.

Kimmel, M. (1994) "Masculinity as Homophobia: Fear, Shame, and Silence in the Construction of Gender Identity," in Brod, H. and Kaufman, M. (eds), *Theorizing Masculinities.* London: Sage Publications.

Kimmel, M. (ed.) (1987) *Changing men: New Directions in Research on Men and Masculinity.* London: Sage Publications.

Kimmel, M. and Messner, M. (eds) (1989) *Men's Lives.* New York: Macmillan.

Lakoff, G. and Johnson, M. (1980) "Conceptual Metaphors in Everyday Language," *Journal of Philosophy*, 77 (8), August.

Levi-Strauss, C. L. (1966) *The Savage Mind*. Chicago: Chicago University Press.

Mellström, U. (1995) *Engineering Lives: Technology, Time and Space in a Male-Centred World*. Linköping: Linköping Studies in Arts and Science, no. 128.

Merten, D. and Schwartz, G. (1982) "Metaphor and Self: Symbolic Process in Everyday Life," *American Anthropologist*, 84, pp. 796-810.

Rabinow, P. (1986) "Representations are Social Facts: Modernity and Post-Modernity in Anthropology," in Clifford, J. and Marcus, G. (eds), *Writing Culture. The Poetics and Politics of Ethnography*. Berkeley: University of California Press.

Tannen, D. (ed.) (1993) *Gender and conversational interaction*. New York: Oxford University Press.

Traweek, S. (1988a) *Beamtimes and Lifetimes. The World of High-Energy Physicists*. Cambridge, Mass.: Harvard University Press.

Traweek, S. (1988b) "Discovering Machines: Nature in the Age of Its Mechanical Reproduction," in Dubinskas, F. A. (ed.), *Making Time: Ethnographies of High-Technology Organisations*. Philadelphia: Temple University Press.

Turkle, S. (1984) *The Second Self*. New York: Simon and Schuster.

Wajcman, J. (1991) *Feminism Confronts Technology*. Cambridge: Polity Press.

Willis, P. (1977) *Learning to Labour: How Working Class Kids get Working Class Jobs*. New York: Columbia University Press.

Chapter 10

Contingency and Desire: The Ritual Construction of Masculinity in a Right-Wing Political Youth Organization

PHILIP LALANDER

Masculinity as a ritual

Masculinity is something which is done. Men in different positions try, through *rituals*, to describe and define themselves as men, and at the same time to distinguish themselves from what they do not apprehend as being masculine. Through sports, drinking, joking, working and riding motorbikes they try to live up to different images regarding masculinity.

The construction of masculinity is especially problematic in contemporary society, in which earlier definitions of how a man should behave have been challenged. During the 1960s and 1970s women's liberation and the gay movement questioned masculine dominance and rationality (Connell, 1995). Female pop/rock stars such as Janis Joplin, Siouxsie Sioux and Nina Hagen showed that women can behave as men, drink, shout and live on the edge. Male pop/rock stars such as David Bowie, The Sweet and Alice Cooper performed and were dressed in more androgynous outfits than earlier artists. By acting as if they were androgynes their presence questioned what masculinity really is and how it should be acted out.

This questioning of the definitions of gender means, on the one hand, a greater freedom for people: men and women can play with gender roles and are not so restrained by moral rules concerning what is masculine or feminine. On the other hand, it may lead to feelings of uncertainty and "feelings of homelessness" (Berger *et al.*, 1973). People need to be able to describe and define themselves as something. To define oneself as a man gives a man feelings of certainty. But, as masculinity has become blurred, this is not an easy thing to do.

Masculinity thus is not something given, but rather something which is achieved through different types of rituals. Most of these rituals take place in the social group, and people who do masculine things together believe in themselves as being masculine when they are aware of other people's participation in the group or attendance at the ritual. We mirror ourselves through the other. That is, to be seen by others as masculine strengthens our belief in our own masculinity and *identity*. Following the theories of Goffman (1959), people constantly express themselves in ways designed to show other people and themselves who they are. They try to dramatize different *roles* or *characters* in order to reinforce their beliefs in their identities. Identity is thus, in Goffman's sense, far from given; rather it is a matter of ritualizing and dramatizing a character.

In this essay I will analyze a group of young Swedish politicians from a relativelly small town, here called Small Town, in Sweden and another group, from the same political organization but from the neighbor city, here called Middle Town. These two groups belong to the same political organization, with a liberal conservative ideology uniting the members.[1] These groups were intimately related and interacted with each other frequently. The cultures in the groups were very much alike because the Small Town organization was highly influenced by the organization in Middle Town. I will therefore treat the cultures of the groups as one.

Ethnographic methods (see for example Agar, 1980) are used in order to get a comprehensive view of how young people view themselves and their surroundings and how they act in everyday life. I gathered data by conducting approximately 15 interviews, most of which would be characterized as what Burgess (1982) calls "the unstructured interview." These interviews were relatively informal. I did not, for example, arrange close-ended questions. Rather, I tried to make the interview appear like an everyday conversation. The interviews took place in their homes, their club house, in the street, in some restaurants or in a car. I waited until I had gotten to know the respondents before conducting the interviews, because I wanted them to be able to speak to me from their hearts and not from some strategic position. We also held several group discussions in which we discussed topics such as jobs, school, pub life, the family, the future and so on. My main method of data gathering was participant observation, sitting in their club house playing a game, being at the disco or the pub, in order to become familiar with their natural settings. I was in contact with the groups from late summer 1994 until late spring 1995.

This essay is an attempt to problematize culture and identity construction, and to do this I will highlight two characters or roles, which are seen as valuable in their culture: the *Swedish hero* and the *perverted politician*. These characters are closely linked with masculinity and with ritualizing masculinity. Before I discuss these characters in detail, I will review the groups' culture in general, which is important to know if one is to understand the basis for their identity construction.

The liberal conservative ideology

The young politicians I studied despise the state and feel that a free economy is something society can really gain from. In a group discussion they expressed what they think about when they hear the word "socialism":

> JOHAN: I think about coercion, misgovernment and coercion. And I think about imprisonment and I think about non-democracy. And I think about Stalin, Lenin and Marx. That's what I think when I hear the word socialism.
> KICKI: Well, I more think of being choked or so.
> JOHAN: Yeah ...
> STAFFAN: Mean old men telling me how to behave, so I can't say what I want, then they are socialists.

We also discussed the state:

> STAFFAN: We hate the state.
> JOHAN: We have that in common with the neoliberals, to hate the state.
> STAFFAN: Yeah, the state should have three functions: defence, judicial system and infrastructural building. If they take care of that, the rest of Sweden will manage on its own.

Despising the state and the socialists were dominant themes and central symbols in their culture. Another part of their culture was their devotion to Swedish traditions. The Royal family, Swedish party traditions, the bourgeois family, are important for them in order to uphold order in society. It seemed as if they were longing for a Sweden that doesn't exist any more.

This ideology was reproduced through jokes, discussions in their club house, courses on ideology, public campaigns and so on. The jokes very often included irony and sarcasm directed toward the social democrats. After staying in the organization for some period of time, the ideology became naturalized and was seen as the only truth. For example, they discuss why people vote for the social democrats:

KICKI: If you join the Red Rose (the social democrats' children's organization) when you are five, you can't do more than voting for the social democrats later on.

STAFFAN: Then ... that so many people vote for the social democrats doesn't mean that they believe in their politics, but rather that they are stuck in their collectivistic way of thinking. They don't have the energy to learn about the political questions and the differences between different programs and they just see that a lot of people vote for them and then they think: "Well then I better vote for them too."

JOHAN: They don't care about who they vote for either, they sort of ... "now the social democrats have had that many votes, so I better vote for them ..."

KICKI: There is still class voting and habitual voting among older people. In my family it is like that, not my parents, but all mama's brothers and sisters, that "we have voted for the social democrats all our life and we'll do it till we dieeeeeeee."

The ideology thus became more and more legitimized and in the end was naturalized and seen as one of the facts of life. This gave their lives and identities a form of stability, since they may view themselves as enlightened and rational while other people are viewed as being less aware, uneducated and irrational. Their ideology becomes a world map, which helps them to relate their identities to the surrounding world.

The Swedish hero

The organization, which encompasses both Middle Town and Small Town, has a strong masculine dominance. Pictures of political leaders in Middle Town's club house only include men. The men in the organization have leading roles at parties. Kicki, a woman who has a strong position in Small Town's organization, is an exception.

In Middle Town they quite frequently have parties. These parties are very traditionally Swedish and are often held in conjunction with Swedish festival days, such as crayfish-parties, a strong Swedish tradition in which people drink a lot of liquor and eat crayfish. Small Town's organization arranged a crayfish-party and invited people outside the organization, with an invitation formulated like this:

> We hereby have the honor to invite you to our crayfish party the 12th of August in the club house in Small Town. For 100 kronor you will get crawfish, bread, salad and a snaps. We also have snaps and beer to sell for these who so wish ...

What is especially important in this invitation is the snaps. Snaps are offered not only in order to recruit new members, but also as part of rituals constructing Swedish traditions and masculinity. In autumn 1994, the Middle Town organization held a party called Swedish Evening. I asked a member of the organization what this means and he said:

> Well, be a Swede, getting pissed.

At these kinds of parties they often saluted each other and the last snaps was sold by auction. This was a tradition in the organization. At some parties they saluted the King and sang royalist songs. This was done in a collectivistic manner. Before the election in 1994 they made their own beer-bottles, on the label of which they printed a verse from the Swedish national poet Essaias Tegnér. The poem tells a story about King Karl XII, who in the poem is called "den unge hjälte" (the young hero). King Karl, who is famous in Sweden for his many battles, pulls his sword from his belt, and enters the field of battle. The enemies are the Russians, but King Karl doesn't fear them. What is important for the "young hero" is to fight for Sweden.

The Swedish King is a central symbol in the organization. As the text says, he is a hero, someone who doesn't fight shy of anything, who is willing to fight for his beloved Sweden. By having the King as a central symbol and by invoking this symbol in rituals, the men in the organization feel like heroes themselves and like true Swedes. To be a man was therefore equivalent to being a true Swede.

The capitalist was also seen as a hero by some people in the organization. To be able to make a good deal was a highly valued skill. The chairman of the Middle Town organization labeled his video cassettes with his name followed by "private capitalist." Being a capitalist was something to be proud of. He also explained to me once that "what unites us is the collective fight against socialism." They saw themselves as warriors, heroes, fighting against evil, in this case socialism. One can use a metaphor here and say that they were knights fighting dragons. This part of masculinity I call "the Swedish hero." But there was another part of masculinity, which was very different from the part I have just described.

The perverted politician

At the parties in Middle Town the men played the leading roles regarding drinking, joking and singing. When Mia, a member of the Middle Town organization, did a public performance in conjunction with a party, one of the male members shouted: "Show the cunt!!!" Mia was also often imitated because she had such a bright voice. There was a rule that one should not bring a girlfriend to these parties. This can be seen as a strategy by which they constantly maintain masculine dominance in the organization. By describing women as sexual objects, they deny that women can be as rational as "real" men. I also witnessed a number of occasions when younger members bragged about sexual conquests. The women can be seen as a constructed "them," which the men used to reinforce their own feelings of masculinity and to reduce doubts concerning the same.

The experiences from partying were very important in the organization. To take part at these parties could give you a good reputation. A member from Small Town describes these parties:

> First of all there's booze at no cost, free liquor and there's every opportunity for those coming to the party and there's some food too, on top of that. And then you sit down and eat and then you socialize. Then you get loaded, at first 'cause a little whisky tastes good and all that, and then, later, 'cause you're so pissed so you think that, I might just get more pissed ... And the last time we had a party, it ended with Anders Carlsson, who is now our vice chairman or is he the second chairman, he was lying stark naked on the toilet floor and had thrown up, we put him in a taxi to take him home [laughter]. So the next thing of course was that he threw up in the taxi as well, in between the window and the door... Alexander who was a secretary at the time, he suggested we should go over to my place to carry on the party, so that's what we did of course. ... It all ended with one of our members dancing on the roof of a discothèque and the police coming to arrest him. Another member fell flat on his face outside a shop that was still open and so he had to be picked up by the police to sober up. The other member who was with him, he went to McDonald's to grab a hamburger and he ended up being stabbed in the leg ...

This narrative includes myths about how the man in the organization should behave. It is important to be wild and bizarre, to do the opposite of what you "normally" can expect from a politician. At big parties it was more or less a tradition that three well-respected male members carried out a strip-tease performance to the tune of the punk/rock song "Pervers Politiker" (Perverted Politician) by the Swedish band Ebba Grön. This song is about a politician who lies and deceives people. Later in the evening, however, this politician changes character and becomes perverted, spanking, hitting in a bizarre way. In this song the role of the politician is totally inverted compared to how politicians are supposed to act in democratic nations. The perverted politician takes a greater interest in "women in rubber" and in spanking and hard cocks than in ideological debate or income policy issues. At a party I once asked the chairman of Middle Town organization how I could gain respect in the organization. He told me to shock them, to strip nude or do something which they wouldn't expect.

In the club house in Middle Town there were two vacuum cleaners which were kept for special applications. One of them was used to clean up vomit, the other was used in a ritual for male members. On some occasions they captured one of the members, pulled down his trousers and placed the tube around his penis. Then they switched on the vacuum cleaner. This was both a legend and a practice in reality. Relatively new members told me about it, expressing both disgust and fascination. A member who had left the organization told me that it wasn't something to be really upset about, it was more or less part of the game:

BERTIL: There are probably different vacuum cleaners. In the old club house they had the classical one, it's an old vacuum cleaner, which they used to take away vomits with, but the other one is more sexual, as one says.

PL: What do they use it for?

BERTIL: It's for sticking the penis into it, well not masturbation to its full extent, more as a joke or so. I have been the subject of it ... when was that? Well, it was at a big political meeting for the district, I think it was 1991 or something like that, when I was elected to be in the board of directors in the organization, it was the day before my birthday. And Lasse Svensson, he was also in the board, I was his best friend, he had a sister anyway and Leif was chosen to be the chairman of the organization ... Well, anyhow, Lasse gave his sister to

Leif as a gift for his success in the election. But he had to exploit her, we used to call it that, before midnight, because after that it was my birthday, and then I would have her as a birthday gift. Leif and I shared a hotel room, but Leif got very drunk and he was supposed to be a representative too, so he forgot about it. But I managed, though she wasn't really cooporative, to make her follow me to the hotel room and then when we had started to undress, the other members took a taxi to the clubhouse, fetched the vacuum cleaner, and back to the hotel. They rushed into the hotel room, grabbed the vacuum cleaner, wrestled me down, and then they sucked ... It's a classical trick in the organization I believe.

PL: The vacuum cleaner?

BERTIL: Yes, the vacuum cleaner, it's used a lot down there ...

PL: How did you feel when you were a victim to it?

BERTIL: Well, I thought it was kind of funny, or so ... I had been in the organization for a while. I acted as they wanted, so to say. I understood what was going on from the beginning ...

PL: But, what about that girl?

BERTIL: Well, she got dressed and went away, I believe. But she had been around since she was around 14, so she knew everybody quite well.

This is not just a story about perversion, it is also a story about male power. The words Bertil uses indicate that the man is the controller; for example, when he says "exploit her," he indicates that women are quite passive while men are active conquerors. One can quite easily see a homological relation between this story and the song "Pervers Politiker." In both of them the man is the controller of the woman, who is seen as a relatively more or less passive object. The use of the vacuum cleaner fits well with the character of the perverted politician. Bertil's comments also indicate how institutionalized this ritual has become in the organization. It serves two functions: first, to escape from the boundaries of everyday life, to do what is not expected, for example by playing with the penis; second, to exclude women from the inner life in the organization. Women cannot actually take part in the ritual, simply because they don't have a penis.

In this organization, if one wants to be seen as a politician one has to go to parties, brag about sexual experiences, get drunk, tell bizarre jokes and show the character of a perverted politician.

Mixing the characters for masculine dominance

If young men participate in both the Swedish and the perverted rituals they may gain good positions in the organization. Using Bourdieu's (1992) words, perversion and Swedishness are *symbolic capital*, resourses they need in order to improve or establish their position. But the members must be skillful when they move from one character to another. For them to be able to act as ordinary politicians during the daytime, and as nationalists and perverts at night-time, they must have the ability to be both rational and perverted. The language in the organization reflects this switching between characters. This can be seen in some of their remarks:

> "Our dear vice chairman ..." (rational title) "he drank away his shoes" (loss of control) "He puked in a cab ..." (loss of control) "but the organization paid for it" (control). "But Leif got very drunk ..." (loss of control) "and he was supposed to be a representative too ..." (rational behavior).

To act in both a controlled and an almost perverted way is a legendary quality in the organization. One must – so to speak – go from wildness to rationality and back to wildness, to become a legend. But women cannot do that, since they are excluded as possible heroes. The perverted politician whips "women in rubber," King Karl is a man, the snaps songs are about men and the vacuum cleaner makes a fit for the penis. The rituals are thus formed to include men who are wild and rational and to exclude women, because they don't fit into the frame of this culture.

The use of alcohol and the permission to deviate from rules of self-control in modern society have historically been privileges for men in Swedish society. This is reflected in statistics concerning gender-specific drinking: men drank more than twice as much as women during the past two decades (Folkhälsoinstitutet and CAN, 1997). Drinking, for many people, is closely related to masculinity, and from this reasoning one can see drinking as a rite of passage (Turner, 1969) into a masculine order. Alcohol serves as a symbol in this masculine rite of passage, and hard liquor and beer work better than wine, because wine is often drunk by women (Norell and Thörnquist, 1995).

As noted earlier, the pictures of former party leaders on the wall of the club house are all of men. A women cannot have any real success in switching from rationality to perversion, simply because she is a woman. She lacks the symbolic capital necessary to compete for a better position, or, to put it in another way, the interpretation of women's actions follows a logic different from that used to interpret men's actions. The implicit message of the rituals in the organization is that women cannot have dominant positions. All the legendary figures in the organization are men, because a drinking and intoxicated man is seen as a hero, while a woman in the same situation is seen as an object, someone who has lost control. Male dominance is thus reconstructed through partying.

Another important condition to understand if one is to get a good view of the construction of masculinity is how these young men treat transgressions from everyday life. The wild and bizarre practices are kept as *secrets* between the male members. This cements solidarity and tightens the social bonds between the members. It gives them a feeling of knowing something that other people don't know. The fact that the perverted character is so far away from the normal definition of how politicians are supposed to act, makes the secrets even more exciting. Simmel writes about secrets:

> The secret in this sense, the hiding of realities by negative or positive means, is one of man's greatest achievements. In comparison with the childish stage in which every conception is expressed at once, and every undertaking is accessible to the eyes of all, the secret produces an immense enlargement of life: numerous contents of life cannot even emerge in the presence of full publicity. The secret offers, so to speak, the possibility of a second world alongside the manifest world; and the latter is decisively influenced by the former (Simmel, 1950, p. 330).

Thus masculine solidarity is reinforced not just by the fact that the males mostly participate in the perverted and Swedish rituals, but also the fact that they share secrets that they do not share with potential voters. To use Goffman's (1959) words, *dark secrets* are only articulated *back stage*, and never in front of the audience. We must therefore see the culture of this organization as a second world – a secret society – in which men have unrestricted power to construct masculinity and to escape boundaries of everyday life and still get away with it.

The ritual construction of masculinity

The rituals that construct masculinity and male dominance are performed at night-time in conjunction with parties. Drinking alcohol is, to a large extent, a symbolic sign for entering into this imaginative and secret society in which male power is beyond question (Lalander, 1997a and 1998). But what do these masculine characters really mean, and why are they seen as symbolic capital?

For Bauman (1991) the postmodern mentality is characterized by *contingency*. By this he means that today we are quite uncertain about what a good ideology, identity or life plan are. Modern mentality was characterized by certainty, that we knew – at least we thought so – the difference between good and evil, male and female, nature and culture and so on. Modern society was marked by its efforts to find grand solutions to different kinds of social problems, and social engineering was part of that modern mentality. But as ideologies come and go and none of them appear to be the perfect one, the postmodern mentality of contingency is shaped.

> Postmodernity is modernity coming of age: modernity looking at itself at a distance rather than from inside, making a full inventory of its gains and losses, psychoanalysing itself, discovering the intentions it never before spelled out ... Postmodernity is modernity coming to terms with it own impossibility; a self-monitoring modernity, one that consciously discards what it was once unconsciously doing (Bauman, 1991, p. 272).

If our mentalities are categorized by contingency this entails an increased reflection concerning what is good or bad, nature or culture, masculine or feminine. One can see this kind of postmodern society from two viewpoints. On the one hand, individuals may experience increased degrees of freedom, since they can reflect upon their own possibilities from a less fixed frame of reference. This view can be found in theories by Giddens (1991), Ziehe (1986) and Bauman (1991). On the other hand, it is difficult to construct and uphold identity in postmodern society, because different realities coexist (see Berger *et al.*, 1973; Ziehe, 1986; Bauman, 1991; and Giddens, 1991).

To define oneself as a man is one opportunity among others for confirming one's identity. But, since the definition of masculinity is not fixed, it becomes a matter of choice regarding which masculinity to pick. And when a certain type of masculinity is picked one must, using Barthes' (1972) words, try to manifest it or even *naturalize* it. Masculinity must be ritualized, since it is not given, it is not totally evident. It is the same with religious rituals. Since we cannot see God we must ritualize the existence of God, to make the idea legitimate and almost natural.

To be both Swedish and bizarre/perverted are the characters of masculinity held in the political organization I have studied. If one can establish a balanced connection between wildness and Swedishness one can become a legend. These two parts of the image of masculinity in the organization reflect two needs of the individual. First of all it reflects the search for ontological security (Giddens, 1991), a state of mind in which the world is seen as natural and relatively easy to control and understand. Ziehe writes about how young people in contemporary societies strive for *ontologization*. By this he means that contemporary youths, as a consequence of de-traditionalization, try to find something with which they may explain and rationalize their own existence and identity. They solve their problems of homelessness and contingency by creating what they believe are true and natural traditions. In their micro-culture, the Swedish hero is a central character. Their culture may be seen as an alternative and imaginative society – constructed in order to repair their identities and make them more solid. In this community they have the power, and not somebody else. It can be seen as a temporary vaccination against feelings of uncertainty and ambivalence.

Perversion, however, represents the second central character in their culture and also in their definition of genuine masculinity. This character can be understood from two points of view. First of all it can be seen as a character through which they demonstrate their independence from adult society, socialism and the state. By doing things that are not accepted by society in general, they gain feelings of independence and supremacy. When they ritualize perversion they experience it as if they have power over their lives and their bodies. By stripping to "Pervers Politiker," they reinforce this feeling of power. Perverted acts can be seen as a form of symbolic resistance, as a resistance through rituals.

On the other hand, perversions may be seen as acts by which young people escape boundaries in everyday life, to experience another dimension of life, to fulfill one's desires. In this perspective drinking can be seen as a rite of passage (Turner, 1969), through which they enter another reality in which many acts not permitted in everyday life are permitted and even approved.[2] By drinking and showing strong independence they get the feeling that they can control their surroundings. When they experience this feeling they also think that they can do things which are otherwise seen as taboo.

Perversions can thus be seen as ingredients in another kind of reality, a *liminal reality* (Turner, 1969), which it is difficult to distinguish from what can be called the paramount reality (Berger and Luckmann, 1966). This liminal reality must, however, be pre-structured (Turner, 1969). Drinking and singing are parts of the pre-structuring process. When these young politicians enter this liminal reality the things which Johan talked about earlier can happen – they may now strip off their clothes and tell bizarre jokes. This is not just due to the toxic effect, but may also be seen as a consequence of a number of rituals which have taken place at the party.

Their culture thus makes it possible for the actors to define themselves, to ontologize and to escape the prison of everyday life. The actors can then experience feelings of both freedom and stability. The definition of masculinity is thus the character of a man who, on the one hand, has good control, yet, on the other hand, may let this control go. One side of this image is a man who is very traditionally masculine, while the other side reveals a man who is closer to being a pervert. In my view the first part of masculinity concerns identity, while the second part is related to *desire* and search for freedom. The young politicians embody a contradiction – getting out of prison and imprisoning oneself. But perhaps that is a typical characteristic of men today, who live with contraditions and ambivalence. The first part of masculinity is, to a large extent, created to deal with and reduce doubts concerning their own sexuality, but the other part contradicts this first part.

In growing up, these men, and some women, experience doubts concerning who they are. These feelings are closely related to contemporary society, which, as Bauman states, makes mentalities contingent and ambivalent. One way to escape from contingency and ambivalence is to pick up, from history, what they think is true masculinity. The hero, the King and Swedish tradition are ingredients in this construction, which they use to stabilize their identities. To believe in them they must ritualize them in the group. But they need something else, something related to their bodies and desires, and therefore they construct the other part of masculinity, "the perverted man."

Notes

1. This group was studied in my dissertation project in which I analyzed three different social groups and their image of alcohol and alcohol consumption. See Lalander, 1998, *Anden i flaskan – Alkoholens betydelser i olika ungdomsgrupper* (The Spirit in the Bottle – The meaning of alcohol in different youth groups) and 1997b, "Gemenskap, frihet och svenskhet – eller ormen i Edens lustgård" (Solidarity, freedom and Swedishness – or the snake in the Garden of Eden).
2. In Lalander, 1997a, "Beyond everyday order; breaking away with alcohol," I analyze how these young politicians use alcohol to transgress the norms of everyday-life. I discuss and use concepts such as liminality (Turner, 1969), carnival (Bakhtin, 1968) and rites of passage (Turner, 1969). This is also done in Lalander, 1998.

References

Agar, M. H. (1980) "The Professional Stranger – An Informal Introduction to Ethnography," Berkeley: Academic Press.

Bakhtin, M. M. (1968) "Rabelais and his World," Cambridge: MIT Press.

Barthes, R. (1972) "Mythologies," London: Vintage, 1993.

Bauman, Z. (1991) "Modernity and Ambivalence," Cambridge: Polity Press.

Berger, P., Berger, B. and Kellner, H. (1973*) The Homeless Mind – Modernization and Consciousness.* New York: Random House.

Berger, P. and Luckmann, T. (1966) *The Social Construction of Reality.* London: Penguin Books, 1987.

Bourdieu, P. (1992) *Distinction – A Social Critique of the Judgement of Taste.* London: Routledge.

Burgess, R. G. (ed.) (1982) *Field research: a Sourcebook and Field Manual.* Boston and Sydney: Allen & Unwin.

Connell, R. W. (1995) *Masculinities: Knowledge, power and social change.* Berkeley: University of California Press.

Ebba Grön (1980) "'Pervers Politiker,' on the record We're only in it for the drugs," Sweden: Mistlur Records.

Folkhälsoinstitutet and CAN (1997) "Alkohol- och narkotikautvecklingen i Sverige – *Rapport 97* (The development of alcohol and narcotic use in Sweden)," Stockholm.

Giddens, A. (1991) *Modernity and Self-Identity.* Cambridge: Polity Press.

Goffman, E. (1959) *The Presentation of Self in Everyday Life.* London: Penguin Books, 1974.

Lalander, P. (1997a) "Beyond everyday order; breaking away with alcohol," *Nordic Studies on Alcohol and Drugs* (Nordisk alkohol and narkotikatidskrift).

Lalander, P. (1997b) "Gemenskap, frihet och svenskhet – eller ormen i Edens lustgård," *Socialt perspektiv*, 2-3.

Lalander, P. (1998) *Anden i flaskan – Alkoholens betydelser i olika ungdomsgrupper.* Stockholm/Stehag: Symposion Förlag.

Norell, M. and Törnquist, C. (1995*) Berättelser om ruset, alkoholens mening för 20-åringar.* Stockholm/Stehag: Symposion Förlag.

Sernhede, O. (1994) "Ungdomskulturen och det Andra – Identitet, motstånd och etnicitet," Göteborg: Daidalus.

Tegnér, E. (1876) *Samlade skrifter:* Nationalupplaga. Stockholm: Norstedt & Söner.

Turner, V. (1969) *The Ritual Process – Structure and Anti-Structure.* Chicago: Aldine Publishing Company.

Ziehe, T. (1986) "Inför avmystifieringen av världen. Ungdom och kulturell modernisering," in M. Löfgren and A. Molander (eds), *Postmoderna tider.* Finland: Norstedts förlag.

Chapter 11

A Death Mask of Masculinity: The Brotherhood of Norwegian Right-Wing Skinheads

KATRINE FANGEN

At a party arranged by the right-wing skinhead subculture in Norway, a band is playing, and young men gather in front of the stage. Some men are drunk, and have difficulty standing upright. From time to time, the men stretch out their right arm in a salute to the band. Some men bang their heads, and others hold their arms around each other. One boy pushes another into the mass, stumbles and falls, and is stamped on by the others. A friend pulls him out of the mass and he stands confused. Later in the evening, several boys remove their T-shirts, revealing their bare upper bodies, tattooed with Vikings and nationalist symbols.

At the first glance, this symbiosis of community and violence might seem like a dislocated and archaic construction of masculinity. For example, Clarke (1976) talks of the skinhead subculture as the magical recovery of past working-class community. Willis (1977), on the other hand, sees racism and violence as distinct parts of working-class young people's counterculture in school. It is common for both of these writers and the other researchers from the so-called Birmingham school of youth research (CCCS: Centre for Contemporary Cultural Studies) to see racism and violence as distinct parts of the "shop-floor culture." They say that the original working-class communities have been broken up, and that working-class young people reconstruct different features of what they imagine to be typically working-class by their subcultural participation. Such subcultures constitute a bricolage where elements from different origins are brought together to produce a new unity, expressing a protest against society, but at the same time reproducing core values of their own class. According to the CCCS researchers, class is still a major structure which serves to distinguish people, and they show that protest subcultures might express conflicts hidden in contemporary society, especially processes of unequal opportunities for young people.

The thesis of class as a major structuring principle in the selection of who will succeed within the school system, and who will not, is supported by the extensive quantitative research of Bourdieu and Passeron (1990) and their colleagues. The claim to take responsibility for one's own life, which opens up many possibilities, might in many respects be considered a myth rather than a reality. There are still considerable class differences in the range of possible choices, the school often being more important as the very institution that selects the already privileged from the already excluded, than as an institution supporting equal opportunities for everyone. This holds true for more clear-cut class societies like France and the UK, but as shown by Jørgensen (1994), some of these processes are highly relevant also in Norway. Young men who act aggressively, who drop out of school, and who commit violence or express antagonism against foreigners might be understood also, as shown in the studies of Willis (1977) and Hebdige (1979), as constructing an image of working-class masculinity.

This thesis stands somewhat in contrast to the way Giddens (1991) and Ziehe (1981) describe the processes of individualization and self-actualization, as being typical of late modernity. Ziehe uses the term individualization to point to the current emphasis on the responsibility of the individual to construct an identity. As Ziehe describes this process, tradition and class no longer determine the identity of young people. They become responsible for their own choices more than ever before. This leads to an intensified vulnerability in young people, but, on the other hand, it provides them with a hitherto unknown freedom to choose their own lifestyles. According to Ziehe, this process might be achieved by cultural experimentation, that is, using the modern to creat something new. Another solution is to become neo-conservative by idealizing the past. Here, Ziehe's argument is parallel to the CCCS researchers' interpretation of skinheads as recovering a class identity that no longer has a material basis, and therefore must be communicated in a symbolic way. The skinheads idealize a lumpen identity (Hebdige, 1979) and they create what Clarke (1976) interprets as a magical recovery of community.

Giddens (1991) does indeed see class as a structuring principle in late modernity, although in his discussion of self-identity and the consequences for the individual of modernity, class seems to be less important. According to Giddens, the uttermost consequences of modernity hit us harder than ever before. Our era is defined by a heightened risk and at the same time a threat to the feeling of ontological security and trust. Identity is not something passively inherited from one generation to another, but rather it has the quality of being a project which continuously must be constructed and reconstructed during the life-span. Since changes between life-phases are no longer regulated by ceremonies, an important task of the individual is to tackle the identity crisis that life offers. The popularity of self-therapy books and courses are, according to Giddens, a mark of the centrality of this aspect of mastering such threats to the feeling of a congruent self and the feeling of ontological security.

Ziehe, like Giddens, rejects the view that we are living in a postmodern society. According to Ziehe, modernity creates a horizon of possibilities, as the individual is expected to choose and form his or her own life and identity. This also leads to insecurity. As with Giddens's focus on the individual working toward self-actualisation, Ziehe pays most of his attention to youths who creatively (in the aesthetic sense of the term) use the diversity of lifestyle choices in their cultural experimentation. A failure in the discussions of both Giddens and Ziehe is that they do not focus much on the importance of class in defining who is profiting in this rapidly changing and highly pluralistic era.

Class still plays a major factor in distinguishing between those who successfully profit from the break with traditions, and those who are more directly hit by the insecurity of our time. Bourdieu shows that the view that school and education are democratic institutions that provide all youths with equal opportunities, is totally wrong. On the contrary, the education system is the very system that serves to select those already privileged, from those who already were excluded from the dominant classes. This finding is supported by ethnographic studies from the CCCS, such as Willis's study of counter-school-culture, and by Norwegian studies like Jørgensen (1994).

The problem with studies such as the one by Willis is not the failure to recognize the significance of class, but rather the failure to recognize the complexity of masculinity, and how class today is constructed in diverse ways. As shown by Connell (1995), working-class boys may often come from more postmodern families, in the sense that the mother is the breadwinner, than do middle-class boys, and boys with almost equal backgrounds may construct their "working classness" in a multitude of ways, many of them breaking with traditional expectations of what it means to be working class.

In Willis's study, racism is seen as one important quality of the proletarian "shop-floor culture". Connell shows that many other qualities are present in the various ways through which working-class identity might be constructed. Deterministic socialization theories fail to show the more paradoxical expressions of class. Also, as pointed out by Connell, many working-class boys today do not orient themselves toward a future on the shop-floor. Many of them face a future marked by unemployment, and therefore they stay within their subcultural lifestyle project which gives no hope for future working-class jobs, or they orient themselves toward educated middle-class jobs. Racism might of course be prevalent in all classes, but is perhaps most directly expressed within the working-class. A study by Pedersen (1996) shows that working-class young people express more prejudices toward foreigners than do middle-class young people. It is possible, however, that the racism of the middle-class is not shown up in a survey.

According to Bauman (1991), racism is a feature of modernity, whereas postmodernity is marked by tolerance. The project of modernity is to rule out ambivalence, and within such a project the Holocaust was the most tragic expression of the modern world. The modern idea of equality means that everything which is not equal must either be assimilated, deported or exterminated. Bauman, in contrast to Ziehe and Giddens, is talking of current society as being postmodern, but at the same time he says that modernity is still with us (p. 270). In Bauman's view, what is new in the current era, is that we are now able to look at modernity from a distance, discovering the impossibility of modernity. In these terms, racist youth subcultures such as the community of right-wing skinheads represent those who still believe in modernity, those who do not want to accept the possibility of living with ambivalence. By celebrating a rigid division between us and them, right-wing skinheads actively reject the more "postmodern" identity projects of individuals who accept the diversity and ambivalence of multiple belongings.

My analysis is inspired by Connell, Wetherell and others who see masculinity as something men negotiate in ongoing situations. A boy is not passively transformed into a man. Rather, all through his life he has to construct and reconstruct his sense of maleness as resolution to dilemmas concerning expectations from others (both men and women) and concerning the power relations he enters. According to Connell, masculinity is a set of choices about what to wear, what to look like, and how to behave in social situations. Even though females constitute about a third of this subculture,[1] it seems that, in many ways, it is male-dominated and defined. Since I have analyzed the social project of right-wing females elsewhere, to reveal the gendered quality of the identity project of these skinheads, I will now analyze how the male participants of the subculture verbalize the aspect of being a "real man," and I will present an interpretation of certain situations in which they actively construct their versions of masculinity.

By using this analytical frame as a guide for what to look for, I will ask what signals right-wing males give to the outside world by the clothes they wear, by the way they relate to each other, by the way they walk, and more explicitly by the words they use to define themselves in contrast to other men. According to Connell's terminology, right-wing skinheads might be considered a version of marginalized masculinity. In another essay, I discuss the life histories of some of these young men. They come from the working class or the lower part of the *petite bourgeois*. In terms of their own occupation, they are all either working-class or unemployed, living on the dole. They are quite similar to the men discussed by Connell under the heading "live fast and die young." Like such men, they have no expectation of the kind of stable employment around which working-class family life earlier was organized. In this way, they differ from "the lads" described by Paul Willis: they do not participate in a violent, racist counterculture as a preparation for a work-life on the shopfloor, rather they participate because they see no future in the working market. Their participation in a counterculture provides their life with the excitement, community and feeling of honor that they cannot find elsewhere.

My aim is to find out what kind of masculinity they are negotiating, and more generally how a right-wing skinhead male is "made." What should he look like and how should he act, in order to fit in with the others? The way these young males construct their social identity as white "nationalist" men is simultaneously a response to the way people outside their own collective define and react to them. Identity is always defined in contrast to those one does not identify with. However, as pointed out by recent social constructionist writers, most persons belong to many different social categories, and might often feel contradictions within themselves as a result of diverging constraints that their manifold belongings lead to.

When putting some of these lines of thought together, we could say that in the course of modernity masculinity has been questioned, partly as a result of the critiques put forward by the women's movement. At the same time, the working class has continuously been changing. The orientation of people has evolved from collectivism toward individualism. The ritualized version of masculinity among right-wing skinheads is one possible solution to modern dilemmas. The skinhead part of the right-wing subculture can be understood as one typical example of the crisis within masculinity, described by several authors. Connell (1995) speaks of a crisis in the gender order as a whole, with implications for masculinities. This crisis may provoke attempts to restore a dominant masculinity. Theweleit (1987) interprets the sexual politics of Fascism in this way. Gibson (1994) has described similar processes in his study of "paramilitary culture."

In other words, ritualized, dominant, violent forms of masculinity can be interpreted not only as ancient masculinities, displaced in modern society. Rather one can see them as distinct solutions to the dilemmas of modern societies, and the processes of individualization leading to ontological insecurity and the need to cope with the threats against a congruent self-feeling. Such ritualizations are seen in the skinhead dance, drinking, pain, and so on. In this way, a feeling of ontological security is created, which partly takes the form of being a feeling or experience of having an identity. It is the feeling of the lack of identity which leads to various attempts to ritualize and thus bind masculinity. These attempts might take perverse forms, and thus lead to a death-mask of masculinity.

This article examines the ritualized ways in which Norwegian right-wing skinheads construct masculinity. The analysis is based upon material gathered from one year of participant observation during 1993-94, interviews from the period 1993-97, and written material about right-wing skinheads.

The verbalization of an archetypal honor ideal

Images of skinheads vs. middle-class men

The clear-cut division between us and them is seen in the way that right-wing skinheads define their own subculture:

> The skinhead movement emerged among white, national workers in England – not among international students and "self-haters"! Skinheads represent white pride and – in contrast to punks, most skinheads have ordinary work. The styles are also different, as the punks look like a ... Christmas tree ..., whereas skinheads dress like militant workers! Workers that are neither communists nor anarchists (*Einherjer*, No. 1, 1996).

In this way, the skinheads link honor to the social categories with which they define themselves, and invert other categories into representing self-hatred. Thus, being white, being working-class, being militant, being national, and – as might be seen as an internal contrast to some of the former – being ordinary, are all aspects of being honorable. This contrast being being something else, militant rebels or warriors, and at the same time being ordinary, one of the people, is typical of the way in which right-wing skinheads present themselves. Broad categories, such as race and nation, provide them with honor, and make them winners (warriors), rather than losers (victims). By being aggressors, they are assured of not being victims. This self-identity is contrasted to their definition of men with education and international experience. The latter have an ethos more different from themselves than anyone else. In addition, such men are those who have the power to define right-wing skinheads negatively, for example in terms of social inability. To redefine the power of these men becomes crucial for right-wing skinheads. Therefore, they invert the aspect of being international and educated into being a self-hater, being a man who suppresses his instincts. Middle-class men in this way are identified as weaklings, whereas working-class men represent true masculinity.

> The problem of people today is going from words to deed! What right do they have to criticise and judge us, these pigs [de svina] who only think of filling their stomachs! It is the foremost men of action who are really free and alive! ... What people in general only slightly dare to admit to themselves we shout out in the street! In the street, we must fight because that is where the real reality is! A reality which the politician pigs and the couch potatoes think only exists in movies! People accuse skins of being rowdy, but we only claim our right: WHITE POWER! (*Ragnarok*, 1993).

This quotation also redefines true men as men who act and who fight. Men who always stay inside, middle-class men, are unable to contest their status to know anything of "the real reality," the reality of the street. This is in line with Bourdieu (1993) saying that masculinity, defined in terms of physical strength (body capital), is the ground pillar of the identity of the dominated classes. These young men exaggerate their abilities in the sphere of bodily action because their power to define is lacking. To tackle the vulnerability they feel as not fitting into the hegemonic areas of society, the feeling of bodily management (Giddens, 1991) becomes crucial.

The emphasis on the warrior image might, however, seem to be a kind of dislocated masculinity image in todays Western societies. However, as pointed out by Morgan (1994, p. 165), the warrior, despite far-reaching political, social and technological changes, still seems to be a key symbol of masculinity, as shown in its central place in films. Dominating the street by means of physical force is a way to achieve power and dignity. "TV-slaves" represent femininity only partly because they do not partake in the contest of masculinity which is played out in the street. The association of "men of action" with the street indirectly defines the antithesis of the street versus the home; the latter is distinguished as the feminine sphere, and thus men who stay at home (even though they watch TV rather than cook) are unmanly men. This point is also highlighted by Back (1994) in his study of racist youths in Britain. For them, he argues, the home symbolizes the feminine sphere and a social boundness. It is important to add here a point made by Nancy Cott (in Brod, 1994, p. 88) that such constructions of geographically separated male and female spheres are ideological constructions, not distinct physical sites.

The Vikings – or the ethos of real men

Another way that right-wing skinheads conceptualize the ethos of "real men," and thus legitimize their own brute masculinity, is by referring to the conduct of the ancient Nordic Vikings. The Vikings serve particularly well to illuminate the link between brute masculinity and honor:

> Fighting today costs, and everyone must sacrifice something. Those who are at the front-line must receive all the support they need! WE MUST STAY TOGETHER; OUR BROTHERHOOD IS HOLY! We are hated and loved, comrades. We live like real Vikings at any rate! Stand up and continue the fight. Sooner or later we will be strong! (*Ragnarok*).[2]

To fight, to be hated by others, and to stay together in a tight brotherhood – this is their image of how the Vikings behaved.[3] In their view the Vikings were strong because they stayed together and supported each other, because they fought their enemies, and because they sacrificed their personal interests for those of the group. Left alone, even a Viking might be vulnerable. Together with his comrades, however, he will (sooner or later) be strong. According to one skinhead, writing in the skinhead fanzine *Bootboys* (1992),[4] the moral rules of Hávamál are as current today as they were "for our ancestors during their era." Hávamál serves as a guide for how real men should behave:

> For one's friend, one shall be friend; for him and his friend, but for the foe's friend, no man shall ever be a friend.[5]

This is a brutal image of the world. Others are either friends or enemies, there are no categories in between. Seeing the world in this way, it becomes crucial that friends stick together and support each other. If one cannot trust one's friends, then one cannot trust anybody. The threat of one's own friends cheating is therefore the worst threat of all, as the only thing one can be sure of is that enemies are enemies. That friends are friends, however, is not always true, and must, accordingly, be demanded again and again, as in the earlier quotation stating that "we must stick together." Joining forces against those who are against them means diminishing personal differences and disagreements between them. This is in line with the way Bauman conceptualizes the differences between the categories friend, enemy and stranger. There is a logical interdependence between the first two categories: "There would be no enemies were there no friends, and there would be no friends if not for the yawning abyss of enmity outside" (Bauman, 1991, p. 53). This point is very significant for right-wing skinheads. One of them once told me that he did not count any of the other skinheads as friends, but in his fanzine, he often refers to the importance of comradeship within the movement. In other words, there are no real friendships between them, and the only way their comradeship can be realized is by joining forces against their enemies. This is also in line with Bauman (1991, p. 54), who points out that enemies are called into being by the pragmatics of struggle.

As a consequence, the most respected skinhead is the one who joins the ongoing combat with their enemies, who defends the others if attacked, and who is constantly aware of possible enemies wanting to split them, spy on them, or attack them. One ideal among right-wing skinheads is the militant who knows how to handle weapons, and who lets his militant actions be guided more by his ideology or strategic considerations than by his emotions. The headless fighter who is constantly getting beaten up because he is incautious is not an admired figure among them. In contrast, they admire those who manoeuver underground beyond the view of outsiders, hide from the police, or escape when caught. Actions aimed at the whole group should be secretive, such as when a leading skinhead arranges a secret meeting or a trip without the police or the anti-fascists getting to know when and where it will take place. To master various aspects of secret behavior is important. In this way, right-wing skinheads achieve honor by being invisible, by being able to hide.

SØNNER AV ODIN
POSTBOKS 72, 3053 STEINBER(

KONSERT STOCKHOLM 27 AUGUS
Følgende band spiller

SQUADRON (

DIVISJON S

SVASTIKA

VIT AGGRES

Bussprisen for tur
(120,- for de som
ble med sist)

Inngangsbilletten
140 Norske og kan

(NB du kan også ve
bussen,da sparer

Reisedag blir Fredag 26 Au
Hokksund/Mjøndalen kl 18.00

Drammen(samme sted som sist) 18.15

Oslo(---"-----) 19.00

_____

Ingen flere opplysninger vil bli sendt.

Behavior in public – messages to the outside world

Traditionally, men achieve honor through being visible to the gaze of others (Gilmore, 1990). Right-wing skinheads by their very outlook are very visible to the gaze of others. This gaze provides them with a sense of honor, even when it is marked by contempt or fear. Skinheads moving together in a group, walking straight down the middle of the street, are signalling that they "own" it. By behaving like this they are looking the enemy in the eye, confronting him in the street, and standing up to his insults. Using physical force is a way of ensuring that such face-to-face interactions with opponents are resolved honorably. In fact, even to get "beaten up" is in a sense honorable, as skinheads use such events to prove that they can take it like a man.

When the skinheads defended their house in Treschowsstreet against the police and the demonstrating anarchists in 1995, they wore skinhead uniforms, used Norwegian flags, and gave fascist salutes. This backdrop was clearly created in order to communicate certain messages to their outsiders. Their aim was to shock and provoke, and, more generally, to produce a contrast, a frightening image. They managed to be recognized by others, as the press gave them extensive attention. As participants in the underground, they are sure to get negatively defined attention, marked by fear and contempt rather than admiration. Nevertheless, this provides right-wing skinheads with self-confidence and a sense of being part of something important.

The importance of combat

In public situations, combat situations or collective scenes, right-wing skinheads act with self-confidence and pride. By contrast, when gathered in private, with nothing particular happening, just sitting together waiting for the next "peak experience" (Lindholm, 1990), they look bored, lacking in confidence, generally unpleasant. It is combat that provides them with honor – outdoors is the only place where they can prove their manliness. This view of masculinity as being defined by the mastering of the street is a view consciously taken by the ideologists of the underground, as shown in the earlier quotation of the contrast between middle-class and working-class men. In the streets the ideal of the fighting hero can be reconstructed, and all the other established rules (or hegemonic masculinities) (Connell, command of anything when he walks down the street and meets an angry crowd of skinheads. Right-wing skinheads adhere to a lifestyle which provides them with power comparable even to the real men of power in society, because they know that if they wanted to they would be able to control these people in the reality of the street.

A lifestyle of intimidation

Uniforms and group conformity

To enter the right-wing underground is to take up a lifestyle based on a threatening appearance. Although there are minor differences, the appearance of the group members seems highly uniform to outsiders. External conformity protects the individual participants in the same way that any uniform does, by hiding their individuality, inner feelings and thoughts. By looking alike, they are a group, and can act accordingly. Thus, when attacking others they can rely on the morality of the group, without taking into account their own private moral standards. Being part of the underground means that the barriers against which actions the single person may commit are moved many steps away from what would have been the case prior to participation.

The dress itself has connotations of brutality. Shaven skull, heavy Doc Martens boots, "bomber" jackets, camo jeans, Viking symbols and tattoos; all these elements serve to build up an aggressive version of masculinity. The skinhead style also connotes working classness (Hebdige, 1979). Those participants who dress like skinheads are aware of this. They point out, for example, that Doc Martens boots are not military boots, as often described, but working boots made to last. Some wear studded "killing boots" which make them extra dangerous in fights.

The shaven head, either completely shaven, or with just a couple of millimetres left, also connotes brutality. They use the completely shaven head as a mark of aggression. One leading figure who usually preferred to leave a slight crest of hair on his skull once showed up with his head shaven to the bone. I asked him why he had done it. Looking angry, he just said "as a reaction." The impression he gave was one of much more hate than usual. From what he said, I gathered that to shave the head entirely was a reaction against things in his life at that time, which were hard for him to handle. Right-wing skinheads are often called "boneheads" by their opponents, because they shave their heads more than left-wing skinheads. Shaving the head gives a more brutish look and leaves nothing for an opponent to grab hold of in a fight. Some skinheads associate long hair with femininity. They tease the few right-wing activists who have long hair, and call them "girls."[6]

Tattoos are a part of the style meant to communicate masculinity. Merely being tattooed is seen as being tough. As a leading right-wing skinhead explains, the pain which comes with being tattooed marks the barrier one has to cross, reflecting that one is willing to remain loyal to the underground in the future. Belonging to a skinhead group is a conviction which lies in your heart, he said, and which you have to stand for later in life as well. Tattoos are marks of commitment; they cannot be taken off like items of clothing. According to this man, being a "real skinhead" means that "you can't just wear the boots when you go out with your skinhead friends." If you are a skinhead, you are a full-time skinhead, and this aspect is assured by the use of tattoos. To have large parts of the body covered with tattoos is also a mark that one has been a member of the underground for a long time. Leading skinheads have most parts of their upper body covered in tattoos. In order to show off the tattoos to the other men, it is usual for them to remove their T-shirts during concerts. The musicians themselves remove their T-shirts. Doing this may be understood as a ritual greeting from man to man, letting the body confirm their commitment through its tattoos, and also through its muscles, serving as a proof of manliness.

The beer culture

Another aspect of the skinhead lifestyle is what the skinhead calls "beer culture." Meeting comrades at the pub is, in his eyes, an integral part of the working-class lifestyle. When drinking a lot, skinheads become more excited, and late at night noisy quarrels are common. Some skinheads accept the fact that one is more easily provoked when drunk, and may initiate fights more frequently. The ideal, however, is that one is able to drink a lot but still control one's body. The man who "gets pissed" is not reckoned to be manly by right-wing skinheads, and those who frequently lose control through drunkenness are ridiculed by the others. Drunkenness also often leads to exaggerated sentimentality. For example, one of the leading skinheads, when he is drunk, tells others how much he likes them, and exaggerates the content of his message so much that it borders on the pathetic. This kind of sentimentality is also seen in right-wing males watching Second World War movies with huge parades, as they sit weeping together because of how great it all was.

Some right-wing males have less sense of this kind of drunken sentimentality, honoring instead the ability to stay sober and disciplined. In their eyes, drunken skinheads are not serious, and might bring harm to the underground by their uncontrolled, raucous street violence. Committing violence without it being noticed is in their eyes more honorable than fighting the enemy eye-to-eye in the street. Some skinheads take the opposite view: they consider fighting bare-fisted facing an opponent to be more honest and just than underground acts committed out of the sight of others.

The lack of empathy – "horny on violence"

Ray (1972) states that Australian neo-Nazis lack the ability to show empathy with – and, moreover, the feeling of pleasure regarding – the pains of others. This tendency is also prevalent among Norwegian right-wing skinheads. Ray considers that this feature is prevalent among most people, and he uses the faces of the audience at boxing matches as proof. However, what defines the fascist, according to Ray, is his acceptance of these sentiments, even taking a pride in them. Similarly, Theweleit (1987) has produced an illuminating report on men in the German storm-troops describing their enormous desire to see blood flowing. Seeing the result of a massacre aroused pleasurable feelings, and the will to act violently may be due to the fact that the violence itself produces desire.

Such sentiments are clearly present among some right-wing skinheads. A female activist once explained a severe violent act committed by two male skinheads as the result of their being "horny on violence." I have seen skinheads laugh and amuse themselves when seeing people suffer from hunger on television. On the other hand, the skinheads do not dwell on the result of their own violence. There is a code among them that when a victim falls to the ground they must stop kicking him. This is not always the case. Sometimes only one skinhead attacks, but there are also incidents where several others follow the initiator, collectively hitting and kicking one person. Usually, they kick an enemy until he falls, and then run away, giving no consideration to the long- or short-term injuries they have inflicted upon him. The consequences of their violence become diffuse for them.

On the few occasions when they have had to face their victim afterwards, they do not show much empathy. Once when they had beaten up a person from their rival group, the police immediately afterwards caught them and confronted them with the victim, who was to point out which of them had beaten him. Afterwards, a skinhead retold the event.

"He was so badly injured, he couldn't even point," he explained. With a grimace, he tried to illustrate how the victim sat there trying to point with his arm, but unable to do so. Apparently, the event did not arouse any feelings of empathy for the pain the man must have felt. On the contrary, he found it amusing.

Revenge and rebellion

However, for the skinheads, the injuries and pain inflicted on their victims even out, as they frequently get beaten up themselves. They define their own violence as revenge or self-defense, depending on the situation. To participate in a gang fight is almost always interpreted as being just and therefore honorable, probably because they are then acting as a group, and on behalf of the group. Revenge might be defined in a very broad sense. When, for example, a politician participates in anti-racist campaigns, this is seen as an initiative on the part of the system directed against right-wing skinheads. Hence, to attack the house of this politician is another version of revenge. Most acts of violence against political opponents seem to be defined as legitimate and honorable among them. However, they also have ideas of what kind of violence they do not approve of. They do not define beating up single persons or "innocents" (people who are not politically involved) as being honorable. However, if this should happen despite the norm, they often reinterpret it afterwards as a sad result of the effects an oppressive system has on its brave fighters:

> Egil: Our rebellion is a product of the system. We occasionally attack people on their own, but this is a result of the politics of the system ... Terror is all the violence carried out by the system, which we don't even notice. That's terror, the rest is a struggle for liberation.

To be a rebel or a revolutionary who opposes the very system seems to be the most honorable profile, as this quotation might illustrate. In accordance with other kinds of terrorists, right-wing skinheads equate their more severe violence with a struggle for liberation and not as terrorism. In this way they explicitly counteract society's common definitions of them, and present alternative interpretations. They prefer others to see them as victims of destiny rather than as evil authoritarians. In this way, they can neutralize their violence as a production of the "system" – its class-structures, bad environments and so on. In contrast to common people, they dare to fight the unjust Authorities. Here we see an association between violence and honesty. To live out the hatred means being honest, being authentic. They do not suppress their aggression against the suppressing structures; in contrast, they live it out. Violence in this sense is a free-floating energy. This is interesting in the light of Reich's (1972) theory of fascism as a blocking of sexual energies. In the self-interpretation of right-wing skinheads, it is the blocking of the aggressive energies of the common people which is pathological. Hence, in their eyes, to live out violent drives is something desirable. This feature is described in several studies of youth violence (Willis, 1977), and is also acknowledged in group psychology (Le Bon, 1896): "When individuals come together in a group, their individual inhibitions fall away and all the cruel, brutal and destructive instincts, which lie dormant ... are stirred up and find free gratification."

The avoidance of femininity

Masculine ideals

It is indeed a brute masculinity that attracts young boys into the right-wing underground. Their masculinity is brutish, as they describe "real men" as those who act rather than those who speak, and those who fight rather than those who move aside. This image of masculinity stands in contrast to their understanding of softness, weakness, or sometimes more explicitly, femininity. A gentle attitude is something skinheads regard with suspicion, whereas force is something they respect. For male skinheads this underground world dominated by masculine ideals is a safe island in the sense that it provides them with self-confidence. One leading activist reports that a trend is for the boys to have few or no contacts with girls before entering the underground. It is the male community that fascinates them and leads them to join it. The accepting attitude of older males, and their willingness to give the young newcomers positions of responsibility, lead newcomers into ecstatic enthusiasm in the first phase of their participation. Several male skinheads have told me that this milieu was the first one in which they felt really welcome. It was here that they developed a sense of importance. In the first phase, it is the feeling of being included by elder, well-known activists which is important to them. Later on, most males try to establish their own agendas within the underground, and in more or less overt ways oppose the dominance of the eldest activists. In this latter phase, they are usually more self-confident, making contact with the girls participating in the underground and being more prepared to engage romantically with them.

Relations to women

In some respects, then, these male skinheads seem to fit the picture Theweleit (1987) draws of fascist men who participated in the free-corps in Germany prior to the Second World War. According to Theweleit, these freebooters feared women and accordingly idealized the male community based to a great extent on brutality. One conclusion we can draw from Theweleit's extensive analysis, is that when men lack the ability to relate to women in an equal way, the way they dare experience intimacy is more one-sidedly brutal. Therefore, the way the men relate to women is an important measure of their degree of brutality.

In the Norwegian right-wing underground, some male skinheads espouse the view that women ought not to participate in the underground, because they destroy the combat by their sensitivity. At events such as concerts and confrontations, some male skinheads tend to exclude their partners. Often, women remain in the background area at such events, so that the area in front of the stage or the front-line during attacks is occupied solely by males. Norwegian male activists change between total acceptance of the women, saying they are willing to include them in all actions, even saying that some of them are more serious and reliable than many of the men, *and* dividing women uncritically into the Madonna/whore icon. They divide "their own girls" into those who are "straight," and thus suitable as love partners and fellow-combatants, and those who are "mattresses" and thus only suitable as sexual objects and as tagalongs. Most of the leading males have established love relationships. In the original English skinhead subculture, according to Clarke (1976), establishing a love relationship usually meant breaking ties with the male-dominated skinhead community. Girls therefore could only function as tagalongs, the males treating them with extreme chauvinism. In some regards, then, the Norwegian male right-wing skinheads are more pro-women than the original skinheads described by Theweleit. They do not operate with as strict a distinction between the all-pure, almost asexual nurse-sister, and the dangerous sexuality ascribed to their hate object, the proletarian woman, who is not even worthy of serving as a "mattress." They do not demand that their partners should be all-pure idealized objects staying out of the battle. In this regard, they are more similar to the communist men described by Theweleit, in that they can become fellow-combatants by behaving in a masculine manner. The men accept women as long as they are able to live up to the ideals of staying calm, controlling their feelings and being able to deal with weapons.

The combative woman

In the anthropological literature, honor is usually described in terms of competition between dominant men and the passive subordination of women (Lindisfarne, 1994). Typically, women are not felt to be capable of protecting their own honor. Consequently, men must protect women's honor. A common trend is that women's honor is defined solely in terms of sexuality (as a contrast to purity). There are indications that female virginity is important in the Norwegian underground, as both male and female activists tend to divide their fellow females into either straight or mattress. A woman activist has to be straight in order to be taken seriously. There have been occasions when a male skinhead has knocked another one down for kissing his girlfriend. Usually it is not the girlfriend who has offended her partner, but rather the other male. In other words, honor can be achieved only between men.

However, as Lindisfarne argues, the picture is often much more complex than this, and usually several roles are available for both men and women. Right-wing subcultures are usually interpreted as extreme areas in regard to these features. Yet, it is not the passive, pure, subordinate woman who is pictured in Norwegian right-wing fanzines, but rather the female fellow-combatant who acts aggressively. The boys idealize various types of combative women (Fangen, 1997). The women themselves idealize the image of the combative woman, and accept the male, militant values of the underground. In other words, they do not provide a feminine impact that would diminish the underground's brutal potential. These women also want to achieve power through militancy, and undergo, for example, weapons training along with the men (Fangen, 1997). Therefore, the women also construct the picture of a community dominated by aggressive masculine ideals. Nevertheless, they also contribute with a distinctive feminine impact, by defining certain "women's issues" as being important to them, such as fighting prostitution, abortion and pornography, and "securing the future for our children and for girls in the movement" (*ibid.*).

The link between homosexuality and neo-Nazism

The right-wing women support militant practices, but so far have taken part "in the front-line" only to a minor extent. Therefore the movement does not differ much traditional view that "combat and military experience separate men from women while binding men to men" (Morgan, 1994, p. 166). When talking about community and comradeship, these right-wing men most often think in terms of male community and male comradeship. The way they conceptualize their heroes is in many ways an idealization and romanticization of maleness, and it is the male hero they pay homage to. The way these men behave at concerts, standing tightly together, sometimes even holding their arms around each other, pulling off their T-shirts, standing their with naked upper body, has lead outsiders to question whether the community of these young men is based on homosexual desires. Second World War Nazism has been interpreted by several authors in this way (Reich, 1972; Mosse, 1985; Theweleit, 1987; Nissen, 1946; Becker, 1946). The issue of the existence of a congruence between neo-Nazism and homosexuality has been made plausible because some male leaders of neo-Nazi groups, like Michael Kühnen, have been homosexuals. In Norway, one of the leading figures of the 1980s neo-Nazi movement was a bisexual. The neo-Nazi leader Michael Kühnen (who died from AIDS) openly argued that homosexuals were especially useful for the movement, because they did not quit as a result of developing a relationship with a woman (Husbands, 1993).

Aware of the plausibility of such a view about their community, the link between homosexuality and Nazism was one of the first issues that right-wing skinheads brought up and tried to explain to me when I started my fieldwork in August 1993. Their response was that the issue was relevant, and that in the Norwegian underground too there had been homosexual participants. Some of the skinheads were still befriended by them, but in another setting they could just as easily beat up a homosexual. Several of the males emphasized that "I have no such tendencies" and "I like girls." When I asked if they had something against homosexuals, they either said that "no, most of the guys in this milieu are tolerant" or that "we like neither gays nor lesbians. Homosexuality is against the Law of Nature." They recited some cruel jokes about homosexuals, and some of their fanzines include satire on presumably homosexual participants of the underground.

Using homosexuality as a way to weaken the Other is a mode well-known in all hypermasculine communities like outlaw motorbike-clubs (Bay, 1989), and was also an integral part of Nazi ideology and practice. When used in this way, the homosexual has the quality of being a stranger in the sense Bauman (1991, p. 55) gives this term. You cannot know whether or not your friend is homosexual, and accordingly, you do not know whether or not your enemy is a homosexual. It is exactly the indeterminant aspect of homosexuality that makes it threatening to a community ruled by the friend/enemy dichotomy.

Teasing as confirmation and intimidation of masculinity

The association with homosexuality is threatening to the right-wing
skinhead community because it weakens the connotation between
masculinity and strength.[7] Male skinheads associate homosexuality with
femininity, which again is associated with weakness and deviance. Being a
fag is understood as being the opposite of a real male. Male skinheads call
another man "fag" to dishonor him.[8] Once a skinhead who was well
acquainted with the underground, but who did not play a leading role
within it, was teased by a younger activist who had just entered the group.
The younger man said to the other "You look like you enjoy being fucked
in the ass." The other one replied "Yes, I do, but I enjoy being taken in the
front even more." "But you," he added, "you look like a girl, with that long
hair!" "No, it's not girlish to have long hair," replied the younger man. "Oh
yes it is," added one of the younger man's own friends. The younger man
became irritated and launched a long tirade of insults against the older
skinhead, calling him fag in all sorts of ways. The older skinhead did not
deign to respond. He just left the table and began playing billiards. He was
the winner anyway, as the younger man's friends had supported him, so
there was no need to continue the quarrel.

In contests such as this, one could say that the men sexualize each
other. This kind of "kidding" is interpreted by Frøberg (forthcoming) as
relation-work between men. It might also be interpreted as an honor game
(Bay, 1989).

The honors and dishonors of the brotherhood

External and internal threats

The community among right-wing skinheads becomes a tense, aggressive
unit against the outer world. The worst threat to this unity is not attacks
from the outside – on the contrary, these attacks are necessary if the
solidarity among skinheads is to remain strong. The real threat is that this
community consisting of many aggressive, bitter and frustrated men (this
description of them was used by a leading skinhead) will split up as a result
of internal strife. A split in their community is far more threatening than
being attacked by rival groups from the outside.

This is also the reason why "traitors" are a continuous threat to their
community. Several times leading skinheads have been accused of serving
as informants for the police. Usually they try to reaffirm their innocence,

but there are also incidents of some having this reputation for years without trying to prove otherwise. Such men, however, generally tend to loosen their bonds with the core of the underground in order to escape the pressure upon them.

Splits in the community occur, however, not just in such cases as police co-operation. Internal strife is frequent, often due to competition for status and respect, or by differing opinions on strategy. Although comradeship is the most worshipped ideal among them, the intimate comradeship based on mutual trust is more the exception than the rule. On the one hand, male skinheads say that the comradeship is the most attractive feature of the underground, and that they have never felt as accepted anywhere else as they have here. On the other hand, they say that the worst thing about the underground is the quarrels and strife.

Emotional tensions

Directing aggressive feelings outwards is necessary if the antagonism which always lurks beneath the surface of the skinhead community is to be suppressed. Their community is not based on bonds that have grown naturally from a base of mutual sympathy and friendship. Rather, many of the men have entered this underground on their own initiative, without any prior knowledge of those associated with it. They do not have much in common, despite their mutual situation of being attached to an underground which makes people outside their community despise them, attack them, or spy on them. Partly because of pressure from the outside world, and partly because of their community being formed on grounds other than friendship, there is a lot of tension between them, and the ideals of comradeship are hard to realize. They often transform their frustration and suspicion of the outside world into frustration and distrust toward other skinheads. These tensions in turn sometimes lead to physical or verbal feuding between the men. They name-call each other in negative terms, or shout at each other. During the course of a single evening, laughing comrades often turn into silent strangers.

The way skinheads express comradeship often serves to show superiority of status. They commend each other by including one another in important events, praising each other in front of others, or by buying each other beer. However, as Bay (1989) points out, buying somebody a beer underlines the subordination of the recipient of the beer. The man who receives the beer is not supposed to reciprocate the action, and that would amount to challenging the status of the other. For example, a younger self-confident skinhead once borrowed money from one of the leading skinheads. When this older and more experienced skinhead later asked for his money back, the younger one merely bought him a beer, turning his back on him as if there were nothing more to discuss. Although the beer was worth only a fourth of the amount he owed, by acting in this manner he clearly opposed the leading status of the other man.

Comradeship and subordination

This episode is understandable in light of the fact that an experienced skinhead might often ask others to buy him a beer. The alacrity with which the other does or does not do so reflects the degree to which the other skinhead accepts the experienced one as a person rightfully deserving of respect. Consequently, very young and inexperienced skinheads would feel honored by being asked to buy the older skinhead a beer. By contrast, more experienced skinheads would question the authority of the elder, answering his question with a laugh, or by ignoring it, and turning their backs on him, or by later demanding that he return the gesture.

Physical expressions of comradeship might also carry symbolic messages of subordination; for example, when one skinhead pushes another skinhead's head or nudges his shoulder. Skinheads who have more highly placed positions of leadership, despite the norm of equality, can be more physical than the others. One of the leading skinheads becomes quite intimate when he is drunk. He kisses and hugs the other men, puts his arm around them, or pulls their hoods over their heads. The others just shake their heads, look elsewhere, push him away gently, or look a bit sheepish when he puts his arm around them. The reactions of the others reflect the fact that these friendly approaches of his also contain an element of subordination. He confirms that he is the initiator, the one to make contact, the father figure, and his actions show them that they are of lower status. A younger skinhead with less status would not have approached the others in such a direct fashion. It is the leading skinhead who can transgress the boundaries. These actions of the leading figure might be seen as status rituals in the sense Goffman (1972) gives the term, the leading figure confirming through his behaviour that the others must defer to his status. The others more or less passively accept his conduct. By not accepting it too explicitly, they express some of the resentment or ambivalence with which they regard his authority.

The skinhead dance

Another situation that reveals closeness, and at the same time subordination, is the skinhead dance. The dance is a blend of "stomping" (as the dance also is named) and "banging," as the men stamp the ground and bang their heads against each other. The dance looks like a fight, and can become very rough. It may be considered a way of being close without showing tender feelings. In this way, togetherness and intimacy can be simultaneously linked to aggression and masculinity. This kind of male interaction is a safe island for them, the rough way of expressing intimacy being easier to handle than other more gentle forms. Often a participant is wounded if he stumbles and falls and is stamped on by the feet of the other men.

This was the case when one of the younger skinheads linking arms with his friend, a leading skinhead, dragged him into the chaotic mob. The man being dragged stumbled and fell with the pressure, and was trampled on. Finally, someone managed to pull him out, but without his bag. Hunting everywhere for it, I later told him that he had lost it when he was drawn into the mass. This tale amazed him. He seemed proud that his friend had pushed him into the crowd, although he had been badly injured by the episode. This again is a case of a friend acting in a physical manner, but in a way which also pushes the other one down. Even though this skinhead was the one who was pushed down, he was happy about it. He accepted the injury because the event served to build up his masculinity. It was a manly way of being physical, a way that marked inclusion, and at the same time an expression of power.

This kind of brutal intimacy serves as an award, letting the other skinhead prove he can take the pain associated with the insult without any sign of weakness. Instead he is proud because he can take it with a smile. Back (1994) shows that it is expected that the person who is exposed to so-called wind-up rituals will take part in the laughter afterwards. In another situation he will be the one doing the winding up. The function of these rituals is to produce a common identity and to contest and modify the friendship. By not being offended by a wind-up, a skinhead implicitly shows that the other's play with him does not threaten the deference shown to him.

On other occasions younger skinheads might question the authority of an older skinhead more explicitly. A young skinhead once told an older one that "no one in this milieu respects you." The older skinhead promptly wanted to knock the younger one to the ground, replying, "I'll whip you with a chain." Such threats of violence between skinheads are not usually followed up in practice. Their function is to show in certain terms that the other should not dare to push the boundaries of authority any further.

These two examples also illuminate the ambivalence with which younger skinheads view the authority of their more experienced elders. For the most part, they have to subordinate themselves to the authority of the most experienced, but to even out the resentment this produces, on other occasions they try to oppose their authority. As Lindholm (1990) puts it, parricide seethes beneath the surface of abjection.

A collective response to the ambivalences of modernity

The right-wing skinhead subculture provides an atmosphere which is attractive to young boys who long for acceptance and the feelings of honor, power and excitement. In this context, violence and intimidation are made possible as a distinct part of a lifestyle constituted by a stylized version of masculinity. Violence becomes a way of claiming and asserting masculinity. Even though the kind of masculinity constructed among right-wing skinheads resembles the hegemonic masculinity portrayed in Hollywood movies and in the propaganda of the military and war, the expression of such masculinities among young working-class men is a manifestation of what Connell calls the assertion of protest masculinity. Protest masculinity is a response to the feeling of powerlessness; it is an exaggeration of masculine conventions. This protest is a collective practice, and not a quality within the individual person. As aptly put by Connell (1995, p. 111), through interaction within this milieu, young men put together a tense freaky facade, making a claim to power where there are no real resources for it. "There is a lot concern with face, a lot of work put into keeping a front." Even though there are individual variations in how this is done, it is the group which is the bearer of masculinity. Without the group, many of these men would be at a loss (Connell, 1995, p. 107).

Typically, those who enter this environment have little to lose by entering it. They have problems in achieving the same feeling of honor by their performances in other more conventional areas. The right-wing community provides them with the warmth of the brotherhood, which also gives them the sense of being part of something of great importance, something that extends their own vulnerable selves. In so doing, this subculture breaks with the individualization trend described by Ziehe. It also breaks with the self-actualization trend described by Giddens as the typical quality of today's identity projects. Rather, one can see these young men's version of masculinity as a collective response to the feeling of ontological insecurity, as described by Giddens. The group makes these men feel omnipotent; left alone, they feel vulnerable, and worth nothing. They feel secure within the group, which provides them with a collective protective cocoon, and with a collective defense against the threats of the outside world. The war between their own group and its opponents gives their fears a concrete object. Without this, a more generalized anxiety attached to the ambivalence of modern everyday life, would be more complex to handle. By constructing a rigid division of us and them, the world becomes ordered and easily defined. And their own role is transformed from being an individual nobody to being a hero among comrades.

However, the warm brotherhood has its limits. The feeling of distrust in relation to the outside world with all its possible enemies leads to a feeling of distrust between the skinheads as well. Many of them are better in dealing with power than in dealing with intimacy, hence there is only a thin layer between comradeship and intimidation. Their uniforms, their lifestyle, and the way they relate to each other are factors serving to create an atmosphere that makes violence more a regularity than a disruption. To be attacked or to attack are the only possible occasions which provide them with a sense of in-group solidarity, and a feeling of being honorable.

Notes

1. In a previous essay (Fangen, 1997), I asked what role and impact girls in the right-wing underground had. The role of the girls is important, for they are a minority in an underground dominated by ideals traditionally understood as masculine. However, this does not mean that the role and impact of boys in the underground is unambiguous.

2. Ragnarok is a militant national socialist fanzine. In 1996 it was replaced by Einherjer.

3. This image might hold some truth. However, as historian Gunnes (1993, p.178) describes it, another side to the Viking male contests for prestige was their "undimensioned exaggerations, a childish desire to impress, and to hold one's own." This description might even hold for today's right-wing activists.

4. Fanzines are journals edited by an individual or a group. They comprise reviews, editorials and interviews produced on a small scale and as cheaply as possible (Hebdige, 1979, p. 111).

5. Hávamál, Verse 43, quoted in Bootboys /Ragnar^k, 12 (2) (1992).

6. In other words, they do not try to copy the Viking man in their appearance.

The connotation between hair and gender was probably the opposite among Vikings, as some of the best known and legendary Vikings had long hair, and on one occasion even hair that continued to grow after the man had died. Harald Hårfagre (Harold with the fair hair), presumably one of the bravest and most masculine of Vikings, letting his hair grow until he had conquered the whole kingdom, personifies this view.

7. Fags might be experienced as competitors and intruders in a male community like the right-wing underground. According to Nissen's (1961) analysis of such features male communities are marked by an outwardly directed tendency to combat. In a male community based on homosexual sentiments, this competitive attitude might be directed inwards as jealousy between the men.

8. Feminine and ethnic attributes may function to lower another man's status, to provoke, or tease him. This means that femininity, homosexuality and being from an ethnic minority are all qualities which the activists consider negations of real masculinity, defined in terms of the white, race-conscious front-soldier.

References

Back, Les (1994) "The White Negro Revisited. Race and Masculinity in South London," in Lindisfarne, A. C. and N. (eds), *Dislocating Masculinities. Comparative Ethnographies*. London: Routledge.

Bauman, Zygmunt (1991) *Modernity and Ambivalence*. Cambridge: Polity Press.

Bay, Joy (1989) "Honor and Shame in the Culture of Danish Outlaw Bikers," presentation at Annual Meeting of the American Society of Criminology: Crime in Social and Moral Contexts. Reno, Nevada.

Becker, Howard (1946) *German Youth - Bond or Free*. London: Kegan Paul, Trench, Trubner & Co.

Bourdieu, Pierre (1993) *Sociology in Question*. London: Sage.

Bourdieu, Pierre and Passeron, Jean-Claude (1990) *Reproduction in Education, Society and Culture*. London: Sage.

Brod, Harry (1994) "Some Histories of some Masculinities. Jews and Others," in Brod, H. and Kaufman, M. (eds), *Theorizing Masculinities*. London: Sage.

Clarke, John (1976) "Skinheads and the Magical Recovery of Community," in Hall, S. (ed.), *Resistance through Rituals*, London: Hutchinson.

Connell, R. W. (1987) *Gender and Power. Society, the Person and Sexual Politics*, Cambridge: Polity Press.

Connell, R. W. (1995) *Masculinities*, Cambridge: Polity Press.

Fangen, Katrine (1997) "Separate or Equal? - the Emergence of an All-Female Group in the Norwegian Rightist Underground," Terrorism and Political Violence, 9, p. 3.

Frøberg, Sissel (forthcoming) *Mellom menn i militæret. Om kropp og seksualisering, makt og samhold i relasjoner mellom menn*, in Institute of Sociology, Oslo: University of Oslo.

Gibson, James William (1994) *Warrior Dreams. Paramilitary Culture in post-Vietnam America*, New York: Hill and Wang.

Giddens, Anthony (1991) *Modernity and Self-Identity. Self and Society in the Late Modern Age*, Cambridge: Polity Press.

Gilmore, David D. (1990) *Manhood in the Making. Cultural Concepts of Masculinity*, New Haven, Conn.: Yale University Press.

Goffman, Erving (1972) *Interaction Ritual. Essays on Face-to-Face Behaviour*, London.

Gunnes, Erik (1993) *Rikssamling og kristning, ca. 800-1177*, Oslo: Cappelen.

Hebdige, Dick (1979) *Subculture. The Meaning of Style*, London: Routledge.

Husbands, Christopher T. (1993) "Racism and Racist Violence: Some Theories and Policy Perspectives," in. Bjørgo, T. and Witte, R. (eds), *Racist Violence in Europe*, Basingstoke: Macmillan Press.

Jørgensen, Gunnar (1994) *To ungdomskulturer. Om vedlikehold av sosiale og kulturelle ulikheter*, Sogndal: Vestlandsforsking.

Le Bon, Gustave (1896) *The Crowd. A Study of the Popular Mind*, London: T. Fisher.

Lindholm, Charles (1990) *Charisma*, Oxford: Basil Blackwell.

Lindisfarne, Nancy (1994) "Variant Masculinities, Variant Virginities: Rethinking 'Honor and Shame'," in Cornwall, A. and Lindisfarne, N. (eds), *Dislocating Masculinity: Comparative Ethnographies*, London: Routledge.

Morgan, David (1994) "Theater of War: Combat the Military, and Masculinities," in Bord, H. and Kaufman, M. (eds), *Theorizing masculinities*, London: Sage Publications.

Mosse, George L. (1985) *Nationalism and Sexuality. Middle-Class Morality and Sexual Norms in Modern Europe*, Madison, Wis.: University of Wisconsin Press.

Nissen, Ingjald (1946) *Psykopatenes diktatur*, Oslo: Aschehoug.

Nissen, Ingjald (1961) *Absolute Monogamy. The Attitude of Woman and War*, Oslo: Aschehoug.

Pedersen, W. (1996) "Working-Class Boys at the Margins: Ethnic prejudice, Cultural Capital, and Gender," *Acta Sociologica*, 39, pp. 257-79.

Ray, John (1972) "Is Antisemitism a Cognitive Simplification? Some Observations on Australian Neo-Nazis," *New Community*, 1, pp. 207-13.

Reich, Wilhelm (1972) *The Mass Psychology of Fascism*, London: Souvenir Press.

Theweleit, Klaus (1987) *Male Fantasies*, Minneapolis, Minn.: University of Minnesota Press.

Wetherell, Margaret (1996) "The Making of Masculine Identities," in Wetherell, Margaret (ed.) *Identities, Groups and Social Issues*, London: Sage Publications.

Willis, Paul E. (1977) *Learning to Labour. How Working-Class Kids Get Working-Class Jobs*, Farnborough: Saxon House.

Ziehe, Thomas (1981) *Narziss ein neuer Sozialisationstypus?* Bensheim: Päd. Extra Buchverlag.

Chapter 12

Fathering, Masculinity and Parental Relationships

VICTOR JELENIEWSKI SEIDLER

Breaking with tradition

In the traditional family of the 1950s, in both white middle- and working-class England, fathering was a position rather than a relationship. To be a father was to occupy a position of authority and to be entitled to respect as a father. "Wait till your Dad comes home" could be heard as a threat and a warning, which could be invoked by mothers who were still largely confined to the domestic sphere and to childcare. The father could be appealed to as a figure of authority whose responsibilities as breadwinner and provider took him into the public realm of work where masculine identities were to be affirmed. So traditionally fathers were placed at the boundaries of family life, as figures of authority.

Within an Enlightenment vision of modernity there was a secularization of a largely Protestant vision where reason, as categorically separated from nature, was to order social relations. But, as I have argued in *Unreasonable Men: Masculinity and Social Theory* it was a dominant white heterosexual masculinity which alone could take this conception of reason for granted. This is why for Kant women supposedly need men and the institution of marriage in a way that men do not need women. It is supposedly through accepting the dependency upon men that women gain contact with the guidance of reason and so can aspire to greater freedom and autonomy. So it is that the dependency of men in relationships is hidden and masculinity can be defined in its dominant white heterosexual form as being independent and self-sufficient. So it is that men have to accept their responsibilities toward "others," who like women and children are deemed to be closer to nature and so left with an indirect relation to reason. This also became part of the legitimation of colonialism and came to define what was known as the "white man's burden." The metaphor stuck and it concerned a father's unquestioned authority in relation to "his" children.

Within modernity the father as the source of reason and authority was still to represent God's presence within the family. So it was that the father's word is law. His word is to be obeyed and he is to be respected. To question is already a sign of disobedience and it is to be punished. Women and children had to learn to regulate their behavior in front of the father. If they disagreed they had to keep it to themselves. Fathers were owed respect not for "who" they were but for the position they held. "I am your father and you have to respect me" – this was a respect that fathers were traditionally entitled to expect and they could rightly punish if it was not forthcoming. This was a hierarchical family form that was structured around the authority of the father. It was not easy for others to have thoughts and feelings of their own, for to disagree was already to challenge and to prove yourself disobedient. Learning to behave meant "doing what you were told."

Along with work, fatherhood was another critical way for men to affirm their male identities and to prove that they were "man enough." To have your "own" family and to father a child, especially a boy child, affirmed your transition to manhood. If the respect that was due to you was challenged through disobedience then it was your male identity that was being questioned, and therefore it had to be dealt with firmly and harshly. It is crucial that within modernity masculinity can never be taken for granted, but always has to be proved. Masculinity is something that you have to be ready to defend at any moment. Men have to be constantly "on guard," ready for a challenge that can come from any quarter, including your children. In this context it is difficult for men to trust, especially when a dominant heterosexual masculinity is set in competitive terms so that men can only feel good about themselves, knowing that they have done better than others. As a father you have to be "in control" of your family. You always have to know that your back is covered. Men want to be able to take their families for granted, knowing that male identities are mainly affirmed elsewhere in the public sphere.

If fathers are to exist as figures of authority, they traditionally learnt that they had to be slightly distant and removed from everyday family life, for they had to be impartial and objective. So it is that fathers are of the family, but not really part of what is going on. To get too involved in establishing relationships with your children was to threaten and maybe compromise your position of authority. It was to make you partial and potentially biased in your rulings. Fathers were to exist as one removed, as the protectors and the breadwinners. Many men still pay lip service to the family, but their attention and focus is often elsewhere, for it is mainly at work that men can prove themselves and show their individual success and achievements, which remain critical if you are to "make it as a man" and not feel that you have somehow failed as a man. Fathers traditionally had the role, at least in white middle class families, of mediating the outside world of work, politics and civic life.

Fathers were to be the source of authority within the family and within a hierarchical family form there could only be a single source. So it is also in the State with the Queen in Parliament. But this could mean that it was difficult for men to learn to negotiate with their partners as part of a changed vision of shared responsibility, at least in relation to children. Men could feel threatened because their masculinity was being put at risk. There is still the challenge of "who is wearing the trousers in your family" and at work men can find it difficult to refuse a promotion that involves a move because they can be told "if you do not have authority within your family, getting them to do what you want, possibly you are unsuited to a position of authority within the firm." This is often a source of conflict as middle-class men can find it difficult to accept how changes in family life can have an impact upon life at work. We need a psychology that can illuminate such tensions without assuming that it is a matter of how people learn to cope with their subjective experience alone.

Traditionally it was women's task to look after the home and take responsibility for the everyday care of children. This was women's work and it was defined as feminine so that men would "not be seen dead doing it." A man's responsibilities lay elsewhere. But though this was normative it could not always be realized, for even in the 1950s there was sometimes work for women but not for men. In the Jute factories of Dundee men were often left unemployed as "kettle cleaners" in the home. But there was also a high degree of domestic violence as men still felt that women had "to know their place." Violence was used to affirm a masculinity which could not be affirmed through work. Men might help around the house but they would never help with putting the laundry out because they did not want to be "seen" helping. But traditionally working-class families were organized around men's work and the man expected dinner to be ready when he came home. Often carrying the frustrations and humiliations of work, there would often be considerable tension when he came home and children report how they learnt to keep out of the way and how it was often like stepping on eggs when "he" was around. Children often absorbed the atmosphere of tension and years later they could still feel it in their bodies.

Sometimes it was part of their determination to father in a different way with their own children.

Fathering and authority

With the challenges of feminism and gay liberation in the 1970s, people have been led to rethink the patriarchal family and the traditional authority of the father. There have been radical changes across a single generation within the West in the ways authority is to be refigured within a postmodern world. This is reflected in the changing meanings of respect, for young people more often think of respect as something that has to be earned for the actions and behavior of a person, not simply for the positions they hold. Sometimes this is experienced as a sharp conflict for children who grow up, for instance, within traditional Asian families where respect is tied to honor and shame, and where fathers expect to be automatically respected for their position. Children can feel torn between a sense of obligation and the freedom that the West seems to offer for them to develop relationships of their own. We need a moral psychology which illuminates some of the pain and tension involved, rather than simply celebrates the fluidity of postmodern identities in which people are supposedly free to create new hybrid identities out of what is culturally available.

Tension is also developing in relationships between fathers and children within working-class families where, with the decline of traditional industries, fathers can no longer provide secure job and so a "future" for their sons in particular. So it is that some of the supports of a father's position within the family are undermined and therefore some of the basis of respect. Parents can no longer protect their children from the exigencies of schooling, so that they can feel more at the mercy of their teachers' evaluations, whereas formerly school did not have to matter in the same way, for there was a secure job or apprenticeship waiting for you. But those days are past and working-class children can be left resenting their parents for not feeling able to defend them at school, for they often feel uncomfortable going into a school that left them marked with a sense of failure. It can seem as though middle-class parents are less likely to take the side of the teachers and more able to stand up for their children. This can diminish the authority of working-class fathers in the eyes of their children. This is exacerbated when fathers are unemployed and cannot afford to provide children with the goods they see advertised around them.

This tension between fathers and children is reflected culturally in the challenges to a Protestant ethic that, as Weber grasps it in *The Protestant Ethic and the Spirit of Capitalism,* is tied to a dominant white heterosexual masculinity. Traditionally it is through working that you affirm your male identity and prove that you are not "good for nothing." Work was a crucial aspect of self-respect and it was a key way in which you affirmed you were a "real" man. But if for their sons, in particular, there is no work to get out of bed for, fathers can resent their sons for they assume that "they are not trying hard enough": as far as they are concerned "there is always a job if you try hard enough to get it." But sons and daughters can feel that there is no point talking because parents just do not understand. There is a difference in ethics here that needs to be appreciated within the terms of moral psychology. Where there is a breakdown of communications, children can feel that their parents just are not interested, especially when it comes to such issues as drugs. Runaways report being thrown out of home because their drug use reflects badly on their parents. There seems to be little point in hanging around. Sometimes there is direct conflict with the father, who feels it is his duty to legislate what is right and wrong for his children. Within a different ethic they feel they cannot respect their father unless they respect themselves. This reflects a shift in culture that fathers can find it hard to grasp.

Fathering and parental relationships

Profound cultural changes are opening up issues for the revisioning of fathering as a relation within a more democratic family form. Within a postmodern family authority has to be shared and adults have to learn to relate differently to their children. If we expect children to knock at our doors before they come in they also expect us to do the same. This is part of a different vision of fairness and equality. This means that parental authority needs to be refigured and this can be particularly difficult for men who are being asked to give up the power and authority they often saw their father exercise when they were growing up and which they often internalized as their entitlement "as a father." This is not a matter of different expectations attaching themselves to the "role" of being a father, but of a different vision of parenthood as a relationship.

Some of these changes are reflected around issues of birth. Different images are in play. In the 1960s we still have the image of the father anxiously pacing up and down outside the hospital door where his wife is giving birth. He is waiting for news, possibly with cigarette in hand. He is agitated but also excluded from what is going on. In the 1990s we can have the image of the young father who is sitting next to his partner, possibly his wife, having supported her through the experience of birth. He has prepared with his partner for the birth and he feels part of what has been going on. Sometimes it is inappropriate for a father to be present because he can make the situation more difficult, so it would be wrong for this to be a duty; rather it is a choice that people make according to the feelings they have. In a lesbian relationship women often support each other. In either case it can be a matter of being protective without being intrusive. For men this is often not easy to do for it involves the deconstruction of a dominant masculinity. Men have to accept that they are not the center of the show and that, at least for awhile, the primary bond is between mother and child. His task might be to protect this relationship while developing his own with the baby.

This is to redefine the notion of the father as protector and at the same time to recognize that others can equally play the part. But in heterosexual relationships this is traditionally a relationship of power in which the father's position is reinforced. Though the woman has given birth, the child is the property of the father. But a different vision of protection is at work in a more equal relationship where the new mother is requesting that telephone calls be made and visits be monitored so that she has the time and space that she needs. Until the 1980s it was expected that fathers would go home soon after the birth and it has taken time to recognize how important it can be for fathers to also be part of this process of early bonding. He has to develop his own relationship, while also recognizing that for the time being at least the primary relationship might be between mother and baby.

Again this reflects a break with the sexual politics of the 1970s and the visions of equality that were around. There was a challenge to the notions of "mothering" and "fathering" and the idea that parenting was more usefully thought about as a gender-neutral set of activities that could be more or less equally divided. This helped men recognize that there wasn't anything "natural" in mothering and that mothers had to learn how to bond and breastfeed, how to change nappies and bath a baby. For it was crucial that men learn confidence in these activities from the first, rather than expect their partners to teach them these skills when they came back from hospital. This sets up a dependency that is unhelpful, for women have more than enough to cope with in the early months without also having to instruct their partners.

But in the 1970s it was too easy to think of equality in terms of sameness and to think that nature has to give way to a reconstructed culture. So for instance, if breastfeeding seemed to be in the way of parents being able to establish an equal relationship with the baby, then possibly bottle feeding should be preferred, for this allowed for greater equality. This was a mistaken vision that failed to appreciate the importance of breastfeeding and was part of an intolerance of difference. It is important for fathers to be equally involved from the very beginning and this means, for instance, learning to change nappies and give baths. But we should show a respect for nature through being wary of any technological interventions to sustain an artificial vision of equality. It might be that fathers have to learn their own humility and respect the bond between mother and baby as being in some sense primary, while recognizing that their own parental relationship and possibly priority will come into being in its own time, sometimes when the child is two years old. It can be difficult for fathers to learn how to be involved without feeling that they have to take over or create yet another activity in which they have to prove themselves.

The point is that fathers have to develop their own relationships with babies right from the beginning and this takes time and attention. It has a rhythm and timing of its own, but depends upon spending time and allowing the relationship to develop as you get to know your child. This is part of fathering as a relationship, and like all relationships it goes through different phases and you can feel tested in particular ways. Though men often talk about wanting to develop more of a relationship with their children, it can be difficult not to give priority to work because this is the sphere where male identities are sustained. As men growing up within the terms of dominant masculinity, we can be left feeling that we should be able to cope with whatever situations life presents us with. This is the way that we prove ourselves as men. It can be difficult to realize that we have to make difficult choices, otherwise we are going to be stretched between too many activities, drained and unable to focus our attention. Men often feel that they should be able to cope with these diverse demands and often fail to appreciate how their lives will change with having children.

Often there is resistance to the idea that if men are to be more involved in fathering, they are going to have to think differently about their priorities at work. This is a difficult transition for both women and men within a culture in which it has been possible to develop more equal gender relations, with both partners working and paying into their housing. This equality is often sustained through putting off the time to have children;

there is a sense that this vision of gender equality cannot be sustained with children, for it is built around the notion of individuals as free and equal autonomous agents. It can be difficult to appreciate think the realities of dependency. The assumption is that routines will hardly be disrupted with a new child and that both partners will be able to return to work after a few days and that life will "return to normal." But it never does and the promises of equal childcare are often left behind, as it is often men who return to work after a few days' leave and women are literally left "holding the baby." The situation does not have to be as grim as it is currently, as in England and in Scandinavia there are schemes which allow partners to share a year of leave between themselves. If men do not participate for at least a month then both parents lose the tax concessions available.

Young people in our culture are little prepared for the realities of new parenting. With the breakdown of traditional communities much less support is available from within extended families. The freedom that young people achieved through moving away from home can mean that they are left isolated in a tower block with young children. Often the difficulties of the early months can be a cause of deep resentment, especially when women feel betrayed by the promises of greater equality. Often there is too much to do with the new baby to work anything through emotionally. Often it is about 16 months later when there is a little more space in the relationship that unresolved feelings come to the surface and we find that many relationships break down irretrievably. It is as if it is too difficult to work through the issues that are raised, especially since having children can bring unresolved feelings to the surface from your own childhood experience. This disrupts the neat pattern of relationships which were formerly neatly organized according to reason alone. Often there is little experience to fall back upon and too few people around who can be trusted to give advice. Rationalism that seemed so reliable when it was a matter of organizing tasks before babies came onto the scene, now seems unable to illuminate the emotional issues and conflicts that young couples face. Often they give up trying in the hope that things might turn out to be different with another partner. Or women decide it is easier to bring up their children on their own.

Fathering and masculinity

Important changes are taking place within Western societies in the nature of fathering. The changes are largely the result of the challenges of feminism and gay liberation but they also involve a redefining of heterosexual masculinities. These changes are affecting diverse masculinities across class, "race" and ethnicities. In crucial ways they also relate to larger structural changes and the decline of many traditional industries, which provided work through which men affirmed their masculinities. With the changes in the labor market and many of the new jobs being available to women, men have been forced to renegotiate their involvement in domestic life and childcare. But there is also a feeling that men want to be more involved with their children than their fathers were with them.

Many men seem to feel disappointed at the distance they feel from their own fathers. They grew up feeling that it was "unreasonable" to want more contact with your father because this just proved how ungrateful you were for the work he was doing for the family. So boys learnt not to expect much contact and to feel that their fathers "had more important things to do." Sometimes boys would go to great lengths to help their fathers, for instance handing tools in the shed or stacking shelves in the family shop, just so they could have more contact. But this was a need that was hard for boys to name because they were supposed to be self-sufficient and need is a sign of weakness.

Often older men carry a sense of bitterness, for they had grown up in a culture which left them thinking that it was fine to give priority to work because they could always take up their relationships with their children later. They never learnt that once the emotional distances had been created they would be very difficult to undo. Often they have to live with embarrassment and are uneasy in their relationships with their children. They would wish things to be different and they have grown up thinking, as men, that there is always something that you can *do* to make things better. This is equally true in their relationships with their partners. The idea was that once a relationship had been established, it could be taken for granted as a supportive background. Men could then go out into the public world of work where individual achievement and success, in the middle-class world, were ways of affirming male identities. There was little sense that relationships had to be nourished or that they required time and attention. Men could feel resentful when women expressed dissatisfaction, secure in the self-justification that they were working for the family. They want women to feel grateful and if they complain that they are not getting enough, men can feel bitter and betrayed.

Within modernity a dominant masculinity learns to think of relationships in mechanistic terms. It is only when a car breaks down that it needs attention. So it is with relationships; it is difficult for men to appreciate what time and attention needs to go into sustaining a relationship. At some level men can feel haunted by a sense that they are not very good at relationships, but this echoes a Protestant notion, as I have explored it in *Recreating Sexual Politics*, that at some level men are bad and that their sexualities are "animal." Men are constantly engaged, often through compulsive relations at work, due to feelings that they are good enough. In the family this can mean men becoming competitive with their partners, as they want to prove that they are "good" fathers. This can be an arena for tension, as women often feel uneasy when they feel guilty about the hours they spend at work and whether they are being "good enough" mothers. Often it is difficult to negotiate and in the early years there can be such a focus upon the needs of the child, that the relationship between the adults ceases to exist in its own right as they drift into relating through the child.

We need a moral psychology that can begin to illuminate some of these changes, while recognizing the inadequacy of thinking in terms of changes in the fathering role. The sense of disappointment, or as Robert Bly has talked of it in *Iron John*, the "hunger" that men often carry for contact with their own fathers, is often carried into these new fathering relationships. If we are not thinking about parenting as a set of gender-neutral activities that can be more or less equally shared, we have to think about what is specific in the fathering relationship, recognizing the equal importance that fathers can play in the lives of their daughters and sons. But it might also be that fathers have a different part to play in the lives of their sons, since they have a particular responsibility when it comes to initiating them into manhood. Bly has been helpful in raising some of these issues, though I think he falls for a return to traditional solutions. This leads him in his distinction between the mother's house and the father's house to reproduce the traditional gender division of labor and unwittingly to underestimate how important it can be for fathers to be involved emotionally with their children. If Bly acknowledges this, he cannot place it theoretically.

It might well be that it is through fathering that we are revisioning masculinities. An involvement in supporting their partners through pregnancy and birth has been a powerful transformative experience for many men. This is a participation that cannot be forced, but is only appropriate where men have a feeling for it. Sometimes it strengthens the relationship and allows men to bond . But this can be difficult to sustain as men return to work, since many men are able to split and separate

Among Men

emotionally as soon as the front door closes behind them. Spending time with small children can be difficult, for it involves "slowing down" in a culture that teaches that people have to "speed up" so that they can keep their emotions in check. It can be threatening for fathers to spend time, because this means slowing down and they fear the unresolved feelings that might surface. It can also challenge the vision they have of themselves as, for instance, they find themselves angry with their child, while thinking of themselves as being quite rational and in control. Spending time can challenge men in unfamiliar ways and it might be that they have to create contexts in which they can explore the sources of their anger, that have so long been suppressed.

There is a tension between "who" men have to be at work and "who" they have to be with small children. A different pacing and a different learning has to take place. Unless men can learn to care for themselves, developing more of a relationship with their own bodies, it is going to be difficult to care for others. Unless, as Simone Weil has it in *Gravity and Grace*, they learn to "read" themselves in different ways, it will be hard to read the needs of the child you are with. This has to do with a psychology that appreciates the significance of feelings and sensitivity. Within the rationalist culture of modernity it is difficult for men to appreciate and value their sensitivity and intuition. These capacities are too easily dismissed as "irrational" and "unreasonable." But this often makes boys and then men insensitive to themselves. Too often they tacitly learn this in relationships with their fathers who traditionally feel they have to "set an example" for their sons, in particular, of resilience and strength. Often fathers will not share their sadness and tears, but will keep these feelings to themselves. Psychology has to be able to illuminate how this leaves boys feeling that there has to be something "wrong with them" because they feel sad. Not only do they learn to suppress these feelings, not even acknowledging them to themselves, but they feel guilty and ashamed whenever such "unmanly " emotions surface.

Spending time with small children can work to allow men to accept the nourishment of an unconditional love they would usually reject. The love that young babies give can touch men who have not allowed themselves to receive emotionally before. This is because men learn that they have to be strong for others but should not have emotional needs themselves. This creates an imbalance within many heterosexual relationships, since women are often left feeling bad that they are the ones who express their emotional needs. This can confirm men's power, for needs are too easily identified with weakness and men's superiority can be confirmed through not needing. But this imbalance can encourage women to look for the love and emotional support they are not getting from their partners and men can feel excluded, recognizing that their partners' love seems to be going exclusively to the child. This can create resentment that can lead to jealousy and competition with the new baby and to affairs which become a means of revenge, though not often recognized as such.

Sometimes men can learn to give to their children love that they never received for themselves when they were young. This can be part of a healing process. This can help men to receive and take in love for themselves, thereby giving them a way of learning a new balance between giving and receiving. Paradoxically this might be something they learn in fathering that they might find it harder to learn directly with their partners where they are locked into particular patterns. This is part of what Foucault meant when he talked about caring as a practice in *Caring for the Self*. This is not a matter of attitude alone, but a matter of providing men with different experiences as fathers and thereby with different practices of care that can help to transform their sense of self. A revisioning of fathering as a relationship can help in developing different notions of masculinity, in which men can be both strong and tender, loving and assertive. This involves challenging definitions of masculinity that conceive it as a relationship of power alone. This means that masculinity has to be deconstructed as a relationship of power because it can only be part of the problem and never part of the solution. But it is not enough for boys to be brought up to be anti-sexist: they also need ways of affirming their masculinities. At the moment there is considerable and widespread confusion about how masculinities are to be revisioned.

Authority and parental relationships

Within a postmodern society there is a crisis in traditional forms of authority. An anti-feminist backlash has attempted to blame this on feminism and the challenges it made to the traditional family. It is argued that there is no authority within the family and that children are not being taught the difference between "right" and "wrong." In some movements, for instance Promise Keepers, this has led men to feel that they have failed their partners through having affairs and have failed their children through not being there for them. They are determined to apologise for not keeping their promises and want to return to their traditional positions within the family. Where a change of heart has taken place it is to be welcome, but men will also have to appreciate that the world has moved on and that women are determined to develop their new freedoms and equality. It is yet to be seen how some of these conflicts are to be resolved, but few can doubt the significance of such events as the March on Washington which mobilized so many African-American men.

How are we to think about the nature of authority within the terms of the democratic family? Should we be thinking of intimate relations in terms of democracy? As the traditional notions of authority which underpinned fatherhood as a position are challenged, so we have to rethink fathering in relation to masculinity. Some men find it difficult not to identify authority with being authoritarian. They can find it hard to set boundaries and exert their authority in different ways. Bly's work has been helpful through showing some of the confusions in men's relationships to feminism, though he is too quick to generalize about this in terms of men being "feminized." He is more helpful in giving examples of how men lose their own emotional ground so that they allow others to invade their psychic space, unable to be clear about their needs and wants and so negotiate from a point of clarity in their relationships. Unable to redefine their masculinity it can be as if they are like children in the relationship, leaving it up to women to also exercise an authority which they find difficult to cope with. Sometimes they are fearful of negotiating new fathering relations for they are anxious not to lose the love and relationship they have begun to develop with children and which is so new in their experience.

But it is important for men to recognize their relationships with their partners as being primary, so learning how to also accept and receive the love that is available to them. This can be particularly threatening within an adult relationship because men can find it difficult to acknowledge their emotional dependency without feeling that their sense of male identity is at risk. Men can feel "on guard" against any signs of weakness and vulnerability. It can be difficult to express love without feeling compromised in your sense of independence and self-sufficiency. Rather men often feel that they have to be able to handle their problems on their own and this is often the unconscious message that is passed across generations. So even if boys want to talk about what is happening for them they find it almost impossible to say "I feel … ."

Many people still feel that to talk about what might be particular in fathering is to get men "off the hook" and so allow them to escape from the everyday involvement in childcare. The men's rights movement has been quick to value the traditional breadwinner role of fathering and to suggest that to ask men to be more involved emotionally and relationally with their children is to ask them to be mothers. This is not to say that fathers do not care for their children but to recognize that both fathers and children are entitle to much more from the relationship and that the society has to rethink the organization of work. We have to be careful that notions of gender equality are not established at the cost of children, whose voice is often silenced in the equation. Rather we have to recognize how important it is to evaluate culture in terms of how it treats its children. We need to question the idea of the insatiable child, that however much you give children, they will always want more. If they have the contact and recognition they need, they will know it will be available to them when they need it.

We need to rethink the responsibilities of fathering in different terms, not simply as an obligation but as a relationship in which fathers can also receive for themselves. Often it is too late when men so closely identified with work, begin to re-evaluate their lives and feel what is important to them. It becomes difficult to recover a relationship when it has been lost. Rather we need to refigure men's lives as part of reworking the relationship between public and private life and so the place of relationships within men's lives. We need a psychology that can link masculinities with emotional life and which can validate emotions and feelings as sources of knowledge.

We also need to understand how it is that so many men fail to sustain relationships with children from their earlier families, though some men go to great efforts to sustain their connection with their children. Many men seem able to split off as if the past can be left behind them and life can begin anew. With widespread family breakdowns, there is a great deal of unresolved pain that children carry that is not far from the surface. They can feel abandoned by their fathers and this can be a source of considerable unease and anger that is projected onto those who are still around. Children can often be left feeling that they were somehow to blame for the divorce, and that if only they had behaved differently things might have turned out differently. This is why it is so important to find more open and honest ways of communicating with children. But unless fathers, as men, can be more open about their own feelings and emotions, it will be difficult to share with their children. Rather they will seek to protect their children, often because they cannot face the issues themselves.

Psychology also needs to be able to listen to children and validate their experience. This involves a different vision of respect in which we break with a rationalist tradition, which in Kant's terms can only respect a person for their thoughts and ideas but which cannot respect a person's feelings and emotions. It is not simply the Cartesian rational self, at the core of much psychological theory, which has fragmented with postmodernity, but the vision of reason that has been set so categorically against nature. If our emotions and feelings are not to be denigrated as forms of unreason situated in the body and therefore radically separated from thoughts which are located in our minds, we need different ways of revisioning the self. This involves recognizing the integrity of our emotions and feelings so that in respecting persons we are also acknowledging the hurt and damage that is inflicted emotionally. A new psychology has to broaden its vision of personal identities as it appreciates the different dimensions of experience and relationships.

The gendering of psychology will be part of recognizing the workings of power in relation to emotion. This involves questioning the identification of a dominant, white, heterosexual masculinity with a vision of reason separated from nature, and which within the terms of an Enlightenment vision of modernity has provided the terms on which "others" have been judged and found lacking. Since modernity has been implicitly shaped as a masculine project it has been easy for men to talk in the impersonal voice of reason, before they have learnt to talk more personally for themselves. As men learn to talk in a different voice with their children, they can begin to also open up a dialogue with a diversity of masculinities. It will be part of learning to talk to ourselves as men in different ways. As we explore the relationships between fathering and masculinity, so we hopefully open up some of the pathways for change. Hopefully as men learn to father in different ways, they will learn to revision masculinity as part of this process.

Chapter 13

Men's Lack of Family Orientation: Some Reflections on Scandinavian Research on Families

CHRISTIAN KULLBERG

The aim of this paper is to make a critical review of the Scandinavian research on men and their families, and the "problem" concerning men's "family orientation" reported in studies carried out in the last 10 to 15 years. In this research it has been assumed that women have come "out," and strengthened their positions on the labor market while men have not taken a corresponding step into the family. The male position has been described as "a lack of concern with child rearing and domestic work."

An analysis of the assumed "problem" with men's family orientation can be made by reviewing family research on the prevailing conditions in three different areas: 1) men's actual *work and responsibilities* in the home, 2) the *distribution of paid and unpaid work*, and 3) *the distribution of power*, between men and women. Doing this investigation, it becomes clear that many of the descriptions and explanations of the current "problem" are oversimplified and problematic.

Introduction

In the last 15 to 20 years, the field of research that deals with men's and women's relations to the reproductive sphere has been studied from a feminist perspective in the Scandinavian countries. Great efforts have been made to describe the conditions of women, and research has focused on what Björnberg (1993, p. 13) calls "the conditions of women in their commuting between employment and family." Family research has neglected to investigate the conditions of fathers in the family sphere. One neglected area, for instance, is men's thoughts about and plans for matters concerning family planning (SCB, 1987). It has been noted that "there are few studies of men and their engagement in questions belonging to the 'family sphere' of life. In the industrialised society, family and children have become the domain of women, while men have been made responsible for almost all activities outside the home" (SCB, 1987, p. 13). It is my conviction that there are three main reasons for this lack of attention to the role of men within the family. First of all, "the intimate sphere" of society has by tradition not been regarded as an area in which men have influence. Second, feminist researchers have (quite understandably) concentrated on drawing attention to the conditions of women. Third, and finally, as Jalmert (1993) suggests, male researchers have paid gender studies (as well as family research) very little attention.

In family research, men's family relations often have been interpreted as "a lack of involvement and presence in the family" (Björnberg, 1994a, p. 49). One example of this way of analyzing the question is Björnberg's (1994b) description of the above-mentioned "problem." According to Björnberg, women have to a great extent entered the labor market, while men "have not taken the corresponding step into the family and involved themselves in the low paid housework" (Björnberg, 1994b, p. 127). Other questions taken up are fathers' insufficient participation in child rearing, and their lack of responsibility for the work of co-ordination being done in families (e.g. Brandth and Kvande, 1993).

It could be claimed that the premises underlying many of the studies made of the family are asymmetric. By this I mean that research in this field has a tendency to be one-sided, in two different respects.

First, this vein of research (as the quotation from Björnberg, 1994a implies) has a tendency to regard positions taken and actions carried out by men as being problematic, while women's strategies and actions have often been seen as unproblematic. Men's deviations from the expected level of participation in household work and other routines have been used as an argument supporting the view that men are a "problem." Women's possible lack of orientation to the labor market, however, has attracted far less interest.

Secondly, in some cases, feminist research has neglected the dynamic aspects of men's and women's relations to working life and the family, and to some extent treated "gender/sexual relations [as if they were] shaped by a single overarching factor" (Mac an Ghaill, 1996, p.1). From my point of view, this is a simplistic way of approaching the problem. The problem of inequality between men and women is a truly "relational" or "interactional" phenomenon, and should therefore be studied from this perspective. By neglecting the dynamic aspects of the problem, "social mechanisms" that constitute the "gender system" remain hidden.[1] The gender system is maintained in different ways within different spheres of society, and with different logics, involving intricate processes which are contextually shaped (Connell, 1995; Cedersund and Kullberg, 1996; Kullberg, 1998a, 1998b) and should be studied on these premises. To cite Connell, it seems relevant to ask:

> if it is actually masculinity that is a problem in gender politics? Or is it rather the institutional arrangements that produce inequality, and thus generate the tensions that have brought "masculinity" under scrutiny? (Connell, 1995, pp. 42-3).

Both the above-mentioned tendencies have to some extent led to stereotyping. Results from studies of patriarchy have partly given the impression that only men contribute to the reproduction of inequality between the sexes. The tendencies mentioned here have also created the impression that gender relations in capitalist societies favor all men unilaterally, and disfavor all women. These results might led to a "victimization" of women as a group, and an understanding of men as fundamentally responsible for the gender order (some researchers have criticized explanations of this kind, e.g. Holter and Aarseth, 1993; Kullberg, 1994, 1997).

An objection that can be made to feminist research on family relations is that some of these studies have a "functionalist" or "normative-ideological" tendency, a criticism that feminist researchers themselves (e.g. Björnberg and Bäck-Wiklund, 1990) have made of traditional sociological concepts of the family in the Parsonian (e.g. Parson and Bales, 1955) version. This means that some feminist researchers tend to treat women's experiences and women's interpretations of relations within the family as norms for this area. Such perspectives can lead to an uncritical approach to the questions at hand. Åström (1992, p. 50) discusses this problem and claims that there is a possibility that feminist research turns "gender blind" if it pays too short-sighted attention to questions of power relations in the gender area. This blindness might result in the neglect of other determinants on a macro (e.g. the class structure) and a micro level (e.g. specific fields of activity).

This article will deal with research on the family and specifically research on men's family orientation. In doing so, I will try to give an explanation of the "problem" that takes into consideration what I have earlier called "relational" or "interactional" aspects of the relation between women and men.

The assumed "problem"

It is not uncommon for feminist research on mothers and fathers or women's and men's work and involvement in the family to describe the family as an area in which men have considerable power over women (e.g. Björnberg, 1994b; Haavind, 1982, 1985; Holmberg, 1993; Jónasdóttir, 1991a, 1991b). According to Haavind, men's power in other spheres of society has an impact on the relations within the family. Haavind states that men's greater authority and higher status in society leads to their domination over women within the family. Women are in a "relatively subordinated" position to men, meaning that they can choose to do whatever they like as long as they remain subordinate to men. Women's career choices are, for example, beneficial to men as long as their aspirations do not conflict with those of men. Within marriage, the subordination of women is expressed through the unjust division of work. Haavind (1982) describes the union between wife and husband as an unequal relationship in which the love and care of women is the driving force that makes them ignore the unfairness of the division of work within the family. Haavind, as well as Björnberg (1994b, p. 126) uses the fact that women in their work within the family adapt to the demands of their husbands' work as an indication of the existence of an asymmetrical power relation between men and women.

With references to Holter and Aarseth (1994) and Haavind (1882), Lindgren (1996, p. 10) claims that paid work is a "very important and desirable power-centre for men." According to Lindgren, it is of vital importance for men that it is accepted that there is a clear-cut division of working life and family life. This strict division is the foundation of men's superior position. Lindgren seems to claim that men intentionally stay on the periphery of the family as a strategy for preserving energy for activities they value more highly (especially working life), and that in the same way they strive to keep their family life and their wife separate from their working life since these parts of their lives could harm their superiority at work.

Other researchers (Holmberg, 1993), who have focused on the daily life of married and unmarried couples without children, claim that women, from a social-psychological perspective, are more dependent on men, than men are on women. Bosseldal (1995) reaches a similar conclusion. By studying narratives of unmarried couples in love, she concludes that men have more influence on the relationship during this period than do women. She also claims that the men to a higher degree than the women had the opportunity to have their own "tastes" satisfied (Bosseldal, 1995, p. 33). Women, on the other hand, seemed more inclined to adapt their tastes to those of their fiancés.

The conclusions from these three studies (Haavind, 1982, 1985; Holmberg, 1993; Bosseldal, 1995) are in line with the findings in Jónasdóttir (1991a, 1991b). She claims that the heterosexual love relation is founded on the fact that women give a proportionally greater amount of love, care and lust to their partner, than men do. Friberg (1993) builds her description on the same theme, and claims that mothers giving love (and care) to other members develop "strategies of adjustment" of their actions (household work, care-taking and paid work) within the family.

Other researchers (Lundén Jacoby and Näsman, 1989, p. 285; Ohlander, 1993) have found that women, in comparison with men, in families use proportionally more time on work which includes maintaining and preserving strategies in relation to material subjects (e.g. cooking, cleaning and doing the laundry) or in relation to other individuals (e.g. nursing). The researchers claim that these circumstances lead to negative consequences for women's career opportunities.

The results from these studies all seem to point in the same direction. In close relations, men are superior and women are subordinate. An important factor contributing to this seems to be men's aspirations on the labor market and women's adaptive/assisting/supplying strategies within the family.

An alternative view

Studies focusing on the constant weakening of men's positions within the family since the industrial revolution can be seen as a contrast to the above-mentioned explanations of the power relation between men and women within the family.

Some researchers have pointed to the fact that fathers in agrarian society, when the family as a unit was of primary importance to both production and reproduction, had an unquestionably close relation to their children (Frykman and Löfgren, 1979; Gillis, 1993). Men's close relation to their children included both the daily care of children (Gillis, 1993) and the socialization of boys in the work done by men (Frykman and Löfgren, 1979).

The breakthrough of the industrialized society led to a separation of production and reproduction in time and space. Reproduction remained within the family, while production was moved outside. When men became employed by others, they also became "absent fathers" (Sandqvist, 1993), and they were clearly separated from the ongoing responsibility for the care of their children. According to Sandqvist, the consequences of this change led to a definitive loss of power within the family which men until then had held. The era of men's patriarchal power within the family ended, and "the mother became the key-character of the home" (Sandqvist, 1993, p. 36). Kortteinen (1982) and Falk (1983), who have studied the situation of men in Finland, claim that working conditions in industrialized society have contributed to the estrangement of the father from the home. Kortteinen's explanation of this phenomenon is that paid work in industrialized urban society provides few opportunities for either women or men to take part in unconstrained creative activities. At the same time, life within the family does not offer the same opportunity for traditionally male activities as it does for traditionally female activities. "Male tasks" have to a greater extent been moved outside the home, and many of the remaining activities are of a kind that women often take more responsibility for. This means that few tasks remain which are not controlled by women and over which women do not exert some kind of "model-power." Since men are uncomfortable with many of these tasks, there is an obvious risk of there being too few activities in the family which are considered by men to be concrete and meaningful.

To summarize, this research shows that men have lost their traditionally strong position in the family. Instead, women have gained in influence in this area.

Life within families

Along with other relations within the family, relations between men and women, wife and husband and mother and father are characterized by intricate processes of negotiations (Haavind, 1982, 1984, 1985; Kimmel, 1987; Björnberg and Bäck-Wiklund, 1990; Bäck-Wiklund and Lindfors, 1990; Brandth and Kvande, 1993; Aarseth and Holter, 1993). Decisions on the division of work within the family, and men's involvement in family matters are not exceptional areas in this respect, and it is important to refine the picture that family research has given of men and their families.

Three areas are of special concern in this scrutiny. First, descriptions of men's interest and involvement in families seem to have been too pessimistic. Studies carried out in recent years indicate that men today are more family-oriented than had previously been suggested. Secondly, the premises for much of the existing research on men's and women's involvement in the family matters can be questioned. Thirdly, a closer examination of research on women's and men's power within the family is important. The question that should be asked is whether men really do possess, and exercise, more power than women within the family.

Men's family orientation

Research has indicated that men's interest in the family sphere has increased. Men orient themselves to the family (Jalmert, 1984; Hwang, 1987; Björnberg, 1996). At the same time, this research indicates that some "traditional" lines of action still remain (Bäck-Wiklund and Bergsten, 1996). Björnberg (1992) claims, on the basis of a very large survey, that Swedish men today regard their family life as being more important than their working life. More and more fathers are also reflecting on the relation between time spent at work and time spent with their children. When fathers describe this "dilemma" they see it as a "lack of time" (Bäck-Wiklund and Bergsten, 1996). Men do not seem to be able to get enough time for care-taking, household work and employment to the extent that they would like. Sandqvist (1993) estimates that today, Swedish men do 40 per cent of all the work within the family. Another Swedish study (Flood and Gråsjö, 1995) indicates that young fathers are reducing the time spent at work and increasing time spent on household work.

Holter and Aarseth (1993), who conducted a study among Norwegian fathers (age 25-45 years) with small children, found that the men interviewed took part in household work and advocated an ideal division of work in which both sexes contribute equally. Despite this, their wives seemed to have the greater part of the responsibility for the co-ordination of different functions within the family. In a study of fathers in three generations, Åström (1990) found that changes have occurred from generation to generation. Today's fathers take part in everyday duties to a greater extent than their fathers and grandfathers did. Today's fathers also have a closer relation to their children when they carry out their paternal responsibilities. The change that Åström's study indicates can best be described by men's decrease in "orientation toward achievements" and increase in "orientation toward relations." These results are also to some extent confirmed by statistics which show that men's use of parental leave is increasing (RFV, 1994).

Research also shows that men are capable of performing household duties and care-taking (Lamb, 1976; Hwang, 1985a; Lamb, 1987; Huttonen, 1995). Children's images of their fathers are also positive. Hyvönen (1993) has found that Swedish children feel that their fathers have many responsibilities within the family, and that they have considerable practical and emotional involvement in the daily lives of their children. The children interviewed ascribed a good caring ability to their fathers. When the children were asked who was the most appropriate parent to take care of them in the case of a divorce, 50 per cent of the children stated that both of their parents were equally appropriate, 25 per cent mentioned their mothers, and 16 per cent mentioned their fathers as the most appropriate.

Premises of studying power relations within the family

The premises of studies on time spent in the family (household work and child-rearing) have been questioned. McKee (1982), for instance, has objected that time-studies focus narrowly on specifically physical aspects of the care of children (e.g. breast-feeding, cooking, bathing). These studies, however, shed little light on qualitative aspects of the care that is given. Two other premises of studies of this kind can also be questioned. One objection is that some of these studies do not include the *total* amount of time spent in (any) type of work, but only time spent in domestic work. A second objection is that it is complicated to almost automatically apply (as has been done in some cases) macro explanations of power relations between men and women to relations within the family.

Regarding the amount of time spent by men and women at work, there are studies indicating that the differences between the two groups are very small. If household work and paid work are considered to be two areas that should be regarded as equal when estimating work effort, a comparison shows that Swedish men and women spend approximately the same amount of time at work. Men, however, spend more time doing paid work and women spend more time doing unpaid work (SCB, 1986, 1992).[2] Results from 1982 to 1985 indicate that the difference between the time that men and women spend on work is less than, or equal to, two hours a week. This means that women spend insignificantly more time than men on work.[3]

In the case of the figures on total time spent at work by men and women, it can be questioned whether it is reasonable to treat the lower amount of time spent by men on activities within the home as more problematic or inequitable than the lower amount of time spent by women in paid employment. From a strict time-consuming perspective, it can instead be argued that both sexes make a comparably large effort for the good of the family.

Regarding power-relations within the family, it is my opinion that it is problematic to consider (as has been done, for example, by Ohlander, 1993, p. 31) men as having more power within the family on the basis of their position in the labor market and as "economical providers" within the family. Taking only quantitative aspects (income) into consideration, it might be true that the party with the greatest material resources has the strongest position. However, this is true only if the resources acquired and accumulated by means of employment are not (re)distributed in an equitable way within the family.

One could also wish that analyses of this type take into consideration the fact that certain "qualitative" aspects of power are associated with being responsible for the decisions in the reproductive area, and with the co-ordination of social relations within the family (areas in which women have more influence). If the power relation between wife and husband is to be discussed, a comparison should be made between the kind of qualitative resources which women more often control and the kind of more "quantitative" aspects that participation in working-life generates. Such a comparison would probably reveal that women in modern society have a considerable influence on men's relations to their children, and that men often feel that they are dependent on women in the field of "intimacy" (cf. Lennéer-Axelsson, 1989; Gidden, 1992), while women feel that they still have not gained equality in the financial area. This means that the current situation within the family places both men and women in "disadvantageous" positions. Men suffer from their lack of competence in the sphere of intimacy, while women are deprived in the financial area.

Another distinction that should be made in this comparison of men's and women's power within the family is the difference between men's and women's own "subjective" notions of the situation within the family and the "objective" stand that researchers take. By this I mean that the conclusions reached by researchers concerning the amount of power that men and women possess in the family sphere sometimes do not correspond with the participants' own understanding of the situation. Bäck-Wiklund and Bergsten (1996), for example, have found that today's young families are aware of the discourse on gender equality, and have placed it on the agenda. At the same time, they have given the concept of equality a slightly different meaning than the researchers cited here have done. Ideals of equality in this new sense do not necessarily mean that wife and husband should carry out the same household duties. Rather, they refer to equality in the sense of an equal amount of spent time in (any) work (in the home or on the labor market), and that men and women have equal opportunities to participate in the decision-making process within the family. Bäck-Wiklund and Bergsten (1996) have also found that there is a correspondence between fathers' and mothers' conceptions of the key aim of their families (good conditions for their children). In this respect, both participants are striving in the same direction. There is, however, a discrepancy between the claims the parents make regarding the ways they are using to achieve these goals. The care of the mothers seems to be more "direct," while the care of the fathers can be described as "indirect." The mothers claim that they bear the bulk of the responsibility for the household work and other duties belonging to the home, while the fathers claim that they take their responsibility by providing their families with a good material standard, and by working with material things (e.g. doing repair work) within the family.[4]

Power relations within the family

In studies of power relations within the family that tend to lead to a "conventional" division of work, research indicates that "static" explanations are problematic. The actions of men and women are, instead, interdependent. A crucial factor when trying to understand this area seems to be the orientation of men and women toward the two spheres, working-life and family life.

The position of women on the labor market

Some results indicate that women's position on the labor market plays a central role for men's involvement in the home. Findings indicate, for example, a connection between an increase in the mother's time spent in paid work and the father's time spent in domestic work (Sandqvist, 1987; Petterson, 1981; Coltrane, 1988). Kaul (1991) as well as Bäck-Wiklund and Bergsten (1997) hold the opinion that the amount of time that mothers spend at work is not really the key factor that influences the fathers' orientation to the family. Rather, it is the strength of these women's work identity that is the most powerful determinant for the involvement of their husbands.

Findings indicate that women with a strong work identity and a strong incentive to hold on to their job even in periods when their children are very young have husbands who take relatively long parental leave. Studies concerning "non-traditional cross-class families" have shown that women in this kind of marriage have a more non-traditional role within the family, in terms of both economy and household work (Leiulfsrud, 1991). This means that women with incomes equal to those earned by their husbands whose marriage places them in a higher social class and gives them a higher status compared to their husbands, also have husbands who share the domestic work on more equal terms than do men in traditional marriages.

Holter and Aarseth (1993) also point to the fact that young men in

Norway today do not want women who, through their reproductive work, complement them in their own job aspirations. In this sense, today's fathers' aspirations seem to deviate from their own fathers' preferences. The men in the study by Holter and Aarseth described their ideal wife as a career woman who is successful in many areas of life, a picture that fitted pretty well with the way in which the men interviewed pictured themselves. The drive behind their wish to have an "independent" wife or partner was not merely the men's considerations for their partners, but also their own thoughts about having to live up to a "bread-winning role." The men interviewed wanted their families in the future to be less dependent on them as "economic providers." The men also hoped that they would be able to benefit from their wive's success by being able to work part-time or to stay at home from work for longer periods in the future.

Nilsson (1992) has obtained similar results. His study implies that an increasing number of men have a positive attitude toward their partner's aspirations for a work career. The men interviewed reported that they had no problem with having a partner who earned more and had a higher status at work compared with themselves.

Men's involvement in family matters

Some studies (Brandth and Kvande, 1993) have indicated that fathers strengthen their position within the family by exercising their right to parental leave. Those men who choose to spend some time with their children gain a better position in the negotiations with their wives on the question of how, and when, household work and child-rearing should be carried out.

In family research, however, it has sometimes been claimed that men themselves feel that their spouses have a kind of "model power" (Sw. "modellmakt") concerning household work, caring and "social relations" within the family sphere (Holter and Aarseth, 1993, p. 156). Men in this study also describe their own mothers as the main or pivotal figures having a firm grip over the family, while their fathers are described as having peripheral influence (Holter and Aarseth, 1993, pp. 44ff, 124ff). The study also indicates that the men interviewed withdraw and try to avoid potential conflicts that could arise if they demand to participate in decision-making on equal terms with their wives. The subordination of men in this respect can best be described by their avoiding responsibility for household duties, and their entrenchment in their working life.

Others (Haas, 1987) suggest that prevailing ideologies concerning child rearing and the way that this activity should ideally be accomplished (e.g.

breast-feeding and other practical matters) have great influence on decisions regarding the question of fathers' use of parental leave. In the negotiations preceding decisions on this subject, women still seem to have the initiative.

Despite their stronger position on the labor market, it seems evident that women in general still have initiative in, and a steady grip on, the household. Feminist researchers (Haavind, 1984; Holter and Aarseth, 1993; Björnberg, 1994b; Bäck-Wiklund and Bergsten, 1997) have, for instance, revealed that women have a proportionally larger amount of responsibility for both practical work within the family and social relations between the parents and/or the children. One explanation of this could be that women from the beginning have obtained (through education and experience) essentially better knowledge of how caring can and should be carried out (Hwang, 1985b).

Researchers claim that women of today to a certain degree have a "housewife ideology," meaning that they still hang on to, and have difficulties in liberating themselves from, the role of being responsible of making family life work smoothly (Karlsson and Jacobsen, 1993; Rahbeck, 1987).

Some male researchers claim that the power held by women in the family sphere gives rise to conflicts between wife and husband (Carlsen, 1990a). These conflicts are rooted in the difference between men's (fathers') and women's (mothers') goals. Men are looking for opportunities to develop their own fatherhood, while women are trying to control men's behavior according to their definitions of what should be accomplished, and how this should be done within the family. In some cases, this conflict is manifested in women's wishes that their husbands do more of the household work, while men want to spend more time with their children. This conflict is rooted in the different understandings of men and women of the routinization and organization of everyday life. Carlsen (1990b) has pointed out that men who feel that their alternatives are reduced involve themselves less than they would have done in other circumstances.

Other researchers claim that mothers have a role as gate-keepers in regard to the opportunities men have to develop their skills in domestic work (Marsiglio, 1991; Huttonen, 1996). Some research also indicates that Swedish working-class women do not believe that their husbands are capable of child-rearing, and that the conditions at their husbands' workplaces will not allow them to do so (Liljeström and Dahlström, 1981).

Limitations to men's opportunities to actively take part in family life as a result of working conditions is a subject that has been relatively little investigated (Pleck, 1987). However, some results suggest that men's plans for parental leave are met by direct sanctions, or lead to other negative consequences in their work (Hwang, Eldén and Fransson, 1984; Hwang, 1985b; Holter & Aarseth, 1993, pp. 277ff). Other studies show that there are men who give up their plans for parental leave, even though they do not want to, because of their wives themselves want to remain on their own parental leave for as long as possible (Kugelberg, 1993, pp. 80ff). It has been suggested that many of these women have marginal positions in the labor market and accordingly do not consider their jobs to be particularly meaningful.

Two other factors which could be claimed to have been disregarded in traditional family research are men's uncertainty when assuming a "new" role of being responsible for child-rearing, and the family-related financial considerations that affect the choices that families make concerning the division of paid work and unpaid work between wife and husband. A closer look at the first of these questions shows that many of today's fathers have themselves had fathers who, to a great extent, have been "absent." Fathers of today lack adequate role-models in their search for a "new identity" (Jalmert, 1884; Björnberg, 1994a). Findings also indicate that many of today's fathers have had negative experiences of their fathers in their childhood (Holter and Aarseth, 1993, pp. 32ff). Regarding the significance of family-related financial considerations, Ellingsæter (1991) has demonstrated that there is a connection between the fact that fathers in (Norwegian) families with small children have to increase the time they spend at work to meet the growing costs these families are faced with.

Conclusions

This essay indicates that family researchers in Scandinavia have paid much more attention to men's position on the labor market and the potential power that this leads to than they have to the actual relations between wife and husband, or mother and father, and the significance that these relations have with respect to men's family orientation.

This examination of family research leads to three conclusions. The first conclusion is that studies of families carried out in recent years show that Scandinavian men today are more family-oriented than studies carried out during the last 10 to 15 years have indicated.[5] The second conclusion is that the premises of many of the studies of power relations within the family and men's and women's involvement in household work are oversimplified. A possible reason for this might be that these studies usually build on the assumption that the existing male dominance over women, which gender studies have uncovered on the macro level, almost automatically can be applied, or extrapolated, to conditions on a micro level of society. But sociologists as well as other scientists have opposed such mechanistic explanations of the relation between macro and micro level (Sayer, 1992). Relations on the macro level of society do not necessarily create the conditions for the micro level (in the family). As Gullerstad (1994, p. 290) expresses it: "families are not only merely consequence receivers but to a certain degree also premises deliverers in society."

A third conclusion is that the descriptions given of the role of fathers and mothers within the family are too static and do not take in consideration the dynamic aspects of the "current problem." It can be questioned, for example, whether it is actually men (as some research has suggested) who have the greatest influence on the process that leads to a decision on a "conventional" division of work within the family. When examining the family from this alternative perspective, it becomes clear that men's "lack" of family orientation can hardly be explained by attributing decisions made in the family sphere solely to men's "rational choice," "hegemonic masculinity" or "free will." Rather, there is no clear-cut division between women's orientation toward the labor market and men's orientation toward family life. Just as the theoretical notions of "masculinity" and "femininity" are inherently relational concepts which have meaning in relation to each other (Connell, 1996, p. 44), so men's and women's lives within the family are intertwined and dependent on each other. This means that the problem with "men's family orientation" is integrated with a corresponding "problem with women's lack of work aspirations" and power within the family. It seems obvious that women's career aspirations in the labor market and their attempt to firmly establish themselves in this sphere (along with men's re-evaluation of their relation to their children) are key factors in men's family orientation. Reflections on this lead to the issue of whether one question for family research today should be women's aspirations regarding working life, rather than focusing merely on men's orientation toward the family. One might expect that today's men become more family-oriented when their partners take (and at the same time are given) the "bread-winning role" in the family.

The results indicate that women still have a firm grip on the relations within the family sphere, and that they have not given up their over-arching responsibility of the family. Women also seem to possess a kind of "gate-keeping" role concerning men's further involvement in the family. Men are still on the periphery of the family. However, this is perhaps not very surprising since household duties are by tradition in the woman's domain. In general, today's men have weak or, as some of them express it, "negative role models" for involvement in the everyday life of the family (Holter and Aarseth, 1993). At the same time, men's involvement, in some cases, is obstructed by prevailing "segregating ideologies." One example of these conservative modes of thought is the negative opinion held by some employers concerning non-traditional men's involvement in family work and child rearing (Hwang, Eldén and Fransson, 1984; Hwang, 1985b; Holter and Aarseth, 1993, pp. 277ff).

Research carried out in recent years indicates that conditions in working life no longer have a strong impact on, or form the guidelines for, family life. The studies by Holter and Aarseth (1993) and Bäck-Wiklund and Bergsten (1997) point to the fact that today's young families value tasks within the family (household work as well as responsibility for children) in a completely different way compared to their fathers and mothers. The studies by Holter and Aarseth (1993) and Bäck-Wiklund and Bergsten (1997) show that the principle that man and woman should share the responsibilities for work is highly valued. At the same time, there are signs that a shift has occurred from families who were organized on the basis of men's working conditions, to families in which household work is paid attention to and valued. Today's men also seem willing to spend time on this work.

The above-mentioned changes in the family can be interpreted in two different ways. On the one hand, the results could indicate that women's power within the family has been strengthened, since it seems to be women who have the active and governing role and men who adapt in these types of family (cf. Holter & Aarseth, 1993, pp. 137ff). On the other hand, it can be expected that men's "re-evaluation" of family life will slowly lead to a "come-back" for men in the reproductive sphere.

Notes

1. This second tendency can be seen in research on the family and on "gender and social welfare" (Pringle, 1995).
2. Studies in other Western countries have given the same result (Connell, 1996, p. 82).
3. There are, however, big differences in time spent on paid work by parents (men and women) with children of pre-school age. A large proportion of the fathers of small children, both in Sweden (SCB, 1986) and in Norway (Ellingsæter, 1991), are among those men having the longest working hours. Many of these fathers spend more than 40 hours at work, while many of the mothers mentioned (70 per cent) work part-time.
4. These findings can be compared with Gullerstad (1984) who has found that

some men consider overtime work as an alternative to involvement in household duties, and seem to consider the extra income as a compensation for their lower degree of family involvement.
5. Studies describing conditions in other Western countries (e.g. the United States) indicate, however, that men's total responsibility within the family is still low (Lamb and Oppenheimer, 1989).

References

Bäck-Wiklund, Margareta and Bergsten, Birgitta (1996) "Moderna fäder mellan tradition och relation," *Sociologisk forskning*, 33 (1), pp. 48-70.

Bäck-Wiklund, Margareta and Bergsten, Birgitta (1997) *Det moderna föräldraskapet. En studie av familj och kön i förändring*. Stockholm: Natur and Kultur.

Bäck-Wiklund, Margareta and Lindfors, Hans (1990) *Landsbygd, livsform och samhällsförändring*. Göteborg: Diadalos.

Björnberg, Ulla (1993) "Inledning," in Agell, Anders, Arve-Parès, Birgit and Björnberg, Ulla (eds), *Modernt familjeliv och familjeseparationer*. Stockholm: Socialvetenskapliga forskningsrådet.

Björnberg, Ulla (1994a) "Mäns familjeorientering i förändring," in Björnberg, Ulla, Kollind, Anna-Karin and Nilsson, Arne (eds), *Janus och genus. Om kön och social identitet i familj och samhälle*. Stockholm: Brombergs Bokförlag.

Björnberg, Ulla (1994b) "Hur påverkas psykisk hälsa av arbete och familjeliv?" *Socialvetenskaplig tidskrift*, 1 (3-4), pp. 114-29.

Björnberg, Ulla and Bäck-Wiklund, Margareta (1990) *Vardagslivets organisering i familj och närsamhälle*. Göteborg: Diadalos.

Bosseldal, Ingrid (1995) "Skillnaden mellan ideal och praktik i förälskelsen," *Kvinnovetenskaplig tidiskrift*, 16 (4), pp. 25-36.

Brandth, Berit and Kvande, Elin (1993) "Når likhet blir ulikhet. Foreldrers forhandlinger om barnomsorg," in Haukaa, Runa (ed.), *Nye kvinner, nye menn*. Oslo: Ad Notam.

Carlsen, S. (1990a) "Mandens rolle i den moderne familie," *Kvinden og samfundet*, 106 (1), pp. 6-7. (Reference in Unenge, Gun (1994) *Pappor i föräldrakooperativa daghem. En deskriptiv studie av pappors medverkan*. Göteborgs universitet: Institutionen för pedagogik. Göteborg studies in educational science no. 97.)

Carlsen, S. (1990b) "Far-skal-hjem-strategien," in Bonde, Hans and Rosenbeck, Bente (eds), *Mandekultur*. Kobenhavn: Varia. (Reference in Unenge, Gun (1994) *Pappor i föräldrakooperativa daghem. En deskriptiv studie av pappors medverkan*. Göteborgs universitet: Institutionen för pedagogik. Göteborg studies in educational science no. 97.)

Cedersund, Elisabet and Kullberg, Christian (1996) *Arbetsvärdering. Teori, praktik, kritik*. Stockholm: Arbetslivsinstitutet.

Coltrane, Scott (1988) "Father-Child Relationships and the Status of Women: A Cross Cultural Study," *American Journal of Sociology*, 3, pp. 1061-95.

Connell, Robert. W. (1995) *Masculinities*. Cambridge: Polity Press.

Ellingsæter, Anne Lise (1991) "Hvorfor jobber pappa overtid? Om årsaker og konsekvenser av fedres lange arbeidstid," in Haukaa, R. (ed.), *Nye kvinner, nye menn*. Oslo: Ad Notam.

Falk, Pasi (1983) "Humalan historia: juomisen merkitysten historiallisuus. Lisensiaatitutkielma. helisingin yliopiston sociologian laitos." (Reference in Peltonen, Eeva (1986) "Finländska sociologer om mannens kris i nya lönearbetarfamiljer," *Sociologisk forskning*, 23 (2), pp. 32-44.)

Flood, L and Gråsjö, U. (1995) "Changes in time spent in work and leisure: The Swedish experience," Göteborgs universitet: Nationalekonomiska institutionen. Stencil.

Friberg, Tora (1993) "Den moderna kvinnan och hennes strävan att få kontroll över vardagen," in Agell, Anders, Arve-Parès, Birgit and Björnberg, Ulla (eds), *Modernt familjeliv och familjeseparationer*. Stockholm: Socialvetenskapliga forskningsrådet.

Frykman, Jonas and Löfgren, Orvar (1979) *Den kultiverade människan*. Malmö: Gleerups.

Gidden, Anthony (1992) *The transformation of intimacy. Sexuality, love and eroticism in modern societies*. Cambridge: Polity Press.

Gillis, John, R. (1993) "Alltid lika problematiskt att göra fäder av män," *Kvinnovetenskaplig tidskrift*, 14 (1), pp. 3-21.

Gullerstad, Marianne (1984) *Kitchen-table society*. Oslo: Universitetsforlaget.

Gullerstad, Marianne (1994) "Familieforskning mellom positivisme og fortolkning" (Family research between positivism and interpretation), *Nordiskt sosialt arbeid*, 4 (4), pp. 289-300.

Haas, L. (1987) *The effect of fathers' participation in parental leave on sexual equality in the family*. Paper presented at the symposium on Nordic intimate couples – love, children and work in Stockholm. (Reference in Kugelberg, Clarissa (1993) "Kvinnor och män. Mammor och pappor på en arbetsplats," in Agell, A., Arve-Parès, B. and Björnberg, U. (eds), *Modernt familjeliv och familjeseparationer*. Stockholm: Socialvetenskapliga forskningsrådet.)

Haavind, Hanne (1982) "Makt och kjærlighet i ektenskapet," in Hakaa, Runa, Hoel, Marit and Haavind, Hanne (eds), *Kvinneforskning: bidrag till samfunnsteori*. Oslo: Universitetsforlaget.

Haavind, Hanne (1984) "Fordeling av omsorgsfunksjoner i småbarnsfamiljer," in Rudie, Ingrid (ed.), *Myk start-hard landing. Om forvaltning av kjØnnsidentitet i en endringsprosess*. Oslo: Universitetsforlaget.

Haavind, Hanne (1985) "Förändringar i förhållanden mellan kvinnor och män," *Kvinnovetenskaplig tidskrift*, 6 (3), pp. 17-27.

Holmberg, Carin (1993) *Det kallas kärlek. En socialpsykologisk studie om kvinnors underordning och mäns överordning bland unga jämställda par*. Göteborg: Anamma förlag.

Holter, Øystein Gullvåg and Aarseth, Helene (1993) *Mäns livssammanhang*. Stockholm: Bonnier Utbildning.

Huttonen, Jouka (1996) "Full-time fathers and their parental leave experiences," in Björnberg, Ulla and Kollind, Anna-Karin (eds), *Men's Family Relations*. Stockholm: Almqvist and Wiksell International.

Hwang, Philip (1985a) "Småbarnspappor," in Hwang, Philip (ed.), *Faderskap*. Stockholm: Natur and Kultur.

Hwang, Philip (1985b) "Varför är pappor så lite engagerade i hem och barn?" in Hwang, Philip (ed.), *Faderskap*. Stockholm: Natur and Kultur.

Hwang, Philip (1987) "The changing role of Swedish fathers," in Lamb, Michael E. (ed.), *The father's role. Cross cultural perspectives*. Hillsdale, New Jersey: Lawrence Erlbaum.

Hwang, Philip, Eldén, C. G. and Fransson, C. (1984) "Arbetsgivares och arbetskamraters attityder till pappaledighet." Göteborgs universitet: Psykologiska institutionen. Rapport nr 1.

Hyvönen, Ulf (1993) *Om barns fadersbild* (Diss.). Umeå Universitet: Studier i socialt arbete vid Umeå Universitet nr 16.

Jalmert, Lars (1984) *Den svenska mannen*. Stockholm: Tidens Förlag.

Jalmert, Lars (1993) "Likgiltighet största hindret för mansforskning," *Kvinnovetenskaplig tidskrift*, 14 (1), pp. 57-64.

Jonasdottir, Anna. G. (1991a) "Könsbegreppet i samhällsvetenskapen. Tre kontroverser," in *Könsrelationernas betydelse som vetenskaplig kategori*. Stockholm: Delegationen för jämstäldhetsforskning (Jämfo-rapport 21).

Jonasdottir, Anna. G. (1991b) *Love Power and Political Interest. Towards a Theory af Patriarchy in Contemporary Western Societies*. University of Göteborg: Department of Political Science. Göteborg Studies in Politics, no. 25.

Karlsson, Jan, Ch. and Jacobsen, Liselott (1993) *Arbete och kärlek. En utveckling av livsformsanalys*. Lund: Arkiv Förlag. (Reference in Björnberg, Ulla (1994b) "Hur påverkas psykisk hälsa av arbete och familjeliv?" *Socialvetenskaplig tidskrift*, 1 (3-4), pp. 114-29.)

Kaul, H. (1991) "Who cares? Gender inequality and care leave in the Nordic Countries," *Acta Sociologica*, 34 (2), pp. 115-25.

Kimmel, Michael S. (1987) "The contemporary 'crisis' of masculinity in historical perspective," in Brod, Harry (ed.), *The Making of Masculinities. The New Men's Studies*. Boston: Allen and Unwin.

Kortteinen, Matti (1982) *Lähiö, Tutkimus elämätapojen muutoksesta*. Hilsinki: Otava.

Kugelberg, Clarissa (1993) "Kvinnor och män. Mammor och pappor på en arbetsplats," in Agell, Anders, Arve-Parès, Birgit and Björnberg, Ulla (eds), *Modernt familjeliv och familjeseparationer*. Stockholm: Socialvetenskapliga forskningsrådet.

Kullberg, Christian (1994) *Socialt arbete som kommunikativ praktik. Samtal med och om klienter* (Social work as communicative practice. Talking with and about clients) (Diss.). Linköpings Universitetet: Linköping Studies in Arts and Science, 115.

Kullberg, Christian (1996) "Swedish Fathers and the Welfare State Institutions," in Björnberg, Ulla and Kollind, Anna-Karin (eds), *Men's Family Relations*. Stockholm: Almqvist and Wiksell International.

Kullberg, Christian (1997) "Arbete eller socialbidrag? Socialsekreterares samtal med och om kvinnliga och manliga klienter," in Bladh, Christine, Cedersund, Elisabet and Hagberg, Jan-Erik (eds), *Kvinnor och män som aktörer och klienter. En antologi som skildrar tidigt 1800-tal och framåt.* Stockholm: Nerenius and Santérus Förlag.

Kullberg, Christian (1998a) "Vilket ansvar har män för samhällets sociala problem? Maskulinitet och socialt vård- och omsorgsarbete," *Socionomen, forskningssupplement* (in press).

Kullberg, Christian (1998b) *Far efter skilsmässan. Familjerättssekreterares föreställning om fäders förmåga att klara av omvårdnaden om sina barn.* Högskolan i Örebro: Institutionen för socialt arbete (in press).

Kullberg, Christian and Cedersund, Elisabet (1996) "Forskning om värdering av kvinnors och mäns arbeten," in Cedersund, Elisabet and Kullberg, Christian, *Arbetsvärdering. Teori, praktik, kritik.* Stockholm: Arbetslivsinstitutet.

Lamb, Michael E. (1976) "The role of the father; An overview," in Lamb, Michael E. (ed.), *The role of the father in child development.* New York: John Wiley and Sons.

Lamb, Michael E. (ed.) (1987) *The father's role. Cross cultural perspectives.* Hillsdale, New Jersey: Lawrence Erlbaum.

Lamb, Michael, E. and Oppenheimer, D. (1989) "Fatherhood and father-child relationships: five years of research," in Cath, Stanley H., Gurwitt, Alan and Gunsberg, Linda (eds), *Fathers and their families.* Hillsdale, N.Y.: Analytic Press.

Leiulfsrud, Håkon (1991) *Det familjära klasssamhället. En teoretisk och empirisk studie av blandklassfamiljer.* Arkiv avhandlingsserie nr 38. Lund: Arkiv Förlag.

Lennéer-Axelsson, B. (1989) *Männens röster i kris och förändring.* Stockholm: Sesam.

Liljeström, Rita and Dahlström, Edmund (1981) *Arbetarkvinnor i hem- arbets- och samhällsliv.* Stockholm: Tiden.

Lindgren, Gerd (1996) "Broderskapets logik," *Kvinnovetenskaplig tidskrift*, 17 (1), pp. 4-14.

Lundén Jacoby, Anna and Näsman, Elisabet (1989) *Mamma, pappa, jobb. Föräldrar och barn om arbetets villkor.* Stockholm: Arbetslivscentrum.

Mac an Ghaill, Mairtin (1996) "Introduction," in Mac an Ghaill, Mairtin (ed.), *Understanding masculinities.* Buckingham: Open University Press.

Marsiglio, W. (1991) "Paternal engagement activities with minor children," *Journal of Marriage and the Family*, 53 (4), pp. 973-86.

246   *Among Men*

McKee, Lorna (1982) "Father's participation in infant care: A critique," in McKee, Lorna and O'Brien, Margaret (eds), *The father figure*. London: Tavistock.

Nilsson, Arne (1992) "Den nue mannen-finns han redan?" in Acker, Joan et al., *Kvinnors och mäns liv och arbete*. Stockholm: SNS Förlag.

Ohlander, Ann-Sofie (1993) "Den historiska konflikten mellan produktion och reproduktion," in Agell, Anders, Arve-Parès, Birgit and Björnberg, Ulla (eds), *Modernt familjeliv och familjeseparationer*. Stockholm: Socialvetenskapliga forskningsrådet.

Parson,Talcott and Bales, Robert F. (1956) *Family Socialisation and Interaction Process*. London: Free Press.

Peltonen, Eeva (1986) "Finländska sociologer om mannens kris i nya lönearbetarfamiljer," *Sociologisk forskning*, 23 (2), pp. 32-44.

Petterson, M. (1981) "Deltidsarbete i Sverige," Rapport 23. Stockholm: Arbetslivscentrum.

Pleck, Joseph H. (1987) "American fathers in historical perspective," in Kimmel, Michael, S. (ed.), *Changing Men. New Directions in research on Men and Masculinity*. Beverly Hills, CA: Sage Publications Inc.

Pringle, Keith (1995) *Men, Masculinities and Social Welfare*. London: University College London Press.

Rahbeck, Lone (1987) "Hver vore veje," Odense: Etnologisk forum. (Reference in Björnberg, Ulla (1994b), "Hur påverkas psykisk hälsa av arbete och familjeliv?" *Socialvetenskaplig tidskrift*, 1 (3-4), pp. 114-29.)

RFV (1994) *Från moderskap till föräldraskap*. RFV Redovisar 1994 (1). Stockholm: Riksförsäkringsverket.

Sandqvist, Karin (1987) *Fathers and Family Work. Antecendents and Concomitants of Fathers' Participation in Child and Household Work*. Stockholms universitet: Institutionen för lärarurbildning. Studies in education and psychology 23.

Sandqvist, Karin (1993) *Pappor och riktiga karlar. Om mans- och fadersrollen i ideologi och verklighet*. Stockholm: Carlssons Bokförlag.

Sayer, Andrew (1992) *Methods in social science. A realist approach*. London: Routledge.

SCB (1986) *Kvinno- och mansvär(l)den. Fakta om jämställdhet i Sverige 1986 (The World of Women and Men. Equal Opportunity in Sweden 1986)*. Stockholm: Statistiska Centralbyrån (Statistics Sweden).

SCB (1987) *Make och far. Forskning och statistik om familjebildning och re-produktion – med speciell inriktning mot män*. Demografisk rapport 1987: 2. Stockholm: Statisktiska centralbyrån.

SCB (1992) *I tid och otid*. Levnadsförhållanden. Rapport 79. Stockholm: Statistiska centralbyrån.

Åström, Lissie (1992) "Könsblindhet en fara också för kvinnoforskare," *Kvinnovetenskaplig tidskrift*, 13 (3), pp. 49-57.

Chapter 14

Fatherhood and Masculinity: Non-resident Fathers' Construction of Identity

THOMAS JOHANSSON

Introduction: fatherhood and masculinity

It is well-documented that a large proportion of non-resident fathers tend to loose contact with their children (Öberg and Öberg 1992; Ihinger-Tallman *et al.* 1995). The contact between father and child also declines considerably over time (Wallerstein and Kelly 1980). Looking at this research, it is easy to draw the conclusion that the bond between non-resident fathers and their children is weak and fragile. However, it is necessary to investigate these questions in more detail before drawing such conclusions. For example, a number of circumstances seem to affect the quality and duration of the bond between father and child, such as conflicts between divorced parents, geographical separation and the non-resident father's psychological, social and economic conditions. I will, however, focus specifically on the relation between fatherhood and masculinity.

Today there is a growing literature dealing with questions concerning changing parental roles and identities. There is still a great discrepancy between images of the ideal father and children's actual experiences of their fathers. The ideal father is supposed to be available to the child as much as the mother, and he is also expected to take an equal responsibility for and to share household work. In reality, there are still great differences between men's and women's involvement in child care and domestic work. Although traditional gender identities seem to be rather persistent, it is nevertheless possible to discern changes in attitudes and behaviors among men and women.

Today certain researchers argue that contemporary men face a "crisis in masculinity." What they mean is simply that men have lost some of their power in society and that they are increasingly forced to reflect upon themselves and to defend their positions. Masculinity is no longer taken for granted or given as a "fact," but has to be articulated and fought for. It would lead too far afield to discuss these issues here, but obviously different men tend to deal with this identity crisis in different ways. Some tend to defend a more traditional masculinity, whereas others try hard to change their lifestyle and to develop a more equal gender identity.

Many men have to develop new strategies in order to cope with changing cultural conditions and ideals. In certain critical situations – as for example a divorce or separation – questions concerning the relation between masculinity and fatherhood are problematized. These men's roles as fathers are no longer taken for granted, and there are no easily available role-scripts for non-resident fathers. In order to develop a bond between themselves and their children, these men must actively construct an identity as non-resident fathers.

According to Arendell (1995), divorced fathers' situations can be understood only by focusing on their notions about their identities as men. Divorces tend to put questions concerning the construction of masculinity on the agenda. When discussing men's relations to their ex-partners and to their children, it is therefore necessary to consider such aspects of masculinity as reflexivity, emotions and ideals. Both men and women are trapped between old role models and new demands, and modern individuals often feel confused by their own contradictory and ambivalent attitudes and behaviors. According to Beck and Beck-Gernsheim (1990/1995), many people today are trapped in the stage between "no longer" and "not yet." Divorced and separated men face great difficulties when they try to put their lives together, finding an identity as non-residential and non-custodial fathers.

I will focus on non-resident fathers' construction of identity. I am using the concept of identity to capture some of the ways these fathers try to articulate their notions of themselves as non-resident fathers. In order to adapt to the post-family situation these men must more or less consciously articulate a discourse about the non-resident father. Within the growing bulk of literature on masculinity it is possible to find a number of assumptions about contemporary men. I will take my point of departure from some of these assumptions and then try to elaborate an analysis of three different stories of fathers. At the end of the article I will also say something about the absent father.

The three fathers portrayed here by no means exclude other possible stories; they should merely be regarded as attempts to understand how non-resident fathers develop different strategies in order to cope with their situations. Using these three stories as a starting point, it is possible to analyze the impact of hegemonic masculinity on the construction of non-resident fathers' identity. The theoretical principle guiding the writing of the three stories is the assumption that the construction of fatherhood and masculinity are to be regarded as an intimately interwoven process. The stories in question may, of course, also apply to resident fathers.

The empirical material used in this article is collected from a qualitative Swedish study of non-resident fathers' living conditions supported by HSFR. The three case studies presented here are carefully chosen from a study of 24 fathers. My intention is to use these three cases as a starting point for a discussion of the construction of the relation between masculinity and fatherhood in the particular case of non-resident fathers.

Hegemonic masculinity: emotions and reflexivity

Connell (1995, p. 77) defines hegemonic masculinity as "the configuration of gender practice which embodies the currently accepted answer to the problem of the legitimacy of patriarchy, which guarantees (or is taken to guarantee) the dominant position of men and the subordination of women." When talking about hegemonic masculinity I am referring to dominant patterns of values, norms, ideas *and* actions produced within a patriarchal gender order.

Most men do not actually meet the normative standards reproduced within the discourse of hegemonic masculinity; in order to relate to their partners' demands for equality they have to develop a more nuanced way of approaching masculinity – but nevertheless they benefit from a particular gender order. At the same time that men benefit through certain advantages regarding career, individual lifestyle and self-fulfilment, they are also disadvantaged in other respects, however. This is particularly evident in the case of non-resident fathers. These men often voluntarily refrain from taking a primary responsibility for their children, and consequently they often become marginalized.

Hegemonic masculinity works in many different ways. On the one hand, it contributes to the reinforcement of the overall male power in society, while on the other hand it promotes certain lifestyles and identities among men. Non-resident fathers may either put a lot of effort in keeping a good relation with their children or put all their time and energy into their own life and into their own private plans and goals and consequently neglect their children. In choosing the first alternative they must struggle to construct an identity as non-resident fathers and to confront themselves with the problems inherent in this particular project. But in choosing the other alternative they may instead defend the claims of masculine hegemony. Being an active non-resident father means that one has to reflect upon certain aspects of masculinity, aspects which promote the reproduction of hegemonic masculinity, but which create difficulties in maintaining a good emotional relation to significant others.

When discussing the reproduction of hegemonic masculinity in this particular context, I will focus on four different aspects: *emotions, reflexivity, men's relations to their own fathers* and *gender ideals*. These aspects make a good point of departure when focusing on non-resident father's construction of identity. Most men have to confront these issues in one way or another, but in the case of non-resident fathers it becomes very urgent to deal with them. In order to keep a good emotional contact with their children these men have to restructure certain aspects of their masculine identity. One of the explanations of why many men fail to keep their relation with their children and instead become absent fathers is probably to be located in their inability to adapt to the new situation and to reconstruct their masculinity. A common theme in research on masculinity is the suppression of emotional and bodily signals.[2]

The construction of masculinity is intimately tied to rationalization and more or less conscious attempts to transform emotional signals into rational decisions.[3] Whereas men often tend to suppress feelings, there is, however, the possibility of expressing hostility and anger. These feelings are, in general, more accepted. Consequently, feelings of sadness or sorrow tend to appear in the form of verbal or behavioral aggression. In the case of non-resident fathers, questions concerning emotional capability become highly relevant. These men live with a constant feeling of lack. Even if they meet their children on a regular basis, they have to develop a way of dealing with the fact that they often disappoint them just by not being there when needed. Consequently, these men must be able to confront their own feelings of sorrow and their inability of fathering.

According to Giddens (1992), modern identities are inherently self-reflexive. That is, contemporary individuals more or less actively construct their identity and biography, using available information and knowledge in order to reflect upon their life plans. The process of reflexivity involves different degrees of insights into one's self identity, but it does not automatically lead to the development of more flexible gender identities. In order to make a difference, reflexivity must lead to actual changes in men's behavior and lifestyles. Many men have certainly understood that they must change and try to become more equal, but these cognitive insights are not always combined with an emotional preparedness to develop a different lifestyle.

In psychoanalytic theory the father is often regarded as one of the primary sources in the development of the super ego. However, this is merely one aspect of the childs' relation to the father – where "the law of the Father" and the development of culture are intimately related to each other. The other aspect, that is, the formation of the ego ideal, is often neglected. Peter Blos, in his book Sons and Fathers (1985), has directed our attention to the aspects of the childs' relation to the father which are related to the development of the ego ideal. Here the father is not primarily regarded as the one who embodies prohibitions and the law, but as someone who gives the child a positive image to relate to and as a person who may be used as a role model. In order to handle the great emotional stress when having to part from one's children, non-resident fathers probably to a higher extent than resident fathers need a good emotional relation with their own fathers. As this often is not the case, there is a great risk that these men reproduce the feeling of lack they have felt in relation to their own fathers, and they become in some sense absent fathers.

Today many men have started to question the traditional forms of masculinity. However, this does not automatically lead to the development of "new men" or "new fathers."[4] At the same time as gender ideals are changing, it is also obvious that traditional identities and strategies show a high degree of persistence. In order to analyze the relation between the "no longer" and "not yet," it is necessary to develop a critical approach to contemporary masculinity. One way of doing this is to differentiate between different masculinities and to develop analysis of the power relations between these different types of men (Connell, 1995). This kind of approach involves a careful study of how hegemonic masculinity continues to influence the formation of new variations in men's identities.[5]

In the following case studies I will focus in more detail on how non-resident fathers struggle with their identities and succeed or fail in adapting to being a father.[6]

"Man on the run": between tradition and reflexivity

Tim is 38 years old. He has recently separated from his girlfriend and his two children (twins). At the moment Tim is living in a big apartment in

Gothenburg, whereas his ex-partner Eva and their children live in Stockholm. He tries to visit his children every third week. These visits are often quite problematic, because he has to meet them in Evas' flat. In order to sort out the problems involved in this arrangement, Tim and Eva are seeing a family therapist on a regular basis. Tim is not satisfied with the current situation, but at the moment he finds no other alternatives. However, in the near future he is probably going to move to Stockholm.

Tim actually never believed that his relationship with Eva was going to last, and they did not plan to have any children. When Eva got pregnant they never thoroughly discussed the consequences of this pregnancy. It all happened very quickly, and when Tim started to react, it was already too late to stop the process. In some ways he is quite open about his feelings, that is, he expresses a certain sorrow when talking about his children, but in the interview he also tells us that he finds it very difficult to relate to his own feelings in certain situations. This is particularly evident when he refers to the moment when he had to confront his feelings regarding the separation from Eva.

> I was convinced that we were going to split, but I have always had great difficulties separating from people. Yes, it's really problematic. Maybe one tries to hold back, and refrain from telling the other person what one really feels. ... You don't wanna hurt the other person.

When talking about his feelings, Tim uses expressions such as "hold back", "what one really feels," and so on. But at this time it seems as if the emotional and cognitive aspects of Tim's person were somehow disconnected. He is confused and partly paralyzed. At the same moment Tim becomes a father, he runs away and experiences a temporary crisis.

When talking about the construction of a masculine identity, one of the important influences may be found in the person's relation to his own father. There are many literary descriptions of the relationship between sons and fathers. The traditional father is often described in terms of his absence and the discipline he embodied. There are few descriptions of emotionally close and enriching relationships between sons and fathers in film and literature.[7] In The Invention of Solitude Paul Auster (1982, p. 20) gives the following description of his own father:

> One could not believe that there was such a man – who lacked feeling, who wanted so little of others. And if there was not such a man, that means there was another man, a man hidden inside the man who was not there, and the trick of it, then, is to find him. On the condition that he is there to be found.

The absent father is a very problematic role model. It is a great difference between having an emotionally distant father in the home and having a father who is not there at all, a father who has "run away." Tim describes his father as a traditional and absent father. He says:

> My daddy left my family when I was six years old. In some sense I was, of course, sad, but on the other hand, I wanted to become a man. Life is cruel, but one has to survive. ... My father was absent. He wasn't good, but not bad either. He was just there - the most traditional father one can imagine. ... Well, he just ran away, and this has surely contributed to my opinion that a father does not necessarily have to be there for his children all the time.

Dealing with emotions in a rational way is a significant characteristic of masculinity, where affects are effectively suppressed (Seidler, 1989). The question is: in which way is the ego ideal influenced by the absence of the father? Tim has great difficulties in relating to his children and to form an identity as a non-resident father. He is still at the beginning of a long process, and he openly talks about his own insecurity and lack of a stable sense of identity as a father. When visiting his children in Stockholm, he often feels alienated and uncertain about how to relate to them. He says: "I don't feel that I ... well if one can say so ... love my children as much as I would have done if we would had been a family."

When talking about gender roles and identities, Tim tends to develop contradictory statements concerning differences between men and women. In one way, he presents some quite traditional views on masculinity, but in another way, he emphasizes individual differences to a greater extent than differences between men and women. He states:

> There are big differences between men and women. A man is more stable, but it all depends upon what ideals you cultivate, of course. A man should not be weak, and he should be able to make decisions. There should also be some form of logical thinking and structure related to masculinity. ... But there are probably more differences between individuals, than between men and women. In a sense, I really regret my statement concerning differences between men and women.

To some extent Tim seems to have incorporated more traditional ego ideals, but he also seems to adhere to a more individualized way of looking at gender and identity. In this sense Tim can be said to embody a clearly ambivalent masculinity; he is both a "traditional man", and a "new man." Tim's own relation to his fatherhood and to his masculine identity is clearly complex and contradictory. He is partly struggling with putting these

fragments together and thus developing a more stable sense of masculine
identity, and partly using his biography and lifestyle as an explanation of
why he finds it difficult to be a father. He tries to explain his situation:

> I am 38 years old and time is running out. ... I am not particularly sad about
> being a bad father, I am aware of the fact, and I think it's worse if one does
> not acknowledge the fact, and there is also a certain "comfort" in not being
> able to fulfil all the demands (this is meant as an ironic statement).

Although Tim is not a "traditional man," he embodies some traditional
male characteristics, such as the high valuation of individuality, the
suppression of emotions and a weak sense of fatherhood. He could be
described as an adventurer, who finds it hard to adapt to the demands of
everyday life and who all the time seeks out new sensations and
experiences.[8] On the one hand, Tim is aware of the ongoing discussion of
"the new man," but on the other hand he clings to certain traditional
masculine strategies. Tim clearly finds it hard to adapt to being a non-
resident father, but at the same time he really struggles to deal with his
emotional difficulties and to secure the bond between himself and his
children. As mentioned, he agrees to see a family therapist and takes the
train to Stockholm every third weekend. Considering his relationship to his
own father, which is quite problematic and distant, Tim really puts up a
fight, trying hard to maintain a relationship with his children.

"Fighting the authorities": blaming the other

Ken is 34 years old. He is a sailor, which means that he spends a lot of
time away from home. Five years ago he met Jeanette. They were quite
happy in the beginning, and Ken really tried to live a regular life. However,
this only lasted for a while. At the same time as Jeanette realized she was
pregnant, Ken went away to a job in England. This was also a turning-point
in their relationship. He told us that Jeanette threw him out. This was the
beginning of a long and bitter fight between Ken and Jeanette. According
to Ken, Jeanette has constantly prevented him from seeing his daughter.
Consequently, Ken has been involved in legal processes, trying to work out
a schedule for his contact with his daughter.

When talking with Ken it becomes clear that he has great difficulties
fitting his life together. On the one hand, he works as a sailor, which means
that he spends a lot of time away from his daughter, but on the other hand,
he constantly fights for his right to meet his daughter on a regular basis.

When he talks about home and family, he seems to cultivate two different images of a father: on the one hand the "caring father," and on the other the "absent father." Talking about these issues he says:

> As a non-resident father one of the most important issues is that one spend actual time with one's child, but one must also be able to relate to her. ... If there are several children involved, one must be able to spend time with each one of them. ... In my occupation people are often away both one and two years. During the war people could stay away for five years. ... In the beginning it was fun when daddy returned to the home, but then, after a while, he was just gone.

It is quite obvious that Ken has great difficulties combining these different models of fatherhood in his everyday life. When talking about his problematic relationship to Jeanette, Ken says that he finds it really difficult to communicate with his ex-partner. So, when he is not able to communicate with her, he turns to lawyers and other professionals, hoping they will be able to help him with the visiting arrangements. When there are no results, Ken becomes more and more desperate and at rare occasions even violent. On one particular occasion he banged at Jeanette's door. He told us: "I went mad, it was lucky the doors were made of iron." Jeanette felt threatened and called the police, and this resulted in a legal process, where Ken was prohibited from meeting his daughter.

> We had a conflict at that time, because I never knew when I was supposed to meet my daughter. I was prohibited to visit my daughter. All of a sudden I had become aggressive and hostile.

Ken could not understand why he was prohibited from seeing his daughter. His world suddenly turned into a nightmare. When we met Ken, he was still involved in this long and bitter fight for his rights to his child. He had recently met a new woman and had a new child – a two-year-old daughter. But his life still was chaotic. Describing his situation he said:

> Today I am involved in a conflict with my new girlfriend, which is one of the reasons why I am not staying with my new family in Gothenburg. It has to be this way until I have settled the arrangements with my ex-wife. I really feel mutilated as a father.

Ken's story contains many different problematic issues. It seems as if he has great difficulties in forming some sort of identity as a father in a stable relationship with a partner. He gets involved in constant fights with his ex-partner and is also incapable of handling his new relationship. So, he withdraws to his mother's house in the middle of Sweden.

Ken's relationship to his own father was quite problematic. His father died a few years ago and he really misses him, but at the same time he still feels angry at him. His father left the family when Ken was only ten years old, and at this point Ken's life became quite problematic.

> My parents divorced when I was ten years old. At that time I only met my father once in a while. Then my mother met a new man, so I stayed with them for a while. It didn't work out well. ... I moved to my dad in the south of Sweden. He was 46 years old at that time and had recently married a 23 years old woman. So I even had a half-brother in Malmö. ... My dad gave all his attention to this new family, so I wasn't even allowed to stay with him. I rented an apartment, and tried to get on by my own, minding my own business. My dad lied and told my mother that he took good care of me.

Ken shows a low degree of reflexivity. Almost without exception, everyone working in the social welfare or at the lawyers are considered to be parts of a big conspiracy against him. He has great difficulties in relating his problems to his own behavior. It is quite clear that this man lacks a developed sense of a masculine identity. He has no stable ego ideal to guide him in difficult situations. His feeling of being alone in a hostile world may be related to his earlier experiences of being left all alone, abandoned by both parents at an early age. When he fails to communicate with his ex-partner and to develop an identity as a father he loses control and becomes violent.

His relationship with Jeanette and his daughter is problematic, and this causes great stress in his life. When talking about his daughter he says: "My relation to my daughter is forever damaged. It is not obvious for me that she is my daughter, the feeling is there, but each time I see her, I get the feeling that I am only borrowing her from her mother." One way of developing a good relation with his daughter would be to confront and reflect on his masculine identity. Even though his relationship with his ex-partner is very problematic, it would be good if he could develop skills in communicating with her and learn to control his aggression. This means that he has to deal with his own sense of loss and his confusion regarding his identity as a father.

Tradition and reorientation

Bob is 42 years old. He had been married for almost 20 years, but recently divorced from his wife. Bob and Ann have six children. The last three children were not exactly planned: in 1992 the triplets were born. This was also the beginning of an unsolvable crisis in the marriage. Bob was working quite hard to save his construction firm, but at that time there was a deep economic crisis in Sweden, so he had to let it go. The family had great problems surviving, the communication between Bob and Ann was almost non-existent, and then Ann became involved with another man. At that time Bob understood that the best solution was to get a divorce.

Bob and Ann got joint custody, but the children are actually staying with their mother. Bob tries to meet his children as often as possible. His oldest children have their own keys to his apartment, so they may visit him whenever they like. He has a bad conscience about the triplets, because he finds it very hard to treat them as three separate individuals when meeting them. However, he meets his three youngest children every second weekend. All in all Bob finds his situation quite satisfying. He has lots of time to invest in his construction firm, and he meets his children on a regular basis.

Bob's masculinity and fatherhood could to some extent be characterized as traditional. His ex-wife was taking care of the children and the home, whereas Bob was putting his energy into his construction firm. At the time of the divorce he regarded it as "quite natural" that the children were to live with their mother. However, he shows a certain degree of reflexivity, when talking about his feelings of guilt towards his youngest children and when reflecting upon his earlier relationship to Ann. He says:

> Today I believe that it is important to have a proper dialogue with my children. A dad has to engage himself in his children, but one does not necessarily have to turn into a stereotypical dad, that's only stupid. Commitment is important. But my wife handled these things better. She took care of school-work, homework, etc. I was more engaged in my work. ... I lost contact with what happened in my home, but then you are in bad trouble. Today I firmly believe that it's good to be engaged in these everyday life concerns.

Although Bob's reflections on his earlier life do not necessarily lead to the development of a new type of masculinity or fatherhood, it is quite obvious that he is aware of his earlier neglect. Bob has quite a firm belief in the family. He has grown up in a traditional working-class family, and has always been quite negative toward the whole thought of getting a divorce.

However, when his marriage broke down, and his wife left him for another man, he was in a sense quite satisfied with the whole development. Although his wife had deceived him and been unfaithful, he told us that he handled the whole situation in a quite "reasonable way."

> I never experienced the divorce as a personal crisis. If we would have argued a lot before, but we didn't do that. ... If I have to do something, I rather get done with it. So, it all went quite well, the worst bit of it, was to tell my parents. I found it very problematic to tell them about the divorce. I went there together with one of my daughters, but I just couldn't tell them. So, my daughter kicked my leg and pushed me into telling them. Then I told my parents about the divorce, and I was almost crying. ... I really felt ashamed.

Bob shows a high degree of self-discipline and inner control, but he also feels shame and embarrassment in relation to his parents. The divorce is a threat to Bob's fundamental values and his ego ideal. After the divorce Bob started reflecting upon his own way of being a father. Like most of the men we interviewed, Bob considers himself to embody a totally different way of being a father from his own father (Johansson, 1996). When talking about his own father he says:

> My dad has been working all his life in construction, exactly as I have. My mother has always been at home. At that time, most working class families had bad economies. ... There were no "alternative fathers." My father was clearly not so engaged in his children. ... I have never talked with him about emotions or relations.

Even though Bob shows a certain degree of reflexivity, he could be characterized as a man who has to some extent adjusted to new values and ideals, but who at the same time cultivates quite traditional values and ideals about manhood. Bob has always put a lot of his effort and energy into his work, and his new life has even made it easier for him to combine family and work. He is quite satisfied with his life and even though he sometimes feels guilty for not being able to spend as much time as he would like with all his children, he firmly believes in being able to create a good situation for all his children.

Conclusions: fatherhood and masculinity

When talking about hegemonic masculinity, we are touching upon matters concerning all men. Although many contemporary men actively reflect upon their own masculinity and also try to change their lifestyle and become more equal with women, there are also other and more worrying tendencies in contemporary culture.

Especially when talking about the situation of non-resident fathers, it is necessary to focus on the problematic construction of masculinity and to identify aspects of manhood which are making it difficult for men to maintain a strong relation with their children. I have focused on men's ways of handling emotions, their reflexivity, relations to their own father and gender ideals. These aspects certainly do not exclude other possible analyses of the reproduction of hegemonic masculinity. They must be regarded as parts of a first tentative approach to a more extended exploration of the relation between masculinity and fatherhood. What we call hegemonic masculinity influences men in different ways. The three case studies presented here illustrate some of these differences.

Tim shows a high degree of reflexivity. He is constantly involved in new projects, trying out new lifestyles. He is quite aware of the fact that he does not live up to the image of the "new father," but nevertheless he really tries to develop a stable relationship with his children. Although he puts a lot of effort into this project, he constantly feels insecure about his role as a father and his identity. His description of his own father shows great similarities with Paul Auster's auto-biographical statements about his father – the invisible man. Tim has great difficulties relating to his new situation. Even though he really feels engaged in his children, trying to adjust to his role as a non-resident father, he often feels lost and incapable of handling the whole situation. Tim lacks a stable sense of masculinity and a stable identity as a father. These feelings are partly related to his family background and his lack of a close relation to his own father. When talking about his father, he expresses a certain resentment and disappointment. Tim is clearly trapped in a stage between the "no longer" and "not yet." He is quite aware of the importance of being in contact with his emotions and developing a stable relation with his children, but this does not make it easier for him to achieve his goals.

The father in the second story may be described in terms of his problematic relation to the world. He often feels that the whole world has turned against him. Whereas Tim constantly reflects upon his life and his values, Ken is acting out his ontological insecurity in his fight against authorities and ex-partners. His sense of masculinity is rather weak. On the one hand, he idealizes the image of the adventurous father, who spends all his time away from home, while on the other hand, he cultivates an idealized image of a caring father. However, he is not ambivalent, that is, he does not suffer from a feeling that these two images are impossible to combine in one identity; he is rather trying to uphold both images at the same time.

Studying Ken's relation to his own father, it becomes obvious that he lacks an internalized image of a good father. He feels abandoned and has great difficulties relating to the image of his father. Instead of spending his time and energy on his new family, he is involved in a long and bitter fight with his ex-partner, social workers and lawyers. Rather than working through feelings of sorrow and lost, this man engages in a constant fight against the world. However, this type of fatherhood is not only a result of psychological processes, but also of circumstances which are related to a particular occupational role and to the cultivation of a certain type of masculinity – a traditional masculinity which has great difficulties handling emotions and developing a caring attitude.

Bob show a stable sense of fatherhood and masculinity. He is aware of the existence of new gender ideals, and is able to combine them with certain more traditional ways of being a man and a father. He believes in having a dialogue with his children and caring about their emotional problems. Although Bob feels sad about his divorce, he has adjusted well to his new lifestyle. Earlier his work interfered with his family life, but now he finds it much easier to fit these two parts of his life together. His new lifestyle in no threatens his sense of fatherhood. He feels quite secure in his role as a non-resident father. Whereas Tim is trapped in the stage between "no longer" and "not yet," Bob has succeeded in keeping his traditional values and identity in his new role as a non-resident father. He has incorporated a certain sense of reflexivity, and this reflexivity has both a cognitive and an emotional character.

The three cases presented in this article are not merely idiosyncratic, but also have a more general character. Many of the men we met during the time we worked with our empirical material fitted into the patterns of the stories presented here. When studying non-resident men's relations to their children, it is important to focus on the problematic aspects of masculinity. I have focused on some specific aspects, though a more complete analysis could include more qualities and characteristics of masculinity. Using this type of approach, I believe it is possible to get closer to the problematic issue of the absent father.

Epilogue: the absent father

One of the men in our study had great problems relating to his son. Although he told us that he thought of his son, who was now a teenager, every day, he did not contact him or try to develop a good relationship with him. Looking at this man's construction of masculinity and his relation to his own father, it became clear that he showed a reluctance to confront his masculinity and to change. However, the difference between this particular man and the other case studies presented in the article, is that he did not try at all to create a relation with his child. Compared to the other types of fatherhood discussed above it is possible to describe the absent father from a more general point of view. He had a weak or non-existing relation to his own father, cultivated traditional gender ideals, showed a low degree of reflexivity and had great difficulties in expressing emotions. At the end of the interview this man talked about his feelings of guilt in respect to his failure as a dad. He said:

> I am often saying to myself: well you couldn't handle this, could you? This is one of the most important aspects of life, and ... What ever happens, I mean divorces and children and so on, one should really try to develop a relationship to one's child, and I have failed in doing this.

Many men today have difficulties in constructing a sense of masculinity and in developing an identity as fathers and men. When studying non-resident fathers and their relations with their children, one way is to focus on these questions. One of the key aspects of many fathers' failure to develop long-lasting relationships with their children may probably be located in the problematic construction of a contemporary masculinity and fatherhood.

Even though it may seem to be problematic to use the concept of hegemonic masculinity when studying men who have lost their positions as heads of the family, I would suggest that the problematic issue of absent fathers must be studied in this perspective. Instead of putting up a struggle for their relationship with their children, "absent fathers" avoid change and instead devote their time to their own careers and life-plans. In this way they reproduce a traditional male position and they contribute to the strengthening of a certain type of limited rationality and hegemonic masculinity. In this article I have focused on how different men dealt with the problematic issues of being non-resident fathers and men of today (see also Johansson, 1996d). A more elaborate study of these matters may contribute to knowledge which can be used to strengthen the bond between fathers and children and work toward the dissolution of hegemonic masculinity. In the end, this can only be achieved through a dialogue between men and women.

Notes

1. This question has been dealt with in a number of different ways (see, for example, Bly (1990), Segal (1990), Badinter (1992), Keen (1991), Kipnis (1991), Middleton (1992) and Lennéer-Axelson (1994)).
2. For a thorough discussion of masculinity, emotions and the body, see, for example, Theweleit (1978) and Johansson (1996c).
3. Within social theory, Victor Seidler has thoroughly discussed the relation between modernity, rationality and masculinity. See, for example, Seidler (1989, 1994).
4. For a discussion of the Nordic debate about masculinity and fatherhood, see, for example, Holter and Aarseth (1993) and Ekman (1995).
5. For a discussion of hegemonic masculinity, see Johansson (1996a, b).
6. The empirical material of this study was collected during 1995 and 1996. Together with my colleague, Lars-Erik Berg, I have conducted qualitative interviews with 24 non-resident fathers. The investigation is designed as a longitudinal qualitative study and at the moment we are interviewing the same men once again, but this time we are also talking to their children, trying to focus on the relation between father and child.
7. For a more thorough discussion of these questions, see Johansson (1997).
8. For a description of the adventurer, see, for example, Simmel (1971), Johansson (1995) or Öhman (1995).

References

Arendell, Terry (1995) *Fathers and Divorce*. London: Sage.

Auster, Paul (1982) *The Invention of Solitude*. London: Faber and Faber.

Badinter, Elisabeth (1992) *XY: Om mannens identitet* (XY: On masculine identity). Stockholm: Månpocket.

Beck, Ulrich and Beck-Gernsheim, Elisabeth (1990/1995) *The Normal Chaos of Love*. Cambridge: Polity Press.

Blos, P. (1985) *Sons and Fathers. Before and Beyond the Oedipus Complex*. New York: The Free Press.

Bly, Robert (1990) *Iron John: A Book about Men*. Reading: Addison-Wesley.

Connell, Robert. W. (1995) *Masculinities*. Cambridge: Polity Press.

Ekman, Daniel (1995) *En mans bok: Om manlig identitet – teorier, ideal, verklighet* (A man's book: Masculine identity – Theories, ideals and reality). Stockholm: Natur och Kultur.

Giddens, Anthony (1992) *The Transformation of Intimacy*. Cambridge: Polity Press.

Holter, Øystein G. and Aarseth, Helen (1993) *Mäns Livssammanhang*. Stockholm: Bonniers.

Ihinger-Tallman et al. (1995) "Developing a Middle-Range Theory of Father Involvement Postdivorce,". In Marsiglio, William (ed.), *Fatherhood, Contemporary Theory, Research, and Social Policy*. London: Sage.

Johansson, Thomas (1995) "Det stora äventyret: Om manlig adolescensutveckling," in Bolin, Göran and Lövgren, Karin (eds), *Om unga män*. Lund: Studentliteratur.

Johansson, Thomas (1996a) "Gendered Spaces: The Gym Culture and the Construction of Gender," *Young*, 3, pp 32-47.

Johansson, Thomas (1996b) "Masculinities at the Crossroads: Gym Culture and the Construction of Masculine Bodies," unpublished paper.

Johansson, Thomas (1996c) "Kroppens sociologi: En introduktion," *Sociologisk Forskning*, no. 2-3.

Johansson, Thomas (1996d) "Den goda viljan. Om separation, faderskap och manlighet," *Fokus på familien*, 4, pp. 222-36.

Johansson, Thomas (1998) *Den skulpterade kroppen. Gymkultur, friskvård och estetik*. Stockholm: Carlssons förlag.

Jung, Carl Gustav (1989) *Aspects of the Masculine Soul*. London: Ark Books.

Keen, Sam (1991) *Fire in the Belly. On Being a Man.* New York: Bantam Books.

Kipnis, Aron R. (1991) *Knights Without Armor: A Practical Guide for Men in Quest for Masculine Soul*. Los Angeles: Jeremy P. Tarcher, Inc.

Lennéer-Axelson, Barbro (1994) *Männens röster i kris och förändring* (Men's voices: in crisis and change). Stockholm: Natur and Kultur.

Segal, Lynn (1990) *Slow Motion: Changing Masculinites, Changing Men*. London: Virago Press.

Seidler, Victor (1989) *Rediscovering Masculinity: Reason, Language and Sexuality*. London: Routledge.

Seidler, Victor (1994) *Unreasonable Men: Masculinity and Social Theory*. London: Routledge.

Simmel, Georg (1971) *On Individuality and Social Forms*. Chicago: University of Chicago Press.

Theweleit, Klaus (1978) *Male Fantasies*. Cambridge: Polity Press.

Wallerstein, Judith and Kelly, Joan B. (1980) *Surviving the breakup. How parents and children cope with divorce*. London: Grant McIntyre.

Wernick, Andrew (1991) *Promotional Culture. Advertising, Ideology and Symbolic Expression*. London: Sage.

Öberg, Bente and Öberg, Gunnar (1992) *Pappa, se mig! Om förnekade barn och maktlösa fäder* (Daddy, look at me! On rejected children and powerless men). Stockholm: Förlagshuset Gothia.

Öhman, Anders (1995) "Äventyraren, passionen och kvinnan" (The adventurer, the passion and the woman) *Kvinnovetenskaplig tidskrift*, 4, pp. 3-13.

Chapter 15

Masculinity and Paranoia in Strindberg's *The Father*

JØRGEN LORENTZEN

In September 1887, August Strindberg (1849-1912) submitted his play The Father. Strindberg sent the play first to Bonniers, who had published several of his previous works, but Bonniers turned it down. He sent it to the Stockholm theaters, but the play was simply returned. Finally, Hans Österling at Helsingborg published the piece without paying Strindberg a royalty, and the play had its premiere at the Casino Theatre in Copenhagen in November 1887.

One reason for the resistance Strindberg was now encountering was that many felt that he had gone too far in his diatribes on the women's issue, even though the prosecution against Strindberg over Getting Married (Giftas I, 1884) was for blasphemy and not immorality. The Getting Married stories came out in 1884 and 1886, and his venomous tone toward women had shocked the public. Elias Bredsdorff, writing on the relationship between Getting Married and Getting Married II (Giftas II, 1886), says: "The humor that characterized the first part, had now been supplanted by an indomitable rage, and Strindberg's pronounced misogyny was, for the first time, clearly expressed in this collection" (Bredsdorff, 1973, p. 154). Strindberg was an active participant in the debate about moral issues, and his loathing for Bjørnson's abstemious morality was undeniable. Getting Married contains the story "The Wages of Virtue" (Dygdens lön), in which Strindberg literally picks up Bjørnson's gauntlet and hurls it back with stinging irony. His foreword to Getting Married II, redolent in its aphoristic style with contempt for womanhood, contains the declaration: "Another matter. The girl who is seduced suffers no injury other than that she loses the respect of other women, on account of her foolishness. Men marry seduced women, widows and prostitutes. They are not the least fastidious. It is only the women and Bjørnson who must now have unsullied offspring" (Strindberg, 1984, p. 181).

At the time of writing The Father, Strindberg was frenetically involved with the sexual issue, politically, artistically and personally. Olof Lagercrantz in his biography of Strindberg, mentions the unhealthy suspicions Strindberg entertained about his wife Siri at this period. His jealousy grew and caused such serious problems for his virility that he had to have it publicly measured and confirmed. In a letter to Pehr Staaff on 21 August 1887, Strindberg wrote: "Excited right to the tips of my genitals, I travelled to Geneva and went to a brothel taking a doctor with me. Underwent a test of strength – not, as a matter of fact, for the first time – which I will call the Rape of Proserpina (picture the situation yourself as a bit like Bernini's statue). Examined my semen, which turns out to be virile and was measured in excited condition (= 16 x 4 centimetres)" (Strindberg, 1958, p. 252).

Strindberg completed The Father in the course of a couple of months. The play was written in the midst of an ongoing social discussion about women and men; it was written in dialogue with a number of other literary works, principally Henrik Ibsen's naturalistic dramas A Doll's House (Et dukkehjem, 1879) and The Wild Duck (Vildanden, 1884); it was written under the pressure of a heated matrimonial crisis (with Siri von Essen) and it was written as part of a proposed dramatic trilogy. Strindberg had already written The Comrades (Kamraterna, first published in 1888, later renamed The Marauders (Marodörer)), which deals with painter Bertha's adult life with the artist, Axel. According to Strindberg The Companions was to be the second part, the first part having been about Bertha's father and childhood, while a comedy and reconciliation was to form the third part (Ollén, 1982, p. 88). The Father was therefore planned as the first part of a trilogy, the third element of which was never written. The notion of reconciliation may have seemed too remote.

The Father is a play in three acts which in essence examines fatherhood in the character of Captain Adolf Lassen, who has been married to Laura for 20 years. Their daughter Bertha has come of age, and her future is discussed. The dispute about their daughter's education reveals that for many years Adolf and Laura have engaged in a dogged struggle for domestic supremacy. Adolf has been the decision-maker by virtue of his position as a man, but now, in the battle over their daughter, who means everything to Adolf, it is the woman who gains power by virtue of her nature. In the course of three acts and 24 hours the reader sees how Laura, by using her allies in the household, and by playing a shrewd game of intrigue, wrests power from Adolf, who finally relinquishes his authority and ends up as a broken man.

In this essay I want to concentrate on the Captain's being as a man, in particular in relation to his demasculinization and paranoia.

You're all born of woman

During the first act a paradoxical side to the Captain has been introduced: his essence as both great and small. He is a man of consequence as an officer and the head of his household. His rhetoric is that of power, and he addresses the others as subordinates, including his wife Laura. But already at the end of the first scene the Pastor calls the Captain "gubbe lilla" – literally "my boy" – a form of address that hints at something other than the Captain's natural authority and dominance. Well into the first act this line is strengthened by Laura's comment to Adolf in the ninth scene: "I've never been able to look at a man without feeling that I am stronger than him" (p. 46), but even more by the Nurse's contribution at the end of the act.

The Nurse makes her first entrance with the words "Now, listen, Mr. Adolf, pet" (p. 40). She has been the Captain's wet-nurse, and addresses him as her own little boy in an attempt to talk him round. She continues this gooey infantilization of the Captain toward the end of the seventh scene: "Old Margaret loves her big, big boy best of all, and when the storm comes he'll creep back to her like the good little child he is" (p. 42) – a form of address that does indeed soothe the Captain's injured narcissism, and makes him express himself more calmly. The reason the Nurse thinks and speaks like this is revealed a little later on when the Captain seeks an explanation for women's ability to treat men as if they were children: "Don't ask me. I suppose it's because, whether you're little boys or grown men, you're all born of woman" (p. 47).

The Nurse here touches on what I would characterize as the second of the two pivotal problems of the play. The first is the Captain's association with time, which is linked largely to his relationship with Bertha. The other is the Captain's sexual standing: either as a man set above woman, or as woman's eternal child and subservient to her. This is what I would describe as a demasculinization problem. The man is demasculinized by being turned into "pet," "boy," or quite simply "born of woman."

The play's second act is short and extremely intense. It is here that these two sets of problems take effect, having been presented as themes in the first act. I will deal with the Captain's demasculinization first.

The question of what it means to be a man is raised several times in the second act. The act is set at night, after the Captain has returned home. It contains several short monologues from the Captain, with dramatic references to Hamlet and several of Shakespeare's other plays, as well as to Ibsen's psychological, modernistic dramas. The act provides considerable insight into the Captain's dilemmas: Is he a man? What kind of man? What are the costs of being a man? Such questions arise in the wake of the doubt Laura has sown about Adolf's paternity, a doubt that has struck home and shaken Adolf's unreflective patriarchal gestalt. The question of his fatherhood is not brushed aside as folly, as all the other attacks from the women have been, but leads to a qualitative shift in the Captain's being. He moves from unphilosophical creature, a man by dint of his actions, to insecure sexual identity because of doubts about his patriarchal authority. The Captain's identity as a man is therefore deeply bound up with his power, and as soon as that power is shaken, his essence as a man is threatened.

This transition may strike us as surprising. Why not simply reject Laura's hypothesis as a speculative one specifically aimed at trying to topple him? Why is the play's second act not focused on Laura and her deceit? Why does the Captain not question her motives? The surprising thing is that attention does not dwell on Laura in the second and reflective act, but on the Captain. In the Captain's own inner drama it is he who is beginning to doubt and deliberate on himself and his being.

The literature on paranoia emphasizes a simultaneous, and often paradoxical, manifestation of opposing forces. The paranoid can frequently display both steadfastness and hypersensitivity, or grandiosity and smallness, or great self-assertion and lack of self-assurance. Such contrasts enable the individual with paranoid characteristics to fluctuate between wide extremes. He may see himself as a victim: weak, helpless, vulnerable and small, and as strong: masterful, dominant, manipulating and powerful (Meissner, 1994, p. 20). Both aspects will always be present in a paranoia, but one side or the other will dominate alternately. Birgitte Diderichsen writes: "The paranoid temperament consists of a personality conflict with on one side a pronounced lack of self-assurance and on the other a need for self-assertion" (Diderichsen, 1987, p. 413). Even something that makes the ego change from the grandiose to the uncertain, can be characterized as a key situation that will lead to an "ethical reverse."

This is the sort of situation the Captain finds himself in, an especially humiliating situation that intensifies his pride, and gives more room to his lack of self-assurance than to his notions of greatness. As a result, it is the Captain who starts questioning himself as a man. In his conversation with the Doctor, the latter advises him against developing unhealthy fantasies about women, and by way of reply the Captain says:

> If I were not a man I would have the right to accuse – or, as the polite phrase is, to lay a complaint. Then I might perhaps be able to give you a complete diagnosis of my illness, and, what is more, its history. But unfortunately, I am a man, and so I can only, like a Roman, fold my arms across my breast and hold my breath until I die (p. 55).

The Captain is reflecting on the possibility of not being a man, and the openings this would provide. If he were "not a man," he would be able to make a diagnosis and tell the whole story of his illness, but as "unfortunately, I am a man," he must just keep his mouth shut and resign himself. The Captain, who spent the entire first act accusing the women, has now lost his ability to accuse, but worse still, he can neither explain nor give a history of himself. He has been deprived of his position of power – of being the one able to articulate the truth. In his own eyes he is no longer simply a man, but says "unfortunately, I am a man." Masculinity has become something to be lamented – he has become less than a man. The humiliating position he feels himself placed in creates a sense of subordination. We are witnessing a double polarization in which the Captain feels his authority compromised by Laura's speculations, but in which the feeling of powerlessness brings with it a contemplation of sexuality, a contemplation that ends in a manliness to be bemoaned.

Though the Doctor in his next reply assures him that to explain will not injure his manly honor, the Captain refuses to speak. His sense of injury begets not only a problematic masculinity, but also suspicion and a preconception about others' willingness to listen to his story. If he were not a man, he could have spoken and been believed, but because he is a man, no one will believe him, so he may as well lie down and die – he has become a victim of his surroundings, his reason for existence has gone.

The next sequence witnesses the radicalization of the Captain's problem with being a man. In the fifth and last scene of the act there is a lengthy dialogue between him and Laura, in which Adolf, in desperation, begs Laura to tell him the whole truth about his child. Laura has turned, and swears to God he is Bertha's father. But now it is too late. The Captain:

> What good will that do, when you have already said that a mother should commit any crime for the sake of her child? I implore you, by the memory of the past – I beg you, as a wounded man begs for mercy – tell me everything!

Don't you see that I am as helpless as a child, can't you hear me crying for pity like a child crying to its mother, can't you forget that I am a man, a soldier who with a word can tame men and beasts? I ask only for the pity you would extend to a sick man, I lay down my power and cry for mercy – for my life (p. 59).

After a lengthy exchange with Laura, the Captain gives up. His cry for pity marks the turning point of the play. The Captain breaks down and begs for mercy. He lays down his symbols of authority and begs for pity and compassion. Yet again we see how tightly bound up is the sign of power with being a man. If Laura is to comprehend his impotence, she must forget he is a man. If she views him as a man, it will be impossible to see his helplessness. He relinquishes his symbols of authority at the same time as abdicating his position as a man.

At that moment he bursts into tears. The Captain forgets that he is a man, and weeps. "What! Man, you're crying!" says Laura. This weeping alters something else about the Captain. He stops falling, and seems almost to assume a new identity. By crying, the Captain shifts from head to body. In his next lines, which we must call his feministic appeal, his rhetoric, from being based on the rationale of authority, turns to follow the warm logic of the body:

Yes, I am crying, although I am a man. But has not a man eyes? Has not a man hands, limbs, heart, thoughts, passions? Does he not live by the same food, is he not wounded by the same weapons, warmed and cooled by the same summer and winter as woman? If you prick us, do we not bleed? If you tickle us, do we not laugh? If you poison us do we not die? Why should a man be forbidden to complain, or a soldier to weep? Because it is unmanly? Why is it unmanly?

The Captain turns. In a moment of truth he wishes to insist that he is a man in spite of his tears: "Yes, I am crying, although I am a man." He is a man in spite of his body: "Has not a man eyes ... hands, limbs." The Captain's shift propels the drama into a new phase. His resignation of power causes an ambivalence about his condition as a man, which again brings his body into the limelight. Weakness creates an unstable sexual identity and an obtrusive physical proximity. His body, which had no place in the Captain's consciousness while he ruled over man and beast, has now become a problem. For a man, the body belongs to the realm of helplessness and pity. Only when the man is helpless does his body take on an existence, and that is a physical nearness the Captain finds unmanly.

His reply opens up yet another dimension, because the Captain's ardent and lyrically formulated question is a paraphrase of Shylock the Jew's speech in Act III, Scene I of Shakespeare's *The Merchant of Venice* (1596). Shylock seeks to argue that a Jew is just like a Christian: "Hath not a Jew hands, organs, dimensions, senses, affections, passions? Fed with the same food ..." and so on. But Shylock's object is to show that a Jew is as vengeful and grasping as a Christian, and, in the spirit of Shakespeare, he turns out far worse. Shylock is a flat and one-dimensional character suffused with miserliness. He is the power his money gives him. So a comparison between the Captain and Shylock does the Captain no credit. But the reference also points up an interesting development in the history of drama. Strindberg's modern, naturalistic play contains a totally different order of psychological richness from Shakespeare's character comedy. In Shakespeare, Shylock's lines represent a claim on his right to greed, despite the humanistic appeal of his statement. In Strindberg's drama the humanistic appeal is more distinct, imparting a new dimension to the Captain and representing a break in the text.

The Captain's reflections on manliness also mark a reversal in the relationship between him and Laura. Not simply in the sense that Laura assumes superiority and Adolf inferiority, but because they change sides in the Aristotelian sexual dichotomy: the man becomes the body and the woman the head. She becomes the cold, calculating and rational wielder of power; he the subservient, humble and corporeal being. The man literally collapses into his body, and once there, his masculinity becomes attenuated and his sexual identity unstable. "Why is it unmanly?" is the Captain's despairing cry from the threshold of losing his masculinity. His question enables him for the first time to confirm, and partially expose, patriarchy's extreme limitations *vis-à-vis* the concept of being a man. The guidelines he has followed blindly so far, now turn against him and become his foe. The patriarchal ideology of masculinity turns into a prison from which it is impossible to escape. For a brief moment, his tears carry him across to the other frontier, but only long enough for him to see that he now inhabits a no-man's-land. He is moving into a physical area where no man ought to be.

Laura affirms the Captain's physical embodiment when she emphasizes that his body is not whole: "Your big, strong body was afraid" (p. 60). In that instant she marks the Captain's final demasculinization:

Weep, my child. Your mother is here to comfort you. Do you remember, it was as your second mother that I first entered your life? Your big, strong body was afraid. You were a great child who had come too late into the world, or had come unwanted (p. 60).

As the Captain takes over the body, he becomes a child on his mother's knee. Again the woman is mother and the man child in a dyadic physical relationship. Closeness and caring flow between them. If he is a child, she will be his mother and intimacy will spring up; if a man, the woman will become his enemy and aloofness will intervene: "The mother was your friend, you see, but the woman was your enemy" (p. 60). The Captain strips off his manliness and becomes a child in order to receive womanly care. As a man he cannot accept care, he must conquer: "But when, later, I awoke and looked about me and saw that my honour had been sullied, I wanted to wipe out the stain through a noble action, a brave deed, a discovery, or an honourable suicide" (p. 60).

The Captain's acute demasculinization is therefore not simply a one-off event that occurs just now, at the moment he falls from power, but a recurrent theme in his life. Throughout his time with Laura he has continuously oscillated between the manly and the unmanly. On this fateful night he has been demasculinized for good. No longer can he raise himself to perform a "noble action, a brave deed, a discovery."

Demasculinization and paranoia

The next question is how to link this demasculinization to the Captain's paranoid characteristics. Demasculinization or "Entmannung" is a key element in Freud's Schreber analysis (Freud, 1990), based on the memoirs of Daniel Paul Schreber. Schreber himself returns to the theme of demasculinization on a number of occasions, and the term may be said to have two meanings for Schreber. First, he uses it negatively where others are attempting to demasculinize him. Second, he gives it positive meaning, in that he must undergo a demasculinization in order to seduce God and save the world. In this second definition, demasculinization is likened to feminization, in the sense that Schreber must be transformed into a woman so that he can seduce God. Diderichsen emphasizes that Freud blurs these two definitions, consistently equating "Entmannung" with feminization: "This is precisely where Freud makes his crucial error, concluding as he does – based on those parts of Schreber's text where the Entmannung theme is genuinely presented as a feminization – that all patients' thoughts on demasculinization *are* fantasies about femininity" (Diderichsen, 1982, p. 384). Freud commits this error so that the analysis will better fit his theory of latent homosexual tendencies (a theory which, incidentally, has now been thoroughly rejected). Diderichsen then goes on to write about the other aspect of the demasculinization theme: "The Entmannung motif is thus particularly marked at, for example, a stage in the patient's disease during which his clothes are removed and he undergoes forcible feeding and consequently feels totally degraded and *dependent*."

In the analysis of Schreber's paranoia it is therefore possible to distinguish between two types of demasculinization. One is bound up with being disenfranchized, the experience of having rights removed. The other is linked to the desire to become a woman, able to seduce God. Elias Canetti touches on the latter form when he criticizes Freud's theory of homosexuality, stressing that it is *power* that plays the decisive role in the paranoia. "It was in order to disarm God that he wanted to transform himself into a woman; to become a woman for his sake was to flatter him and submit to him. Just as others kneel before him, Schreber offered himself for God's enjoyment. To win him over to his side and make sure of him, he lured him to approach and then used every means to keep him there" (Canetti, 1984, p. 450).

Here Canetti is highlighting Schreber's seduction strategy. By turning himself into a woman, he can seduce God and thereby also be with God. The necessity of becoming a woman is related to Schreber's view of femininity as "consisting of a constant feeling of sensuality" (Freud, 1990, p. 97). As God's rays possess a "very high sensuality" for Schreber (*ibid.*, p. 117), contact with God necessarily presupposes a demasculinization. Schreber is clearly operating within the traditional division of man and woman, in which the man is intellect and the woman body. If being conquered by God means being irradiated by sensuality, man must be demasculinized and become woman in every respect.

The fact that Canetti uses the term "disarm" (entwaffnen), also points to the unequal relation between God and Schreber, in which Schreber chooses becoming a woman to avoid the uneven contest with God. Diderichsen teases out the problem even further, maintaining that "Through feminization one can actually avoid competition with other men" (Diderichsen, 1982, p. 386). Male paranoia's demasculinization thus becomes a strategy for avoiding a battle one sees as unequal, and in which the paranoid perceives himself to be inferior.

This brief look at Schreber and his paranoia will help throw light on the problem of the Captain's demasculinization. Though in a somewhat different way to Schreber, it is possible to divide the Captain's demasculinization strategy into two strands: one negative and one positive. The Captain's desire to forget that he is a man and behave in an unmanly way can be linked to his feeling of disempowerment. The Captain's rights to the most precious thing he possesses, namely his daughter, have been stripped from him, so he relinquishes all his symbols of masculinity: "don't you see that I am as helpless as a child" (p. 59). The Captain's helplessness and humiliating position lead to a demasculinization. But in addition to this, we discover another type of demasculinization, not specifically connected with the loss of Bertha, but one which has been a constant factor in his relationship with Laura. The Captain strips off his masculinity and becomes a child in order to be close to Laura. As soon as he becomes a child, she gathers him to her and nurtures him. We can call this the Captain's positive demasculinization strategy, since it provides him with warmth and affection. By becoming a child he can "seduce" Laura, and enjoy her physical proximity, a closeness she denies him when he is a man of power. So the Captain vacillates between an infantile propinquity and love, and an adult absence and hate. He plays a game with his masculinity, in which its presence creates war, though perhaps also great "sublimated" exploits, and its absence brings proximity and tenderness, not to mention sensuality. The Captain therefore gets the chance to be irradiated with sensual feeling too – but only, it must be stressed, after he has undergone a necessary demasculinization. As a result, the Captain's demasculinization cannot be seen as being motivated by a wish to avoid unequal contests with other men, as in Diderichsen's rationale. The other men are relatively insignificant in the Captain's case. For him it might be more a desire to avoid doing battle with a woman – Laura. This would indicate that for some time the Captain has had a physical experience of Laura as his superior, a superiority he avoids confronting by becoming a child in her arms. Thus his seducing is also motivated by a wish to distance himself from an insufferable balance of power, one in which Laura is actually his superior, a fact hinted at in some of her words. "I've never been able to look at a man without feeling that I am stronger than him" (p. 46). Schreber and the Captain undergo two different types of demasculinization. Whereas Schreber's feminization was the expression of a hope of disarming God, the Captain's infantilization (it is important to stress that there is no question of feminization in the Captain's case) is a desire to disarm Laura.

When positive and negative demasculinization meet, the Captain's demasculinization is final. Act II, Scene V marks the play's turning point. From here the nature of the drama changes; from this point onward the Captain is sinking. Demasculinization marks his loss of power and authority as well as his forfeiture of masculinity. He is left like a struggling capon.

Man and time

Before I turn to the Captain's relationship with time, I should mention that there is an alternative interpretation of the Captain's demasculinization. Such a reading is to be found in Ronny Ambjörnsson's guide to the paradoxes of masculinity. Ambjörnsson links the Captain's infantilization with his physical inadequacy and his desire to become part of eternity. Ambjörnsson also starts from the assumption that man represents head and intellect, while woman is body and nature. The woman's physical centeredness affords her a place in eternity: "breast, pudenda, womb" is extended to "progeny, the child, the link with the future" (Ambjörnsson, 1987, p. 22). This link women have with the future through their bodies is not so simple for men. Ambjörnsson claims that the man's route to the future is through the woman's sexual organs. Consequently, man's association with woman is ambiguous because of his own conception by woman, his own potential for future extension through another woman and his bond with that woman as lover. "For the man, mother and lover merge; seen from this perspective, his devotion is a longing for nature and his origins: to lose his identity" (*ibid.*, p. 23).

This implies that the man's need to be anchored in time engenders a double lust, one that harkens back and one that drives forward. He longs to relive his conception, that first fusion with his mother in which no distinction existed, and he wants to live on through his child – so that he can create a continuum of his own life. Both strategies, however, are erected on extremely flimsy and problematic foundations: one, on the renouncing of masculinity, and the second on the relationship to another – the woman.

Ambjörnsson's ideas are interesting, but I do not want to pursue his line of argument here. I shall let his theories about man's yearning for his origins lie, while in my further analysis of *The Father* following up the problems he raises about men's relationship with time, and with the future in particular.

I shall discuss the Captain's attitude to time in regard to three different phenomena in *The Father*: his relationship with Bertha, the Captain as a scientist, and his study of meteorites. I will start with the Captain's relationship with his daughter Bertha.

A parable from India may serve to set the scene for the account of men's attitude to time. In *The Masks of God* (1960-68), Joseph Campbell relates how the Indian pundit Saubhari dedicated himself to a life of isolation and meditation. His place of meditation was a small lake, in which he sat immersed for several years. One day he was sitting watching an old fish that was totally immersed in its numerous offspring: first and second generation. Saubhari thought that he, too, would like to experience such enjoyment, and decided to return and live amongst his fellow men once more. In his search for a wife, the wise man met a king who had 50 beautiful daughters. The pundit employed his talents and seduced every one of them, and their father had to agree to allow him to marry all 50. He built 50 palaces in the forest and began the job of begetting children. He fathered 50 sons, after which he dedicated himself wholeheartedly to his desire for grandchildren, and thereafter for great-grandchildren. He was absolutely determined to share the experience of the old fish. Suddenly Saubhari realized that his expectations were boundless:

> What a fool. There is no end to my desires. Even though for ten thousand years or a hundred thousand years, all that I wish should come to pass, there would still be new wishes springing to my mind. For I now have seen my infants walk, beheld their youth, manhood, marriage, and progeny, yet expectations still arise and my soul yearns to behold the progeny of their progeny. As soon as I see those a new wish will arise, and when that is accomplished how am I to prevent the birth of still further desires? (Campbell, 1962, p. 217).

Saubhari's desire for children is not linked to any wish to play with them, or to stand in ethical relation to them, or to watch them develop as individuals, but is bound up with a longing to see himself in ever newer generations, in the progeny of his progeny. Saubhari sees himself as never being able to share in the immediate present, but being forever ruled by an unquenchable passion for the future. Saubhari's new life, his bid to be like the old fish, is built on the same model as his former one in isolation. Both are motivated by a wish to be part of a greater whole than the circumscribed life that is Saubhari's lot on earth. Either he attempts to meditate himself into a spiritual existence, or he lives with his offspring in a never-ending continuum of generations. In both cases he finds himself on the outside of life.

Children's importance for the lives of men can also be found in the stories Lévy-Bruhl tells in *The "Soul" of the Primitive* (1965). A father from a South American Indian tribe is not allowed to work or go hunting after his child is born, because the arrow may pierce the child. Should the father need to climb over a tree trunk, he places two little twigs as a bridge for the baby's spirit, which always comes with him. Should he encounter a jaguar, instead of running away, he approaches the animal fearlessly. The child's life is totally dependent on such an action. No matter how badly he has been bitten by insects, he must scratch himself very carefully in order that his nails will not hurt the child. Father and child are so closely linked that everything that befalls the father also affects the child. They are almost a single being, though at the same time clearly distinct. The child always follows its father, though it may actually be sleeping in its mother's bed at home, and it can even happen that the father has never seen the child yet. Even so, it accompanies him all the time (Lévy-Bruhl, 1965, p. 183). The father's consciousness of the ties between him and his child are strong, but this consciousness of how he, as a man, lives with his progeny, does not make him remote from present existence, as it does with Saubhari. On the contrary, his imaginary link with the child increases his being in the present.

These stories highlight men's attitudes to their offspring and to time. Both mythologize the same set of problems, but provide two widely differing images of how the two men tackle them: one, by abandoning himself to time as an abstract quantity, the other by linking time to definite contemporary events.

The Father throws up the same problem in the Captain's endeavour to perpetuate his soul in Bertha: "You see, it isn't enough for me to have given the child life. I want to give it my soul too" (p. 41). Although the Captain tries to involve himself in his daughter's actual life – "but when you come, father, it's like throwing open the window on a spring morning!" (p. 43) – he is actually nearer Saubhari's problem of yearning than the South American father's spiritual closeness to his child. Bertha assumes greater importance for the Captain as *daughter* rather than as Bertha. It is not his daughter's independence and autonomy that makes the Captain fight for her, rather his involvement is brought about by her ties with, and extension of, himself. The Captain's life will extend with and through Bertha. This he will do both spiritually and physically, and his relationship to Bertha becomes more radical throughout the action of the play, as his responsibility for her diminishes.

At the opening of the play the Captain's intention is to provide his daughter with an education that will enable her to look after herself. He seems to have no desire to make her into a copy of himself: "You mustn't imagine I want to build the child into ... a copy of myself" (p. 31). Toward the end of the first act the Captain is more uncompromising. He feels himself persecuted and has to demonstrate his authority. He tells the Nurse, who wants him and Laura to reach an agreement, "You see, it isn't enough for me to have given the child life. I want to give it my soul too" (p. 41).

The Captain's laid-back approach to Bertha in the exposition has already been altered considerably by his encounter with the women. There is no more talk about her not becoming a copy of him, now that she is to be the bearer of his soul. She is to perpetuate his spirit and rationality, as an antidote to the womanish irrationality that rules the house. A further radicalization of the fusion with Bertha occurs in the third act, now that the Captain not only wishes to transfer his soul to Bertha, but his body as well:

> I grafted my right arm, half my brain, half my spinal cord on to another stem, because I believed they would unite into a single, more perfect tree, and then someone comes with a knife and cuts beneath the graft, so that now I am only half a tree – but the other tree goes on growing with my arm and half my brain, while I wither and die, for I gave the best parts of myself (p. 70).

His fantasy of fusion with his offspring is complete. She has had the best half of his body, and previously she was given his soul. He is in her, and when Laura cuts short the fantasy by removing his right to Bertha, she is slicing him in two. The Captain experiences no feeling of separateness. He does not see himself as autonomous in relation to his daughter, or vice versa, his daughter divorced from him. They are as one because he continues his life through her. This makes the Captain both great and small at the same time. He is grandiose as he views Bertha as a part of himself, and he is small in the instant he is riven from her. Her autonomy means that he will be just half a man. His investment in Bertha costs him dearly: he wants to become double, but is threatened with being halved. This wholly concrete investment of body and soul in Bertha is the central theme of the play – what the Captain terms his *idea of immortality*. In his conversation with Laura in the second act the Captain says: "I do not believe in resurrection, and to me this child was my life hereafter. She was my idea of immortality – perhaps the only one that has any roots in reality. Take her away and you cut short my life" (p. 58).

Ambjörnsson says of this idea of immortality: "Children are a man's connection with the future. The Captain calls Bertha his 'idea of immortality'. Bertha anchors him in time, to the line that links the past with the future. Without this anchor he would float free, like a balloon in the upper regions of the spirit" (Ambjörnsson, 1987, p. 23). Ambjörnsson is neatly emphasizing men's position outside the unbroken line of physical descent that runs from mother to daughter, mother to daughter in endless succession. The Captain realizes he is excluded from this physical condition, an experience he attempts to compensate for with a phantasmatic over-investment in Bertha. Men are unable to incorporate

life, and therefore incapable of giving life. This explains why they are
lonely, according to Ambjörnsson. This severance from children is
reflected by the Captain toward the end of his life. In Act III, Scene VII
Laura asks if he would like to see his child one last time: "My child? A
man has no children. Only women have children, and so the future belongs
to them, while we die childless" (p. 76).

The Captain's philosophy, and the basis of his existential crisis, is that
a man has no children and therefore no future. Because he has no future, he
is alone in the universe. He tries to overcome this loneliness by dedicating
his life to rationality, to things outside the body, so that the body can be
forgotten and sublimated. This train of thought leads Ambjörnsson to
conclude that a man is an incomplete woman – he does not possess the
bodily functions that enable him to live with children. Such a philosophy
means that the gender question is reduced to turning on the same point. If
he is not a whole man he must be an incomplete woman. The idea that
everyone turns into women, or into men in other theories, is a line of
thought that is unable to justify their differences. The man's position in
time and his physical distinction from the child-bearing woman does not
make him an incomplete woman, but it does create a different ethical and
existential set of problems for men. His "deficiency" does not make him a
woman – on the contrary it makes him radically different from her, a
disparity both man and theory find difficult.

The body and rationality

The Captain is an example of a man who, in a desperate attempt to
maintain his patriarchal power, has become remote from his body. He has
wedded himself to rationality and renounced his body. A perception of his
body has only been possible in the form of a demasculinization, an
infantilization, through which he is able to experience fusion with the
mother's body. His renunciation of his body has created loneliness, as
Ambjörnsson points out, a loneliness enhanced in the Captain by his
rationalistic view of the world. He attempts to repair this isolation by
investing in his daughter, by giving her his rational soul and,
phantasmatically, his body as well. This investment encompasses the
Captain's idea of immortality. Bertha becomes the bearer of his idea of
immortality, his notion of life.

But the Captain does not only invest in Bertha, he also strives to
extend his life beyond death by means of research. The Captain's work as a

scientist is an attempt to make his knowledge survive into the future. He will discover something that will outlive him and give him a place in eternity. The fact that his speciality is meteorites can also be interpreted symbolically. Meteorites are the celestial bodies that, severed from their origins, travel freely between planets and move through space without any fixed orbit. The Captain believes he has discovered coal, or traces of organic material in the meteorites, and can therefore trace them back to an organic form of life. Seen like this, his research is an attempt to give meteorites some sort of origin. Similarly, one can view the Captain as a man thrust out into empty space, beyond the organic continuum, who drifts round struggling to create a meaning for himself in existence, a meaning that brings with it an attachment to the infinity of the universe.

The problems surrounding the Captain's association with time are thus compounded in the drama. He is working on the same problem in different ways: in relation to meteorites, the propagation of knowledge, and the relationship with his daughter. But the paranoid power struggle he enters into with the women brings about his defeat on all fronts: Laura withholds his letters so that he does not receive the literature from Germany that he needs to complete his research, she takes away his right to their daughter, and finally she declares him mad and asks for him to be certified (in the final scene of Act II). With the charge of madness, she has also stripped him of his rationality. His body was severed when the doubt about Bertha was sown, and now his reason is also in jeopardy.

The third act is dedicated to the culmination of the intrigue against the Captain, and his total breakdown. The die has been cast in the final scene of the second act, now all that is necessary is for Laura to reap her reward. But before I move on to that, there are still some questions that need answering. Why do Laura's musings about the child's father have such an effect on the Captain? How can Laura have the Captain certified with such minimal opposition? How does madness arise? Who is the driving force of the play's dramatic nerve – Laura or the Captain? What relevance has paranoia to the problems of man and time?

I have attempted to show how the Captain's attachment to Bertha is based on a strong desire to become part of eternity. She is his idea of immortality. This idea of immortality is to be affirmed by breaking with her mother's will and body and yielding to her father's wish to send her to town. She is to be an extension of his rationality in a break with the mother's irrationality. The Captain attempts to realize this idea of immortality by wielding his power. As a man and the household's patriarch he has the right to rule over it and its members – not least the coming generations. He tries to stifle disagreement by standing on his authority and rights. But there is an authority more powerful than the Captain's, and that is physical authority. The paradox is that this awareness has already been vouchsafed to the Captain. He has seen his own vulnerability. He has experienced his own rejectability in terms of eternity, and tries to overcome this through the exercise of power. When once the female body's link with time is threatened, Bertha's mother retaliates by joining battle on the grounds where she knows she is strongest. The Captain is doomed to defeat. The incongruity for him is that his ability to understand the male problem makes him blind. He experiences his distinctness, his vulnerability, but is not capable of relating ethically to them. He is dazzled in his attempt to maintain power over his daughter, and can no longer see clearly what is taking place around him. This also applies to the paranoid: "He [the paranoid] lacks the flexibility of mental processes that engender openness and shrewdness. Instead, his understanding is clouded by an intense emotional engagement in that aspect of life which for him has become the one 'justifying' his existence on earth" (Diderichsen, 1987, p. 429). He tries to solve the problem by using power – the means he, as a man, has at his disposal within the patriarchal system. He engineers his own downfall. He has experienced his non-corporeality in repeated situations of demasculinization, and consequently does not realize that he must fulfil his desires in the world of male rationality. He wants to be made body through Bertha, refusing at the same time to give up his male authority; therefore he has to eradicate the mother in her. He invites a battle between the body and rationality, or nature and culture, in which rationality is doomed to lose.

The Father is a drama built wholly on an inversion. In Act I the Captain is presented as having power, he gives the orders, he keeps the accounts. By the third act, however, Laura is the one holding sway. She now, quite literally, is at the desk issuing orders. She has assumed the same authoritative tone as the Captain in the first act. Their relationship has been inverted. The same kind of reversal lies at the heart of the paranoid structure. The Captain sees himself as being persecuted by the women in the house, who are out to get him, and want to tear him to pieces like tigers in a cage. The Captain's love for Laura has been inverted. Both predicate and subject/object have been swapped. In his Schreber analysis Freud describes how persecution mania converts the sentence "he loves her" into "she hates me," *ergo* I can hate her. Of this inversion Freud writes: "In persecution mania the distortion lies in an emotional transformation; what should have been felt as love from within, is perceived as hate from without" (Freud, 1990, p. 61).

But the inversion does not bring any liberation; subject and object are just as tightly locked in an infernal power struggle. Thus paranoia is described as a *relational* problem, where the significance of the persecutor, rather than diminishing, actually increases. As the Captain's situation becomes more acute, his relation with the outside world will merely intensify. Hurt does not lead to retreat into an intra-narcissistic melancholy, but to an interpersonal persecution mania. When his relationship with the outside world becomes strained, his daughter's significance will increase. The question of compromise is an impossible one; there is no half-way house or in-between stage for the Captain: fear of losing the symbolic object, or the thing that gives the Captain worth – Bertha – makes it impossible to strike a compromise with the person who threatens to take that object of value away. In a paranoid structure there is neither trust nor intimacy: love is turned to hate.

In a sense therefore, it may also be claimed that the Captain foresees the resistance he will face. Diderichsen says that the paranoid anticipates things before they have happened: "His ability to anticipate is developed to such a pitch that he can actually elicit in others the behavior he expects and fears" (Diderichsen, 1987, p. 425). Even in Act I the Captain harbors an expectation of losing. He goes to war with the women, who are capable of tearing him to shreds. In the first act he does not want Bertha to tell Laura that she would like to live in town – as the Captain, too, wishes. If she is allowed to, he knows that Laura has the power to change Bertha's mind: "I happen to know she wants to leave home. But I also know that you have the power to alter her will at your pleasure" (p. 44). The Captain adds that Laura has a malevolent gift for getting her own way: "You have a satanic genius for getting what you want" (p. 44). The Captain has foreseen his own defeat. If Laura is given the power to get her own way, it will be impossible to oppose her. He is unwilling to bend in her direction, at the same time acknowledging her power, which in a sense he is challenging her to use, and he gets what he expects and fears: a demon for an adversary, to borrow a concept from Strindberg literature.

As we can see, an entire complex of notions is being denied and projected: the power struggle, the body's inadequacy, male loneliness, the child's autonomy, time and eternity. The Captain is incapable of seeing his own vulnerability or exposure, but projects the threat onto the women, with Laura at their head, and they become the actors in his experience of a narcissistic violation. The Captain is never able to see the others as they really are, but perceives a distorted image of them characterized by mistrust, prejudice, bias and aggression. Both Meissner and Diderichsen describe how the paranoid's inadequate understanding of his surroundings results in poor self-knowledge, because the two aspects are closely interconnected. This also applies to the Captain. He does not see the others, and therefore cannot see himself. Instead, he attempts to close in on himself using his tunic as protection against his pursuers.

It is tempting, naturally, to guess at the cause of the Captain's paranoia. Especially as the play itself provides clues that can be followed. In the key exchange between the Captain and Laura in Act II, the Captain says:

> Yes, I suppose it was that. Father and mother had me against their will, and so I was born without a will. When you and I became one, I thought I was making myself whole; so I let you rule; and I who, in the barracks, among the soldiers, gave commands, was, with you, the one who obeyed. I grew up at your side, looked up to you as though to a superior being, listened to you as though I was your ignorant child (p. 60).

The Captain himself provides the explanation: born without will, without an aim or purpose in life. Even so, he attempts as a husband, as a patriarch, to create his own will, a will that melts in the physical fusion with Laura. As psychoanalysis has provided some clues in analyzing the paranoid, it would be tempting to speculate on the Captain's relationship with his mother and father, but I will leave this kind of psychology alone, and join with Deleuze and Guattari (in *L'Anti-Oedipe*, 1972) in their criticism of Freud's Schreber analysis: Why reduce such wonderfully rich material to a parental topic?

Paternal love

I have reached the point at which my analysis must take a new direction. I have tried to plot the unfolding tragedy and the Captain's nervousness and to explain his paranoid relationship to the others, linked as it is to a desire for eternal existence. Now I must ask myself some other leading questions: Is there anything in the text that points in another direction? What principles of life does the Captain breach? Which ethical problems does the text raise? The necessity of putting these questions lies in the fact that paranoia is no accidental madness, but an elemental process everyone undergoes during the genesis of the ego. The mere separation from the Other (the mother) and the experience of a self independent of the Other, implies paranoid problems in the relation of the self to the Other. Furthermore, the very question "Am I the child's father?" has paranoid overtones. The question harbors a suspicion very close to paranoia. Paranoia's universal nature necessitates searching for traces of something else, something that points toward a harmony between the characters, where insanity's persecutional relationship is supplanted by equitable consideration.

Is there anything in the text that points to something other than the unyielding struggle between the Captain and Laura? Is there perhaps a compromise? Everyone, except for the Captain, proposes a practical compromise. Even Laura seeks a compromise in Bertha's case, a suggestion ridiculed by the Captain. Compromise is shown as the place where the protagonists can meet and be reconciled. Compromise is envisaged as part of the sphere of reconciliation. Compromise, however, is flatly rejected by the Captain. He has the power, and shall therefore decide: compromise would be a meaningless capitulation. Here, power is the Captain's enemy. He falls back on authority's traditional sovereignty and right, without listening to people or sense. Masculine rationality becomes the opposite of reason. Compromise is not a necessity for the decision-maker, but a sign of weakness.

The drama plays this out, as the text shows how the power that masculine rationality rests upon begets a counter-force that can grow mightier than itself. Certainly, the text elegantly demonstrates how, toward the end, this counter-force resembles the original authority, perhaps because Laura becomes just as obstinate and uncompromising as the Captain. Laura's authority emerges as a pure replica of the Captain's, and thus the play ends in the paradox of role-reversal. The new authority takes over from the power that has already fallen, and therefore carries within itself the seeds of its own destruction. Viewed in this light, the entire play is hung on a paranoid framework, closed in on itself, where the counter-force will have to use the old power's protective mechanisms to ward off potential persecutors. The paranoid is characterized by a lack of openness toward others, and it is just such a lack of openness toward *anything else* that the structure of the drama displays – the Captain's power is reproduced and reiterated in Laura's new power.

Besides the conciliatory philosophy of the compromise there are other clues that should be followed up. Early in Act II the Doctor, who otherwise emerges as quite a phlegmatic character in the play, expresses an ethic that points well away from the Captain's paranoid attitude to women. The Captain asks the Doctor if he ever doubted whether his children really were his own, and the Doctor replies: "Indeed I did not! Has not Goethe written: 'A man must take his children on trust'?" (p. 54). The Doctor never doubts. His life is run on a different principle, to a different rule, in a different relation to the Other. The child is an act of good faith, an act that begets fondness. The Doctor is describing a relationship founded on another ethic, a fertility ethic that acknowledges the child as different from himself, while at the same time being tied to him.

Jacques Lacan reflects that the father's role in the family has two key functions: to forbid and to love. The father must forbid the child to take his place with the mother. The father's no is the guarantee that the child will leave the mother. "Le nom du Père" – the father's name – becomes "le non du père" – the father's no. But the father must also love, so that the child can identify with him, as the other person in its life. The father assumes a commitment before the birth, before the conception of the child. By loving the Other, the mother, he takes on the role of creator. He is able to create something different, something he is ignorant of, something that is not based on knowledge or work, something that is not part of a project, but something that simply arrives, something quite new. The father can only take the arrival of this new thing in good faith, says Lacan, because no one except the mother can guarantee it. Marcelle Marini in his interpretation of Lacan says: "Such a Father can only be the object of an 'act of faith': 'there is no Other of the other' to guarantee him" (Marini: 75). If the father must act in good faith, the child must act in double good faith, since the child has no option but to take the word of both its parents.

The uncertainty that arises when the child is born is based in the dichotomy that the child is a stranger, while at the same time being part of oneself. This duality is the kernel of Levinas's philosophy of fecundity, in relation to the eternal future. In *Totality and Infinity* he writes that the parents discover that the child's self is different. The child is the mother's and father's creation, which gives them a feeling of being in the child – I am there – but the child is both mine and something else, unfamiliar. "He is me a stranger to myself," says Levinas (Levinas, 1969, p. 267). He is me and a stranger, an ambiguity that can raise doubts in someone who does not wish to understand the world. The child is a possibility for me and for someone else, both mine and not mine, incomprehensible to a normal logic of rationality.

Levinas distinguishes between two approaches to the world, or two ways of seeking truth. In Peter Kemp's words in *Levinas* (1992): "Cognition at experiencing a reality that overreaches one's ability to contemplate it ... and cognition as the free development of a thought process that can make all it encounters fit within its categories" (Kemp, 1992, p. 37). In the second version everything unknown is reworked into familiar categories and thus brings no experience with it. Thought utters itself as truth the whole time. This attitude of mind attempts to be autonomous, sovereign, independent, and feels threatened by whatever it finds hard to reconcile. Such a mentality is recognizable, not only in the whole of our Western philosophical tradition, but also in the Captain. A threatened autonomy, trying to foist itself on the Other, so that she can be ruled and controlled. The child, Bertha, is conceived in this philosophy. Her otherness cannot be tolerated. She is partly the Captain's self and partly a stranger to that self, a strangeness the Captain cannot endure and so must obliterate. Bertha must only be the bearer of the Captain's self: she is to be him.

If Bertha were to be just him, nothing would change and time would become static. She, like him, would make time stand still. His desire to be her is at odds with his desire for eternity. Only through her otherness can he grow into the future. For according to Levinas's first mode of thought, or method of seeking truth, only that which exceeds understanding, that which is beyond planning and logical possibility, can point toward eternity. "The relation with the child – that is, the relation with the Other that is not a power, but fecundity – establishes a relationship with the absolute future, or infinite time" (Levinas, 1969, p. 268). Relationship with the future, with an infinite being, is only possible through such parenthood, and in this context let me use the term "fatherhood," a fatherhood linked to the child's being, both as a part of himself and as a stranger, quite outside control. Such an attachment to another being (the child) will be a link to an eternity that is both a continuum (continuation of myself) and a perpetual renewal (different from myself). Such an eternal being will not perish or become obsolete, but rejuvenate itself as something ever better, manifest in the child's openness and eternal youthfulness. It is not one individual remaining constantly the same, as in the Captain's desire for Bertha to *become* him, but one constantly becoming the Other. Fecundity is therefore an ontological category for Levinas, and only by a devotion to the child's duality, as both a stranger and myself, can the father link himself with eternity. "Paternity is a relation with a stranger who while being Other *is* me, a relation of the I with a self which yet is not me" (Levinas, 1969, p. 227). In this duplication of oneself in the child, the I is transcended and becomes part of eternity: "The fecundity of the I is its very transcendence" (*ibid.*, p. 277).

The Captain realizes that only through his child can he live forever –

this I would term the Captain's insight; but he attempts to conquer the child and make it resemble him completely in both body and soul – and this is the Captain's blindness. He cannot comprehend that only by acknowledging the child's otherness, as something new in continuation of his own self, can he share in that eternity as a father. He breaches both the ontology of fecundity and the basis of ethics. Laura is no better, she is incapable of seeing that time is discontinuous and that "in time" something new must always come. She, too, wishes to maintain Bertha in her own image, while replicating the Captain's eternity and making it her own.

In Levinas' philosophy the child is unique, it is something utterly different, and each child is inimitable in its parents' eyes. The child's uniqueness makes it totally special and thus irreplaceable. This is the source of a distinctive kind of paternal love: love of that which is irreplaceable. This love exists even though the child must free itself from the father and break with him; but because of this love the child can always come home, seek security and find itself in that space where it can always grow in an irreplaceable love. In this way we can say that fatherly love is the basis of all love: love of the Other as an irreplaceable being.

So we can conceive an ethical relation in the family as an extension of the Doctor's statement that one must take one's children in good faith. Such an ethic would be fundamentally at odds with the Captain's paranoid attempts at eternal being. His defective understanding of his surroundings, his fear of the others, means that his self-knowledge is poor and this, in turn, causes him to cling to power in the hope that it can save him and enable him to gain control over his closest relative, Bertha, and thus afford him a piece of eternity. This is the ethical conflict played out in the drama, *The Father*, where the struggle for power, embodied in the battle between woman and man, turns fatherhood paranoid and cannibalistic, rather than making it the foundation of all love.

References

Ambjörnsson, Ronny (1987) "Strindbergs *Fadren* og *Fordringsägare*: Lockelse och äckel," *BLM årg.* 56 (1).

Bredsdorff, Elias (1973) *Den store nordiske krig om sexualmoralen.* Copenhagen: Gyldendal.

Campbell, Joseph (1962) *The Masks of God: Oriental Mythology.* Viking Penguin.

Canetti, Elias (1984) *Crowds and Power*, trans. Carol Stewart. New York: The Noonday Press.

Deleuze, Gilles and Guattari, Felix (1977) *Anti-Oedipus. Capitalism and Schizo phrenia.* New York: Viking Press.

Diderichsen, Birgitte (1982) "Hinsides forstanden," *Agrippa*, 4.

Diderichsen, Birgitte (1987) "Paranoia og erkendelse," *Psyke and Logos*, 8 (2).

Freud, Sigmund (1990) *Schreber. Psykoanalytiske bemærkninger om et selvbiografisk beskrevet tilfælde av paranoia,* trans. Steffen Jørgensen. Copenhagen: Hans Reitzels forlag.

Kemp, Peter (1992) Levinas. Denmark: Forlaget Anis.

Lagercrantz, Olof (1979) *August Strindberg.* Stockholm: Wahlström and Widstrand.

Levinas, Emmanuel (1969) *Totality and Infinity*, trans. Alphonso Lingis. Pittsburgh: Duquesne University Press.

Lévy-Bruhl, Lucien (1965) *The "Soul" of the Primitive*, trans Lilian Clare. London: Allen and Unwin.

Marini, Marcelle (1992) *Jacques Lacan. The French Context*, trans. Anne Tomiche. New Jersey: Rutgers University Press.

Meissner, W. W. (1994) *Psychotherapy and the Paranoid Process.* New Jersey: Aronson.

Ollén, Gunnar (1982) *Strindbergs dramatik.* Stockholm: Sveriges Radios förlag.

Strindberg, August (1958) *August Strindbergs brev 6.* Stockholm: Albert Bonniers förlag.

Strindberg, August (1984) *Giftas I-II. Samlade Verk 16.* Stockholm: Almquist and Wicksell.

Strindberg, August (1986) *The Father*, trans. Michael Meyer. London: Methuen.

Chapter 16

Phallic Lovers, Non-phallic Lovers: Stereotyped Masculinities in Women's Novels of the 1970s

HELENA WAHLSTRÖM

While "images of women" have been given much attention by feminist literary criticism, female-authored representations of masculinity have largely been neglected. Looking at the ways in which various kinds of masculinities and masculine ideals are activated in a number of "women's novels" of the 1970s can contribute to filling this critical gap.

How do female authors represent masculinity in texts that deal primarily with female liberation and "coming to consciousness"? Exploring a number of popular women's novels from the 1970s – the era of the feminist breakthrough as well as that of the so-called sexual revolution – will provide some answers to this question. Novels like Erica Jong's *Fear of Flying*, Lisa Alther's *Kinflicks*, Gail Godwin's *Glass People*, Gael Greene's *Blue Skies, No Candy*, and Judith Rossner's *Looking for Mr Goodbar* deal with a female protagonist's quest for personal emotional and sexual liberation. However, since the plot in almost every case presents a woman who leaves her husband in order to have one or several love affairs, these novels also offer a map of contemporary stereotyped masculinities – the macho man, the successful businessman, the cowboy, the rebel, the hippie – in the role of lover. What is the significance of representing lovers as stereotypes in the texts? What is the meaning of female-authored "sexist" representations of masculinity? I suggest that representations of masculinity in women's novels function as sites for (sexual) political and social critique. The ambiguous and multifaceted aspects of the novels' representations of gender and sexuality, as well as their destabilization of ideals of masculinity, deserve critical attention.

Dictionary definitions of "lover" reveal connotations and semantic content that are diametrically opposed to those given for "husband":

husband a master of a house; the male head of a household; a man joined to a woman by marriage; correlative of wife (*Oxford English Dictionary*). A married man; a prudent or frugal manager (*Random House Dictionary*). **lover** a person who is in love with another. A person who has a sexual or romantic relationship with another. A person with whom one conducts an extramarital sexual affair (*Random House Dictionary*) One who loves illicitly; a gallant, paramour (*Oxford English Dictionary*). A sexual partner. One who loves another, esp. one who feels sexual love (*Heritage Dictionary*).

Contrary to "husband," "lover" carries no connotation of economy and control; instead, the defining features focus on emotion and sexuality. This lexical "distance" between the two positions has a parallel in the representations of the two types of masculinity in the novels under investigation, in that the socially acceptable (licit) ideal of masculinity is embodied predominantly by the husband (the "in-law"), while the socially unassimilated (illicit) ideal of the rebel is embodied predominantly by the lover (the "outlaw").

Unlike the relationship of husband and wife, the lover relationship is not subject to regulations and restrictions, nor is it officially sanctioned by society or regulated by laws. In her essay "Thinking Sex" (1984), Gayle Rubin enumerates the forms of sexuality that belong to what she terms the "charmed circle" in patriarchal American society, that is, the forms of sexuality that are socially accepted, even promoted, by patriarchal culture. She sets these up against those forms of sexuality that exist on "the outer limits" in patriarchal culture, that is, forms which are not sanctioned by that culture. Rubin writes: "[m]arital, reproductive heterosexuals are alone at the top of the erotic pyramid. Clamoring below are unmarried monogamous heterosexuals in couples, followed by most other heterosexuals" (279). Heterosexuals, in turn, are followed by homosexuals, lesbians, and other "transgressives" in Rubin's model. The differences between the socially sanctioned sexuality within marriage and the unsanctioned sexuality between lovers clearly affect female-authored representations of lovers and set them apart from representations of husbands in women's novels of the 1970s.

The reaction against patriarchal restrictions on female sexuality, and the new surge of feminist critiques of marriage as a patriarchal institution that had begun with Friedan's *The Feminine Mystique* (1963), grew stronger and more radical in the early 1970s. The critique of the institution of marriage was paralleled by the new "discovery" of female sexuality and the female potential for multiple orgasms in, for example, Masters and Johnson's *Human Sexual Response* (1966) and *The Hite Report* (1976).

These two factors combined can be seen to play into the representations of lover figures and lover relationships in the novels.

In *Adultery in the Novel* Tony Tanner claims that adultery is an act that transgresses, and thereby undermines the authority of, social rules:

> If society depends for its existence on governing what may be combined and what should be kept separate, then adultery, by bringing the wrong things together in the wrong places (or the wrong people in the wrong beds), offers an attack on those rules, revealing them to be arbitrary rather than absolute (Tanner, 1992, p. 13).

However, writing in the late 1970s, Tanner maintains that contemporary novels are produced in a society which has largely lost interest in marriage, and which has also lost "contact with the sense of intense passion," to the extent that adultery "no longer signifies" (*ibid.*, p. 89). I would argue that Tanner's assumption is mistaken. It is true that "the novel of adultery" sounds stale in the context of American women's novels of the 1970s, but the act of adultery – for want of a better term – still is still significant. Although the lover relationship does not signify the "intense passion" that Tanner, perhaps nostalgically, refers to, it certainly serves as a critique of the limitations on female sexuality and "femininity" imposed by patriarchy, for which marriage stands as a symbol in the novels in question. Thus, Tanners claim concerning adultery as attack on social rules does have bearing on the womens novels that I am investigating, where representations of adultery and single women's illicit sexual relationships call into question the rules of patriarchal society, "revealing them to be arbitrary rather than absolute" (*ibid.*, p. 13).

Tanner claims that the "mythology" of marriage is the central subject of the bourgeois novel (*ibid.*, p. 15). However, he also notes that perhaps it is "the unstable triangularity of adultery, rather than the static symmetry of marriage, that is the generative form of Western literature as we know it" (*ibid.*, p. 12). Although Tanner is concerned with nineteenth- and early twentieth-century literature by male authors, his words seem relevant for the present study as well. In the novels I discuss, the protagonist's desires for husband and lover carry very different implications, which are emphasized in the characterization of the two forms of masculinity. First, while the husband is represented as linked to a restricted, often routine, sexuality, the lover is represented as offering the protagonist a new kind of sexual experience. Second, the lover is also positioned – temporally and spatially – very differently from the husband, which indicates that he represents a possibility for mobility for the protagonist. Third, the representations of lovers typically build upon cultural ideals other than those which inform representations of husbands. While representations of husbands in women's novels often build upon the masculine ideal of the breadwinner/male professional, representations of lovers, in contrast, often build upon the masculine ideal of the rebel/outlaw.

The outlaw aspect of the lover signals the protagonist's illicit desire as opposed to the licit and socially sanctioned desire for her husband. Furthermore, the appearance of several lovers in the narrative, each of whom is linked to a specific kind of sexual behavior, signals the desirability of sexual variation. This sexual variation is linked in the novels to the "personal growth" of the protagonist and to her achievement of individuality (a notion which was promoted at the time when the novels were produced by, for example, Alex Comfort in *The Joy of Sex*).

In my investigation of representations of lovers, I focus particularly on two main types: the phallic and the non-phallic lover. "Phallic lover" denotes a lover who is sexually active, aggressive, perhaps even violent, and who embodies a powerful masculinity. "Non-phallic lover" indicates a lover who may be involved in sexual interplay, but who is primarily attractive to the protagonist for his emotional, spiritual and intellectual qualities. This lover is often impotent or uninterested in penetrative sexuality and thus, in a sense, fails to fulfil his "lover's contract."

The phallic and non-phallic lovers in the novels are based on images from popular culture, particularly from film. Thus, culturally specific masculine ideals (for example the businessman, the cowboy and the hippie) are employed in the representations of lovers. The question that presents itself is: are writers who use these ideals in fact shattering or perpetuating them? By exploring the ways in which these masculine ideals are used in the texts, I argue that the ideals are given new meaning when they are envisioned in the context of female desire in women's novels. In the novels, this new meaning is above all signalled through the choice of representing lovers as stereotypes of masculinity. How does the representational concept of stereotype relate to the figurations of a cultural ideal? What political or ideological significance does the stereotyping of male characters entail? Is the protagonist's stereotyping of her lover presented as empowering for her? Unlike men's stereotyping of women, the phenomenon of women's stereotyping of men has (with very few exceptions) hardly been recognized by literary and cultural criticism.

The phallic lover I: the businessman

In the novels some representations of lovers, or even potential lovers, similar to representations of husbands, build upon the breadwinner ideal. The link between lover and marriage is signalled most clearly by the lover proposing marriage to the protagonist, but also by the protagonist imagining them together in a marriage situation.

The characterization of the lover in Gail Godwin's *Glass People* (1972) adheres to other representations of lovers in 1970s women's novels: he is above all described as being different from the husband; he offers the protagonist "male variation." The lover in *Glass People* is linked to a time/space continuum other than that of the husband and he is portrayed as a "generic male" rather than as a nuanced individual. He is linked to certain transitory spaces (hotel rooms), to a time zone of his own, and to the east coast and the metropolitan city. In contrast, the husband, Cameron, is linked to other, more permanent rooms in his own house, to the west coast time zone, and to the suburban landscape of the west coast. The lover, in other words, is contrasted to and positioned as being physically/sexually different from the husband. Francesca's first impression of the lover is his physical distinctness from Cameron. With his youth, good looks, and smart attire, he provides specular pleasure for Francesca. He is described as a "young executive with so many colors in his face and hair. A firm, clear face with very dark, alert eyes, and thick brown-gold hair, sunbleached" (Godwin, 1972, p. 70), as opposed to Cameron, whose hair is graying, and whose body is "dead white" (*ibid.*, p. 7).

One of the most significant things about Francesca's lover is his lack of specificity. At first he is only mentioned as "a man" (*ibid.*, p. 50), which suggests generic masculinity and a sense that his appearance on the scene is to a large extent arbitrary. Francesca has continuous difficulties in "identifying" the lover. The two of them take a room at the airport, where she is frustrated by not knowing who he is.

> He was the tenderest, most thoughtful lover she had ever known, but he was *maddeningly impersonal* in conversation. ... She knew no more about him – except that he called himself Mike – than she had when they met on the plane. What he did for a living, whether or not he was married, where he came from, where he was flying off to, none of this had he volunteered (*ibid.*, p. 81, emphasis added).

Later, going through his wallet at night, she cannot quite discern the name on the driver's licence: "Facts and figures jumped before her eyes, she must focus on one. Birth date, January something, 1937 ... Michael S. ... what? ... Rushing, Reusing?" (*ibid.*, p. 91). The man's anonymity guarantees his functionality as lover, as object, as projection of desire in a way that would perhaps be impossible should he reach the level of individuality that a specific name and personal history endow.

From the moment she first sees him, Francesca's gaze not only surveys Mike's exterior, but also probes inward toward that which cannot be seen, toward the more abstract qualities of importance and power that she connects to masculinity: "There would be important papers in his case. He would be expected, awaited somewhere. When he walked into a room with that smile, someone would look up and think happily, 'Here's, back at last!' He had the sort of appearance that could bring only good news" (*ibid.*, p. 71). This man embodies the businessman ideal; he is a stereotype of the successful man busy doing important business, a yuppie before the yuppie had been defined.

Given the protagonist's initial "distancing" of her lover from her husband, it seems paradoxical that she is unable to think of the lover without imagining that he is a replacement for the husband, or that they give the impression of being married: "Francesca liked walking beside Mike, making a couple. Most of the other people walking were in couples. ... She imagined herself married to him and even went so far as to imagine the dog they would have. ... Another couple, not so handsome, turned to stare enviously" (*ibid.*, p. 88). The lover is simply seen as replacing the husband and immediately takes on the same position in relation to Francesca, the position of teacher, judge, guide: "He put his arm around her shoulder and guided her up and down various streets and avenues, pointing out sights, examples of good architecture, bad architecture. Perhaps he was an architect, she thought" (*ibid.*, pp. 88-9). As in her first meeting with Cameron, Francesca remains mute, imagining the course of events rather than asking questions.

When Francesca eventually returns to California, however, Mike's connection to marriage takes a more menacing turn as she begins to imagine that the two men, Mike and Cameron, are secretly allied against her.

> She often thought of Mike. She liked to think of him best in daylight, when the sun was shining. ... When she thought of Mike at night, he became sinister. ... At night he still seemed a fateful emissary, but not one who came in spontaneous sunshine and joy. He seemed somehow in league with Cameron, part of Cameron's mysterious plans, "sent" by Cameron himself (*ibid.*, p. 205).

To Francesca, Mike is obviously made more attractive by the fact hat he is linked to marriage, although the attraction is partially disrupted toward the end of the novel as the link to marriage is transformed into a link to Cameron.

The power of the phallic lover/businessman is thus social, economic and "civilized." In this way, then, he is not unlike the typical husband figure in 1970s women's novels. Embodying a different set of characteristics and a different kind of masculine power is another, and more prevalent, type of phallic lover: the macho man. In the novels under investigation, the macho man is given the shape of a cowboy, a biker, or a delinquent, and his power, in contrast to that of the businessman, is physical, sexual and "uncivilized."

The phallic lover II: cowboys, bikers, and delinquents

The rebel is an ideal of masculinity that connotes speed, force and lawlessness. This ideal also encompasses suggestions of violence, the precedence of body over mind and strict gender roles, as well as phallicism and potency. In the novels, the phallic rebel is represented as a cowboy, biker, delinquent, or "hood." The latter categories are modern adaptations of the cowboy which build upon cultural images of masculinity exemplified by James Dean and Marlon Brando in the 1950s and 1960s, and by Peter Fonda and Jack Nicholson in the 1970s.

The macho man or tough guy is a commonplace of American culture and, in a sense, he is also an ideal for masculine behavior. He has appeared in numerous books and films and he is also brought into women's novels in the 1970s in order to envision the protagonist's dream of a man who is always sexually ready and available. Although the similarities are by no means all-encompassing, some parallels can be drawn between the cowboy/Jason in Gael Greene's *Blue Skies, No Candy* (1976), the cowboy/Douglas in Hilma Wolitzer's *In the Flesh* (1977), Tony in Judith Rossner's *Looking for Mr Goodbar* (1975), and Clem Cloyd in Lisa Alther's *Kinflicks* (1976).

The lovers in *Blue Skies, No Candy*, *In the Flesh*, and *Looking for Mr Goodbar* are all described as being physically attractive, forceful men. The cowboy-lover Jason in *Blue Skies, No Candy* is described, repeatedly, by the protagonist Kate as a beautiful man, often clad in blue jeans, boots and a Stetson hat. In Wolitzer's novel the protagonist Paulie's description of her lover's body and clothes is evocative of a "cowboy" masculinity. He is a handsome man, "quite beautiful, with dark golden curls and a wonderful smile" (Greene, 1976, p. 234). He is unusually tall, and wears tight, faded jeans and cowboy boots. He comes from "the West," from a ranch in Montana. He has also spent time "looking for himself" in the West (*ibid.*, p. 234), a rite of passage connected to establishing a masculine identity. Another contender for the position as Paulie's lover is a married man with a family of his own. Choosing between the two of them, she decides that "[m]y cowboy would be easier. He had his own room, no visible attachments" (*ibid.*, p. 239), and what he offers her is "the relative simplicity of plain lust" (*ibid.*, p. 240). His apartment, the place to which they "limit [their] lovemaking" is "a mess," in "disorder" (*ibid.*, p. 250). It has not been prepared for impressing a visitor and its temporary quality is intensified by the fact that Paulie never spends the whole night there.

Paulie is represented as being highly aware that the love affair functions in ways dissimilar from those of marriage. She says that they are not "like a real family at all. There weren't any of those terrible complexities of mood, of power struggle and ambition that seem built into marriage. We were more like Tarzan and Jane ourselves, intelligent savages in a primitive jungle existence, a day-by-day pursuit of survival and pleasure" (*ibid.*, p. 250). In this brief passage, we are presented with the perceived opposition between the situation of marriage and the relationship between lovers, as well as ideas about the phallic lover being pleasurable, transitory, and uncomplicated.

According to Theresa in *Looking for Mr Goodbar*, her lover Tony is "a punk but a cute one" (Rossner, 1975, p. 152). He has dark hair and dark eyes, broad shoulders and a slim torso. Reflecting upon her choice of Tony over James – a sensitive man – Theresa makes the observation that:

> Something there was that couldn't really be interested in a man who liked powerful, intelligent women. Something there was that wanted a man from Marlboro Country. Smart only in the way he subordinated his girls. Swaggering, suave. With a dick so long you rode it as though it was a horse (*ibid.*, p. 178).

Here the protagonist aligns her lover, the "punk" Tony, with the image of the Marlboro Man, a widespread "cowboy" image. The physical looks of the macho lover can be very diverse, from tall and blond to short (but strong) and dark, but the descriptions in all the novels share an avoidance of detail and a sense of clear-cut simplicity that enhances the impression that we are presented with a stereotype.

The cowboy example of macho masculinity has a long history in

American popular culture. An emblem of rugged manliness and a master of such "masculine" traits as silence, physicality, and violence, the Western hero is a representative of the reliably stable masculinity that says that "a man's gotta do what a man's gotta do." The lover in all three novels is reductive in his view of the protagonist, as expressed by his renaming her. The cowboy/Douglas calls the protagonist of *In the Flesh* "Babe," in *Looking for Mr Goodbar* Tony reduces Theresa to her sex by calling her "cunt," and the cowboy/Jason does the same to Kate in *Blue Skies, No Candy*. The interests of this type of man lie within the realm of physicality, not within that of intellect and emotion. He is often linked to nature and to a problematic relationship to society, or civilization, which he may well defend, but never really belong to.

As Jane Tompkins has pointed out in *West of Everything* (1992), the Western is a genre that celebrates phallicism. The cowboy's foremost attribute is his gun, but in the context of the novels discussed here, his six-shooter is exchanged for his extraordinary sexual force and appetite; the cowboy is never impotent. Sexually, Douglas, the lover in *In the Flesh*, "was as reliable as an Eveready battery, as persistent as a drill" (Tompkins, 1992, p. 174). At night, the protagonist Paulie is awakened by "the reckless insistence of his penis, hammering for entry at all my doors" (*ibid.*, p. 174). Theresa's lover Tony in *Looking for Mr Goodbar* is equally potent and persistent. When they have sex, Tony is easily aroused and indefatigable: "He didn't come until what seemed like hours had passed" (Rossner, 1975, p. 155).

In the case of Kate's lover Jason in *Blue Skies, No Candy*, the cowboy appears as an almost fantastical symbol of virility and potency. Much differently forged than in Wolitzer's novel, this cowboy is connected to danger and, more predictably, he is the discoverer and tamer of the protagonist's sexual persona. This cowboy, too, is always ready for sex, "turned on in an instant" (Greene, 1976, p. 207). Kate says that she has "never been so full, never felt so much pressure" as when she has sex with him; it goes on for "hours" and "his cock is still steel battering into [her]" (*ibid.*, p. 177). Being a screenwriter, Kate speculates about who she would cast as the Cowboy in a movie: "McQueen. Paul Newman, maybe. If only Eastwood were more urbane. Robert Redford is too handsome. Maybe Jack Nicholson" (*ibid.*, p. 173). The appearance of "real" models for masculinity, whether these are film stars (as in the case of Greene) or the Marlboro Man (as in the case of Rossner), signals the status of these masculine icons as being instantaneously recognizable for their macho qualities.

Through Kate's descriptions of the cowboy, which focus more on his penis and its power than on any other part of his body or on his mind, and through the narrative's insistence on explicit (pornographic) descriptions of sexual innovations or "conquests," the cowboy is reduced to a sex object (an object for sexual pleasure/his sex, detached). Kate even asks him if she makes him "feel like a sex object" (*ibid.*, p. 220), to which he answers that he does not mind. At times she also seems to forget that he has a professional life, that he, like herself, is part of the film industry. By ignoring her lover's professional identity, Kate seems to be attempting to limit him to his sexual existence and sexual significance through a process of stereotyping.

The biker/delinquent is a modern rendition of the phallic rebel that has some characteristics in common with the cowboy ideal. Similar to the cowboy, the delinquent is a figure posed in opposition to civilization and community. He is often associated with the working class, and is often less well educated than the protagonist. In *Kinflicks*, the introduction of the "town hoodlum" (Alther, 1976, p. 113) Clem Cloyd is a move toward greater sexual excitement and heightened sexual expectations. Clem is tall, dark and handsome, but due to an accident he has a deformed leg and, consequently, a limp. In contrast to Joe Bob, Clem is vaguely dangerous and he quickly reduces Ginny from a named individual to "woman." When they first have sex, he thrusts himself into Ginny "savagely time after time, like a murderer stabbing a still stirring victim" (*ibid.*, p. 127). The violence in this scene is disturbing, and is complicated by Ginny's expressed fear of violence; the desirability of Clem as lover thus becomes ambiguous.

In *Looking for Mr Goodbar* Theresa sees Tony as the uncomplicated, all-body male. Tony has a violent and exaggerated body language, while his verbal communication is incoherent and monosyllabic. Theresa finds this a commendable quality in him: "Talking was so much more complicated than making love ... fucking, she should call it, since it was hard to see how anything she did with [Tony] could be about love" (Rossner, 1975, p. 167). Later, she feels "the need of a man. A Tony ... A good hard fucking and no words.... . Just pick up some anonymous muscular type and get laid. And never see him again" (*ibid.*, p. 245). In the novels, female desire is presented as the need for a man who will provide sex (Alther), who is an uncomplicated sex object (Greene, Rossner, Wolitzer). How can we read the fact that the lover's body is desired, while his mind is neglected? Before returning to the implications of this preference, I will turn to the representations of another type of lover that appears in my selection of women's novels, whose desirability does build upon his mind rather than his body.

The non-phallic lover

While the phallic lover is identified largely through his powerful but potentially menacing body and through his sexual ability and persistence, there is another type of lover who, although "rebellious" like the phallic figures, stands in opposition to phallicism. This non-phallic lover is most often brought into the novels in the shape of the hippie. The hippie is a recent stereotype that embodies a disavowal of much of what the traditional rebel/cowboy stands for, as his masculinity privileges emotionality, cerebrality, and mysticism. However, this new kind of masculinity is treated with suspicion in female-authored texts.

Except in the capacity of dissenter, the hippie is an unassimilated (and perhaps unassimilable) character in American culture, in that he is represented as rejecting traditionally idolized traits of masculinity such as forcefulness, physicality, and aggression. Representations of lovers as hippies are the result of a preoccupation with a contemporary ideological context that causes the author to bring current political events into her fictions. Therefore this character can be said to be typical of the times in which the novels are written and, in a sense, the hippie is linked to the present rather than to a historical past. Although he – like the cowboy – is a rebel, he symbolizes a form of "untraditional" rebellion. What makes the hippie a desirable man for the protagonist differs from one novel to the next, but in each case he initially symbolizes liberation for the protagonist. In Erica Jong's *Fear of Flying* (1973), Adrian is first perceived by Isadora as a purely sexual being who offers erotic escape from her husband. Similarly, in Alther's *Kinflicks*, Hawk symbolizes adventure for Ginny, who is getting tired of the regularity of married life. In Alison Lurie's *The War Between the Tates* (1974), Erica is drawn to Zed because he is sweet and undemanding, intelligent and sensitive; he also offers her a possibility to retaliate against her husband's adultery.

When Isadora meets Adrian Goodlove, she notices his "Indian sandals and dirty toenails ... The corners of his eyes crinkled into about a hundred tiny lines and his mouth curled up in a sort of smile even when he wasn't smiling" (Jong, 1973, pp. 29-30). This hippie figure immediately arouses Isadora, who believes that she is going to experience her imagined ideal for sexual interaction, the "zipless fuck," sex without the complication of emotional involvement: "I knew I'd say yes to anything he asked. My only worry was: maybe he wouldn't ask soon enough. ... Sweet Jesus, I thought, here he was. The real z.f. The zipless fuck par excellence" (*ibid.*, p. 30). In stating that "[h]e didn't look like a shrink at all" (*ibid.*, p. 29), Isadora distances the lover Adrian from her husband Bennett, a psychoanalyst; she positions the lover as being different from her husband. However, she speculates that perhaps Adrian and Bennett "only represented the struggle within me. Bennett's careful, compulsive, and boring steadfastness was my own panic about change, my fear of being alone, my need for security. Adrian's antic manners and ass-grabbing was the part of me that wanted exuberance above all" (*ibid.*, p. 80). Isadora is aware that, for her, Adrian and Bennett embody opposed sexual economies. As it turns out, while Bennett never fails to have an erection, Adrian is impotent.

In *The War Between the Tates*, Sandy/Zed is the hippie lover that Erica takes as a form of revenge on her husband, Brian, who is having an affair with one of his students. Erica knew Sandy when they were young, and remembers that he was "rather pathetically stuck on her for a while," that he had always been unconventional and looked different, and that he was "sweet ... amusing to talk to, and intelligent – but sort of a lost soul even then" (Lurie, 1974, p. 103). When he resurfaces in her life, he is a mystic who runs the Krishna Bookshop and has changed his name to Zed. Erica sees Zed as possessing a "shyness and lack of social initiative" (*ibid.*, p. 166), which endears him to her, but which also presents difficulties, since, unlike her husband, he does not adhere to social conventions and therefore does not behave in expected or traditional ways. Erica is not alone in setting Zed up as a contrast to her husband Brian, for Zed does so himself, among other things by pointing out to Erica that "I'm not like your husband; I don't like to be worshipped. It gives me claustrophobia" (*ibid.*, p. 242). Zed's mode of lovemaking is also unlike Brian's. When Zed and Erica kiss for the first time,

> it is hardly like being kissed at all; then Zed, with a clumsy, half-blind gesture, pulls her closer, and shifts his mouth so that it meets hers more accurately. Erica remembers the look in his eyes a few moments ago ... she remembers Brian, and waits for Sandy to crowd, to grab. But he only holds her, stroking her face and hair, kissing her gently and intermittently. Gradually she relaxes, rests against him... . Erica looks up at him in a way *which would have informed Brian, or any other man, that he should kiss her again*. But Zed doesn't move (*ibid.*, pp. 247-8, emphasis added).

Zed is not only different, then, from all other men, including Erica's husband, but the ways in which he is different lead Erica to suspect that he is perhaps also "less than a man."

Hawk, the final lover to appear in *Kinflicks*, is another example of the hippie. When he turns up at her house, Ginny is alone; her husband Ira is away with the National Guard at Camp Drum. In a pattern similar to other women's novels, the lover Hawk is represented as an antithesis to the husband Ira. As opposed to Ira's immaculate militant masculinity, he is a free-floating army deserter who lacks a permanent address, but who also belongs most to the "present" time in the narrative. Is Hawk, then, the "new man"? Is he the "present" that the modern woman should expect? While Hawk is the immediate reason why Ginny leaves Ira, he proves to be an unreliable partner who suddenly disappears during their journey. Ginny later finds out that he has been placed in an insane asylum. It becomes clear that the new man is inadequate and "damaged." In a move that is rather unusual for the genre I am discussing, Alther includes a larger political context in emphasizing the disastruous effects of the Vietnam war on a generation of American men.

In Lurie's novel, Erica is faced with an ultimatum: Zed asks her to leave Brian and their children and join him in his search for "the Path." However, Zed/Sandy is not somebody who would be able to provide for Erica, who has become used to being cared for in her marriage to Brian. Erica therefore decides against a life with Zed, who is not only socially "impractical" for her, but also most often sexually impotent. Instead she chooses Brian, who is socially and sexually potent, and sexually even somewhat demanding. In *Fear of Flying*, Adrian, who throughout the European odyssey is impotent more often than not, is abandoned by Isadora when she realizes that he is actually asking her to leave Bennett definitively behind. Bennett is her final choice – Bennett, her (relatively) immobile, but ever-potent husband, who always manages to give her an orgasm. In *Kinflicks*, Hawk is also an example of a representation of an impotent lover – a sexually "unwilling" man, while Ginny's husband Ira conscientiously does his "duty" three times per week.

The protagonists in these cases are sexually active, even aggressive, while the lover in a sense breaks his contract as lover by failing to perform sexually. This is an illustration of role-reversal, where the man takes the (traditionally feminine) passive role, and the woman the (traditionally masculine) active role. In a passage that portrays the woman as empowered, active, tireless, and unafraid, Isadora Wing offers the comment that "the older you got, the clearer it became that men were basically terrified of women. Some secretly, some openly. What could be more poignant than a liberated woman eye to eye with a limp prick? All history's greatest issues paled by comparison with these two quintessential objects: the eternal woman and the eternal limp prick" (Jong, 1973, p. 97). The protagonists in these novels experience their own desire as powerful, and the desire of their lovers as vague or weak. While the non-phallic lover is emotionally (and sometimes intellectually) desirable, his failure to perform sexually is frustrating for the protagonist. It is worth noting that in these novels about women's liberation, that appear to be critical of traditional gender values, male characters who refuse to enact traditional masculinity (involving an active or even agressive sexuality) are not, finally, desirable for the protagonists, but are treated with suspicion and, eventually, rejected.

Sandy/Zed has qualities and interests that are similar to Erica's, and she finds that they can do many more things together than she and her husband ever have:

> Sandy is nicer than Brian in many ways, Erica thinks... . He is kinder and more considerate, with a better sense of humour, and he knows much more about gardening and carpentry and art and music and old children's books. Though he has refused to attend any more parties, he will go with her to places and events Brian used to scorn: an art opening or a tour of the new fire station or a house sale or a bird walk (Lurie, 1974, p. 271).

However, instead of feeling reassured that this is a man she can live with and take comfort in, Erica "for the hundredth time in six weeks ... thinks of something [her friend] Danielle said about Sandy: that he is not only nice but 'too nice to be a man'" (ibid., p. 272). Erica's reservations are partly based on the fact that their attempts to have sex are embarrassing failures because of Zed's impotence. Thus, although he is "nicer" than the protagonist's husband, and despite the possibility he offers for emotional rapport, this lover is finally rejected.

This rejection of the sensitive or "nice" man occurs in other women's novels as well. In Looking for Mr Goodbar, the protagonist Theresa has parallel relationships with the "punk" Tony and with James, a man who is characterized as Tony's opposite. James is orderly, middle-class, and employed with a law firm; he takes care of his old mother and wants to marry Theresa. Since the protagonist's perception of married women is that they are usually busy "telling stories to prove who had it worse. Whose husband was more demanding" (Rossner, 1975, p. 136), her rejection of James is evidently based upon her wariness of the contract of marriage, and of the role-transformations that marriage could bring. Another reason, however, is that she perceives James as not being "man enough," for he is not sexually aggressive, and she experiences her own sexual desire as stronger than his. James, besides being a provider and connoting marriage, exemplifies a sensitive type of man whom the protagonist rejects as a lover in favor of the insensitive man, Tony.

Another example of the sensitive man appears in Helen Yglesias's *How She Died* (1972). The protagonist Jean has a date with a deaf man. Unlike the protagonist's lovers, who are seemingly uninterested in her feelings, the deaf man is nice, polite, and wealthy, and his behavior signals security, affection and dependability. However, Jean finds his deafness to be embarrassing and annoying, and although she is divorced she lies, using her marriage as a shield against the deaf man. The deaf man is never considered as a lover, and Jean rejects him as completely uninteresting, never even bothering to find out what his name is. Since the deaf man is the only sensitive male character in the novel, it would seem that Yglesias pairs sensitivity with disability.

The topos of defective masculinity recurs in Marilyn French's *The Women's Room* (1979), where the only male character who is presented as a reliable friend of the protagonist Mira is Biff, who once rescues her from being gang-raped. Biff also happens to be physically crippled; he has had polio, and he is also socially crippled, because he is, and looks, poor, with "haggard cheeks" and a "tattered jacket" (French, 1979, p. 35). He is never a contender for Mira's desire, who knows that "he would never approach her sexually. Because of his limp, probably" (*ibid.*, p. 35). French seems to tell us that friendship and sexuality are incompatible, and that sensitivity makes for an asexual masculinity.

It would seem, then, that when a sensitive man is introduced and compared to more aggressive and sometimes even violent lovers, he is often given characteristics of being either physically disabled or at least physically inadequate (Yglesias, Lurie) or dysfunctional in a social context (Lurie), and he is sometimes perceived as an unreliable provider by the protagonist. In other cases, the "niceness" of the man is perceived as "unmanly" (Rossner, Yglesias, Lurie, French). In these cases, the sensitivity and the predominance of intellectual rather than physical qualities in the lover finally negate his "manliness." Through these representations of masculinities and the representations of the protagonists' suspicion and rejection of such masculinities, the authors present sensitive masculinities as anomalies, exceptions to the "rule" of masculinity. These representations undermine the idea, emphasized for instance by the *Hite Report*, that female desire is directed towards sensitivity and friendship. Instead, many of the novels present the aggressive, phallic type of lover as embodying the masculinity that is most desirable to the protagonist.

What, then, does the protagonist's act of taking a lover imply? Given that both the husband and the institution of marriage are represented in the novels as positioned within the law (of patriarchy and societal authority), and that the protagonist is aware that she has been conditioned to desire marriage, the protagonist's act of taking a lover is in itself an act of rebellion, an act of breaking or transgressing the boundaries of the law. In this sense, the lover becomes an instrument through which the protagonist rebels against the law; he is a tool and a vehicle in her struggle for a position outside the boundaries of marriage/law/patriarchal rule. Taking a lover is often presented as an act to spite the husband and the controlling and economizing force linked to "husbandry." Not least, the protagonist's affair with the lover is a subversive act because it emphasizes sexual and sensual pleasure above all other criteria for desirability, and because it is not subject to official regulations or demands. The lover's sexuality is not linked to reproduction, nor does it impose specific temporal or spatial restrictions on the protagonist.

However, in several of the novels, the rebelliousness of the act of taking a lover is given a second dimension through the choice of a specific type of lover. The lover in these novels is cast as a rebel or "outlaw," whether as a phallic cowboy or as a non-phallic hippie. The rebel is an ideal of masculinity that is linked to individuality and to dissent from society. In relation to the husband or "breadwinner," the rebel as ideal is located at the opposite end of the spectrum of legal, economic, familial and erotic constructions of masculinity. Cultural ideals such as the biker, the cowboy, and the hippie, despite their varying degrees of phallicism, are similar in that they all exist outside of, or even in opposition to, official law.

As I have tried to demonstrate, the macho lover and the hippie lover signify very different types of masculinity and male sexuality in the novels. Yet, for different reasons, they can be gathered under the same rubric: the rebel. However, something remains to be said about the ending of the love affairs of the protagonists. The protagonists who do not die (that is, the overwhelming majority) decide to end the love affair and either return to the husband, or else live alone. The lover is, after all, not the final choice of the protagonists. Signifying a stage in the protagonists' quest for self-discovery, the lover is finally abandoned for a more potent provider. Marriage, in the end, seems to win out over adultery.

Cultural ideals reassessed

We have seen that the non-phallic lover is typically impotent and can thus be said to be a representation of masculinity that disrupts traditional, patriarchal conceptions of masculine sexuality. The impotence of the lover eventually becomes a frustrating problem for the protagonist, rather than being positively presented as a non-aggressive alternative masculinity.

It seems significant to note that not only the non-phallic lovers, but even the lovers that I have called phallic, are somehow connected to physical wounds and defects. Clem Cloyd (*Kinflicks*) has a limp following a farming accident, and Tony (*Looking for Mr Goodbar*) has shrapnel in his leg, a souvenir from the Vietnam war, intimately a part of his own body. Wolitzer's cowboy has an unmarked body, but is instead likened to a child. Douglas's child-like quality is reinvoked throughout Paulie's narration. She describes him dressing and "buttoning himself up wrong like a thick-fingered, sleepy child" (Wolitzer, 1977, p. 251). The youthfulness and innocence evoked by the image of a dressed-up boy is emphasized further by Paulie's discovery that "there wasn't any silver in his mouth. He didn't even have any cavities!" (*ibid.*, p. 234) and she finds his naked chest "as gorgeous as a laborer's, as vulnerable as a child's" (*ibid.*, p. 270). The "child-like" quality is also brought into Theresa's description of Tony, who, when jealous, sounds "like a little kid staking out territory" (Rossner, *Looking for Mr Goodbar*, 1975, p. 180), and into Erica's description of Zed in *The War Between the Tates* as having a "childlike directness" (Lurie, 1974, p. 165). While at first Erica appreciates this quality in him, Zed's sexual "hesitancy" and his "childish diffidence" (*ibid.*, p. 272) later become increasingly troubling for her. The element of childishness in the characterization of the lover undermines his adult masculinity.

Another issue that is brought up in the novels and that seems to question the force of the macho man, is that of unreality. In *Looking for Mr Goodbar*, the protagonist and the lover venture out into the world together on one occasion but Tony ends up insulting Theresa in public, and the event is a disaster. Theresa concludes that "Tony was unreal. ... They'd gone out together into the real world, she and Tony. And it hadn't worked" (Rossner, 1975, pp. 219-20). Similar scenes of private pleasure and public humiliation occur in *Blue Skies, No Candy*. Douglas and Paulie in *In the Flesh* never meet outside of their apartments. In all three cases, the lover can only be "real" in bed, in the limited space of a room or an apartment, in isolation from the outside world and other people.

In addition, the lover's mental abilities are often derided as being insufficient or inferior to those of the protagonist; he is presented as pure body. This dualism is commented on by Isadora Wing:

I thought of all those centuries in which men adored women for their bodies while they despised their minds. ... Now I understood it. Because that was how I so often felt about men. Their minds were hopelessly befuddled, but their bodies were so nice. Their ideas were intolerable, but their penises were silky (Jong, 1973, pp. 96-7).

Ginny, in *Kinflicks*, tolerates intellectual inferiority in Joe Bob, whom she calls the "body beautiful of Hullsport High" (Alther, 1976, p. 46), and Theresa appreciates the mindless quality of her lover Tony in *Looking for Mr Goodbar*. The separateness of mind and body is, in other words, a recurring theme in these representations of men. Is this an ironic move? Are these women writers mimicking a "male" strategy for representation in their portrayals of men, in order to disarm it as a "useful" strategy for representing desire? Certainly, irony is involved in these representations, but I think it is important to stress that the male body/sex object offers a kind of pleasure for the protagonists that has been a taboo pleasure in the context of female desire: the pleasure of "pure" sex.

The hippie belongs to the category of the rebel but, although he shares some elements with the more traditional (phallic) rebels, he is above all a new man, a phenomenon of the late 1960s and early 1970s. Appearing in the 1970s novel, the hippie connotes the open road and an existence that is materially unbound, and he is thus far removed from the ideals of bourgeois marriage. However, although the protagonist may be critical of marriage when she first encounters the hippie lover, it is in fact often his offer of a life on the "open road" and of material "freedom" that finally causes her to abandon him.

To return to my discussion of the lover as outlaw in the context of patriarchal societal and sexual patterns, I would argue that the impotent lover is positioned as "outlaw" not only in his active rebellion against the middle-class standards and values of an "orderly" society (which the protagonist has aligned herself with through her marriage), but also in his rejection of phallic masculinity and "machismo," which is expressed by the focus on cerebrality, mysticism, and emotion. He rebels also against the sexual economy of patriarchy.

In the context of the present investigation, the representations of lovers coincide with images that I have called ideals of masculinity. How subversive is the use of a cultural ideal in constructing an image of female desire? Can it be "subversive" to uphold a certain ideal, like the Western hero or the macho man? Is this not to once again affirm the status of the macho man as a desirable ideal, not only in the eyes of men – as for example in Western movies produced almost exclusively by men – but in novels by women for women? Does the appropriation of the macho man by female authors in the 1970s have political significance?

By appropriating the image of the macho man, and by positing the male lover as the transitory party and the female protagonist as the stationary party in the narrative, the traditionally celebrated ideal is transformed. The macho man becomes, as it were, an instrument for erotic satisfaction that takes its force of recognition from cultural history, while at the same time fulfilling a role in the female protagonist's fantasy: the ever available, "hard" lover. Thus, a masculinity that has traditionally been idolized is picked up by women writers and transformed according to strategies for imagining female desire. It can certainly be argued that, in the process, the stereotyped masculinities are affirmed as ideals, since they figure as the "chosen ones" in the narratives. Simultaneously, however, these ideals are destabilized, in two ways: first, they are represented as incomplete, as less than perfect and, second, they are represented through stereotypes.

Stereotype is a form of representation which carries largely negative connotations. In "Rethinking Stereotypes," T. E. Perkins explains that the pervasiveness of a stereotype derives from three factors: its simplicity, its immediate recognizability, and its implication of an assumed consensus. Stereotypes are thus "prototypes of 'shared cultural meanings'" (Perkins, 1979, p. 141). Perkins also points out that there is "such a strong ... tendency to define stereotypes as pejorative that pejorativeness has become almost built into the meaning of the word 'stereotype'" (*ibid.*, p. 144). The pejorative element in stereotypes is taken for granted by Judith Levine in her catalogue of male stereotypes in *My Enemy, My Love*. Levine concludes that all representations of men by women are stereotypes grounded in misandry, and that while this representational strategy is unknown to men it is shared knowledge among women.

Although it is impossible to ignore the derogatory element of stereotypes in cultural representation, I believe that masculine stereotypes in female-authored texts carry much more complex implications than misandry. Using gender stereotypes in representing masculinity does perhaps signal a certain amount of sexual-political anger or frustration, but the stereotypes are also part of a general cultural landscape that permeates male- and female-authored texts. What is of interest here is to disclose what the stereotypes signify in the context of women's novels.

Recently, some critics have produced problematizing readings of the concept of stereotype in order to link it to ideological issues. According to Homi Bhabha, a notion central to an understanding of the concept of stereotype is ambivalence. In "The Other Question: Stereotype, Discrimination and the Discourse of Colonialism," Bhabha (1994) specifically discusses racial stereotypes, but invites other applications of his argument. I take his occasional use of "sexist" in connection with "racist" as an encouragement to attempt an extension of his theories for feminist concerns. Bhabha suggests that "the stereotype is a complex, ambivalent, contradictory mode of representation" (Bhaba, 1994, p. 70). He warns against an exclusively negative reading of the act of stereotyping, for "[s]tereotyping is not the setting up of a false image which becomes the scapegoat of discriminatory practices. It is a much more ambivalent text of projection and introjection, metaphoric and metonymic strategies, displacement, overdetermination, guilt, aggressivity" (*ibid.*, pp. 81-2). He goes on to argue the ambivalence of the stereotype by saying that it functions as both "phobia and fetish" (*ibid.*, p. 72) in that it is something simultaneously unknown and familiar: "For the stereotype is at once a substitute and a shadow. By acceding to the wildest fantasies (in the popular sense) of the colonizer, the stereotyped Other reveals something of the 'fantasy' (as desire, defence) of that position of mastery" (*ibid.*, p. 82). How can the positionalities of stereotyper/stereotyped, or to speak with Homi Bhabha, colonizer/colonized, be rethought for the present argument? Although Bhabha's theories are perhaps not easily applicable to a discussion of gender and "role-reversal," I nevertheless take seriously his suggestion that ambivalence is a crucial component in strategies of stereotyping.

Viewing the stereotype as an ambivalent mode of representation is helpful in trying to explain female-authored stereotypes of masculinity. Through the act of choosing and defining their lovers, the protagonists in the novels I have discussed are involved in a similarly ambivalent and complex movement. In their relationships to the lovers, the protagonists seem to alternate between perceptions of masculinity as familiarity and as otherness, between desire and rejection, and between heroic idealization and disruption of traditional masculinities.

The choice to represent masculinities in this way exposes the constructedness of gender, and can potentially disrupt the hegemony of masculinity, emphasizing not only the ambivalent position of a protagonist caught in yet resisting traditional gender roles, but also the lack/power of masculinities that have traditionally been idolized in patriarchal culture. However, in the context of the present investigation, the stereotypes of lovers coincide with rather more romanticized and, as such, strongly upheld ideals of masculinity. This tendency certainly complicates the discussion of stereotyping as an empowering strategy in women's novels.

The representations of phallic lovers point to the desirability of a masculinity where the body is emphasized and the mind repressed. Needless to say, male authors who have treated female characters in this way have been widely criticized by feminists not only for stereotyping and misrepresentation, but also for misogyny. Is female authors' stereotyping, then, of the same kind, or how can we understand it? What does the male sex object signify? How does a macho masculinity fit into narratives of women who are trying to establish selfhood and affirm their own sexuality? In the cases that I have presented, the cultural ideal is the raw material upon which the protagonists project visions of erotic pleasure. The protagonist actively stereotypes her lover by calling him "cowboy" instead of using his name, and by "reducing" him to a sexual being, ignoring, for example, his professional identity, his connections to the world outside of the bedroom. In the process, the macho man becomes a visionary ideal that embodies erotic availability and lawless pleasure.

However, the protagonist's stereotyping of the lover is accompanied by her own transformations as she enters her relationship with him. Her wish to manifest her independence through an act of "breaking" her marriage contract and "taking" a lover is rendered problematic by her wish to annihilate her individuality and identify completely with her sex – a desire voiced in several of the texts. Kate longs for the annihilation of her own identity, and when she has sex with her cowboy, it is the transformation from "Kate" into "woman" or "cunt" that she experiences as the most fulfilling.

It seems that the protagonists are involved in a double movement – not only are they stereotyping their lovers, but they are also performing a kind of self-stereotyping. After taking a lover, an act that transgresses the culturally assigned role of women as sexually passive and monogamous, and that seems to affirm selfhood and erotic pleasure, the protagonist assumes the role of submissive mistress. In the cases I have described here, it is, after all, the lover who sets the tone for the relationship and its development. His is the aggressive sexuality; the woman becomes passive. This development could be read as a refutation of the possibility, or indeed of the desirability, of a sexual revolution for women. It would be easy to suggest that the protagonists' self-stereotyping and ultimate disappointment in sexual exploration mean that no gratification is to be found through varieties of masculinity/sexuality. We have also seen that the protagonists also are stereotyped by their lovers, evidenced by the derogatory naming that they are subjected to. This fact, taken together with the protagonist's submission, or self-stereotyping, stresses stereotyping as an act that is not only ambiguous, but also has an element of reciprocity.

The representation of ideal masculinities as stereotypes in women's novels can thus be said to be an ambiguous practice that finally disrupts those masculinities and questions their validity as ideals. Moreover, the multiple instances in which "ideal" lovers are represented as stereotypes may also be seen as pointing out the narrowness of choices available to women. By this I mean that the alternative masculinities popularized by American culture are limited in number. Perhaps it could be said that one of the functions of the various masculinities in women's novels is to puncture cultural ideals, to expose American culture as offering stereotypes as ideals. The recurring theme of ultimate disappointment for the protagonist implies that the ideals which have functioned most prominently and effectively as focal points of (largely male) desire for decades are inadequate when adopted for a female erotic discourse. Yet, the ideals are the same ones that appear in male-authored texts. As Marcus Klein has pointed out, these are masculine figures that are "indisputably contemporary" (Klein, 1994, p. 3) but, as we have seen, their meanings shift when they are appropriated for women's novels.

The protagonists' choices from among alternative masculinities are marked by tension and paradox. One possible explanation is that the models on which these ambiguous desires of the protagonists build emanate from very diverse sources. In the novels, pornography, consciousness-raising groups, sexual fantasies, and literary precedents (D. H. Lawrence in *Fear of Flying* and *The Story of O* in *Blue Skies, No Candy*) crowd each other for space and power as the basis and determiners of the image(s) of female desire. The ambiguity can also can be read as a consequence of the irreconcilability of American popular culture's conflicting ideals of promiscuity on the one hand and marriage on the other. The ideals clash as exciting tough guys and rebels, from Western heroes to James Dean, meet the culturally condoned desirability of a husband and a nuclear family, part of the foundation of Western patriarchal ideology.

While the novels I have discussed can be seen as instrumental in mapping out the protagonist's attempt to gain self-knowledge and liberation through sexual experience, they are also effective in mapping out ideal (American) masculinities. In the novels, the lover figure – whether a phallic or a non-phallic type – is ultimately marked by inadequacy and is rejected by the protagonist. Through the female protagonist's relations to the men she encounters, the desirability of certain masculinities is undercut, and the lovers are revealed as "dysfunctional" in some sense. The dysfunction may be emotional, sexual, or social – in each case it is a part of the representation of the lover which undermines the stability of traditionally idolized masculinities.

Nevertheless, the lover symbolizes the protagonist's rebellion against patriarchal law, and through the introduction of several lovers, the diversity of female sexuality is emphasized in the novels. Although her power of agency is seldom unproblematic, the protagonist herself is positioned as having the ability to choose, discard, judge and exchange lovers. Consequently, the lover characters can function as loci for the female protagonist's wish to live out various personalities, various sexualities, and various impersonations of her desiring self. While the subversive force of these representations of lovers can certainly be questioned, especially in view of the ideal/sterotype problematic, the ambiguous "nature" of lovers in women's novels of the 1970s serves to question cultural formations of masculinities in their various molds.

Acknowledgment

This article has previously been published in a different form as a chapter in Helena Eriksson's study *Husbands, Lovers, and Dreamlovers: Masculinity and Female Desire in Women's Novels of the 1970s* (Uppsala: Almqvist and Wiksell, 1997).

References

Alther, Lisa (1976) *Kinflicks*. New York: Knopf.
Bhabha, Homi (1994) "The Other Question: Stereotype, Discrimination, and the Discourse of Colonialism," *The Location of Culture*. London: Routledge, pp. 66-84.
French, Marilyn (1977) *The Women's Room*. New York: Summit Books.
Godwin, Gail (1972) *Glass People*. New York: Knopf.
Greene, Gael (1976) *Blue Skies, No Candy*. New York: Morrow.
Jong, Erica (1973) *Fear of Flying*. New York: Holt, Rinehart, Winston.
Klein, Marcus (1994) *Easterns, Westerns, and Private Eyes: American Matters, 1870-1900*. Madison: University of Wisconsin Press.
Levine, Judith (1992) *My Enemy, My Love: Men, Women, and the Dilemmas of Gender*. New York: Doubleday.
Lurie, Alison (1974) *The War Between the Tates*. New York: Random House.
Perkins, T. E. (1979) "Rethinking Stereotypes," in Barrett, Michèle *et al.* (eds), *Ideology and Cultural Production*. London: Croom Helm, pp. 135-59.

Rossner, Judith (1975) *Looking for Mr Goodbar*. New York: Simon and Schuster.

Rubin, Gayle (1984) "Thinking Sex: Notes for a Radical Theory of the Politics of Sexuality," in Vance, Carol (ed.), *Pleasure and Danger: Exploring Female Sexuality*. Boston: Routledge and Kegan Paul, pp. 267-319.

Tanner, Tony (1992) *Adultery in the Novel: Contract and Transgression*. Baltimore: Johns Hopkins University Press.

Tompkins, Jane (1992) *West of Everything: The Inner Life of Westerns*. New York: Oxford University Press.

Wolitzer, Hilma (1977) *In the Flesh*. New York: Morrow.

Yglesias, Helen (1972) *How She Died*. Boston: Houghton Mifflin.

Chapter 17

Fathers – The Solution or Part of the Problem? Single Mothers, their Sons and Social Work

THOMAS JOHANSSON

Representations and practices

In late modern society many of the previously uncontested narratives of the family have been called into question. Whereas alternatives to the traditional nuclear family was frequently discussed in the 1970s, today we can see how these alternatives have become social reality (Lasch, 1977; Johansson, 2000). Traditional ways of living and constructing gender roles are clearly contested, not only discursively but also in social life.

Social work with families touches upon central issues concerning gender, family and contemporary identity. Although it is often possible to discern and identify hegemonic discourses, social reality is, of course, complex. The client and "the problem" are constructed in a multi-discursive reality. This paper analyses how images of fatherhood and masculinity are drawn into social work. The main object of the study is to explore social work with single mothers and their sons.[1] The empirical material used in the paper is collected in a Swedish study. Altogether twelve persons were interviewed.[2] Thus, the material consists of three case studies (mothers, sons, social workers and contact persons).

Single Mothers have been the focus of a considerable amount of research and debate (Bortolaia 1996, Duncan and Edwards 1999, Bak 2001). Moral and political issues are often raised in relation to this group. So, when approaching this category, we are clearly touching upon a large range of social issues. In this paper I particularly focus on one issue, the part played by the father in the family. In the cases I refer to, the fathers are more or less absent. An issue often raised is what impact this has on the sons. The need of a male "role-model" or a surrogate father is often discussed.[3] Even when this is not the case, social workers tend to work in the direction of creating a point of identification between the son and an adult man.

Against this background I focus on how different discourses of fatherhood and the family intersect and intervene in discussions of and the treatment of "problematic" single mothers and their families.

Hegemonic representations

The traditional nuclear family still holds its position. Although the rate of divorces is increasing and alternative models of the family are appearing, the classical, heterosexual nuclear family is a hegemonic structure in late modern societies. The notion of the nuclear family thus has a strong impact upon people's imagination and attitudes.

According to the social workers we interviewed there are often strong demands from the client – in these cases the single mother – to somehow recreate the nuclear family.

> When dealing with single mothers with small children, there is often a demand to recreate the "family." They want to give the child something we cannot provide them with, a nuclear family and all that goes with it. I guess this is the most common desire (Social worker).

In Sweden there are also clear socio-political ambitions to locate and work with the original family, especially the often "absent" father. In certain cases social workers also succeed in "bringing home" the father.

> The father is important, not least because he is the biological father, and blood is thicker than water. He clearly has a responsibility, as a member of this society. The biological parents should also be the people who care about and take care of their children: bonds, and so on. And in most cases the fathers we succeed in tracing are quite okay. They are often sad and they also have a guilty conscience (Social worker).

The social worker has to form his or her opinion. This is done in a context where professional demands and discourses of motherhood and fatherhood intersect and form complex patterns. Social workers try to create free space where they can analyse and work with different cases. Sometimes it is a good idea to contact the father, but not always. According to our informants the nuclear family is not an automatic solution to all problems. Children do not always need their fathers, and sometimes there is also a need to protect the children from their fathers. The social workers we interviewed are unwilling to discriminate against any type of "family." They are highly aware of normative ways of looking at gender and the family, and they want to contribute to a more up-to-date way of seeing these issues. However, the solutions suggested are not based on a *reflexive* gender perspective, but in arguments concerning the correct type of pragmatic solutions to specific social problems.

However, when we interviewed the clients, another picture was brought forward. The single mothers experiences and needs are explicitly formulated in terms of gender. These mothers feel that nobody listens to them or take them seriously. Whenever there is a man present, the authorities clearly pay attention, however. Single fathers are always regarded as competent and capable, whereas single mothers are considered a problematic category.

> No one pays enough attention to a single mother. They won't spend any energy on us. It is a dead race they think. "She will just spend her time on social welfare, and cost us a lot of money. We cannot accept that." That is the way see it. Single mothers have to take a lot of shit (Mother).

Among the contact persons there is also a tendency to formulate the problem in terms of gender, more specifically as an absence of male role models. These male contact persons regard the absence of a father and the lack of stability in the family as two sides of the same coin. However, at the same time there is also a strong awareness that a present father would not solve all problems.

The nuclear family is thus constantly present, even when it is absent. At the same time, the social workers are aware that it is necessary to see the problem from many different angles. Different images of the family, gender and masculinity/femininity influence the different actors: single mothers, their sons, social workers and contact persons. Although there is an awareness of this complexity, pragmatic solutions are often put to work. The formula: "a lousy father must be replaced by a good male role model" forms a general discourse in practical social work. But it is not made explicit.

Masculinity

Whereas the importance of gender is underplayed in some situations, it is clearly present in others. The more we approach material reality and concrete activities, the more importance is put on gender. Activities are governed by an obvious logic of gender. Young boys are occupied with totally different activities than little girls. And this is also supported by social workers. The conception of gender differences follows quite a strict logic.

> Hans, whom you met earlier, says: "what kind of activities could I do with a girl?" He is pretty much oriented towards activities. It could be difficult to bring her on a fishing trip, or to go to the Laserdome. That is the situation, roughly. Spending time with a group of girls is different. They are into cosmetics, and just talking about guys and sex and so on. They are also watching specific films. Boys are more into go-carts. So, in that way we are different (Social worker).

The construction of gender becomes clearly visible when we approach the sphere of activities and action. There is often an absolute division between male or female activities and responsibilities. When the social workers have to deal with an aggressive client, the men are often asked to step forward and deal with the problem. The idea that men are more competent in this area is often emphasised.

Gender issues are often redefined as practical problems. For example, single mothers approach the social worker with a specific definition of the problem: "my son needs a father figure." In social workers' terminology this need is redefined as a need for a person (no gender) who can assist the young boy in school work and stimulate him to be active in different ways. In reality, this person often tends to be a male person. The young boys we interviewed all said that it is easier to spend time with a man. "We have the same interests."

However, sometimes the need for a male role model is put on the agenda. Certain traits are then regarded as masculine: the ability to uphold certain norms and rules, to react towards violent behaviour and to demand changes in behaviour. But we may also note a reflexive attitude towards this:

> A male role model? That is difficult. (He laugh and cracks jokes about being a chauvinist.) Well, I am probably not a male role model. We often joke about this. Anyhow. A male role model is a guy who shows a lot of confidence, and who won't tolerate any attempts to escape. Anders keeps a strong grip on this young boy. He is straightforward and he will not put up with any fuss (Male social worker).

The need of a male role model is often brought up when the social workers are dealing with single mothers who show difficulties in controlling their young sons. Sometimes the presence of a man is regarded as part of the solution. These men may then function as communicative links between the mother and "society."

I have experienced this as really crucial. I could make my voice heard then. I felt that no one listened to me, as a mother. Nothing I said really mattered. But Erik helped me out. I could use him. He helped me to make my voice heard. And when he told them this or that, things started to happen (Mother).

Although the importance of gender is frequently underplayed, this structure is constantly present. Gender makes a difference. The concept of the male role model is regarded as a problematic category. Gender issues are transformed into technical issues. For example in this case: "Maybe they will say it was thanks to my masculinity I did this, but I would rather refer to the technique I used to communicate." The considered awareness that gender is constantly transformed in late modern societies, that masculinity and femininity are social and historical constructions, is constantly present in our interviews. But there is also another discourse that cuts through all this: the absent father. Absence means something. We are thus approaching the loss of a parent and the question of mourning.

Absent fathers and sons

To delve into and investigate people's experiences of loss and their mourning is a difficult matter. Most people have developed psychological mechanisms to protect them from psychological suffering. What does it mean to lose a parent, or to meet a father once or twice a year? The young boys we met had very irregular contact with their fathers.

Well, he is my father, so he should call me. That is what I think. And he thinks I am his son and that I should call.

A year ago he lived in the same city. /.../ That was more fun, because then I could meet him regularly, and visit him during the weekends. Now I can't see him during the weekends, it's too far away. I only see him during vacations.

Among these young boys it is possible to discern a silent acceptance of the fact that their fathers are absent. So why do they not complain? Often we find deep conflicts between the mother and the father. The child's silence may also be an expression of solidarity with the father or a cultural acceptance of the fact that fathers disappear and leave their families.

Every year, a large number of children and teenagers lose contact with their fathers (Berg and Johansson, 1998; Bradshaw et al, 1999). In some cases this is a gradual and slow process, and in other cases it happens quite quickly. The fathers we indirectly "meet" in our project have often abused their partners. However, there are also families in which the "absent" father is not so absent. He may even be experienced as a positive role model.

The young boys' stories about their fathers are often complex and filled with contradictory details. On the one hand, they are sometimes afraid of their fathers. On the other hand, they long for him and want to see him more often. However, the irregular contact with the father makes it difficult for the sons to form a coherent picture of him. The father is therefore often "read" through the mother's gaze.

> He is afraid of his dad. Scared to death. But at the same time he wants to see his dad. /.../ He believes that he can change his dad. He thinks that all the time. That is no good. He feels quite bad about it, very bad (Mother).

The young boys often have difficulties in expressing their feelings and their desires. One of the boys only saw his father a few times every year. He said he regarded this as sufficient contact. He also pointed out that he had a good relationship with his father; they often called each other and talked. This boy clearly considered himself to have a good and emotionally sufficient relationship with his father. While the sons accepted their fathers, their mothers told a totally different story.

> If his father had been there, it would have been a lot easier. Anthony needs a father figure. He recently said: "I need a father. I wish my dad was like Erik" (his contact person). /.../ He was very sad about this. He has had many disappointments (Mother).

One of the young boys we met had had a serious conflict with his father. This father had physically abused the boy's mother. Although there had been other potential "fathers" in the family, stepfathers, none had fulfilled the family's expectations. There had also been more male violence. The hope of a whole family and a new "father" had successively vanished. Instead, the son had become a sort of father substitute in the family. The mother had given up her adult position in the family, and her two boys ruled the family.[4]

The general expectations upon fathers are complex. On the one hand, there is an image of the absent father. This discourse may sometimes even contribute to creating a defence for absence. Absence becomes a normal condition. On the other hand, expectations on fathers have increased. The nurturing and caring father is no longer an exception. We have to interpret the complex patterns we meet in social work against this background.

Do families actually need fathers? This question is often raised today. We have new family patterns where the father sometimes becomes redundant. There is always the possibility of finding other ways of compensating for the absent father (Silverstone and Rashbaum, 1995). If the sons of lesbians can manage without a father, and if single mothers are better off alone, then why should social workers always consider the father or the male role model as a solution? These questions are clearly important to ask today. The different discourses of fatherhood cut into each other and form complex patterns. On a practical level it is possible to use the arguments and discourses which fit into specific solutions and actions.

Sources of identification

The reactions within social work to the concept of "male role models" or sources of identification are obviously ambivalent. Sometimes the mothers express a strong need for a father figure for their sons: a person who can uphold rules and norms. "The Father's Law," as Jacques Lacan calls it.

> I have always tried to find a good man for my son. I have missed having a father who could bring discipline into the family. I grew up with my mother, so I have never learned anything about discipline. Therefore, I lack it and consequently, Janos also lacks this (Mother).

Janos had developed a good relation to a male contact person. He describes this man as follows: "He is a funny guy, and ugly as hell. He is tall, ugly and fleshy. A real meatloaf." The mother's expectations were fulfilled. The contact person was in this case a big, strong police officer. The social workers handling this "case" did not argue in terms of a male role model. They reasoned in terms of the boy's need for someone who could work with this kind of client.

It has gradually become difficult to establish what a good family or a father figure is. The differentiation of masculinity has complicated the picture. This brings the whole concept of male role models into doubt. What is a man?

> You advertise for male of female employees for different reasons. Well, "the male role model" is a tricky concept. But you always want a mixture of men and women. However, men and woman seldom fit into gender stereotypes. I am responsible for this project /.../ and there are two guys working in the project: Anders and Kalle. The boys call them Andrea and Karin. They don't

think of them as "real" men. We consider them men, because we are used to this type of man. But they (the young guys) look at their cars and laugh (Social worker).

Different masculine ideals are brought together here. Here we have the young boys' image of "real" men and the social workers' ideal – the gentle and man who believes in gender equality. So what is a male role model?

At the same time as we may observe that the question of male role models and potential sources of identification has become a problematic issue in contemporary society, such models are still in use. Or as one male contact person expressed it: "First and foremost they lack male role models. That is, men who uphold norms and rules and who can function as a supportive structure in the family. These mothers need whatever help they can get."

The male role model is often defined in terms of functions. This person does certain things with the young clients. Plays football, tennis or some other sport.

> Sometimes these young kids only need to be out with an adult and have some fun, to be out with a surrogate dad. Do things they wished their own dads would do, but never does. And sometimes their dads try to do this stuff, but then they get drunk and spoil everything. Dad starts off with a beer and then he is drunk by bedtime (Male contact person).

The good role model is often defined as the opposite of the biological father. The role model does not drink or beat his wife. The aim is to show these young boys that adults can act in a responsible way.

As we have seen, many of the concrete supportive acts in social work tend to strengthen rather than weaken the idea of the need for a male role model. Thus, we have a complex pattern where gender is either made visible or kept hidden. The social workers own experiences are sometimes important influences, as in this case:

> Each time I meet a new family I introduce myself and tell them about my own family. I grew up with my mum. I missed my dad throughout my childhood. No one could help me with my motorbike, for example. So I have my thoughts about all this, my life without a dad. I use this experience when talking to these families, and especially when approaching the guys. My memories (Male contact person).

Personal experiences are filtered through and mixed with societal discourses of fatherhood. This forms a powerful background to social work.

Absence as presence

In everyday life we find different and often contradictory ways of looking at and defining gender identities. There is, of course, still a gender order, which regulates the relations between men and women. However, this "order" is not static or stable.[5] On the contrary, radical changes in our ways of defining and considering gender and sexuality are taking place in late modern societies.

This paper is exploratory. By analysing how people involved in social work – both clients and professionals – relate to the concept of "the male role model" and how they define fatherhood, I am interested in exploring how gender is present or absent in social work.

The importance of gender is seldom highlighted as an important issue, and particularly not as a discursive formation. As one social worker expressed it:

> We have not discussed this, not in my group anyhow; the importance of male role models. It is just one component among many others (Social worker).

Although the father is seldom mentioned and is also not physically present, he is very much present in the lives of the single mothers, their sons, the social workers and the contact persons. The gestalt of the father or his symbolic structure casts a shadow over the families. The arguments used when dealing with social problems in these families vary, but the result is often that the young boys are referred to a male contact person. The need for certain activities is translated into the need of a male person, a role model. There is a certain awareness of the discrepancy between different ways of seeing the concept of male role models. But this awareness is still at a pre-reflexive level. Gender matters, but there is no discussion or established standpoint in this question.

The discussion of male role models, and of the father's function and importance for young boys in particular, is complex. Societal changes in the family and in ways of looking at gender have clearly influenced and changed the position of the father. Sometimes the father is treated as a redundant category, and sometimes he steps forward as the "new caring father." Fathers are absent in many ways, in particular in these boys' lives, but this absence sometimes leads to a presence. Social workers have to deal with this *"gestalt"* They have to develop strategies and ways of handling these questions. What we have seen in this exploratory investigation is attempts to find pragmatic solutions, influenced and impregnated by discourses of fatherhood and gender.

Notes

1. The concept of "single mothers," is, of course, not unproblematic. In fact, these "mothers" are often not alone, but they often have the sole responsibility for their children.
2. This paper was written within the project "Male Role Models in Social Work," a project funded by *The Swedish Council for Working Life and Social Research*.
3. The concept of the "male role model" has a long history, see for example Mitscherlich (1969), Lasch (1977), Bly (1996) and so on. This concept is often used in order to defend the patriarchy.
4. For a discussion of this phenomenon, see for example, Garbarino (2000).
5. For a discussion of these changes, see for example Gillis (1993), Connell (1995), Bordo (1999), Hwang (2000), Johansson (2000, 2001).

References

Bak, M. (2001) Barns vardagsliv i ensam-mor familjer. I Bäck-Wiklund and Lundström, T (eds.) *Barns vardagsliv i det senmoderna samhället.* Stockholm: Natur och Kultur.

Berg, L-E. och Johansson, T (1998) *Den andre föräldern. Om deltidspappor och deras barn.* Stockholm: Carlssons förlag.

Bly, R. (1996) *Syskonsamhället.* Helsinki: ICA bokförlag.

Bordo, S. (1999) *The Male Body. A New Look at Men in Public and Private.* New York. Farrar, Strauss and Giroux.

Bortolaia, S.E. (1996) *Good Enough Mothering? Feminist Perspectives on Lone Motherhood.* London: Routledge.

Bradshaw, J. Stimson, C. Skinner, C. och Williams, J. (1999) *Absent Fathers?* New York: Routledge.

Connell, R.W. (1995) *Masculinities.* Cambridge: Polity Press.

Duncan, S. and Edwards, R. (1999) *Single Mothers, Paid Work and Gendered Moral Rationalities.* London: MacMillan.

Garbarino, J. (2000) *Pojkar som gått vilse. Varför våra söner blir våldsamma och hur vi kan rädda dem.* Stockholm: SfPH.

Gillis, J. (1993) *A World of Their Own Making. Myth, Ritual and the Quest for Family Values.* Cambridge: Harvard University Press.

Hwang, P. (red.) (2000) *Faderskap i tid och rum.* Stockholm: Natur och Kultur.

Johansson, T. (2000) *Det första könet? Mansforskning som reflexiv praktik.* Lund: Studentlitteratur.

Johansson, T. (2001) "Fadern som försvann". I Ekenstam, C. Johansson, T. och Kuosmanen, J. (red.) *Sprickor i fasaden. Manligheter i förändring.* Gidlunds.

Lamb, M.E. (red.) (1987) *The Father's Role. Cross-Cultural Perspectives.* New Jersey: Lawrence Erlbaum.

Lasch, C. (1977/1983) *Den belägrade familjen.* Stockholm: Norstedts.

Mitscherlich, A (1969) *Society without the Father. A Contribution to Social Psychology.* London: Tavistock Publications.

Silverstone, O. och Rashbaum, B. (1995) *Mödrar och söner. Att våga strunta i givna könsroller.* Stockholm: Norstedts.

Index